MANAGING YOUR PERSONAL FINANCES

JOAN S. RYAN

Willamette High School
Eugene, Oregon

Published by

HO3 **SOUTH-WESTERN PUBLISHING CO.**

CINCINNATI   WEST CHICAGO, IL   DALLAS   PELHAM MANOR, NY   PALO ALTO, CA

ISBN 0-538-08030-2

Library of Congress Catalog Card Number: 83-51153

1 2 3 4 5 6 7 8 D 1 0 9 8 7 6 5 4

Printed in the United States of America

Cover photograph by R. D. Randolph/Uniphoto

PREFACE

MANAGING YOUR PERSONAL FINANCES is a multidisciplinary approach to personal financial management for high school students. The text incorporates a variety of topics in the areas of business, economics, law, business education, home economics, and social studies. These materials were first developed in 1978 and have been used in my personal finance classes since that time. The materials have undergone several major revisions, plus yearly updates. Activities that did not work well have been discarded; others have been developed and tested. The result is a text that offers high school students a chance to master basic financial and economic concepts needed for survival in the modern world.

The approach to the study of personal finance and consumer economics offered in this text focuses on the student's role as citizen, student, family member, consumer, and active participant in the world of work and business. The intent is to inform students of their various economic and financial responsibilities, as well as of opportunities for self-awareness, expression, and advancement in a progressive and highly competitive society.

High school students in many states are required to take a course in personal finance and economics. In Oregon, personal finance is a full-year requirement that can be covered by the six units presented in MANAGING YOUR PERSONAL FINANCES. These six units can be fitted into 36 weeks of instruction. MANAGING YOUR PERSONAL FINANCES can be used for a full-year course, two half-year courses, or three trimester courses.

Unit one, "Employment and Income," covers how to get a job, how to keep it, and employee benefits. Unit Two, "Money Management," includes financial planning and legal documents, checking accounts and miscellaneous banking services, income tax, savings, investments, and insurance. Unit Three, "Credit," studies all aspects of credit in America, including availability, costs, and responsibilities of using credit. Bankruptcy, sometimes the unfortunate result of credit, is also covered. Unit

Four, "Consumer Rights and Responsibilities," deals with the role of the consumer in the marketplace, consumer protection, and legal protection. Unit Five, "Purchasing Goods and Services," emphasizes consumer decision making, living arrangements, housing options, family decisions, and contingency planning. Unit Six, "Economics," is a comprehensive overview of economics and economic systems. The Appendix includes the annual percentage rate formula and the Rule of 78, with several practice problems. A glossary of terms used throughout the text is also provided.

Learning objectives given at the beginning of each chapter are fulfilled through study of the chapter narrative and completion of selected end-of-chapter activities. Vocabulary, review questions, applications, and case problem activities provide a variety of opportunities for students to apply the concepts presented. Exercises provided in MANAGING YOUR PERSONAL FINANCES—STUDENT ACTIVITIES serve as reinforcement for the text. Through the numerous practical applications offered, students gain a thorough understanding of the basics of personal finance and consumer economics.

Effective consumers are aware of the significance of their role as consumers, from the selection of personal purchases and construction of a meaningful budget to participate in the American business system and total economic picture. To capture this understanding, students need to read, study, and apply the principles presented in MANAGING YOUR PERSONAL FINANCES. After studying this text, students will have a better grasp of their financial responsibilities to themselves and to society. They will also have a better understanding of their own wants, needs, values, and how these elements affect personal financial decisions. Finally, by understanding the wise use of credit and how economics affects all citizens personally, students will be able to make wise decisions to affect future financial goals for themselves and for the country.

Each person belongs to and has a rightful position in our economic system, but each person must also strive toward top achievement so that maximum contribution can be made toward both self-actualization and contribution to the American system. The marketplace belongs to all of us, but only those of us who understand it and know how to use it wisely will benefit from it and make significant contributions to it as well.

Joan S. Ryan

CONTENTS

Unit One—Employment and Income

Unit Two—Money Management

Unit Three—Credit

Unit Four—Consumer Rights and Responsibilities

Unit Five—Purchasing Goods and Services

Unit Six—Economics

UNIT ONE
EMPLOYMENT AND INCOME

CHAPTER 1

YOUR JOB, YOUR FUTURE

CHAPTER OBJECTIVES
After studying this chapter and completing the activities, you will be able to:

1. Identify and describe good job search techniques.
2. Complete self-analysis and goal activity steps in career planning.
3. List sources of job opportunity information and formulate a personal plan of action to get the job you want.

WHY PEOPLE WORK

Two-income families are common.

Most of you will work at sometime during your life. After completing high school and other forms of additional training or education, many of you will work for twenty-five to forty years. Today it is common to see two-income families, teenagers with part-time jobs, and family members with more than one job.

People work to meet their needs, wants, and goals. They work to provide themselves with everything from food, clothing, and shelter to vacations, education, and luxuries. If working does not make it possible for a person to meet personal goals, that person is likely to become frustrated or unhappy in her or his job.

Work is a central life activity.

People also work to gain a sense of *identity*—of who and what they are. Because a person's work is most often life's central activity, it often becomes a way of life, or a person's main identity in life. For example, as a student, your main activities center around school. Your identity is that

2

of student. When you are asked what you do, you describe activities, classes, grades in school, and events related to your education. When you are out of school, your main identity will be based on your career. When adults are introduced, the first question asked is usually "What do you do for a living?" When one person answers, "I'm a financial economist," and another says, "I'm a sports announcer," two entirely different images come to mind.

FACTORS AFFECTING CAREER CHOICE

Because your career will have an impact on nearly every part of your life, the choice of a career is a very important decision. Many factors affect your career decision; some of these are values and life-style, aptitudes and interests, and personal qualities and traits.

Values and Life-Style

Values are the things in life that are important to you. While you are living at home, your values will probably reflect your parents' values. During your years in high school, you begin to form values of your own—keeping many of your parents' values and rejecting others. For example, you may retain your parents' value that it is proper to wear a tie while

During high school you form your own values.

attending a religious service. But you may reject a value that modern music is worthless.

Life-style may be defined as the way people choose to live their lives, based on the values they have chosen or rejected. Your life-style is displayed to others by the clothes you wear and by the things you buy, rent or use, do, enjoy, and feel. A career is considered an important value in most peoples' lives because it dictates life-style. With careful planning, a career can be rewarding and satisfying and also provide the money needed to support the life-style you desire.

A career can make possible a desired life-style.

Aptitudes and Interests

An *aptitude* is a natural physical or mental ability that permits you to do certain tasks well. Examples of aptitudes include *finger dexterity*, the ability to use your fingers to move small objects quickly and accurately; and *manual dexterity*, the ability to move your hands skillfully. Certain types of work require certain types of aptitudes. Aptitude tests are valuable tools in career planning because they help you to become aware of your strengths and weaknesses. Aptitude tests can be taken through counseling or career guidance departments of most high schools. You may want to test your physical and mental abilities before you begin making career plans.

Aptitude tests are valuable tools.

In addition to your aptitudes, you should also think about your interests—the things you like to do and the reasons why you enjoy doing them. By examining the types of things you enjoy, you can better choose a career that has activities that are similar and will be satisfying and enjoyable. For example, a person who enjoys being with large groups of people and helping others will likely prefer a job working with others rather than one working alone. Consider the options listed in Figure 1–1.

Choose a career that offers things you like to do.

FIGURE 1–1
Types of Work Activities

Which of these work activities appeal to you?	
indoor work	outdoor work
physically active work	physically inactive work
various tasks	same tasks
manual work	thinking work
working with machines	working with others
working alone	leading and directing
following directions	creating and designing
helping others	presenting or speaking
self-motivated work	analyzing and recording

Personal Qualities and Traits

Your *personality* is made up of the many personal qualities and traits that make you unique. Personal qualities include such things as your appearance, intelligence, creativity, sense of humor, and general attitude. Many times a certain position requires an individual with a particular set of personal qualities and traits. For example, a person who represents a company to the public or to potential customers needs a different set of personal qualities and traits than does a machine operator. Examining your personal qualities and traits can help you to choose a career that's right for you. How many of the traits listed in Figure 1–2 apply to you?

Your personality is a job qualification.

FIGURE 1–2
Personality Traits

1. Has a good attitude toward own work and toward others' work.
2. Shows courtesy and respect toward others.
3. Is dependable and will do what is promised.
4. Has a desire to succeed and do a good job.
5. Has enthusiasm for the job and for life.
6. Is clean and has a healthy appearance.
7. Is friendly and helpful.
8. Has a good sense of humor and cares about others.

CAREER PLANNING

Planning for your future career is an important task. Consider the total time spent in life's central activity of working. Eight hours a day, five days a week, 50 weeks a year totals 2,000 hours each year. If you work the average career span of 43 years (from age 22 to age 65), you will have spent 86,000 hours on the job. In addition, you will have spent time in traveling to and from work, in getting ready for work, in overtime (paid and unpaid), and in other work-related activities performed away from the workplace. Because your work will likely take so much of your time, you will want to choose and plan for your career carefully.

The average worker spends 86,000 hours on the job.

Steps in Career Planning

Effective career planning involves careful investigation and analysis—a long process that may take years to complete. Career planning involves self-assessment, research, and a plan of action.

Self-Assessment. Using resources available to you (at schools, employment offices, testing services, etc.), you can explore personal factors that relate to your career choice. You should:

What is your desired
life-style?

1. Determine your wants and needs.
2. Determine your values and desired life-style.
3. Assess your aptitudes and interests and how they match job descriptions and activities.
4. Analyze your personal qualities and traits—those you have and those you need to improve.

Research. Based on a good self-assessment, you can determine which careers interest you most and which suit you best. You should:

1. Seek information in books, pamphlets, articles, and other resources available from libraries, counseling centers, and employment offices.
2. Compare some of your interests, abilities, and personal qualities with job descriptions and requirements. Most careers can fit into one of the nine classifications shown in Figure 1-3. Can you choose one or more of these areas that you might want to pursue in which you would be able to meet the requirements? Can you decide which cluster the job of your choice would fit into?
3. Interview people in the fields of work you find interesting.
4. Observe occupations, spend time learning about jobs and companies, and seek part-time work to get direct exposure and experience.

Set a plan to meet your
goals.

Plan of Action. After you have done some job research, you will need to develop a plan of action that will eventually bring you to your career goals.

1. Use good job search techniques: get organized, make a plan, follow through, and don't give up.
2. Develop necessary skills by taking courses and getting exposure to the area in which you want to pursue a career.
3. Seek a part-time or volunteer job to gain experience.
4. Evaluate what you have done. If at any point you think you are following the wrong career path, change your mind before you stay too long in an occupation.

Don't get locked into a
job.

Choosing and planning for a career in the method just described may seem confusing and complicated. Most people do follow this method, however, either consciously or unconsciously. Those who do not give career choice and planning the proper thought often spend years in a job not really suited for them before they finally discover their error. Others discover their mistake, but are unable to correct it.

The Importance of Goals

A *goal* is an end toward which efforts are directed. People need to have goals to have a sense of direction and purpose in life. There are three types of goals: short-term goals, intermediate goals, and long-term goals.

JOB CLASSIFICATION	DESCRIPTION OF ACTIVITIES	TRAINING NEEDED	WORKING HOURS	BEGINNING SALARY	EXAMPLES
Clerical/Secretarial	Work in office setting. Involves contact with people and machines. Must type, have telephone skills, etc.	High school diploma plus special training in typing, shorthand, accounting, etc.	40 hours/week during normal business hours	$800+/month	Secretary, typist, word processor operator
Professional	Involves use of highly specialized knowledge. Often stressful. High-level responsibility implied.	4+ years of college. May require special training and/or apprenticeship.	40 hours/week during normal business hours plus overtime	$15,000/year to unlimited	Physician, lawyer, teacher, accountant
Skilled Labor	Emphasis on use of highly specialized skill. Special clothing required. Involves use of tools, machines, etc.	High school diploma plus special training, apprenticeship, licensing, or bonding.	40 hours/week plus overtime	Minimum wage to set salary. $1,000–1,200/month	Builder, mechanic, construction worker
Sales and Marketing	Emphasis on persuading others to buy products and services. Salesperson represents company, self.	High school diploma plus special training. License usually required.	Varied. Often seasonal.	Commission. Often self-employed.	Real estate agent, insurance agent, retail salesperson
Service	Involves labor that does not produce a material good. May or may not involve personal contact.	None to specialized 2-year degree program	Varied. Split shift, as needed	Minimum wage to $1,000/month	Custodian, barber, chef, police officer
Management	Emphasis on supervision of operations, decision making, and direction giving.	College degree plus in-service training.	40 hours or more/week.	$2,000/month or salary plus percentage of profits	Store manager, bank officer, supervisor
Semiskilled and Unskilled Labor	Involves assembly line and other manual work. Physical fitness and good health needed.	In-service training or vocational diploma.	40 hours/week plus overtime	Minimum wage. $10–$15/hour when advanced.	Assembly worker, farm laborer
Entertainment and Recreation	Emphasis on entertaining people. Special quality or talent needed.	None required. Dancing, singing, and music lessons helpful.	Varied. Often under contract.	$0 to unlimited.	Singer, dancer, athlete
Military Service	Emphasis on defense of the country. Discipline and training stressed. Ability to follow orders needed. Must fulfill minimum service requirement.	High school diploma usually required.	Daily during set number of years' commitment.	$7,000/year and up, depending on rank.	Armed Forces service people

FIGURE 1– 3 Job Clusters

Short-term goals take care of daily living.

A *short-term goal* is one that is set to happen in the next few days or weeks. You will work consistently and with certainty to achieve it because you will have to account for the results in a very short time. A short-term goal could be preparing to pass a math test next week—you know you must plan your studying to be ready for the test or suffer the consequences.

Intermediate goals are those you wish to accomplish in the next few months or years. Some examples are graduation from high school, a trip you would like to take, or your plans for the coming summer.

Long-term goals include college, career, marriage, and family planning goals. All are activities or plans that will materialize in five to ten years or longer.

Work on your goals every day.

If they are to be meaningful, goals should be defined and worked on every day. If goals are to give direction to your life, they must be carefully considered, clearly defined, and actively sought after in an organized manner. Many people find a checklist a handy way to keep on target. For example, your goals, which you would look at and work on daily, might be listed as in Figure 1–4.

A checklist keeps you current on your goals.

You might want to make up your own checklist form and include your own short-term, intermediate, and long-term goals. Remember: if you don't know where you're going, you'll probably end up somewhere else.

Making the Right Choices

How do you know what kind of job you will be best suited for? How can you possibly decide now, while in high school, what you will want to do for the rest of your life? You may not be able to decide. Yet, unfair as it may seem, the fact is that what you do now can greatly affect what you will do in the future.

What you learn to do, you gain *experience* doing—knowledge, skills, and practice from direct participation in a certain area. Furthermore, the more experience you gain, the more qualified you become, and the more you learn. The more experience and expertise you gain in one area, the

Experience makes you a valuable employee.

more desirable you become as an employee in that area. Thus, you can, in effect, "set yourself up" for a career in a certain area, make yourself worth more to an employer, and increase your earnings by continuing in that area. Then you must design your life-style around that work and salary.

Unfortunately, the longer you work at one type of job, the greater the chance of becoming *locked into* that job—of feeling that you cannot change to another type of work because you cannot afford to take the cut in pay that may accompany starting over. This is true even of part-time

FIGURE 1–4
Checklist Plan

CHECKLIST
Week of _____

Accomplished

Short-term goals (today/this week)
1. Buy birthday gift for Mom. _____
2. Get haircut (Saturday). _____
3. See counselor about chemistry class. _____

Intermediate goals (next month/year)
1. Get a C or better on Chemistry test (test in 2 weeks). _____
2. Prepare for SAT test (test in October). _____
3. Finish term report (due November 9). _____
4. Complete college admission forms (by January 15). _____

Long-term goals (future)
                                                                Things to do now
1. Graduate from college.   __Extra work in science
                             __Bring up GPA to 3.5
2. Begin full-time job.   __Update placement folder
3. Buy a car.   __Get part-time job (save $50 a month)

work. If you take a job as a clerk, for instance, rather than take a job that pays less but would prepare you for your preferred career, you are in the process of locking into the clerk job. Taking a temporary position to earn a living while you are preparing for your chosen career is a common practice. However, to achieve your career goals, you must continue to pursue jobs in your field.

Through a careful self-assessment, thorough research, a good plan of action, and well-defined goals, you will be able to choose the career that is right for you. These steps are essential for obtaining employment in the job that you want and in the career field that you want.

SOURCES OF JOB OPPORTUNITY INFORMATION

There are several sources of job opportunity information available: word of mouth and personal contacts; school counseling and placement services; periodicals, books, and other publications; public and private employment agencies; and newspaper, telephone book, and private job listings.

Word of Mouth and Personal Contacts

Most job openings are filled by word of mouth.

Many job openings are filled before they are ever advertised. They are filled from within the company, or by people outside the company who have been privately informed of the opening by a friend or other contact within the company. Each of you has a certain amount of exposure to *contacts*. Relatives, friends, people you have worked for, and others may be able to provide you with inside information on job openings. Therefore, the more people you know, the better your chances of hearing about a job opening before it is made public and of getting the job because you had a contact.

If you are seeking a job in an area in which you have no contacts, it may be necessary for you to make contacts within that work area before you will be able to find an opening. If, for example, you want to work in a bank, you will find it to your advantage to get to know people who work in banks and to make yourself known to the personnel manager and other key employees.

School Counseling and Placement Services

Many schools have programs to assist students in preparing for careers, in making career choices, and in securing part-time and full-time work. One such program is the *cooperative work experience program*. In this program, students receive high school credits for on-the-job experiences that directly relate to classroom studies in a chosen career area. Students placed in work situations are given grades on their work and are paid minimum wages for their efforts. Employers receive tax credits for the wages the students receive during training.

Employers get tax credits for some wages paid.

School counselors and teachers are also good sources of job opportunity information. They often know about specific job openings and are asked by employers to recommend students for job openings. If you are interested in an office job, you should talk to counselors and business teachers as you complete business courses.

College and universities (and some high schools) offer *placement services*. Placement services help students find employment; they are usually offered free of charge. These services include keeping a placement folder on each student that contains school records employers most often ask for. Records kept include: attendance, academic, and discipline. Job openings are posted at the school, and qualified students are given information so that they can apply. When employers ask for information about a student, they are given copies of information kept in a student's placement folder. If your school offers a placement service, perhaps through the counseling center, you should examine your folder and have teachers and other adults write recommendations to put in your folder. You should also see that all school records are in the folder. Be sure to check at your school to see what other types of assistance are available to you.

Employers ask about attendance.

Periodicals, Books, and Other Publications

Your library has much information about jobs.

Your local public library and your school library are good resource centers where you can find information about jobs. You can find facts about which jobs will be available in the future and about which jobs may not be around very long. You can read job descriptions, opportunities for employment, benefits, and requirements.

One good job sourcebook is the *Occupational Outlook Handbook*, published yearly by the U.S. Department of Labor. This book contains current information about most jobs throughout the country. At the library you will also find many government and industry publications that present information about job trends, kinds of jobs, employment possibilities, skills needed, and education requirements. Your librarian can assist you in finding and using such publications.

In addition, many current periodicals contain timely information about selected occupations. You might want to look at magazines such as *Time, Newsweek, U.S. News & World Report, Fortune,* and *Business Week.* The library's *Guide to Current Periodicals* will assist you in locating information by topic, article title, or author.

Public and Private Employment Agencies

All major cities have private and public employment agencies whose business is to help you find jobs for which you are prepared and help employers locate the best applicants for job openings. Private employment agencies may or may not charge a fee for their services. Such fees vary within a community; so you should compare prices before you sign with an agency. Some of these employment agencies charge a fee to the employer, others charge the person seeking work a fee when a job is found, and still others divide the fee between the employer and the person hired. The state employment office does not charge a fee because it is a government agency.

Employment agency fees vary greatly.

At the state employment office, you can also obtain information about government jobs training assistance programs, YES (Youth Employment

Services), Youth Corps, Civil Service (state and federal), and apprentice-ship boards, as well as other government employment programs that exist from time to time. You may qualify for one or more of these types of work programs.

Newspaper, Telephone Book, and Private Job Listings

The ***help wanted ads*** in the classified section of your local newspaper consist of job openings in your area. Brief descriptions of the positions are given, often with salary ranges specified. By keeping close watch on these ads, you can tell when a new job enters the market and be quick to respond. Both employers and employment agencies advertise job openings to attract qualified applicants. You may be asked to send a letter of application and a résumé to an employer before you will be granted an interview. In the next chapter you will learn how to prepare a letter of application and a résumé.

Job openings are often advertised.

The ***Yellow Pages*** of the telephone book is an alphabetic, subject listing of businesses advertising their services. If you are looking for a job in a certain field, determine the subject heading under which that type of work might be classified. Under that heading, you will find a list of companies to help you begin your job search. You may want to send letters of application and résumés to all those listed, asking to be considered for the next opening.

Many companies, government offices, and schools place job opening announcements on bulletin boards, circulate them within the company, and post them in other special locations. Checking in these places may give you inside information to apply for a position at the right time. Often the first persons to apply for a job opening have an advantage over those who apply at the last minute.

JOB SEARCH TECHNIQUES

Finding and getting the right job does not happen by accident. It takes hard work, careful planning, and often a great deal of time. Nevertheless, it is important that you put in sufficient time and effort to ensure that you get a job you enjoy and can stay with. Dissatisfaction leads to frequent job changing, which may damage your employment chances in the future. Your ***work history***, a record of the jobs you have held and how long you stayed with each employer, will be important to future employers. If your record shows that you changed jobs six times in six months, you will appear immature and unstable to future employers. Thus, your

Your work history should show stability.

work history, in this example, will hurt your chances of getting a job you might want very much.

Job search techniques that will help you to find and get the right job are discussed in the following paragraphs.

Get Organized

Gather all the information you can about a job.

After you have decided what kind of job you want, the first step is to get organized. Gather together all the information you will need about the type of work you want to do. Get a list of prospective companies for which you would like to work. Gather your sources of information and research job descriptions, skills and aptitudes needed, and other job requirements. Make lists of personal contacts, places to go, and people to see. Type a current résumé and letter of application. Ask previous employers, teachers, or others to write letters of recommendation for you. Update your placement folder at school. You may want to prepare a checklist of things to do and check them off as they are completed.

Make a Plan

A good plan lists all your goals in a time frame.

A plan is important to the success of your job search because it keeps you organized, shows what you have done, and indicates what you need to do in the immediate future. A good plan lists all your goals and shows a time frame for getting them done. As each step or goal is accomplished, it should be checked off. A plan you might want to follow is shown in Figure 1–5.

Follow Through

The most important, yet difficult, step is this one. After you have contacted a potential employer by letter or by filling out an application for a job opening, after you have met a personnel manager, or had an interview, it is important that you follow through. This means checking back from time to time to say you are still interested in the job. Be neatly dressed and well groomed at all times so that you will represent yourself well. Call back in a day or two to check on the job and remain courteous and optimistic.

Don't Give Up

Before you get a good job, you will probably not get several other jobs for which you applied. When your first and second efforts appear to be fruitless, remain calm and courteous, and keep checking back for open-

FIGURE 1–5
Plan to Get a
Job

Job Leads: ___ State employment office
              ___ Help wanted ads (newspaper)
              ___ School placement office
              ___ Marketing teacher

Contacts: ___ Uncle Henry (knows manager of local Penney's)

Time Line—Week 1
    Day 1:   ___ Type résumé and letter of application.
              ___ Check help wanted ads.
              ___ Make list of local stores from Yellow Pages.

    Day 2:   ___ Send two application letters.
              ___ Get two personal references.
              ___ Call Uncle Henry to set a date for lunch.

    Note: Any planned activities that are not completed this
              week should be brought forward to next week's plan.

Check with your con-
tacts frequently.

ings. Try all your job leads. Be prepared at all times, so that if you are called to come in for an interview on short notice—even the same day— you can do so. Continually check the want ads for new openings. Call back when you have established a contact, and check with your contacts frequently. Although a good job search may take several weeks or months, it will pay off. With careful planning and research, you can find the job that will meet your needs, wants, and goals.

VOCABULARY

Directions: Can you find the definition for each of the following terms used in Chapter 1?

identity	goal
values	contact
life-style	placement service
aptitude	work history
personality	

1. The things in your life that are important to you.

2. A natural physical or mental ability.

3. Personal qualities and traits that make you unique.

4. Person you know in a business to give you inside information about a job.

5. The record of jobs you have held.

6. A description of who and what you are.

7. The way you choose to live your life, based on your values.

8. An end toward which efforts are directed.

9. A service that sends out school records and other information used to help students secure employment.

ITEMS FOR DISCUSSION

1. Why do people work?

2. What is your identity at this time in your life? (You may have more than one.)

3. Define *values*. List three of your parents' values and three of your own.

4. Why is choice of a career considered to be an important decision?

5. What is manual dexterity? Why might it be important to you to know if you have manual dexterity?

6. What is meant by *personal traits*? List three.

7. What are the three major steps in good career planning?

8. Why do people need to set goals in life?

9. What are (*a*) short-term, (*b*) intermediate, and (*c*) long-term goals?

10. What is meant by the term *locked in*?

11. How can you establish personal contacts within a business where you don't know anyone?

12. What are placement services? What types of placement services are available at your school?

13. Who publishes the *Occupational Outlook Handbook*? What does it contain?

14. Why should you check around with different private employment agencies before signing up with one of them?

15. Describe the Yellow Pages of your telephone book. What does it contain? How is the information listed?

APPLICATIONS

1. From Figure 1−1, list the activities that appeal to you. Can you think of several occupations that offer these types of activities?

2. Make a list of personality traits that would be important in three different types of work (for example, secretary, accountant, mechanic). Your best source of information is someone in these types of work. Ask what personality traits are more successful.

3. Describe your desired life-style in ten years. Include the things you want to have and what you want to be. Consider such factors as marriage, family, housing, job title, etc. Will the job you want to work at support the life-style you desire?

4. Research three different types of careers, using the resources available to you. (Suggestions: *Occupational Outlook Handbook*, current periodicals.) List for each occupation: job description, job requirements (including education), working hours, salary range, and other information.

5. Using Figure 1−4 as an example, prepare a checklist that contains short-term, intermediate, and long-term goals. At the end of the week, check to see what you have accomplished.

6. Cut these types of want ads from the classified section of your local newspaper: three ads by private employers; three ads by private employment agencies, one ad for someone to make a cash investment, one ad for someone in a sales position (to work on commission rather than for a salary), and one ad that gives the beginning salary in a dollar amount.

7. Using your telephone book, list ten private employment agencies, their addresses, and their phone numbers. Also list the address and phone number of the state employment office. Call one of the private agencies and ask a counselor the amount of the fee for a job that will pay approximately $1,000 a month, and ask who would pay the fee.

8. Write a paragraph describing your work history. It can be current or what you would like it to be in ten years.

9. List and describe the four steps in an effective job search.

10. Using Figure 1−5 as an example, prepare a plan to get yourself a job using a one-week timetable. List your job leads, your contacts (or potential ones), and a daily plan to accomplish several things each day.

11. Define the phrase *follow through*.

1. Give five or more activities (see Figure 1–1) that would be a part of the work involved in each of the following occupations: carpenter, forest ranger, teacher, social worker.

2. Using the *Occupational Outlook Handbook* and the following format, prepare a career report for one occupation you are interested in.

CAREER REPORT

Name of career: _____

Year of handbook: _____ Info. located on pp.: _____

1. What is the nature of the work? _____

_____

_____

2. Describe the average working conditions. _____

_____

3. List possible places of employment. _____

_____

4. What training is needed for this type of work? _____

_____

5. What is the employment outlook for this career across the country? _____

_____

6. What salary can you expect to earn as a beginning worker in this career? __

_____

7. What personality traits are needed for success in this career? _____

_____

_____

8. Where can you find additional information about this career? _____

_____

_____

---

3. John Wilson has decided that his long-term goal in life is to become an astronaut. He is now a sophomore in high school and hasn't done any planning. John's grades are average; he is active, outgoing, and bright. What can John do now, in the next few years, and beyond to prepare himself for a career as an astronaut?

4. Using Figure 1-3 as a guide, classify each of the following job titles into one of the nine job classifications. You may have to do some research to determine types of activities performed, skills and education required, working hours, and beginning pay.

   a. log scaler
   b. court reporter
   c. sheet-metal worker
   d. technical writer
   e. building custodian
   f. underwriter
   g. mechanical engineer
   h. sonar operator
   i. cosmetologist
   j. physical therapist
   k. computer programmer
   l. radio announcer
   m. singer
   n. infantry officer
   o. administrative assistant
   p. F.B.I. special agent
   q. tailor

5. Linda Garcia wants to be an accountant when she completes high school. She is taking accounting courses and is working part-time at the ice cream store. What should Linda be doing to prevent herself from becoming locked into her job at the ice cream store?

6. Henry Weinberger would like to work as a merchandising manager for a large department store. He has all the qualifications, education, and skills necessary; but he doesn't know anyone in any large stores, and most openings are filled before he even knows they existed. What can Henry do to find out about job openings in the large department stores?

7. Louise Pitts is a sophomore in high school. She plans to use the placement service of her high school to help get a part-time job in her senior year. What should Louise do between now and her senior year to be sure her placement folder is ready when she is ready to find a job?

8. Jack Adams has worked part-time after school for the past two years. He worked for two weeks as a cook, but rarely got to work on time and was fired. He worked for two months as a busboy but quit because he didn't get enough tips. Jack also worked for three weeks as a janitor but was laid off. Finally, he worked for four months as a plumber's assistant but quit because the work hurt his back. What is Jack's record of job changes called? What does it say to potential employers? Would you hire Jack?

CHAPTER 2
GETTING THE JOB

CHAPTER OBJECTIVES

After studying this chapter and completing the activities, you will be able to:

1. Prepare the necessary job application tools (résumé, letter of application, application form, and thank-you letter).
2. Identify and describe appropriate job interview techniques.
3. Understand the steps in successful application for a job and the proper timing for the application tools.

LETTER OF APPLICATION

Your initial job application should consist of a letter of application and a résumé. The *letter of application* is an important tool in the application process: it introduces you to the potential employer and gives you a chance to sell your qualifications.

Preparing the Letter of Application

Generally, the letter of application should be typed on white, standard size (8 1/2-by-11-inch) paper of a good quality. Use Figure 2–1A as a positioning and spacing model when you type your own letter of application.

You may wish to enclose a copy of your school records or a letter of reference with your letter of application and résumé. Remember to refer to all enclosures within the body of the letter. Enclosures should also be listed at the end of the letter in a separate note.

If a handwritten letter of application is required, be sure to follow the same guidelines. Use standard size plain white paper and leave the same amount of space between parts so that the spacing on the final product looks very much like a typed letter.

Parts of the Letter of Application

There are five basic parts to a letter of application. They are the return address, the inside address, the salutation, the body, and the complimentary close.

Return Address. The *return address* shows the person to whom you are writing your address so that they can return a letter to you. The return address contains your complete address and the date of the letter, but it *does not* contain your name.

Inside Address. The *inside address* contains the name and address of the person or company to whom you are writing. It should be a complete address.

Salutation. Also known as the greeting, the *salutation* addresses your letter to a particular person you want to read the message. The person's name or other form of address is always followed by a colon. "Dear Mr. Smith:" and "Dear Sir or Madam:" are examples of salutations.

Body. The *body* of the letter contains three basic parts and should be in three or four paragraphs. These paragraphs should attract the

Consider the purpose of the letter.

employer's attention, state your interest in the company, arouse the employer's desire to interview you, and request that the employer take action in the form of an interview.

Complimentary Close. Once you have stated your business, you close the letter with "Sincerely yours," or some other appropriate phrase, and your name.

Below the complimentary close, make notations for enclosures that will accompany the letter.

RÉSUMÉ

A *résumé*, also called a personal data sheet, is a concise summary of personal information. It briefly describes your work experience, education, abilities, and interests. The résumé can be a valuable tool for getting a job because it tells the employer neatly and concisely who you are, what you can do, and the names of people who know you and your work. Therefore, it is a good idea to prepare a typed résumé and have it ready to send or give to potential employers. Figure 2–1B shows a commonly used résumé style.

General Guidelines

Keep the following guidelines in mind when planning and preparing your résumé:

Keep your résumé short.

1. Keep your résumé to one page, if possible, by carefully arranging the information you choose to include.
2. Include all information pertinent to the job for which you are applying. Be honest, but emphasize your strong points.
3. Unless a particular employer requests otherwise, type the résumé on good quality, 8 1/2-by-11-inch paper.
4. Use a format that is attractive and that displays the information in an easy-to-read fashion.
5. Proofread the finished copy—there should be no obvious errors. If it is necessary to make corrections, do so with care. The résumé you present to a potential employer should not contain poor erasures or messy correction fluid blotches.

Parts of the Résumé

You may arrange your résumé according to your own preference. In general, however, there are six basic parts to a simple résumé. Your

FIGURE 2–1A Letter of Application

13 (at center)

234 Maple Street
Eugene, OR 97401-4231
June 15, 19--

Mr. Ryler Evans
Magna Music Company
2456 Main Street
Eugene, OR 97401-4302

Dear Mr. Evans:

Please consider this letter an application for the secretarial position advertised in Sunday's Register Guard.

I believe my high school training and part-time office experience while attending high school have prepared me for the position. Enclosed is a copy of my résumé, which details my qualifications. Please feel free to call the references I have listed.

My interests, abilities, and experiences are all in the office administration field. I feel I have gained valuable knowledge while working with people in my previous positions, and I look forward to the opportunity for additional growth.

I shall appreciate the opportunity to talk to you about this secretarial position. I can be reached at (503) 555-9326. I look forward to hearing from you soon.

Sincerely yours,

Terrence B Adams

Terrence B. Adams

Enclosure: Résumé

(Margin=20)   (Margin=80)

FIGURE 2–1B Résumé

TERRENCE B. ADAMS
234 Maple Street
Eugene, OR 97401-4231
(503) 555-9326

CAREER OBJECTIVE

To obtain a position in the office administration field that will provide an opportunity for continuous growth.

EDUCATION

1979-1982   Madison High School; Eugene, Oregon; GPA 3.00 or above
1977-1979   Wilson Junior High School; Eugene, Oregon; GPA 3.5 or above

SKILLS

Typing (70 wpm)   Experienced in use of: calculator, ten-key
Filing   adding machine, IBM
Accounting   word processor, various
Telephone use   copiers, cash register

EXTRACURRICULAR ACTIVITIES

Member of National Honor Society; president, senior year
Senior class student council representative
President of debate team, junior year
Secretary of FBLA (Future Business Leaders of America), sophomore year

EXPERIENCE

June, 1982   Farwest Truck Center; Eugene, Oregon
to   Assistant File Clerk
Present   Duties: filing, typing, operating word processor

December, 1981   Coast Carloading; Eugene, Oregon
to   Office Helper
June, 1982   Duties: errand running, some typing and filing

July, 1980   Pancake House Restaurant; Eugene, Oregon
to   Host/Cashier
October, 1981   Duties: greeting and seating customers, operating
                 cash register

REFERENCES

Ms. Grace Lawton, Manager, Valley Title, 480 Willamette Street, Eugene,
    OR 97401-4278, (503) 555-6121.
Mr. Patrick Bailey, Business Teacher, Madison High School, Eugene, OR
    97402-5223, (503) 555-0731.
Miss Frances Bishop, Work Experience Coordinator, Madison High School,
    Eugene, OR 97402-5223, (503) 555-0731.

résumé should include personal information, career objective, education, experience, additional qualifications, and references.

Personal Information. This section should be placed first on the résumé. Data to be given include name, address, and phone number. You may also wish to include your social security number or other descriptive information. Information such as age, sex, marital status, number of dependents, and ethnic background cannot lawfully be demanded by potential employers, but you may offer it if you wish.

Make the objective statement clear and forceful.

Career Objective. Below the personal information section, you should place a short statement indicating your goal in a particular occupational field or your goal to obtain a particular position title.

Education. List all secondary and post-secondary schools you have attended, giving the most recent first. You may wish to include major areas of study, grade point average, extracurricular activities, scholastic honors, or other pertinent facts that you think will help create a favorable impression on the employer. Extracurricular activities tell an employer that you are a well-rounded person and possess many different abilities, interests, and aptitudes. Listing any offices held in your extracurricular activities will show the employer that you have leadership ability. Be sure to include dates of attendance for each school.

Experience. List all jobs, paid and unpaid, that you have held. Include all that you have done. You may want to write this section of your résumé in paragraph form or in outline form. Include information such as name and address of employer, job title, job description, and specific achievements while with this employer.

Additional Qualifications. Educational and employment records present an overview of your personal and professional qualifications. However, you may have additional skills and abilities that you wish to bring to a potential employer's attention. You may wish to list special equipment you have learned to operate or call attention to an especially high typing or shorthand speed.

Emphasize your special qualifications.

References. *References* are persons who have known you for at least one year, and who can provide information about your character and achievements. References should be over age 18 and not related to you. The best types of references include teachers, school counselors, former employers, adults in business, and others. Be sure to ask permission of the people you wish to list as references before including them on your résumé.

LETTER OF REFERENCE

Ask for letters of reference now.

A *letter of reference* is a statement, in letter form, written by someone who can be relied upon to give a sincere report on your character, abilities, and experience. When you ask someone to write a letter of reference for you, be sure to give the person enough time to compose and type the letter. Be sure to ask a business reference to type the letter on letterhead stationery. A sample letter of reference is shown in Figure 2–2.

FIGURE 2–2
Letter of
Reference

```
                  FARWEST TRUCK CENTER
                         402 First Street, NW
                         Eugene, OR  97402-2143




                                                June 4, 19--


         To Whom It May Concern:

                      RE:  Terrence B. Adams

         I have known Terry Adams as an employee for one and a
         half years.  Terry began working for Farwest as a work-
         study student in the cooperative education program at
         his high school.  He proved to be such a good employee
         that, at the end of the school year, we kept Terry as a
         full-time summer worker.  He now works for us part-time
         after school and on weekends.

         Terry is a fine young man.  I have found him to be hon-
         est and sincere.  He is always on time and is genuinely
         eager to do a good job.  Terry gets along well with
         other employees and customers.  He has filled in for
         vacationing office employees and has been able to assume
         additional responsibilities very quickly.

         Without hesitation I can recommend Terry to you as a
         fine person and an outstanding employee.  He will, I am
         sure, be an asset to any company for which he works.

         If you have any further questions, please do not hesi-
         tate to call me.

                                 Sincerely,

                                 Harriet Williams

                                 Harriet Williams
                                 Manager
```

When you have received the letter of reference, make several photocopies of the original to give to employers along with your résumé and letter of application. Keep the original letter of reference for your files, since you may need additional copies for other job applications. Remember, the most impressive letters of reference usually come from former employers, teachers or other school personnel, adults in business, or other persons over age 18 but not related to you who have known you for at least one year.

APPLICATION FORM

When you visit a company in person to interview or inquire about a job opening, you will probably be asked to complete an *application for employment*. When completing an application for employment, you should follow these steps:

1. Type your answers, or print them using a black or blue ink pen that does not skip or blot.

Fill out the application carefully.

2. Fill in all the blanks. When you cannot answer a question, fill in *N/A* (information not available or not applicable), or use a broken line (- - - - - -) to indicate to the employer that you have not missed or ignored the question.
3. Be truthful. Give complete answers. Do not abbreviate unless the meaning of the abbreviation is clear.
4. Type or print neatly. Keep your responses in the space provided.

Take needed information with you.

5. Have with you all information that might be asked for on the application, such as social security number, telephone numbers, driver's license number, or work permit number. Calling later with the rest of the needed information inconveniences the employer.

A completed application for employment is shown in Figure 2–3.

JOB INTERVIEW

During the job interview, an employer will have in front of him or her your completed job application, together with your résumé, letter of application, letter(s) of reference, and any other information you have provided. You may be asked questions about answers you have provided on the application for employment, or about information contained in the résumé and letters. Therefore, you should spend at least as much time and effort in preparing for the interview as you did in obtaining the appointment.

FIGURE 2-3
Application Form

APPLICATION FOR EMPLOYMENT			
PLEASE PRINT WITH BLACK INK OR USE TYPEWRITER		*AN EQUAL OPPORTUNITY EMPLOYER*	

NAME (LAST, FIRST, MIDDLE INITIAL)		SOCIAL SECURITY NUMBER	DATE
Adams, Terrence B.		643-27-1364	6/24/--

ADDRESS (NUMBER, STREET, CITY, STATE, ZIP CODE)	TELEPHONE NUMBER
234 Maple Street	(503) 555-9326
Eugene, OR 97401-4231	

IN CASE OF EMERGENCY, NOTIFY:	NAME	Thomas and Rita Adams	RELATIONSHIP
	ADDRESS	——— Same as above ———	Parents

EDUCATION

SCHOOL NAME	CITY AND STATE	YEARS ATTENDED
HIGH SCHOOL Madison High School	Eugene, Oregon	1979-1982
JUNIOR HIGH SCHOOL Wilson Junior High School	Eugene, Oregon	1977-1979
OTHER Lane Community College	Eugene, Oregon	1982-1983

SKILLS

TYPING	SHORTHAND	ACCOUNTING	FILING
70 wpm	No	Yes (1 yr.)	Yes

OTHER SKILLS (LIST)
Telephone Use

MACHINES YOU CAN OPERATE (LIST)
Calculator, Ten-Key Adding Machine, IBM Word Processor, Copier, Cash Register

WORK HISTORY (LAST POSITION FIRST)

FROM	TO	EMPLOYER NAME/ADDRESS	POSITION	ENDING PAY	REASON FOR LEAVING
June, 1982	Present	Farwest Truck Center Eugene, Oregon	Assistant File Clerk	$3.95/Hr.	Desire More Responsibility
December, 1981	June, 1982	Coast Carloading Eugene, Oregon	Office Helper	Minimum Wage	More Responsibility
July, 1980	October, 1981	Pancake House Restaurant Eugene, Oregon	Host/ Cashier	Minimum Wage	More Time For School

REFERENCES

NAME	ADDRESS	OCCUPATION	TELEPHONE NUMBER
Ms. Grace Lawton	Eugene, Oregon	Manager, Valley Title	(503) 555-6121
Mr. Patrick Bailey	Eugene, Oregon	Business Teacher	(503) 555-0731
Miss Frances Bishop	Eugene, Oregon	Work Experience Coordinator	(503) 555-0731

I understand and agree that any false statements on this application may be considered sufficient cause for dismissal.

Terrence B. Adams
SIGNATURE OF APPLICANT

Preparing for the Interview

Rehearse before the actual interview.

Preparation is essential to a successful interview. First, you should review your résumé so that all your personal information and qualifications will be fresh in your mind. Be prepared to state this information briefly during the interview.

It is also important to learn something about the company. Find out what the company makes or sells, where its plants and branch operations are located, how rapidly it has grown, and what its prospects are for the future. Think of questions you might ask the interviewer about the company and about the position for which you are applying. The prospective employer will be more interested in you as an employee if you show that you are interested in the company.

Plan your interview strategy.

Information about companies can be obtained from such sources as these:

1. The Yellow Pages of the telephone directory, which may have an advertisement that will list products or services
2. The company itself (simply call and request the information you wish)
3. A friend who works for the company and can describe it to you
4. Annual reports (usually kept on file at public and university libraries), which will describe the company and its financial resources

Making a Good First Impression

Several important details should be remembered in preparing to make a favorable impression.

Arrive on Time. Better yet, arrive five to ten minutes early so that you have time to check your appearance and compose yourself. Never be late for an interview: the interviewer will consider your tardiness an indication of your expected job performance.

Arrive early for the interview.

Dress Appropriately. If you are seeking work in a bank, dress like those who are already employed at the bank. Whatever you wear, be neat and clean. Do not overuse jewelry, perfume, or after-shave. Be modest and conservative in dress and appearance.

Go Alone. Do not bring a friend or relative. Only you will perform the job if hired; therefore, the interviewer wishes to talk to you alone.

Be Prepared. Have copies of your résumé, reference letters, and school transcripts with you. All should be typed neatly and accurately. Carry one or two good pens with you.

Appear Poised and Self-Confident. It is normal to be nervous, but don't let your emotions get the best of you. Do not chew gum, smoke, or display other nervous habits. An occasional smile shows you are relaxed and feel good about yourself.

Smile to show self-confidence.

Be Courteous. Even if you are asked to wait, respond with courtesy and understanding. Convey an attitude of being composed and easy to get along with.

Think before You Answer Each Question. Be polite, accurate, and honest. Use correct grammar; be especially careful of verb tenses. Speak slowly and clearly.

Emphasize Your Strong Points. Talk about your favorite school subjects, grades, attendance, skills, work experience, activities, and goals in a positive manner. Negative comments are unnecessary and reflect badly on your personality.

Be Enthusiastic and Interested in the Company and the Job. Show that you are energetic and able to do what is asked with a willing attitude.

Leave copies, not originals, for the employer.

When the interview is over, thank the interviewer for his or her time. Say you will check back later, then do it. Leave a copy of your résumé, letters of reference, and other information with the interviewer. Exit with a smile and an I-look-forward-to-working-for-this-company type of comment.

Above all, let common sense be your guide throughout the interview.

THANK-YOU LETTER

When your job interview is completed and the employer is left to make a decision, a *follow-up* is essential. Positive contact with the employer after the interview will remind the employer of your appearance, personality, and qualifications, and should improve your chance of getting the job. A ***thank-you letter*** is an excellent tool to remind the interviewer of your interest in and desire to work for the company.

Reaffirm your interest with a letter.

A brief thank-you letter should be written to the employer to express your appreciation for having been given an interview. This letter will also reaffirm your interest in the job and give you an opportunity to restate some of your qualifications for the position. See Figure 2–4 for a sample thank-you letter.

Basic Rules

The thank-you letter should be short and simple. Follow the same format and typing guidelines that you used in preparing your letter of application. You may want to enclose an additional letter of reference or some

FIGURE 2–4
Thank-You
Letter

```
                                    234 Maple Street
                                    Eugene, OR  97401-4231
                                    June 25, 19--


        Mr. Ryler Evans
        Magna Music Company
        2456 Main Street
        Eugene, OR  97401-4302

        Dear Mr. Evans:

        Thank you for the time you spent with me during our inter-
        view yesterday.  I enjoyed the opportunity to meet you
        and some of your office staff.

        Your description of the secretarial position sounded very
        interesting to me.  I am sure this is a position for
        which I am qualified, and I would enjoy working for your
        company.  You can be assured I am a very dependable and
        conscientious worker.  If there is any additional infor-
        mation that I can supply for you, please do not hesitate
        to call me.  I plan to make a career in the office admin-
        istration area and am, therefore, available for long-
        term employment.

        I look forward to hearing from you soon.

                                    Sincerely yours,

                                    Terrence B. Adams

                                    Terrence B. Adams
```

information that may help the interviewer. Remember to address the interviewer by name. If more than one person interviewed you during your visit, write a brief letter to each person.

Body of the Letter

The content of the thank-you letter is very important. The first paragraph should remind the interviewer of your interview by making reference to it. A good way to begin is, "Thank you for giving me the opportunity to speak with you on (date and time of interview) concerning . . . ."

The second paragraph reminds the interviewer of your interest in and desire to work for the company. At this point you should also remind the interviewer of your abilities, goals, and qualifications in a subtle, modest manner.

Remind the interviewer of your strengths.

The final paragraph should express a courteous mention of your eagerness to hear from the interviewer when he or she has reached a decision. This paragraph should end on a positive note.

Keep your letter short and to the point. It must be typed without error. Your final opportunity to represent yourself to the potential employer through a thank-you letter may make the difference that will get you the job.

See Figure 2–4 for a sample thank-you letter.

VOCABULARY

Directions: Can you find the definition for each of the following terms used in Chapter 2?

letter of application	complimentary close
return address	résumé
inside address	personal information
salutation	education
body	experience
references	letter of reference
application for employment	job interview
thank-you letter	follow-up

1. The part of a letter that shows the writer's street address, city, state, ZIP code, and date of the letter.

2. The greeting, using a person's name followed by a colon.

3. The part of a letter that shows the name and address of the person or company to whom you are writing.

4. A summary of personal information, education, experience, additional qualifications, and references of a person seeking a job.

5. A list of schools you have attended, last ones first, appearing on the résumé.

6. People over 18, not related to you, who have known you for at least one year and can report on your character and achievements.

7. A written statement from someone who knows you; it should be typed.

8. A form you fill out when you apply for a job.

9. A procedure whereby you are asked questions and you respond orally.

10. A letter to an employer asking for a job interview.

11. A list of jobs, paid and unpaid, that you have held, which appears on a résumé.

12. A tool to remind the employer of your interest in the job, written after the job interview.

ITEMS FOR DISCUSSION

1. What is the purpose of a letter of application? What action is desired?

2. What size paper should you use for a letter of application or a thank-you letter?

3. List and briefly describe the five basic parts of a letter of application.

4. What is a résumé? Describe the parts you will include in your own résumé.

5. Why should you list extracurricular activities on your résumé?

6. Which kinds of people should be used as references on a résumé?

7. List five rules for filling out an application for employment.

8. What is meant by the term *follow-up* ?

9. What is the content of the body of the thank-you letter?

10. Why is it important for you to type your résumé, letter of application, and thank-you letter?

APPLICATIONS

1. Using Figure 2–1A as an example, prepare a letter of application to a business or company that you would like to work for. Read the instructions on pages 19–21 carefully.

2. Using Figure 2–1B as an example, prepare your résumé, or prepare a résumé of your own design. Include all information that applies to you, emphasizing your strong points.

3. Call, write, or speak directly to each person you listed on your résumé as a reference and ask permission to use their names on your résumé. Ask one person to write a letter of reference for you to use in seeking a job.

4. Obtain from a local business an application for employment, such as the one shown in Figure 2–3, and complete it.

5. Write a thank-you letter for a job interview, using Figure 2–4 as an example. Assume you were interviewed by the person to whom you sent your letter of application (see Question 1). You should know the interviewer's name now. Address the person by name and title.

CASE PROBLEMS AND ACTIVITIES

1. Prepare a basic example of a letter of application, so that when you actually do apply for a job you will have the content outlined for actual use. In red pen, write in the directions for vertical spacing, margins, and letter parts. Use Figure 2–1A as an example.

2. Steve Mason wants to work as a forest ranger when he graduates from college. At present, he knows of no openings, but does know the address of the local Bureau of Land Management, which occasionally hires students during summers to help in the forest. Steve takes science courses and does well. He is available to work all summer, and could even live at a ranger station if necessary. He would even work without pay if his living expenses were covered. Because you are Steve's friend, you have offered to help him write a letter of application. Make up a return address, inside address, salutation, body, and complimentary close using the letter of application in Figure 2–1A as a guide.

3. Melanie Josephs must provide a résumé in order to answer an advertisement in the local newspaper. Write in outline form a summary of the basic rules of writing a résumé. On another piece of paper, sketch a résumé and label its parts. You do not need to insert fictional information, just describe what kinds of information Melanie should use.

4. Jean August tells you that she has a job interview tomorrow. She has never been on a job interview before, and she is very nervous. Jean asks you to point out to her what she should and should not do during her interview. On a piece of paper, make a list for Jean of at least five things she should be sure to do and five things she should avoid doing during her job interview tomorrow.

CHAPTER 3
KEEPING YOUR JOB

CHAPTER OBJECTIVES

After studying this chapter and completing the activities, you will be able to:

1. Understand and complete appropriate work forms, such as W-4, social security application, and work permit application.
2. Understand and recall employee responsibilities at work and employer responsibilities to employees.
3. List and define provisions of basic employment laws enacted for protection and security of workers.

WORK FORMS

When you begin your first paying job, you will need to be aware of a number of forms. Most of these forms ask for information that employers are required by law to keep. Some of these forms can be obtained prior to beginning work (social security card and work permit, if you are under 16), while others are completed by you when you begin working (W-4) and by the employer after you have worked during the year (W-2). You should be familiar with these forms because you may need to make corrections or changes from time to time.

Form W-4, Employee's Withholding Allowance Certificate

When you report to work, you will be asked to fill out a *Form W-4, Employee's Withholding Allowance Certificate*. Form W-4 is for income tax withholding purposes and remains in effect until you make a change. On this form you declare the total number of ***allowances***, persons who are dependent on your income for support. The more allowances you can claim, the less tax you will have withheld. You may automatically claim yourself. Other allowances can be for spouse, children, or if your itemized deductions allow less money to be withheld from your paycheck. You may also claim ***exempt status*** and not have any federal tax withheld from your paycheck, if you qualify, by writing *exempt* as shown in Figure 3–1. You may claim to be exempt from federal tax withholding if you will not earn enough money to owe any federal tax. The amount of maximum earnings varies, but in 1982, the qualifying figure was $3,400 for a single person. Exemption may be claimed if last year you owed no federal tax and had a right to receive a full refund and if this year you do not expect to owe any federal tax and expect a full refund.

Claim exempt status if you qualify.

Social Security Forms

Because all workers in the United States must pay a social security tax from wages earned, all persons must obtain a ***social security number***. Your social security number is your permanent work identification number. While you are working, your employers withhold social security taxes from your pay and contribute matching amounts. All your work life, the amounts you earn and the amounts contributed for social security are credited by the Social Security Administration to your account under your assigned number. When you become eligible, benefits are paid to you monthly based upon how much you have paid into your account.

Withholdings are credited to your account.

FIGURE 3–1
Form W-4, Employee's Withholding Allowance Certificate

Form **W-4** (Rev. January 1982)
Department of the Treasury—Internal Revenue Service
Employee's Withholding Allowance Certificate
OMB No. 1545–0010
Expires 4–30–83

1 Type or print your full name: Marisa M. Clark
2 Your social security number: 682-40-5896
Home address (number and street or rural route): 685 West Circle Avenue
3 Marital Status: ☒ Single ☐ Married ☐ Married, but withhold at higher Single rate
Note: If married, but legally separated, or spouse is a nonresident alien, check the Single box.
City or town, State, and ZIP code: Cincinnati, OH 45227-6287

4 Total number of allowances you are claiming (from line F of the worksheet on page 2) . . . .
5 Additional amount, if any, you want deducted from each pay . . . . $
6 I claim exemption from withholding because (see instructions and check boxes below that apply):
a ☒ Last year I did not owe any Federal income tax and had a right to a full refund of **ALL** income tax withheld, **AND**
b ☒ This year I do not expect to owe any Federal income tax and expect to have a right to a full refund of **ALL** income tax withheld. If both a and b apply, enter "EXEMPT" here . . . . ▶ Exempt
c If you entered "EXEMPT" on line 6b, are you a full-time student? . . . . ☒ Yes ☐ No

Under the penalties of perjury, I certify that I am entitled to the number of withholding allowances claimed on this certificate, or if claiming exemption from withholding, that I am entitled to claim the exempt status.

Employee's signature ▶ Marisa M. Clark Date ▶ January 3, 19

7 Employer's name and address (including ZIP code) (FOR EMPLOYER'S USE ONLY)
8 Office code
9 Employer identification number

Social security isn't just for retirement. If a parent covered by social security dies or becomes disabled, minor children may be eligible for payments. Persons who become severely disabled (unable to work for a year or more) are paid benefits until they return to work. If disability coverage is needed for more than two years, payments are continued under Medicare.

Disability benefits are available.

Figure 3–2 is an application for a social security number card. This application must be filled out completely and sent to the Social Security

FIGURE 3–2
Application for a Social Security Number Card

DEPARTMENT OF HEALTH AND HUMAN SERVICES
SOCIAL SECURITY ADMINISTRATION

Form Approved
OMB No. 0960-0066

FORM SS-5 — APPLICATION FOR A SOCIAL SECURITY NUMBER CARD (Original, Replacement or Correction)

MICROFILM REF. NO. (SSA USE ONLY)

Unless the requested information is provided, we may not be able to issue a Social Security Number (20 CFR 422.103(b))

INSTRUCTIONS TO APPLICANT ▶ Before completing this form, please read the instructions on the opposite page. You can type or print, using pen with dark blue or black ink. Do not use pencil.

NAA 1 NAME TO BE SHOWN ON CARD — First: Marisa — Middle: Melanie — Last: Clark

NAB FULL NAME AT BIRTH (IF OTHER THAN ABOVE) — First: — Middle — Last

ONA OTHER NAME(S) USED —

SST 2 MAILING ADDRESS (Street/Apt. No., P.O. Box, Rural Route No.): 685 West Circle Avenue

CTY STE ZIP — CITY: Cincinnati — STATE: OH — ZIP CODE: 45227-6287

CSP 3 CITIZENSHIP (Check one only)
☒ a U.S. citizen
☐ b Legal alien allowed to work
☐ c Legal alien not allowed to work
☐ d Other (See instructions on Page 2)

SEX 4 — ☐ MALE ☒ FEMALE

ETB 5 RACE/ETHNIC DESCRIPTION (Check one only) (Voluntary)
☐ a Asian, Asian-American or Pacific Islander (Includes persons of Chinese, Filipino, Japanese, Korean, Samoan, etc., ancestry or descent)
☐ b Hispanic (Includes persons of Chicano, Cuban, Mexican or Mexican-American, Puerto Rican, South or Central American, or other Spanish ancestry or descent)
☐ c Negro or Black (not Hispanic)
☐ d North American Indian or Alaskan Native
☒ e White (not Hispanic)

DOB 6 DATE OF BIRTH — MONTH 08 DAY 21 YEAR 64
AGE 7 PRESENT AGE 20
PLB 8 PLACE OF BIRTH — CITY: Cincinnati — STATE OR FOREIGN COUNTRY: OH — FCI ☐

MNA 9 MOTHER'S NAME AT HER BIRTH — First: Mary — Middle: Grace — Last (her maiden name): Jacobs
FNA FATHER'S NAME — First: Richard — Middle: Allen — Last: Clark

PNO 10 a Has the person listed in Item 1 above or anyone acting on that person's behalf ever applied for a social security number card before? ☐ YES (2) ☒ NO (1) ☐ Don't know (1) If yes, when: MONTH YEAR
b Was a card received? ☐ YES (3) ☐ NO (1) ☐ Don't know (1) — If you checked yes to a or b, complete items c through e; otherwise go to Item 11.
SSN c Enter Social Security Number ☐☐☐–☐☐–☐☐☐☐
NLC PDB d Enter the name shown on the most recent social security card — e Date of birth correction (See Instruction 10 on page 2) ▶ MONTH DAY YEAR

DON 11 TODAY'S DATE ▶ MONTH 01 DAY 08 YEAR – –
12 Telephone number where we can reach you during the day. Please include the area code. ▶ HOME (513)555-8684 OTHER

ASD WARNING: **Deliberately furnishing (or causing to be furnished) false information on this application is a crime punishable by fine or imprisonment, or both.**

13 YOUR SIGNATURE: Marisa M. Clark
14 YOUR RELATIONSHIP TO PERSON IN ITEM 1 — ☒ Self ☐ Other (Specify) ____
WITNESS (Needed only if signed by mark "X") — WITNESS (Needed only if signed by mark "X")

DO NOT WRITE BELOW THIS LINE (FOR SSA USE ONLY)
SSN ASSIGNED ☐☐☐–☐☐–☐☐☐☐ — DTC — SSA RECEIPT DATE — NPN
DOC — NTC — CAN — BIC — SIGNATURE AND TITLE OF EMPLOYEE(S) REVIEWING EVIDENCE AND/OR CONDUCTING INTERVIEW
TYPE(S) OF EVIDENCE SUBMITTED — ☐ MANDATORY IN PERSON INTERVIEW CONDUCTED — DATE — DATE
IDN — ITV — DCL

Form SS-5 (7-82) 3

Administration. You are then assigned one social security number for your lifetime, and are issued a card bearing this number. If the original card bearing the assigned number is lost or destroyed, you can obtain a duplicate without charge.

From time to time—every few years—you should check to see that your earnings have been properly credited to your account. The Social Security Administration in Baltimore provides a handy card for you to complete for this purpose (see Figure 3–3). Within 30 days you should receive a report that lists your income according to the Social Security Administration's records. Any mistakes should be reported immediately.

If you have not yet applied for your social security number, you should do so now, so you will have it handy when you are ready to go to work.

Check your social security records periodically.

FIGURE 3–3
Request for Social Security Statement of Earnings

Work Permit Application

A parent must sign the work permit application.

Federal and some state laws require ***minors***, persons under the age of legal majority, to obtain a ***work permit*** before they are allowed to work. The work permit is signed by the parents or legal guardian of persons under 16 years of age. Application for a work permit is obtained from the Department of Labor, a school counseling center, or work experience coordinators. There is usually no charge for obtaining the card, but the applicant will have to provide his or her social security number and proof of birth and have a parent's or legal guardian's signature. Additional information may be required in some states. Figure 3–4 is an example of a work permit application. The form must be filled in completely and clearly. Processing of the work permit application takes three to six weeks, so early application is advisable.

WORK PERMIT APPLICATION

This Is Not A Permit

| 2 | 5 | 2 | – | 4 | 3 | – | 4 | 5 | 5 | 7 |

SOCIAL SECURITY NUMBER

SEE INSTRUCTIONS

PERMIT WILL NOT BE ISSUED
unless all blanks are carefully filled in and are clearly readable

Mitchell B. Lewin   *M*   *3-28-68*
NAME   SEX   BIRTHDATE

1350 Harrison St.   *272-3485*
MAILING ADDRESS   PHONE NO.

Cincinnati, OH   *45227-6308*
CITY AND STATE   ZIP CODE

Cincinnati   *OH*
BIRTHPLACE (CITY)   STATE

Riverside High School   *Cincinnati*   *9*
LAST SCHOOL ATTENDED   LOCATION   GRADE COMPLETED

Janice M. Lewin
PARENT OR GUARDIAN SIGNATURE

1350 Harrison St.   *272-3485*
STREET ADDRESS   PHONE NO.

Cincinnati, OH   *45227-6308*
CITY AND STATE   ZIP CODE

Mitchell B. Lewin
MINOR'S SIGNATURE

Do Not Write Below This Line

Form W-2, Wage and Tax Statement

When you have worked for a business or company during the year, you will receive a *Form W-2, Wage and Tax Statement*, which lists income you earned during the year and all amounts withheld by the employer in your behalf. These amounts include federal income tax, state income tax, and social security tax. Figure 3–5 is a completed W-2 statement. Your W-2 should be compared to payroll slips received with each paycheck to be sure that the right amounts have been reported.

Compare the Form W-2 with your payroll slips.

FIGURE 3–5
Form W-2, Wage and Tax Statement

1 Control number	22222			
2 Employer's name, address, and ZIP code		3 Employer's identification number 93-81256791		4 Employer's State number OH44422
Hanson Motors 85 Briar Street Cincinnati, OH 45230-5162		5 Stat. em-ployee De-ceased ☒ Legal rep. ☐ 942 emp. ☐ Sub-total ☐ Void ☐		
		6 Allocated tips		7 Advance EIC payment
8 Employee's social security number 682-40-5896	9 Federal income tax withheld	10 Wages, tips, other compensation $2,084.00		11 Social security tax withheld $139.63
12 Employee's name, address, and ZIP code		13 Social security wages $2,084.00		14 Social security tips
Marisa M. Clark 685 West Circle Avenue Cincinnati, OH 45227-6287		16		
		17 State income tax $14.04	18 State wages, tips, etc. $2,084.00	19 Name of State Ohio
		20 Local income tax $41.60	21 Local wages, tips, etc. $2,084.00	22 Name of locality Cincinnati

Form **W-2 Wage and Tax Statement 1983**   Copy B To be filed with employee's FEDERAL tax return
This information is being furnished to the Internal Revenue Service.   Department of the Treasury Internal Revenue Service

The employer must provide a W-2 form to you no later than January 31 of the year following the one in which you were employed. This is true even if you only worked part of the year and were not working as of December 31. If you do not receive a W-2 from your employer (and all employers you may have worked for during the year) you should contact the employer to get the W-2. Former employers may not have a current address for you.

EMPLOYEE RESPONSIBILITIES

As a new employee, you will want to do the best possible job. In order to be successful, you will have a number of responsibilities to meet.

Responsibilities to Employers

Your employer hires you and pays you at predetermined intervals. In return for this pay and other benefits you may receive, the employer expects certain things from you.

Plan to meet your job responsibilities.

Competent Work. You should do your best to produce the best possible finished product for your employer. The work needs to be *marketable*; that is, of such quality that the employer can sell it or represent the

McDonald's
Corporation

company by use of your product. If, for example, you type a letter that has so many mistakes and erasures that it cannot be mailed, the letter is not a marketable product.

Be thrifty with your
employer's supplies.

Thrift. When using an employer's materials, you should be as thrifty as possible, conserving supplies and materials with care and diligence as though they were your own. Supplies and other materials are expensive to an employer.

Punctuality. Workers should consistently arrive at work on time, take allotted breaks, and leave at quitting time. Being punctual means being ready to go to work at the appointed time—not rushing through the door at the last minute.

Pleasant Attitude. On any job, it is important to be pleasant and easy to get along with. You should be willing to follow orders and take directions. Your employer also has the right to expect you to be courteous to customers, since you represent the company or store to others.

Loyalty displays respect
for the employer.

Loyalty and Respect. While working for a company, you should never be guilty of spreading rumors or gossiping about your employer or job. As long as you are on the company "team," you are expected to be loyal to the company. Loyalty includes showing respect to the employer and the company on and off the job.

Dependability. When you say you will do something, follow through. The employer should be able to depend on you to do what you are hired to do.

Initiative. You should not have to be told everything to do. Employees who stand idle when a specific job is completed are of very little value to employers. *Initiative* means that you do things on your own without being told to; you're a self-starter.

Interest. It is important for you to show an interest in your job and your company. You should project an attitude of wanting to learn all you can and of giving all tasks your best possible effort. An enthusiastic attitude projects to an employer your sincere interest in being a cooperative and productive worker.

Self-Evaluation. The ability to take criticism and to assess your own progress is important to you and the employer. Everyone has strong points and weak points, but the weak points cannot be improved unless you are willing to admit they exist and begin to work on them. Employers are faced with the task of employee evaluation to determine raises and promotions. Employees should be able to recognize their own strong points and limitations and do a realistic self-evaluation of their job performance.

Be aware of your weak points.

Responsibilities to Other Employees

In addition to the responsibilities that you owe your employer, you also have duties to your fellow workers. These include the following:

Teamwork. You are part of a team when you work with others in a company, and you need to do your share of the work. Employees must work cooperatively in order to produce a quality final product; when friction and personality problems occur, the productivity and efficiency of the whole company decrease.

Do your share of the work.

Thoughtfulness. Be considerate of fellow workers to promote a good work atmosphere for everyone, including customers. Having a pleasant attitude will result in a more enjoyable time for yourself and others. Personal problems and conflicts have no place being displayed at work.

Loyalty. In addition to being loyal to and supportive of your employer, you should also be loyal toward fellow employees. This means not spreading rumors about them. Gossiping leads to a breakdown of teamwork.

Responsibilities to Customers

As an employee, you represent the company. To the customer who walks in the front door, you *are* the company. Thus, your attitude toward a customer often makes the difference in whether he or she returns for future products or services. Therefore, remember that on behalf of your employer you have the responsibility to greet the customer with an attitude of helpfulness and courtesy.

Attitude is very important.

Helpfulness. When customers come to your employer's place of business, they expect to have reasonable help in finding or deciding what to purchase. It is the employee's responsibility to help customers find what they want or to do what is needed. An attitude of helpfulness reflects well on the company and is an important part of any job.

Courtesy. Whether or not you like a customer, that customer actually pays your wages—by keeping your employer in business. Without the customer, the business could not exist. Therefore, your attitude toward the customer should always be respectful and courteous, never hostile or unfriendly. Customer loyalty to a business is often built by friendly, helpful employees.

Being helpful is good for business.

EMPLOYER RESPONSIBILITIES

Employers also have responsibilities to employees. Some responsibilities are required by law, and others are simply good practices to follow for keeping employees happy and on the job. Failure to meet these responsibilities can result in an employer being fined for unfair labor practices or a high turnover rate, higher premiums for unemployment insurance, and costly expenses in connection with the continual need to hire new employees. Some employer duties include adequate supervision, fair personnel policies, safe working conditions, open channels of communication, recognition of achievement, and compliance with civil rights and laws.

Adequate Supervision

Employees need to be properly supervised to be sure they are learning to do a good job on work assigned. Supervision includes providing appropriate instruction in the use of equipment and safety standards, and spending enough time with new employees to adequately train them to do the assigned task.

Fair Personnel Policies

Know what is expected of you.

Hiring and firing policies, salary advancement policies, and procedures for recourse for employee disputes are some of the policies that need to be fair and well defined. Employees should know clearly what is acceptable and unacceptable performance, what the standards are for advancements and raises, and what constitutes grounds for suspension or discharge.

Safe Working Conditions

All employees must be provided safe equipment, a safe working environment, and adequate training for working under dangerous conditions. Special protective equipment and clothing and warning signs must be provided to employees working under dangerous conditions. Minors have stricter working conditions than adults in some industries.

Open Channels of Communication

Employers need to communicate with employees so that all employees have the opportunity to express concerns, ask questions, and make suggestions. Lack of open channels of communication can result in poor morale of workers and low work output. Employees need to know they are an important part of the company and that their opinions are valuable.

Recognition of Achievement

Rewards are work incentives.

Employers need to provide some form of reward for performance by employees. Merit pay raises, as well as advancement on a regularly established schedule, provide encouragement for workers to do their best possible work. When achievement is not recognized, employees lose the desire to be as productive as possible. All human beings need to be rewarded and encouraged from time to time; a salary bonus or raise is an excellent method of encouragement.

Compliance with Civil Rights and Laws

Employers must obey state and federal laws designed to protect workers from discrimination in employment on the basis of race, color, sex,

Employment laws protect workers' rights.

national origin, religion, and, in some cases, age. In the next section we will learn of some of the employment laws enacted to protect workers from unfair labor practices. The employer is responsible for observing workers' rights. Failure to do so can result in severe penalties for the employer. Complaints of discrimination in employment may be filed with the Equal Employment Opportunity Commission.

EMPLOYMENT LAWS

In the last fifty years many laws have been enacted to provide various protections for American workers. Laws enacted are generally enforced by government agencies, such as the Department of Labor or the Social Security Administration.

Major employment acts are called administrative laws. Established by Congress and authorized by the executive branch of government, *administrative agencies* are given the power of law to enforce administrative laws. The Department of Labor is responsible for overseeing several important labor acts and their provisions.

All workers receive benefits.

The main provisions of the laws will generally be in one or more of the following areas *for all workers*:

1. To establish a minimum wage
2. To provide regular working hours
3. To provide unemployment, disability, and retirement insurance benefits
4. To provide equal employment opportunities and eliminate discrimination
5. To establish safe working conditions

Other laws have provisions for specific workers that do not apply to all workers. Minors are given several special provisions:

1. Specific safety precautions and working conditions that are more extensive than for adults
2. Maximum number of hours to be worked and times during which minors can work during the school year
3. Requirement for those under age 16 to obtain a work permit

Legal recourse is available.

If any employee believes that he or she has not received benefits as required by law, *recourse*, or remedy is available. If you think that you have a legitimate complaint, you should call the state Department of Labor, which will assist you without charge. Employers found in violation of labor laws are subject to fine, payment of damages to employees, and other penalties determined by a court of law.

Social Security Act

Originally called the Federal Insurance Contributions Act of 1935, the *Social Security Act* was the first national social insurance program, enacted to provide federal aid for the elderly and for disabled workers. In 1965 the Medicare provision (hospital and medical insurance protection) for elderly retired workers and other qualified persons was added. Five basic types of benefits are paid: (*a*) disability, (*b*) survivor, (*c*) retirement, (*d*) hospital, and (*e*) medical. Benefits received depend on the amount of contributions made. Self-employed workers pay their social security contributions when they pay their income tax. For employees in occupations covered by social security, contributions are mandatory. Social security protection is not yet available for some types of employment. Your local social security office will know if your employment is covered. Social security (FICA) is deducted from your gross pay and sent to the Internal Revenue Service for proper crediting to your social security account.

Benefits depend on contributions.

Unemployment Compensation

An important part of the Social Security Act provides that every state must have an *unemployment insurance* program that provides benefits to workers who lose their jobs through no fault of their own. After a waiting period, laid-off or terminated workers may collect a portion of their regular pay for a certain length of time. Premiums for unemployment insurance are generally paid by employers. Rates vary according to employers' records of turnover, or how often they hire and fire employees. The more often employers let workers go, the higher the premium rate they will pay. Each state has its own regulations as to waiting period, maximum benefits, deadlines for filing claims, and premium rates. Unless otherwise extended by provision of the legislature of the state, benefits are paid for a maximum of 22 weeks, through the local state employment office.

Waiting periods are necessary.

Fair Labor Standards Act

Popularly known as the *Wage and Hour Act*, the Fair Labor Standards Act of 1938 provided that persons working in interstate commerce or a related industry could not be paid less than a minimum wage of 25 cents an hour. A *minimum wage* is the legally established lower limit on wages employers may pay. The minimum wage reached $3.35 an hour in January of 1981. Another provision of the act states that hourly wage workers cannot be employed for more than 40 hours a week. Hours worked in addition to the regular hours are considered *overtime* and must be paid for at one and one-half times the regular rate.

Each state enforces wage and hour laws, which include federal provisions and additional state regulations. These laws, which are regulated by state Departments of Labor, provide that regular paydays must be established and maintained by every employer. Payment of wages to new employees must begin no later than 35 days after the date work has begun. When an employee quits, wages due must be paid within 48 hours of the final day worked. When an employee is discharged, all wages are due immediately. Any employee who requests that his or her paycheck be mailed is entitled to have it mailed to an address designated by the employee. An itemized statement of deductions from wages must be furnished to employees with their regular paychecks. The maximum number of hours that minors may work varies according to state laws. Tips are not considered wages and may not be calculated in the amount of minimum wage due. Any employee who is unduly charged fees or denied any of the preceding legal rights provided by the Fair Labor Standards Act may file an appeal with the nearest office of the Department of Labor. Employees may not be discharged because of a pending wage claim.

The minimum wage law has an exception—those businesses whose annual sales do not exceed $250,000 are exempt from paying the minimum wage. Also exempt are nonprofit and governmental offices that are providing employment as part of a training program.

Workers' Compensation

Workers' compensation, traditionally called workmen's compensation, is the name for statutes (laws) that give financial security to workers and their families for on-the-job injury, illness, or death that occurs as a result of the job or working conditions. This law is often labeled "liability without fault" because the employer is responsible for employee injuries and illnesses that are the result of employment, even though the employer may have done nothing to cause the injury or illness. Today all 50 states have workers' compensation statutes. In some states, the SAIF (State Accident Insurance Fund), or other designated state agency, collects a premium for each working person. The fee is usually based on the number of days worked during a pay period. Employers pay the workers' compensation premium in most states. However, in some states, employees are required to pay all or a part of the premium. The premiums are used to pay benefits to injured employees. Benefits include payments to doctors and hospitals, payment to the employee for temporary or permanent disability, and payment of benefits to survivors in the event of death.

Employers may also elect to maintain their own workers' compensation insurance program, if they qualify. Upon proof that an employer can

Employers may provide their own insurance.

meet the expenses of such a liability, a private company will establish the fund on behalf of the employer to insure against the loss. Large companies may provide their own workers' compensation insurance program within the company benefits package.

VOCABULARY

Directions: Can you find the definition for each of the following terms used in Chapter 3?

Form W-4	allowances
exempt	social security number
Form W-2	marketable
initiative	minors
administrative agencies	Social Security Act
unemployment insurance	workers' compensation

1. Persons who are dependent on your income for their support.

2. Your permanent work identification number.

3. A form completed by your employer and mailed to you no later than January 31.

4. Work of such quality that an employer can use it.

5. Persons under the age of legal majority.

6. Authorized by Congress to enforce administrative laws.

7. Enacted in 1935, it was our first national insurance program to provide financial help for elderly and disabled workers.

8. A part of the Social Security Act, ensuring that benefits are paid to workers who lose their jobs.

9. One of the forms you will fill out when you begin working on which you claim a number of allowances to determine taxes withheld from your paycheck.

10. Persons who will not incur any federal tax liability may claim this status on their Form W-4.

11. The ability to do things without being told.

12. Benefits to protect workers from loss due to on-the-job illness or injuries.

ITEMS FOR DISCUSSION

1. What is the purpose of Form W-4?

2. Why do you need to have a social security number before you begin work?

3. Besides retirement income, what other benefits are provided by social security?

4. Why is it important that your employer have your correct social security number?

5. Where can you obtain a work permit application?

6. Besides yourself, who must sign your work permit application if you are under age 16?

7. What information is listed on Form W-2?

8. By what date must your employers for the past year provide you a Form W-2?

9. What should you do if your employer during the past year does not send you a Form W-2?

10. List at least five responsibilities that the employee has to his or her employer.

11. List at least three responsibilities that an employee has to other employees at work.

12. What responsibilities do employees have to the employer's customers?

13. List and describe three responsibilities that employers have to their employees.

14. What is an administrative agency?

15. What were some of the provisions of the Social Security Act?

16. What is unemployment insurance?

17. List the major provisions of the Fair Labor Standards Act.

18. What is meant by the term *liability without fault*?

APPLICATIONS

1. Obtain a Form W-4 from the closest office of the Internal Revenue Service and complete it properly, claiming exempt status if you are entitled to do so.

2. Obtain an Application for Social Security Number Card from your local Social Security Administration office. Complete the form with the appropriate information.

3. Look up in your telephone directory the address of your nearest Department of Labor office. Go there and pick up a work permit application and fill it in. (Your counseling center or work experience coordinator will probably have work permit forms also.)

4. On a piece of paper list in the order you think most important the responsibilities that employees have to their employers. Then ask your parent or another working person to also list employee responsibilities in order of importance. Compare the two lists. Then, if possible, ask an employer to list in order what she/he considers important responsibilities that employees have to their employers.

5. What responsibilities do you have, as an employee, to customers of your employer?

6. What responsibilities do you think employers should have to employees besides the regular payment of wages you have earned? Interview a person who is working full-time and ask her/him the same question. Compare answers.

7. Look up the Social Security Act in an encyclopedia or historical reference book in your library. Obtain this information: (*a*) why social security was deemed necessary by the president at the time; (*b*) who the president at the time was; (*c*) history of benefits, deductions from paychecks, and purpose of social security.

8. Obtain from your state Department of Labor the provisions of state laws regarding employment of minors. Include: (*a*) maximum hours per week that can be worked, (*b*) latest hour in the evening that a minor can work, (*c*) if a work permit is required for workers under 16, (*d*) any other provisions to protect you as a minor while working part-time or full-time.

9. From your state Department of Labor or from an employer obtain information as to how workers' compensation insurance is handled in your state. Is it by a state agency or private insurance programs? What types of benefits are available? How much are premiums and who pays them? Since all states have workers' compensation laws, determine all you can about the laws in your state.

CASE PROBLEMS AND ACTIVITIES

1. Your friend Mitch has discovered that the amount of wages paid to him during the year appears to be different from the amount listed on the W-2 sent to him by his employer. He asks you, "What shall I do?" What should you reply?

2. Kris McMahan worked for three employers last year. It is now February 1 of the following year, and she has received Form W-2 from only two of those employers. She asks you what she should do about it. What should you tell her?

3. Because last year Sean did not earn enough money on his part-time job to have to pay any federal taxes, his employer has asked him if this year he would like to claim exempt status on his W-4. Explain to Sean how he can claim to be exempt and what this means to him.

4. Margarita, 14, has decided that she wants to work part-time this summer doing whatever kind of work she can find to earn money to buy school clothes. Tell her what things she should do now, several months before summer, to get appropriate numbers and cards she may need to go to work. Also tell Margarita what forms she may have to complete when she begins work.

5. Karen Jacobs just received her W-2 form from her employer and has noticed that her social security number is wrong on the form. What should she do? What can happen if she does nothing?

6. Clarke Jackson worked for over a year for the same employer, then was laid off because business was slow. He is looking for another job, but is in need of income to make his rent payment. You told Clarke that he may be eligible for unemployment insurance payments. Explain how he could qualify and whom he should see to find out about unemployment benefits.

CHAPTER 4
EMPLOYEE BENEFITS

CHAPTER OBJECTIVES

After studying this chapter and completing the activities, you will be able to:

1. Compute payroll deductions and net pay from information and tables provided.
2. Identify optional and required employee benefits and recognize their value as additions to net pay.
3. Understand the role of unions and professional organizations in this country.

GROSS PAY, DEDUCTIONS, NET PAY

Gross pay is the total pay before deductions.

When people work, they agree to perform certain job tasks in exchange for financial remuneration, called gross pay, together with optional and required benefits that go with the employment. ***Gross pay*** is the total or agreed upon rate of pay or salary, before any deductions are made. If a person is working for $800 a month agreed upon salary, that is his or her gross pay. For people who work for an hourly wage or work overtime hours, computations must be made to determine the amount of their gross pay.

Hourly Wage

Perhaps you will be paid for each hour you work. A record is kept of hours worked, and then the number of hours is multiplied by the rate to

determine the amount of gross pay. For example, a person working for $3.35 an hour who works 40 hours during the week will earn gross pay of $134 ($3.35 multiplied by 40 hours).

Overtime

Overtime is defined as hours worked in addition to regular hours of work. A standard workday is eight continuous hours with allowed breaks plus an unpaid lunch period. A standard workweek is 40 hours in a five-day period of eight hours each day. According to the Fair Labor Standards Act, overtime is paid at the rate of one and one-half times the regular rate of pay. If the regular rate of pay is $4.00 an hour, the overtime rate is $6.00 an hour ($4.00 times 1 1/2). For example, a person may work a regular workweek of 40 hours at $3.50 an hour, plus one hour overtime each day. Gross pay will be computed as follows:

$$
\begin{aligned}
40 \text{ hours} \times \$3.50 \text{ an hour (regular pay)} &= \$140.00 \\
5 \text{ hours} \times \$5.25 \text{ an hour (overtime pay)} &= \underline{26.25} \\
\text{Gross pay} &= \$166.25
\end{aligned}
$$

Monthly Salary

Perhaps you will be paid a set amount per month. In most cases you will work regular hours, but you will not receive additional pay for any overtime work. In the event you work overtime on a regular basis, then your employer could, if he or she wished, pay an agreed upon overtime rate computed from your monthly salary. For example, your salary is $800 a month. The agreed upon rate might be $6.82 an hour for overtime ($800 a month divided by 22 average workdays a month, divided by 8 hours a day, times one and one-half). Thus, if you worked a total of 20 hours overtime in one month, your total gross pay would be $800 plus $136.40 (20 hours times $6.82 an hour).

Overtime pay is added to regular pay.

Annual Salary

Perhaps you will agree to an *annual*, or yearly, salary. Annual pay is usually divided into equal amounts paid each month. For example, you agree to work for $10,800 a year. Your monthly gross pay will be $900 ($10,800 divided by 12).

Deductions

Amounts subtracted from your gross pay are known as *deductions*. Some deductions are required by law, such as social security, federal income tax, and state income tax, if your state has an income tax. Other deductions are optional and you may choose them: an automatic deduction to be sent to your savings account or to your credit union for a car payment.

Records are kept by employers.

Employers are required to keep detailed records of wages earned and hours worked for inspection by the Department of Labor. With each paycheck, you must also receive a detailed list of all deductions taken from your gross pay. Deductions may not, except by court order, be withheld from your pay without your written consent. This, of course, does not apply to taxes, social security, and other deductions required by federal and state laws.

Net Pay

When all deductions are taken out of your gross pay, the amount left is known as *net pay*. This is the amount of your paycheck, or what you can actually spend. Net pay is often called *take-home pay* because it is really what you have left over to do with as you wish.

Regular Wages or Salary + Overtime = Gross Pay
Gross Pay − Deductions = Net Pay

Figure 4–1 is an Employee Withholding Sheet, which lists gross pay, deductions, and net pay. By law, an explanation of the pay computa-

Explanations of with-
holdings are required.

tions—including gross pay, deductions, and net pay—must be provided with each paycheck. It is important to save the Employee Withholding Sheet or other form of itemization of withholdings from your gross pay so that you can check the accuracy of the W-2 your employer gives you the following January for filing your income tax return.

To compute gross pay on the Employee Withholding Sheet, the number of regular hours worked is multiplied by the hourly rate. Any

FIGURE 4–1
Employee
Withholding
Sheet

EMPLOYEE WITHHOLDING SHEET

Employee Name _Shari Gregson_ Social Security Number _898-40-7426_

Pay Period: ☑ weekly ☐ bimonthly ☐ monthly

Number of Allowances: _1_ ☐ married ☑ single

GROSS PAY

   1. Regular Wages: _40_ hours at $ _4.00_/hr. = $ _160.00_

or

   2. Regular Salary: = _____

   3. Overtime: _4_ hours at $ _6.00_/hr. = _24.00_

   GROSS PAY ....$ _184.00_

REQUIRED DEDUCTIONS

   4. Federal Income Tax (use tax tables) ....$ _23.20_

   5. State Income Tax (use tax tables) .... _11.00_

   6. Social Security Tax (use 6.70% times gross pay) .... _12.33_

OTHER DEDUCTIONS

   7. Insurance .... _____

   8. Union Dues .... _8.00_

   9. Credit Union .... _20.00_

   10. Savings .... _____

   11. Retirement .... _____

   12. Charity .... _____

   13. Other: _____ .... _____

   _____ .... _____

   TOTAL DEDUCTIONS (total lines 4 through 14) ....$ _74.53_

   NET PAY (subtract total deductions from gross pay) ....$ _109.47_ overtime hours are multiplied by the overtime rate. Gross pay includes either hourly wages plus overtime, or salary plus overtime.

Required deductions include federal, state, and local taxes, and social security. The tax withholding amounts are determined from tax tables such as those shown in Figures 4–2 through 4–5. The more allowances a person claims on his or her W-4 statement, the less the amount of tax the employer will withhold or deduct from gross pay. The social security deduction is withheld at the rate of 6.70 percent of the first $35,700

Withholding amounts are taken from tables.

Weekly payroll period (Oregon)
Amount of tax to be withheld

WAGE		SINGLE			MARRIED		THREE OR MORE SINGLE OR MARRIED											
AT LEAST	BUT LESS THEN	0	1	2	0	1	2	3	4	5	6	7	8	9	10	11	12	13	14+
0--	20	0	0	0	0	0	0	0	0	0	0	0	0	0	0	0	0	0	0
20--	40	1	1	0	1	1	0	0	0	0	0	0	0	0	0	0	0	0	0
40--	60	2	2	1	2	2	1	0	0	0	0	0	0	0	0	0	0	0	0
60--	80	4	3	2	3	3	2	1	0	0	0	0	0	0	0	0	0	0	0
80--	100	6	4	3	4	4	3	2	1	0	0	0	0	0	0	0	0	0	0
100--	120	7	6	4	5	5	4	3	2	1	0	0	0	0	0	0	0	0	0
120--	140	9	7	6	6	6	5	4	3	2	1	0	0	0	0	0	0	0	0
140--	160	10	9	7	8	7	6	5	4	3	2	1	0	0	0	0	0	0	0
160--	180	12	10	9	9	8	7	6	5	4	3	2	1	0	0	0	0	0	0
180--	200	14	12	11	11	9	8	7	6	5	4	3	2	1	0	0	0	0	0
200--	220	15	14	12	13	11	10	8	7	6	5	4	3	2	1	0	0	0	0
220--	240	17	15	14	14	13	11	10	8	7	6	5	4	3	2	1	0	0	0
240--	260	18	17	15	16	15	13	11	10	8	7	6	5	4	3	2	1	0	0
260--	280	20	18	17	18	16	15	13	11	10	8	7	6	5	4	3	2	1	0
280--	300	22	20	19	20	18	16	15	13	12	10	8	7	6	5	4	3	2	1
300--	320	23	22	20	21	20	18	16	15	13	12	10	8	7	6	5	4	3	2
320--	340	25	23	22	23	21	20	18	17	15	13	12	10	8	7	6	5	4	3
340--	360	26	25	23	25	23	21	20	18	17	15	13	12	10	9	7	6	5	4
360--	380	28	26	25	26	25	23	22	20	18	17	15	13	12	10	9	7	6	5
380--	400	29	28	27	28	26	25	23	22	20	18	17	15	14	12	10	9	7	6
400--	420	31	29	28	30	28	27	25	23	22	20	18	17	15	14	12	10	9	7
420--	440	32	31	29	31	30	28	27	25	23	22	20	19	17	15	14	12	10	9
440--	460	34	32	31	33	31	30	28	27	25	23	22	20	19	17	15	14	12	11
460--	480	35	34	32	34	33	31	30	28	27	25	24	22	20	19	17	15	14	12
480--	500	36	35	34	36	34	33	32	30	29	27	25	24	22	20	19	17	16	14
500--	520	38	36	35	37	36	34	33	32	30	29	27	25	24	22	21	19	17	16
520--	540	39	38	36	39	37	36	35	33	32	30	29	27	25	24	22	21	19	17
540--	560	41	39	38	40	39	37	36	35	33	32	30	29	27	26	24	22	21	19
560--	580	43	41	39	42	40	39	38	36	35	33	32	30	29	27	26	24	22	21
580--	600	45	43	41	43	42	40	39	38	36	35	33	32	31	29	27	26	24	22
600--	620	47	45	43	45	43	42	41	39	38	36	35	33	32	31	29	27	26	24
620--	640	50	48	46	46	45	43	42	41	39	38	36	35	34	32	31	29	27	26
640--	660	52	50	48	48	46	45	44	42	41	39	38	36	35	34	32	31	29	28
660--	680	54	52	50	50	48	46	45	44	42	41	39	38	37	35	34	32	31	29
680--	700	56	54	52	53	50	48	47	45	44	42	41	39	38	37	35	34	32	31
700--	720	58	56	54	55	53	51	49	47	45	44	42	41	40	38	37	35	34	32
720--	740	60	58	56	57	55	53	51	49	47	45	44	42	41	40	38	37	35	34
740--	760	63	61	58	59	57	55	53	51	49	47	45	44	43	41	40	38	37	35
760--	780	65	63	61	61	59	57	55	53	51	49	47	45	44	43	41	40	38	37
780--	800	67	65	63	63	61	59	57	55	53	51	49	47	46	44	43	41	40	38
800--	820	69	67	65	65	63	61	59	57	55	53	51	49	47	46	44	43	41	40
820--	840	71	69	67	68	66	64	61	59	57	55	53	51	49	47	46	44	43	41
840-- --	860	73	71	69	70	68	66	64	62	60	57	55	53	51	49	47	46	44	43

10.8 PERCENT OF EXCESS OVER 3560 PLUS --

| 860--OVER | | 74 | 72 | 70 | 71 | 69 | 67 | 65 | 63 | 61 | 59 | 57 | 54 | 52 | 50 | 48 | 46 | 45 | 44 |

FIGURE 4–2 State Tax Withholding Table—Weekly Payroll

earned. This ceiling amount will continue to rise through 1990 because of legislation submitted by President Carter and approved by Congress in 1977.

Additional withholdings may be authorized.

In addition to required deductions, those which an employee has authorized to have withheld will be subtracted from gross pay. Most common of these deductions are insurance payments, union dues, credit union payments, savings account deposits, retirement contributions, and charity deductions. These types of deductions cannot be withheld from pay without the written consent of the employee.

Monthly payroll period (Oregon)
Amount of tax to be withheld

WAGE		TWO OR LESS					NUMBER OF WITHHOLDING ALLOWANCES												
		SINGLE			MARRIED		THREE OR MORE SINGLE OR MARRIED												
AT LEAST	BUT LESS THEN	0	1	2	0	1	2	3	4	5	6	7	8	9	10	11	12	13	14+
0--	40	0	0	0	0	0	0	0	0	0	0	0	0	0	0	0	0	0	0
40--	80	3	0	0	3	0	0	0	0	0	0	0	0	0	0	0	0	0	0
80--	120	5	1	0	5	1	0	0	0	0	0	0	0	0	0	0	0	0	0
120--	160	7	3	0	7	3	0	0	0	0	0	0	0	0	0	0	0	0	0
160--	200	9	5	1	9	5	1	0	0	0	0	0	0	0	0	0	0	0	0
200--	240	11	7	3	11	7	3	0	0	0	0	0	0	0	0	0	0	0	0
240--	280	13	9	5	13	9	5	1	0	0	0	0	0	0	0	0	0	0	0
280--	320	16	11	7	15	11	7	3	0	0	0	0	0	0	0	0	0	0	0
320--	360	19	13	9	17	13	9	5	0	0	0	0	0	0	0	0	0	0	0
360--	400	22	16	11	19	15	11	7	2	0	0	0	0	0	0	0	0	0	0
400--	440	26	19	12	21	17	13	9	4	0	0	0	0	0	0	0	0	0	0
440--	480	29	22	16	23	19	15	11	6	2	0	0	0	0	0	0	0	0	0
480--	520	32	25	19	25	21	17	13	8	4	0	0	0	0	0	0	0	0	0
520--	560	35	29	22	27	23	19	15	10	6	2	0	0	0	0	0	0	0	0
560--	600	38	32	25	29	25	21	17	12	8	4	0	0	0	0	0	0	0	0
600--	640	42	35	28	31	27	23	19	14	10	6	2	0	0	0	0	0	0	0
640--	680	45	38	32	35	29	25	21	16	12	8	4	0	0	0	0	0	0	0
680--	720	48	41	35	38	31	27	23	18	14	10	6	2	0	0	0	0	0	0
720--	760	51	45	38	41	34	29	25	20	16	12	8	4	0	0	0	0	0	0
760--	800	54	48	41	45	38	31	27	22	18	14	10	6	2	0	0	0	0	0
800--	840	58	51	44	48	41	34	29	24	20	16	12	8	4	0	0	0	0	0
840--	880	61	54	48	52	45	38	31	26	22	18	14	10	6	1	0	0	0	0
880--	920	64	57	51	55	48	41	34	28	24	20	16	12	8	3	0	0	0	0
920--	960	67	61	54	58	51	44	37	30	26	22	18	14	10	5	1	0	0	0
960--1000		70	64	57	62	55	48	41	34	28	24	20	16	12	7	3	0	0	0
1000--1040		74	67	60	65	58	51	44	37	30	26	22	18	14	9	5	1	0	0
1040--1080		77	70	64	69	62	55	47	40	33	28	24	20	16	11	7	3	0	0
1080--1120		80	73	67	72	65	58	51	44	37	30	26	22	18	13	9	5	1	0
1120--1160		83	77	70	75	68	61	54	47	40	33	28	24	20	15	11	7	3	0
1160--1200		86	80	73	79	72	65	58	51	44	37	30	26	22	17	13	9	5	1
1200--1240		90	83	76	82	75	68	61	54	47	40	33	28	24	19	15	11	7	3
1240--1280		93	86	80	86	79	72	64	57	50	43	36	30	26	21	17	13	9	5
1280--1320		96	89	83	89	82	75	68	61	54	47	40	33	28	23	19	15	11	7
1320--1360		99	93	86	92	85	78	71	64	57	50	43	36	30	25	21	17	13	9
1360--1400		102	96	89	96	89	82	75	68	61	54	46	39	32	27	23	19	15	11
1400--1440		106	99	92	99	92	85	78	71	64	57	50	43	36	29	25	21	17	13
1440--1480		109	102	96	103	96	89	81	74	67	60	53	46	39	32	27	23	19	15
1480--1520		112	105	99	106	99	92	85	78	71	64	57	50	43	36	29	25	21	17
1520--1560		115	109	102	109	102	95	88	81	74	67	60	53	46	39	32	27	23	19
1560--1600		118	112	105	113	106	99	92	85	78	71	63	56	49	42	35	29	25	21
1600--1640		122	115	108	116	109	102	95	88	81	74	67	60	53	46	39	32	27	23
1640--1680		125	118	112	120	113	106	98	91	84	77	70	63	56	49	42	35	29	25
1680--1720		127	121	115	123	116	109	102	95	88	81	74	67	60	53	45	38	31	27
1720--1760		130	125	118	126	119	112	105	98	91	84	77	70	63	56	49	42	35	29
1760--1800		133	127	121	130	123	116	109	102	95	88	80	73	66	59	52	45	38	31

FIGURE 4–3 State Tax Withholding Table—Monthly Payroll

WAGE-BRACKET WITHHOLDING TABLES

WEEKLY Payroll Period — Employee NOT MARRIED — Effective July 1, 1982

| And the wages are— | | And the number of withholding allowances claimed is— | | | | | | | | | | |
At least	But less than	0	1	2	3	4	5	6	7	8	9	10 or more
		The amount of income tax to be withheld shall be—										
$0	$27	$0	$0	$0	$0	$0	$0	$0	$0	$0	$0	$0
27	28	.10	0	0	0	0	0	0	0	0	0	0
28	29	.30	0	0	0	0	0	0	0	0	0	0
29	30	.30	0	0	0	0	0	0	0	0	0	0
30	31	.40	0	0	0	0	0	0	0	0	0	0
31	32	.50	0	0	0	0	0	0	0	0	0	0
32	33	.70	0	0	0	0	0	0	0	0	0	0
33	34	.80	0	0	0	0	0	0	0	0	0	0
34	35	.90	0	0	0	0	0	0	0	0	0	0
35	36	1.00	0	0	0	0	0	0	0	0	0	0
36	37	1.10	0	0	0	0	0	0	0	0	0	0
37	38	1.30	0	0	0	0	0	0	0	0	0	0
38	39	1.40	0	0	0	0	0	0	0	0	0	0
39	40	1.50	0	0	0	0	0	0	0	0	0	0
40	41	1.60	0	0	0	0	0	0	0	0	0	0
41	42	1.70	0	0	0	0	0	0	0	0	0	0
42	43	1.90	0	0	0	0	0	0	0	0	0	0
43	44	2.00	0	0	0	0	0	0	0	0	0	0
44	45	2.10	0	0	0	0	0	0	0	0	0	0
45	46	2.20	0	0	0	0	0	0	0	0	0	0
46	47	2.30	.20	0	0	0	0	0	0	0	0	0
47	48	2.50	.30	0	0	0	0	0	0	0	0	0
48	49	2.60	.40	0	0	0	0	0	0	0	0	0
49	50	2.70	.50	0	0	0	0	0	0	0	0	0
50	51	2.80	.60	0	0	0	0	0	0	0	0	0
51	52	2.90	.80	0	0	0	0	0	0	0	0	0
52	53	3.10	.90	0	0	0	0	0	0	0	0	0
53	54	3.20	1.00	0	0	0	0	0	0	0	0	0
54	55	3.30	1.10	0	0	0	0	0	0	0	0	0
55	56	3.40	1.10	0	0	0	0	0	0	0	0	0

| And the wages are— | | And the number of withholding allowances claimed is— | | | | | | | | | | |
At least	But less than	0	1	2	3	4	5	6	7	8	9	10 or more
56	57	3.50	1.20	0	0	0	0	0	0	0	0	0
57	58	3.70	1.40	0	0	0	0	0	0	0	0	0
58	59	3.80	1.50	0	0	0	0	0	0	0	0	0
59	60	3.90	1.60	0	0	0	0	0	0	0	0	0
60	62	4.10	1.80	0	0	0	0	0	0	0	0	0
62	64	4.40	2.00	0	0	0	0	0	0	0	0	0
64	66	4.70	2.20	.20	0	0	0	0	0	0	0	0
66	68	5.00	2.50	.40	0	0	0	0	0	0	0	0
68	70	5.30	2.70	.60	0	0	0	0	0	0	0	0
70	72	5.70	3.00	.80	0	0	0	0	0	0	0	0
72	74	6.00	3.20	1.00	0	0	0	0	0	0	0	0
74	76	6.30	3.50	1.20	0	0	0	0	0	0	0	0
76	78	6.60	3.70	1.40	0	0	0	0	0	0	0	0
78	80	6.90	3.90	1.60	0	0	0	0	0	0	0	0
80	82	7.30	4.20	1.90	0	0	0	0	0	0	0	0
82	84	7.60	4.50	2.10	.30	0	0	0	0	0	0	0
84	86	7.90	4.80	2.40	.60	0	0	0	0	0	0	0
86	88	8.20	5.20	2.60	.80	0	0	0	0	0	0	0
88	90	8.50	5.50	2.80	1.00	0	0	0	0	0	0	0
90	92	8.90	5.80	3.10	1.20	0	0	0	0	0	0	0
92	94	9.20	6.10	3.30	1.50	0	0	0	0	0	0	0
94	96	9.50	6.40	3.60	1.70	0	0	0	0	0	0	0
96	98	9.80	6.70	3.80	1.90	.10	0	0	0	0	0	0
98	100	10.10	7.10	4.00	2.10	.30	0	0	0	0	0	0
100	105	10.70	7.60	4.60	2.60	.80	0	0	0	0	0	0
105	110	11.50	8.40	5.40	3.40	1.60	0	0	0	0	0	0
110	115	12.30	9.20	6.20	4.20	2.30	.50	0	0	0	0	0
115	120	13.10	10.00	7.00	5.00	3.10	1.10	0	0	0	0	0
120	125	13.90	10.80	7.80	5.80	3.90	1.90	0	0	0	0	0
125	130	14.70	11.60	8.60	5.60	4.70	2.80	1.60	0	0	0	0
130	135	15.50	12.40	9.40	6.30	3.40	1.10	0	0	0	0	0
135	140	16.30	13.20	10.20	7.10	3.80	1.60	0	0	0	0	0
140	145	17.10	14.00	11.00	7.90	4.90	2.30	0	0	0	0	0
145	150	17.90	14.80	11.80	8.70	5.60	2.90	.60	0	0	0	0
150	160	19.10	16.00	13.00	9.90	6.80	3.80	1.50	0	0	0	0

WEEKLY Payroll Period — Employee NOT MARRIED — Effective July 1, 1982

| And the wages are— | | And the number of withholding allowances claimed is— | | | | | | | | | | |
At least	But less than	0	1	2	3	4	5	6	7	8	9	10 or more
		The amount of income tax to be withheld shall be—										
$160	$170	$20.70	$17.60	$14.60	$11.50	$8.40	$5.30	$2.70	$.40	$0	$0	$0
170	180	22.60	19.20	16.20	13.10	10.00	6.90	3.90	1.60	0	0	0
180	190	24.50	20.80	17.80	14.70	11.60	8.50	5.40	2.80	.50	0	0
190	200	26.50	22.60	19.40	16.30	13.20	10.10	7.00	4.00	1.70	0	0
200	210	28.50	24.60	21.00	17.90	14.80	11.70	8.60	5.60	2.90	.60	0
210	220	30.50	26.60	22.80	19.50	16.40	13.30	10.20	7.20	4.10	1.80	0
220	230	32.50	28.60	24.80	21.10	18.00	14.90	11.80	8.80	5.40	3.00	.60
230	240	34.50	30.60	26.80	22.90	19.60	16.50	13.40	10.30	7.20	4.10	1.90
240	250	36.50	32.60	28.80	24.90	21.20	18.10	15.00	11.90	8.90	5.80	3.10
250	260	38.50	34.60	30.80	26.90	23.10	19.70	16.60	13.60	10.50	7.40	4.30
260	270	41.40	36.80	32.80	28.90	25.10	21.30	18.20	15.20	12.10	9.00	5.90
270	280	43.60	39.00	34.80	30.90	27.10	23.20	19.60	16.80	13.70	10.60	7.50
280	290	46.60	41.60	37.00	32.90	29.10	25.20	21.40	18.40	15.30	12.20	9.10
290	300	48.60	44.60	39.40	34.90	31.10	27.20	23.40	20.00	16.90	13.80	10.70
300	310	51.00	46.40	41.80	37.20	33.10	29.20	25.40	21.60	18.50	15.40	12.30
310	320	53.40	48.80	44.20	39.60	35.10	31.20	27.40	23.50	20.10	17.00	13.90
320	330	55.80	51.20	46.60	42.00	37.40	33.20	29.40	25.50	21.70	18.60	15.50
330	340	58.80	53.60	49.00	44.40	39.80	35.20	31.40	27.50	23.70	20.20	17.10
340	350	61.80	56.10	51.40	46.80	42.20	37.60	33.40	29.50	25.70	21.80	18.70
350	360	64.80	59.10	53.80	49.20	44.60	40.00	35.40	31.50	27.70	23.80	20.30
360	370	67.80	62.10	56.30	51.60	47.00	42.40	37.80	33.50	29.70	25.80	22.00
370	380	70.80	65.10	59.30	54.00	49.40	44.80	40.20	35.50	31.70	27.80	24.00
380	390	73.80	68.10	62.30	56.50	51.80	47.20	42.60	38.00	33.70	29.80	26.00
390	400	76.80	71.10	65.30	59.50	54.20	49.60	45.00	40.40	35.70	31.80	28.00
400	410	79.80	74.10	68.30	62.50	56.80	52.00	47.40	42.80	38.10	33.80	30.00
410	420	82.80	77.10	71.30	65.50	59.80	54.40	49.80	45.20	40.50	35.90	32.00
420	430	85.80	80.10	74.30	68.50	62.80	57.00	52.20	47.60	42.90	38.30	34.00
430	440	88.80	83.10	77.30	71.50	65.80	60.00	54.60	50.00	45.30	40.70	36.10
440	450	92.30	86.10	80.30	74.50	68.80	63.00	57.30	52.40	47.70	43.10	38.50
450	460	95.70	89.20	83.30	77.50	71.80	66.00	60.20	54.70	50.10	45.50	40.90

| And the wages are— | | And the number of withholding allowances claimed is— | | | | | | | | | | |
At least	But less than	0	1	2	3	4	5	6	7	8	9	10 or more
460	470	99.10	92.60	86.30	80.50	74.80	69.00	63.20	57.50	52.50	47.90	43.30
470	480	102.50	96.00	89.50	83.50	77.80	72.00	66.20	60.50	54.80	50.30	45.70
480	490	105.90	99.40	92.90	86.50	80.80	75.00	69.20	63.50	57.70	52.70	48.10
490	500	109.30	102.80	96.30	89.80	83.80	78.00	72.20	66.50	60.70	55.10	50.50
500	510	112.70	106.20	99.70	93.10	86.80	81.00	75.20	69.50	63.70	57.90	52.90
510	520	116.10	109.60	103.10	96.50	90.00	84.00	78.20	72.50	66.70	60.90	55.30
520	530	119.50	113.00	106.50	99.90	93.40	87.00	81.20	75.50	69.70	63.90	58.20
530	540	123.00	116.40	109.90	103.30	96.80	90.30	84.20	78.50	72.70	66.90	61.20
540	550	126.60	119.80	113.30	106.70	100.20	93.70	87.20	81.50	75.70	69.90	64.20
550	560	130.40	123.20	116.70	110.10	103.60	97.10	90.50	84.50	78.70	72.90	67.20
560	570	134.10	126.90	120.10	113.50	107.00	100.40	93.90	87.40	81.70	75.90	70.20
570	580	137.80	130.60	123.50	116.90	110.40	103.80	97.30	90.80	84.70	78.90	73.20
580	590	141.50	134.30	127.20	120.30	113.80	107.20	100.70	94.20	87.70	81.90	76.20
590	600	145.20	138.00	130.90	123.70	117.20	110.60	104.10	97.60	91.00	84.90	79.20
600	610	148.90	141.70	134.60	127.50	120.60	114.00	107.50	101.00	94.40	87.90	82.20
610	620	152.60	145.40	138.30	131.20	124.00	117.40	110.90	104.40	97.80	91.30	85.20
620	630	156.30	149.10	142.00	134.90	127.60	120.80	114.30	107.80	101.20	94.70	88.20
630	640	160.00	152.80	145.70	138.50	131.40	124.20	117.70	111.20	104.60	98.10	91.50
640	650	163.70	156.50	149.40	142.20	135.10	128.00	121.10	114.60	108.00	101.50	95.00
650	660	167.40	160.20	153.10	145.90	138.80	131.70	124.50	118.00	111.40	104.90	98.40
660	670	171.10	163.90	156.80	149.60	142.50	135.50	128.20	121.40	114.80	108.30	101.80
670	680	174.80	167.60	160.50	153.40	146.20	139.10	131.90	124.80	118.20	111.70	105.20
680	690	178.50	171.30	164.20	157.10	149.90	142.90	135.60	128.50	121.60	115.10	108.60
690	700	182.40	175.00	167.90	160.80	153.70	146.50	139.40	132.20	125.10	118.50	112.00
700	710	186.10	178.70	171.60	164.50	157.40	150.30	143.10	136.00	128.80	121.90	115.40
710	720	189.60	182.40	175.30	168.20	161.10	154.00	146.80	139.70	132.60	125.50	118.80
720	730	193.30	186.10	179.00	171.90	164.80	157.70	150.50	143.40	136.30	129.20	122.10
730	740	197.00	189.80	182.70	175.60	168.50	161.40	154.30	147.10	140.00	132.90	125.80
$740 and over		198.80	191.70	184.60	177.50	170.30	163.20	156.10	149.00	141.90	134.80	127.60
		37 percent of the excess over $740 plus—										

FIGURE 4–4 Federal Tax Withholding Tables—Weekly Payroll

WAGE-BRACKET WITHHOLDING TABLES

MONTHLY Payroll Period—Employee MARRIED—Effective July 1, 1982

And the wages are—		And the number of withholding allowances claimed is—										
At least	But less than	0	1	2	3	4	5	6	7	8	9	10 or more
		The amount of income tax to be withheld shall be—										
$0	$200	$0	$0	$0	$0	$0	$0	$0	$0	$0	$0	$0
200	204	.20	0	0	0	0	0	0	0	0	0	0
204	208	.70	0	0	0	0	0	0	0	0	0	0
208	212	1.20	0	0	0	0	0	0	0	0	0	0
212	216	1.70	0	0	0	0	0	0	0	0	0	0
216	220	2.20	0	0	0	0	0	0	0	0	0	0
220	224	2.60	0	0	0	0	0	0	0	0	0	0
224	228	3.10	0	0	0	0	0	0	0	0	0	0
228	232	3.60	0	0	0	0	0	0	0	0	0	0
232	236	4.10	0	0	0	0	0	0	0	0	0	0
236	240	4.60	0	0	0	0	0	0	0	0	0	0
240	248	5.30	0	0	0	0	0	0	0	0	0	0
248	256	6.20	0	0	0	0	0	0	0	0	0	0
256	264	7.20	0	0	0	0	0	0	0	0	0	0
264	272	8.20	0	0	0	0	0	0	0	0	0	0
272	280	9.10	0	0	0	0	0	0	0	0	0	0
280	288	10.10	.10	0	0	0	0	0	0	0	0	0
288	296	11.00	1.00	0	0	0	0	0	0	0	0	0
296	304	12.00	2.00	0	0	0	0	0	0	0	0	0
304	312	13.00	3.00	0	0	0	0	0	0	0	0	0
312	320	13.90	3.90	0	0	0	0	0	0	0	0	0
320	328	14.90	4.90	0	0	0	0	0	0	0	0	0
328	336	15.80	5.80	0	0	0	0	0	0	0	0	0
336	344	16.80	6.80	0	0	0	0	0	0	0	0	0
344	352	17.80	7.80	0	0	0	0	0	0	0	0	0
352	360	18.70	8.70	0	0	0	0	0	0	0	0	0
360	368	19.70	9.70	0	0	0	0	0	0	0	0	0
368	376	20.60	10.60	.60	0	0	0	0	0	0	0	0
376	384	21.60	11.60	1.60	0	0	0	0	0	0	0	0
384	392	22.60	12.60	2.60	0	0	0	0	0	0	0	0
At least	But less than	0	1	2	3	4	5	6	7	8	9	10 or more
392	400	23.50	13.50	3.50	0	0	0	0	0	0	0	0
400	420	25.20	15.20	5.20	0	0	0	0	0	0	0	0
420	440	27.60	17.60	7.60	0	0	0	0	0	0	0	0
440	460	30.00	20.00	10.00	0	0	0	0	0	0	0	0
460	480	32.40	22.40	12.40	2.40	0	0	0	0	0	0	0
480	500	34.80	24.80	14.80	4.80	0	0	0	0	0	0	0
500	520	37.40	27.20	17.20	7.20	0	0	0	0	0	0	0
520	540	40.60	29.60	19.60	9.60	0	0	0	0	0	0	0
540	560	43.80	32.00	22.00	12.00	2.00	0	0	0	0	0	0
560	580	47.00	34.40	24.40	14.40	4.40	0	0	0	0	0	0
580	600	50.20	36.80	26.80	16.80	6.80	0	0	0	0	0	0
600	640	55.00	41.60	30.40	20.40	10.40	.40	0	0	0	0	0
640	680	61.40	48.00	35.20	25.20	15.20	5.20	0	0	0	0	0
680	720	67.80	54.40	41.10	30.00	20.00	10.00	0	0	0	0	0
720	760	74.20	60.80	47.50	34.80	24.80	14.80	4.80	0	0	0	0
760	800	80.60	67.20	53.90	40.60	29.60	19.60	9.60	0	0	0	0
800	840	87.00	73.60	60.30	47.00	34.40	24.40	14.40	4.40	0	0	0
840	880	93.40	80.00	66.70	53.40	40.00	29.20	19.20	9.20	0	0	0
880	920	99.80	86.40	73.10	59.80	46.40	34.00	24.00	14.00	4.00	0	0
920	960	106.20	92.80	79.50	66.20	52.80	39.50	28.80	18.80	8.80	0	0
960	1,000	112.60	99.20	85.90	72.60	59.20	45.90	33.60	23.60	13.60	3.60	0
1,000	1,040	119.60	105.60	92.30	79.00	65.60	52.30	39.00	28.40	18.40	8.40	0
1,040	1,080	127.20	112.00	98.70	85.40	72.00	58.70	45.40	33.20	23.20	13.20	3.20
1,080	1,120	134.80	119.00	105.10	91.80	78.40	65.10	51.80	38.40	28.00	18.00	8.00
1,120	1,160	142.40	126.60	111.50	98.20	84.80	71.50	58.20	44.80	32.80	22.80	12.80
1,160	1,200	150.00	134.20	118.30	104.60	91.20	77.90	64.60	51.20	37.90	27.60	17.60
1,200	1,240	157.60	141.80	125.90	111.00	97.60	84.30	71.00	57.60	44.30	32.40	22.40
1,240	1,280	165.20	149.40	133.50	117.70	104.00	90.70	77.40	64.00	50.70	37.40	27.20
1,280	1,320	172.80	157.00	141.10	125.30	110.40	97.10	83.80	70.40	57.10	43.80	32.00
1,320	1,360	180.40	164.60	148.70	132.90	117.10	103.50	90.20	76.80	63.50	50.20	36.80
1,360	1,400	188.00	172.20	156.30	140.50	124.70	109.90	96.60	83.20	69.90	56.60	43.20
1,400	1,440	195.60	179.80	163.90	148.10	132.30	116.40	103.00	89.60	76.30	63.00	49.60
1,440	1,480	203.20	187.40	171.50	155.70	139.90	124.00	109.40	96.00	82.70	69.40	56.00
1,480	1,520	210.80	195.00	179.10	163.30	147.50	131.60	115.80	102.40	89.10	75.80	62.40
1,520	1,560	218.40	202.60	186.70	170.90	155.10	139.20	123.40	108.80	95.50	82.20	68.80

MONTHLY Payroll Period—Employee MARRIED—Effective July 1, 1982

And the wages are—		And the number of withholding allowances claimed is—										
At least	But less than	0	1	2	3	4	5	6	7	8	9	10 or more
		The amount of income tax to be withheld shall be—										
$1,560	$1,600	$227.80	$210.20	$194.30	$178.50	$162.70	$146.80	$131.00	$115.20	$101.90	$88.60	$75.20
1,600	1,640	237.40	217.80	201.90	186.10	170.30	154.40	138.60	122.80	108.30	95.00	81.60
1,640	1,680	247.00	227.00	209.50	193.70	177.90	162.00	146.20	130.40	114.70	101.40	88.00
1,680	1,720	256.60	236.60	217.10	201.30	185.50	169.60	153.80	138.00	122.10	107.80	94.40
1,720	1,760	266.20	246.20	226.20	208.90	193.10	177.20	161.40	145.60	129.70	114.20	100.80
1,760	1,800	275.80	255.80	235.80	216.50	200.70	184.80	169.00	153.20	137.30	121.50	107.20
1,800	1,840	285.40	265.40	245.40	225.40	208.30	192.40	176.60	160.80	144.90	129.10	113.60
1,840	1,880	295.00	275.00	255.00	235.00	215.90	200.00	184.20	168.40	152.50	136.70	120.90
1,880	1,920	304.60	284.60	264.60	244.60	224.60	207.60	191.80	176.00	160.10	144.30	128.50
1,920	1,960	314.20	294.20	274.20	254.20	234.20	215.20	199.40	183.60	167.70	151.90	136.10
1,960	2,000	324.20	303.80	283.80	263.80	243.80	223.80	207.00	191.20	175.30	159.50	143.70
2,000	2,040	335.00	313.40	293.40	273.40	253.40	233.40	214.60	198.80	182.90	167.10	151.30
2,040	2,080	345.80	323.30	303.00	283.00	263.00	243.00	223.00	206.40	190.50	174.70	158.90
2,080	2,120	356.60	334.10	312.60	292.60	272.60	252.60	232.60	214.00	198.10	182.30	166.50
2,120	2,160	367.40	344.90	322.40	302.20	282.20	262.20	242.20	222.20	205.70	189.90	174.10
2,160	2,200	378.20	355.70	333.20	311.80	291.80	271.80	251.80	231.80	213.30	197.50	181.70
2,200	2,240	389.00	366.50	344.00	321.50	301.40	281.40	261.40	241.40	221.40	205.10	189.30
2,240	2,280	399.80	377.30	354.80	332.30	311.00	291.00	271.00	251.00	231.00	212.70	196.90
2,280	2,320	410.60	388.10	365.60	343.10	320.60	300.60	280.60	260.60	240.60	220.60	204.50
2,320	2,360	421.40	398.90	376.40	353.90	331.40	310.20	290.20	270.20	250.20	230.20	212.10
2,360	2,400	432.20	409.70	387.20	364.70	342.20	319.80	299.80	279.80	259.80	239.80	219.80
2,400	2,440	443.60	420.50	398.00	375.50	353.00	330.50	309.40	289.40	269.40	249.40	229.40
2,440	2,480	456.40	431.30	408.80	386.30	363.80	341.30	319.00	299.00	279.00	259.00	239.00
2,480	2,520	469.20	442.50	419.60	397.10	374.60	352.10	329.60	308.60	288.60	268.60	248.60
2,520	2,560	482.00	455.30	430.40	407.90	385.40	362.90	340.40	318.20	298.20	278.20	258.20
2,560	2,600	494.80	468.10	441.40	418.70	396.20	373.70	351.20	328.70	307.80	287.80	267.80
2,600	2,640	507.60	480.90	454.20	429.50	407.00	384.50	362.00	339.50	317.40	297.40	277.40
2,640	2,680	520.40	493.70	467.00	440.40	417.80	395.30	372.80	350.30	327.80	307.00	287.00
2,680	2,720	533.20	506.50	479.80	453.20	428.60	406.10	383.60	361.10	338.60	316.60	296.60
2,720	2,760	546.00	519.30	492.60	466.00	439.40	416.90	394.40	371.90	349.40	326.90	306.20
At least	But less than	0	1	2	3	4	5	6	7	8	9	10 or more
2,760	2,800	558.90	532.10	505.40	478.80	452.10	427.70	405.20	382.70	360.20	337.70	315.80
2,800	2,840	571.60	544.90	518.20	491.60	464.90	438.50	416.00	393.50	371.00	348.50	326.00
2,840	2,880	584.90	557.70	531.00	504.40	477.70	451.00	426.80	404.30	381.80	359.30	336.80
2,880	2,920	599.70	570.50	543.80	517.20	490.50	463.80	437.60	415.10	392.60	370.10	347.60
2,920	2,960	614.50	583.60	556.60	530.00	503.30	476.60	450.00	425.90	403.40	380.90	358.40
2,960	3,000	629.30	598.40	569.40	542.80	516.10	489.40	462.80	436.70	414.20	391.70	369.20
3,000	3,040	644.10	613.20	582.40	555.60	528.90	502.20	475.60	448.90	425.00	402.50	380.00
3,040	3,080	658.90	628.00	597.20	568.40	541.70	515.00	488.40	461.70	435.80	413.30	390.80
3,080	3,120	673.70	642.80	612.00	581.20	554.50	527.80	501.20	474.50	447.80	424.10	401.60
3,120	3,160	688.50	657.60	626.80	596.00	567.30	540.60	514.00	487.30	460.60	434.90	412.40
3,160	3,200	703.30	672.40	641.60	610.80	580.10	553.40	526.80	500.10	473.40	446.80	423.20
3,200	3,240	718.10	687.20	656.40	625.60	594.70	566.20	539.60	512.90	486.20	459.60	434.00
3,240	3,280	732.90	702.00	671.20	640.40	609.50	579.00	552.40	525.70	499.00	472.40	445.70
3,280	3,320	747.70	716.80	686.00	655.20	624.30	593.50	565.20	538.50	511.80	485.20	458.50
3,320	3,360	762.50	731.60	700.80	670.00	639.10	608.30	578.00	551.30	524.60	498.00	471.30
3,360	3,400	777.30	746.40	715.60	684.80	653.90	623.10	592.30	564.10	537.40	510.80	484.10
3,400	3,440	792.10	761.20	730.40	699.60	668.70	637.90	607.10	576.90	550.20	523.60	496.90
3,440	3,480	806.90	776.00	745.20	714.40	683.50	652.70	621.90	591.00	563.00	536.40	509.70
3,480	3,520	821.70	790.80	760.00	729.20	698.30	667.50	636.70	605.80	575.80	549.20	522.50
3,520	3,560	836.50	805.60	774.80	744.00	713.10	682.30	651.50	620.60	589.80	562.00	535.30
3,560	3,600	851.30	820.40	789.60	758.80	727.90	697.10	666.30	635.40	604.60	574.80	548.10
3,600	3,640	866.10	835.20	804.40	773.60	742.70	711.90	681.10	650.20	619.40	588.60	560.90
3,640	3,680	880.90	850.00	819.20	788.40	757.50	726.70	695.90	665.00	634.20	603.40	573.70
3,680	3,720	895.70	864.80	834.00	803.20	772.30	741.50	710.70	679.80	649.00	618.20	587.30
		37 percent of the excess over $3,720 plus—										
$3,720 and over		903.10	872.20	841.40	810.60	779.70	748.90	718.10	687.20	656.40	625.60	594.70

FIGURE 4–5 Federal Tax Withholding Tables—Monthly Payroll

BENEFITS

A benefit that employers must provide is national holidays. Full-time employees who are receiving a salary are entitled to have off, with pay, those holidays designated as *paid holidays*. These include Christmas, Thanksgiving, Fourth of July, Labor Day, and Memorial Day. Other holidays that are considered paid holidays by many companies include New Year's Day, Veterans' Day, and Presidents' Day. An employee cannot be required to work on a national holiday, and, if he or she does, the compensation is double or more than double the regular rate of pay.

Pay for work on national holidays is usually double.

Many employers provide one or more of the following *optional* (not required) *benefits*.

Profit Sharing

Profit sharing is usually a plan whereby employees are allowed to receive a portion of the company's profits at the end of the corporate year: the more the company makes (profits), the more the company has to share with employees. Most companies who offer profit sharing consider it an *incentive*, which is a way to encourage employees to do more and better quality work.

Incentives encourage better performance.

Paid Vacations

Most businesses provide full-time employees with a set amount of paid vacation time. While you are on vacation, you are paid as usual. It is common to receive a week's paid vacation after a year, two weeks after two years, three weeks after five years' employment, and so on.

Discounts

Many companies offer to their employees discounts on merchandise sold or made by the company. For example, if you work at a clothing store that allows employee discounts, you can purchase your clothing for a reduced price. A usual discount is 10 percent or more.

Sick Pay

Sick pay is available to full-time workers.

Many businesses also provide an allowance of days each year for illness, with pay as usual for full-time workers. It is customary to receive three to ten days a year as "sick days" without deductions from pay.

Leave of Absence

Some employers allow employees to leave their jobs (without pay) for certain events, such as having children or completing education, and return to their jobs at a later time.

Insurance

Most large companies provide group health insurance plans for all employees. Some plans are paid entirely by the employer, as a part of employee compensation, with full family coverage. Other plans require paycheck deductions if employees elect to participate in the plan. Insurance plans typically include hospitalization, major medical, dental, vision, and life insurance. A typical health insurance plan has a $100 deductible (or more for a family), then pays 80 percent of most doctor bills and prescriptions and 100 percent of hospitalization charges and emergency type bills. Many insurance plans will not cover routine physical examinations because they are not classified as illness or injury.

Coverages vary according to plans purchased.

Bonuses

Bonus plans include stock options or salary incentives based on quality of work done, years of service, or company profits.

Retirement Plans

Some employers provide retirement plans whereby employees contribute a percentage of gross pay, which may or may not be matched by the employer. When an employee retires, he or she receives a monthly check that is partially or wholly taxable. In some cases, an employee may draw against the account, withdraw it early in part or in full, or retire early and begin collecting benefits.

Travel Expenses

Companies that require employees to travel in the course of their work often provide a company car or a mileage allowance if they use their own car. Often car insurance, gasoline, and repair and maintenance expenses for the company automobile are also provided. While out of town, employees are paid a daily allowance, or have their motel and meals paid, as well as other travel expenses.

Mileage is allowed when you drive your own car.

Many of these optional benefits are of great value to employees. Optional benefits generally are not taxable to employees (except bonuses and other benefits paid to employees in cash), yet provide valuable coverages and advantages. Generally, large companies provide more extensive optional benefit packages.

LABOR UNIONS AND PROFESSIONAL ORGANIZATIONS

Membership in unions is sometimes required.

Many employment opportunities also involve union membership or participation in a professional organization as a requirement of employment. *Unions* are units or groups of people joined together for a common purpose. *Labor unions* are groups of people who work in the same or similar occupations, organized for the benefit of all employees in these occupations.

History of Unions

Unions were organized in the United States as early as the late 1800s. The first unions were local units organized by skilled craftspeople to protect themselves from competition of untrained and unskilled workers. In 1886 the American Federation of Labor (AFL) was organized by Samuel Gompers, who served as its president for 37 years.

Unions had a slow and painful start.

Early unions had very little power until 1935, when the National Labor Relations Act (Wagner Act) gave unions the right to organize and bargain with employers. In 1938 John L. Lewis became the first president of a new union—the Congress of Industrial Organizations (CIO). Unions continued to grow in number, power, and size until 1947, when Congress passed the Labor Management Relations Act, commonly called the Taft-Hartley Act. The Labor Management Relations Act was passed to limit the powers of unions and to curb strikes. In 1955 the AFL and CIO merged under the leadership of George Meany and became the largest and most powerful union in the United States.

Functions of Unions

The importance of labor unions in American life cannot be measured by the numbers of workers in unions. Many nonunion employers are influenced by the standards set by union agreements with other employers; and many employees reap the benefits of unionization even though they do not belong to a union.

Labor unions have four major functions: (*a*) recruitment of new members; (*b*) collective bargaining; (*c*) support of political candidates who are favorable to the union; and (*d*) provision of support services for members, including employment, job transfer, membership and employment credentials, and education.

Large unions are usually powerful.

Unions exercise power through large numbers of members. Therefore, new employees in occupations that have unions are strongly urged, if membership is not mandatory, to join the union. Political candidates who express opinions favorable to a particular union may receive campaign funds and/or endorsements from union leaders. These endorsements usually mean large numbers of the union members, locally and nationally, will vote for the candidate. Unions provide support for their members by helping to keep their members employed, negotiating job transfers, providing credentials for job-seeking employees, and providing education necessary to obtain and keep jobs held by union members.

Unions negotiate employment contracts.

The major function of unions is *collective bargaining*, which is the process of negotiating the terms of employment for union members. Terms of the agreement are written in an employment contract. The contract is usually quite detailed and is divided into these major sections: wages and supplements; workers' rights on the job; union rights in relation to the employer; management rights in relation to the union; and the grievance procedure when a provision of the contract has not been honored.

Seniority rights are stated in contracts.

The contract stipulates wages to be paid for certain jobs and types of work. Paid holidays, vacations, overtime rates, and hours of work are also specified in the contract. Most contracts also list *fringe benefits*, which are optional or extra benefits provided for union employees. Health insurance, sick leave, and pensions are considered fringe benefits. Union contracts usually provide for *seniority* rights, which state that the last ones hired should be the first ones laid off. In other words, the longer you work, the more job security you are entitled to have. Seniority may be used to determine transfers, promotions, and vacation time according to most union contracts.

When agreement as to meaning of a contract provision cannot be reached between the union and the employer, the dispute must be arbitrated. Through *arbitration*, a decision is made by a neutral third party. When employers and union officials cannot agree on the terms of a new contract, the labor union may make the decision to *strike*, a process whereby the members of the union refuse to work until an agreement is reached.

Types of Unions

Unions are classified into three types: craft unions, industrial unions, and public employee unions.

Craft Unions. Membership in craft unions is limited to those who practice in an established craft or trade, such as bricklayers, carpenters, or plasterers. Major craft unions include those of the building, printing, and maritime trades, and of railroad employees.

Industrial Unions. Membership in industrial unions is composed of skilled, semiskilled, or unskilled workers in a particular place, industry, or group of industries. Examples include the AFL-CIO, Teamsters, and United Auto Workers.

Various occupations have different unions.

Public Employee Unions. Municipal, county, state, or federal employees such as firemen, teachers, and policemen may organize public employee unions.

Unions are self-governing organizations. Major decisions are made by elected leaders. Of the four functions of unions, the most significant is collective bargaining. Many unions have developed a high degree of professionalism and are regarded as powerful. Union leaders often devote full time to their positions. Unions often employ their own lawyers, doctors, economists, educators, and public relations officials; dues collected from members provide the basis for the services of these professionals.

Powerful unions now exist.

Professional Organizations

Professional organizations also collect dues from members and provide support services. In some cases, membership in a professional organization may be compulsory. Most notable of professional organizations include the American Bar Association (required) for lawyers and the American Medical Association (optional) for doctors. Each state bar association provides the testing procedures by which lawyers who pass are "admitted to the bar." Attorneys who are severely disciplined are "disbarred," which means they can no longer practice law.

Purposes of professional organizations are: (*a*) to establish and maintain professional standards, including procedures for self-improvement; (*b*) to support legislation and political action, known as *lobbying*, that is beneficial to the profession; (*c*) to encourage individual growth and achievement; (*d*) to publish a professional journal or magazine; (*e*) to provide pension, retirement, and insurance benefits for members; and (*f*) to keep members up-to-date on current information and procedures. Because most doctors and lawyers are self-employed, they are not regulated as to professional behavior except through membership in these organizations and/or through court procedures. Exams, accreditations, admission procedures, and other standards are administered through these professional organizations.

Dues are used to fund professional organizations.

Another professional organization, sometimes called a union, is the NEA (National Education Association). Membership is not compulsory, but teachers who choose not to belong pay what is known as a "fair share," which is the same as the deduction for dues paid by members. This payment is justified because the organization benefits all teachers, regardless of membership. There are national, state, and local branches of NEA and other professional organizations. Each branch of the NEA charges dues, just as do the national, state, and county bar associations.

Unions benefit all employees.

VOCABULARY

Directions: Can you find the definition for each of the following terms used in Chapter 4?

gross pay	net pay
deductions	optional or fringe benefits
incentive	collective bargaining
labor unions	seniority
strike	professional organizations
lobbying	

1. Similar to labor unions, but membership is required for persons in certain occupations.

2. A process whereby employees refuse to work until an agreement is reached.

3. An effort to support legislation that would be of benefit to a certain group.

4. The total agreed upon salary or pay before deductions.

5. Amounts subtracted from gross pay, some required and some optional.

6. Also known as the amount of the paycheck.

7. Added benefits that are not required by law, but are provided by employers as part of a total wage package.

8. Groups of people in the same or similar occupations, organized for the benefit of all.

9. The process whereby unions and employers negotiate terms of employment.

10. The first hired is the last fired or laid off.

11. Encouragement plan to get employees to do more and better work.

ITEMS FOR DISCUSSION

1. How is gross pay different from net pay?

2. List five optional deductions you may elect to have withheld from your gross pay.

3. How much is the minimum wage?

4. What is required when an employee has worked more than the maximum regular workweek?

5. What is a leave of absence?

6. What are the four major functions of labor unions?

7. What are the three types of labor unions?

8. How are labor unions funded; that is, how are labor unions able to operate—who pays for the services that are provided?

9. What is collective bargaining?

10. What is seniority?

11. What was the significance of the Wagner Act to American labor?

12. What is a strike?

13. Name a professional organization.

14. Explain lobbying.

APPLICATIONS

1. Compute gross pay for these situations:

    (a) Regular hours worked: 40
    Overtime hours worked: 5
    Regular rate of pay: $3.85 an hour

    (b) Regular salary: $800 a month
    Overtime hours agreed upon: 8 a week (four weeks)
    Overtime rate of pay agreed upon: $6.82 an hour

(c) Total hours worked: 43 (in 5 days)
Regular rate of pay: $4.10

(d) Annual salary: $18,000
Compute gross pay (monthly).

2. Using the payroll income tax withholding tables on pages 54–57, locate the following answers:

(a) For a single person, two allowances, who made $110 last week:

State withholding tax: _____
Federal withholding tax: _____

(b) For a single person, no allowances, who made $222 last week:

State withholding tax: _____
Federal withholding tax: _____

(c) For a married person, two allowances, who made $1,120 last month:

State withholding tax: _____
Federal withholding tax: _____

(d) For a married person, six allowances, who made $1,479 last month:

State withholding tax: _____
Federal withholding tax: _____

CASE PROBLEMS AND ACTIVITIES

1. Mike Martinez, social security number 484-40-9876, works for a weekly paycheck. He is single and claims no allowances. Last week he worked five days, for a total of 44 hours. His regular rate of pay is $6.60 an hour. In addition to federal income tax, state income tax (use tables shown in Figures 4–2 through 4–5), and social security tax, Mike also has insurance of $16 a week withheld and puts 6 percent of his gross pay into a retirement account.

Compute Mike's gross pay, deductions, and net paycheck.

2. Lorraine Wong, social security number 444-33-2121, works for a weekly paycheck. She is single and claims one allowance. Last week she worked five days, for a total of 48 hours. Her regular rate of pay is $6.80 an hour. In addition to required deductions, Lorraine also has $10 a week sent to her credit union account and gives $5 a week to United Fund (charity).

Compute Lorraine's gross pay, deductions, and net paycheck.

3. Willard Weinstein, social security number 644-30-2929, works for a monthly salary. He is married and claims four allowances. Last month Willard worked 22 days. He does not get paid for overtime. His monthly salary is $1,780. In addition to required deductions, Willard also pays insurance premiums of $23 a month and sets aside for retirement 6 percent of his gross monthly pay.

   Compute Willard's gross pay, deductions, and net paycheck.

4. Marjorie Wilkinson, social security number 331-84-3139, works for a monthly paycheck. She is married and claims two allowances. Her yearly salary is $14,700. Last month she worked 21 days, without overtime. In addition to required deductions, Marjorie also contributes $14 a week (assume a four-week month) to the Heart Fund and sets aside $50 a month, paid directly to her savings account.

   Compute Marjorie's gross pay, deductions, and net paycheck.

5. Jack King, social security number 414-31-3245, works for a monthly salary. He is married and claims no allowances. His monthly salary is $1,500. When Jack works overtime it is at an agreed hourly rate of $12.75. Last month he worked 10 hours that will be paid overtime. He worked 23 days. Jack has only the required deductions.

   Compute Jack's gross pay, deductions, and net paycheck.

UNIT TWO
MONEY MANAGEMENT

CHAPTER 5
FINANCIAL PLANNING AND LEGAL DOCUMENTS

CHAPTER OBJECTIVES

After studying this chapter and completing the activities, you will be able to:

1. Analyze and understand the budgeting process and prepare personal and case study budget problems.
2. Understand the purpose of personal record keeping and be able to prepare a personal net worth statement and personal property inventory.
3. Explain the elements of legal contracts and negotiable instruments and understand consumer rights and responsibilities.

BUDGETING INCOME AND EXPENSES

How would you like to have unlimited resources to buy all the things you want or need? Unfortunately, for most people personal financial management is not that easy. Careful budgeting and planning are needed to enable you to meet your financial goals. That is why you need to study financial planning and budgeting—so that you will learn how to make the most of your financial resources.

Importance of Financial Planning

Your **disposable income** is the money you have to spend as you wish after taxes, social security, and other required and optional deductions have been withheld from your gross pay. In order to use this income to your best ability, you will need to create a financial plan.

All the money you receive is spent, saved, or invested. You may spend it for things you need or want, save it for future needs, or invest it to earn more money. *Financial planning* is an orderly program for spending, saving, and investing the money you earn. You may already understand the need to save part of your income for the future. Financial planning is important because it helps you to do the following:

1. Determine and evaluate how wisely you are using your money
2. Get the most from your income
3. Prevent careless and wasteful spending
4. Organize your *financial resources* (sources of income) so that you can maintain a plan of personal financial fitness
5. Avoid money worries and problems by understanding the proper methods of saving, spending, and borrowing money

Eliminate waste through planning.

The first step in financial fitness is to set up a plan. *Budgeting* is an organized plan whereby you match your expected income to your expected outflow. The purpose of budgeting is to plan your spending and saving so that you won't have to borrow money to meet your needs. Careful budgeting will enable you to stretch your money to provide for your present and future needs and satisfy your wants.

Preparing a Budget

Figure 5–1 shows a high school junior's budget plan for one month. This student expects to receive a total of $260, and plans to use the money for certain needs and wants and to save part of it as well.

FIGURE 5–1
Simple Budget

Budget for September	
Income	
Work (part-time)	$230.00
Allowance (household chores)	10.00
Lunch money..	30.00
Total income	$260.00
Expenses	
Savings (monthly)	$195.00
Daily lunches	20.00
Miscellaneous: supplies	12.00
snacks	14.00
other	19.00
Total expenses	$260.00

The first step in setting up a budget is to estimate total expected disposable income for a certain time. Include all money you expect to receive. You may wish to use a weekly, biweekly, or monthly budget—whichever best matches how often you expect to receive money.

The second step is to decide how much of your income you want to save—to set aside for future needs. Most financial experts advise saving at least 10 percent of your disposable income each pay period. By saving at least 10 percent, you will have money to pay for future needs, both expected and unexpected.

Set aside for savings each month.

The third step is to estimate your *expenses*, or money you will need for day-to-day purchases; for example, lunches, fees, personal care items, clothing, and so forth.

A Typical Monthly Budget

Figure 5–2 represents the monthly budget of Bill and Mary Anderson, a recently married couple. Bill and Mary have no children, and both are working. The Andersons estimate their expected income by adding together their two take-home incomes (paychecks). They have decided to save at least 10 percent every month, invest some of their income in a home, and use the rest as shown.

To further refine their budget, Bill and Mary could divide their expenses into two groups: fixed expenses and variable expenses.

Fixed expenses are those that remain constant, and to remove them or change them will take a major revision in life-style. Examples are savings, house payments, utilities, car payments, average gasoline and car maintenance costs, and insurance premium payments.

Fixed expenses are difficult to change.

Variable expenses will change according to needs and short-term goals. Sufficient money should be allowed to cover these expenses, since they can change frequently. Examples are telephone, TV cable, groceries, dental or medical bills not covered by insurance, entertainment, recreation, charge account purchases, investments, and miscellaneous purchases.

FIGURE 5–2
Monthly Budget
for Married
Couple

Budget Bill and Mary Anderson		
	Month	Year
Income (monthly)	$1,800	$21,600
Expenses		
Savings	$ 200	$ 2,400
House payment	450	5,400
Utilities (average)	80	960
Car payment	150	1,800
Gasoline	100	1,200
Car maintenance	15	180
Insurance		
Car	30	360
Life and Health	50	600
Telephone	45	540
Cable television	25	300
Groceries	200	2,400
Entertainment and recreation	100	1,200
Vacation fund	75	900
Charge accounts (clothing)	200	2,400
Miscellaneous	80	960
Total expenses	$1,800	$21,600

PERSONAL RECORDS

Efficient personal records are important. They make planning a budget easier; they assure improved long-range financial planning; and they are a basis for properly completing income tax returns, credit applications, and other needed forms. Basically, there are four types of personal records that most families will want to keep: records of income and expenses, a statement of net worth, a personal property inventory, and tax records.

Keep important records in a safe place.

Records of Income and Expenses

W-2 slips sent by employers each January show money earned and deductions made by the employer during the year. The W-2s prove that you had social security withheld. You may need the W-2s later when you want to collect benefits. Other records of income include statements from banks of interest earned on savings. Expense items include receipts listing charity contributions, medical bills, or work-related expenses. All this information will be needed when preparing budgets and tax returns. These receipts and statements are often referred to as *documents* and can be used as *proof*, or evidence, of income and expenses. These documents should be stored in a safe place for future reference.

Keep receipts for tax return information.

Statement of Net Worth

A net worth statement, such as that shown in Figure 5–3, is a list of items of value, called *assets*, that a person owns; amounts of money that are owed to others, called *liabilities* or debts; and the difference between the two, known as *net worth*. If your assets are greater than your liabilities, you are said to be *solvent*, or in a favorable credit position. But if

FIGURE 5–3
Net Worth
Statement

Net Worth Statement		
Wendy Haskins		
January 1, 19--		
ASSETS		**LIABILITIES**
Checking account... $ 58.00		Loan at bank on car $ 600.00
Savings account 80.00		Loan from Mother ... 80.00
Car value 1,000.00		Total Liabilities ...... $ 680.00
Personal property		
(inventory attached) 2,000.00		**NET WORTH**
		Assets - liabilities.... $2,458.00
Total assets $3,138.00		Total $3,138.00

your liabilities are greater than your assets (you owe more than you own), you are said to be *insolvent*, or in a poor credit position.

Net worth information (lists of assets and liabilities) is most often required when you ask for a loan or apply for credit. The bank or other financial institution will want you to be solvent and a good risk who will likely pay back a loan. How does your personal net worth statement compare with the one shown in Figure 5–3?

Personal Property Inventory

The personal property inventory is a list of all the personal property a person owns. Personal property is usually all items inside the home—clothing, furniture, appliances, and so forth. A personal property inventory is especially useful in the event of fire, theft, or property damage, as proof of possession and value. As a further safeguard, a person or family may photograph items of value, attach the photographs to the inventory, and keep this information in a safe-deposit box or other safe place to use as evidence in the event the property is damaged, lost, or stolen. As new items are purchased and others disposed of, the inventory should be revised. Figure 5–4 shows the inventory of personal property of Wendy Haskins.

An inventory is proof of property ownership.

FIGURE 5–4
Personal Property Inventory

Personal Property Inventory
Wendy Haskins
January 1, 19--

Item	Year Purchased	Purchase Price	Approximate Current Value
Acme stereo turntable with speakers in cabinet, Model XJ (SN 54J213)	1980	$ 600	$ 600
Bedroom furniture (bed, dresser, lamp, clock)	1971	800	200
Clothing and jewelry	1980-81	app. 2000	1000
Marvel "Cruiser" 10-speed bicycle (SN 5482164)	1983	120	120
TKO microcassette tape recorder, Model II, (SN 81426)	1983	(gift)	80
Total		$3520	$2000
(photographs attached)			

Tax Records

All taxpayers must keep copies of their tax returns, W-2 slips, and other receipts verifying income and expenses listed on tax returns for six years. Information used in preparing tax returns should be kept in a safe place in the event of **audit**, which is the examination of your tax records by the Internal Revenue Service. The IRS has the legal right to examine your tax returns and supporting records for six years from the date of filing the return (longer if fraud or international wrongdoing on your part can be proved).

The four types of records discussed are important because they enable you to (*a*) evaluate your family or individual spending; (*b*) provide information for tax returns; (*c*) analyze your financial picture and plan for the future; (*d*) provide a basis for determining future goals; and (*e*) provide a basis for maintaining an effective, updated budget.

LEGAL DOCUMENTS

To manage personal finances, you often need to enter into agreements, fill out forms and applications, and provide personal information and records. It is difficult to function successfully in today's society if you do not master these simple documents.

Contracts and Agreements

A **contract** is a legally enforceable agreement between two or more parties to do or not to do something. We all have many transactions in our daily lives that can be properly classified as contracts or lawful agreements. Contracts are involved in personal business situations even though one may not be aware that contracts exist. If you buy a suit and it needs an alteration, a ticket is filled out by the clerk. What change must be made and when completion is promised are written on the ticket. This ticket is a contract under which you, the consumer, promise to pick up the suit and pay for the alteration when it is completed. The store promises to do the work and present it to you on the agreed upon date for the stated price.

Other examples of situations requiring agreements are (*a*) retail credit plans, whereby customers agree to pay for purchases by monthly payments or open a charge account at a store; (*b*) buying a home and paying for it over a number of years by means of mortgage payments; or (*c*) renting an apartment, a duplex, or a house. In each of these cases there is generally an agreement between two or more persons known as an **express** *contract.* Express contracts can be oral or written: what makes them express is that the terms have been agreed upon between the parties.

Figure 5–5 shows a charge application a retail store may require. In addition to giving certain requested information, you are asked to agree to certain conditions before opening an account. Attached to the application

CHARGE APPLICATION

Please print clearly

ACCOUNT IN NAME OF:

First *Richard*   Initial *J*   Last *Washington*

Address *45 Front Street #8*

City *Portland*   State *OR*   ZIP *97201-1072*

Area Code   Number
Phone *(503) 221-1181*   How long at this address? *4 years*

Check one: ☐ Own   ☐ Lease   ☒ Rent   ☐ Live with parents   ☐ Other*

*Explain

Previous address if less than three years:

How long?

Employer *O'Toole Paper Co.*   How long? *4 years*

Employer's Address *Portland, OR 97214-4179*   Phone *221-8342*

Occupation *Administrative Assistant*   Salary *#342*   ☒ Weekly   ☐ Monthly

COMPLETE SECTION FOR JOINT ACCOUNT:

Name
First *N/A*   Initial   Last

Employer   How long?

Employer's Address   Phone

Occupation   Salary   ☐ Weekly   ☐ Monthly

Other income:
Source   Amount

CREDIT REFERENCES:

Name of Bank *First Bank*   Bank Address *Portland, OR*   ☒ Checking ☒ Savings

Name of Creditor *Meier & Frank*   Account Number *818 424961*   Address *Portland*

Creditor *JC Penney*   Number *489 1248369*   Address *Portland*

Creditor   Number   Address

NEAREST RELATIVE NOT LIVING WITH YOU:
Name *Harry Washington*   Address *614 Chevy St., Portland, OR 97216-6172*

I understand the terms and conditions of this credit application, including service charges and fees, which will be charged to this account as explained on the reverse side of this application. I have read it completely and agree to all conditions. I testify that all information contained in this application is true and complete.

APPLICANT'S SIGNATURE *Richard J. Washington*   Social Security Number *481-32-8194*   Date *4/1/--*

FIGURE 5–5   Charge Application

will be an explanation of finance charges and how they are computed. You will sign the application to show that you understand the finance charges and agree to pay them if your balance is not paid in full each month. Be sure you have read everything contained in the agreement *before* you sign it. If something is not clear, be sure to ask for an explanation so that you can understand your rights and responsibilities *before* you enter into the contract.

In addition to written agreements, there are also many unwritten agreements. If you possess a driver's license, a social security card, a work permit, or any of many such items, you have made an *implied agreement*. Whether or not you realize it, you have agreed to certain things by your acceptance of a license or card. When you are issued a driver's license, you agree to abide by laws, drive in a safe and responsible manner, and have the license with you when driving. A violation of one of these unwritten agreements can result in the loss of your license, a fine, imprisonment, or all these.

By accepting certain items you enter into implied agreements.

Essentials of an Enforceable Contract

To accomplish its purpose, a contract must be binding on all persons who enter into it. Some contracts *must* be in writing and signed by all persons involved in order to be legally binding. Examples of contracts that must be written are contracts for the purpose of sale of real property (homes and land); contracts that cannot be fully performed in less than a year; contracts involving $500 and over; and contracts in which one person agrees to pay the debts of another.

To be enforceable, some contracts must be in writing.

To be legally binding, enforceable agreements, contracts must have all of the following elements:

1. Mutual assent
2. Consideration
3. Competent parties
4. Lawful objective
5. An agreed upon period of time
6. Legal format

Let's examine each of these elements in detail.

Mutual Assent. A contract has *mutual assent* when it is offered and accepted. If there is any disagreement, the contract is not legally enforceable. In order to prove mutual assent, two conditions are required by law: a valid offer and acceptance of that exact offer. One person makes the offer, another person accepts the offer. When one person makes an offer and another person changes any part of the offer, the second person making what is known as a *counteroffer.* The counteroffer is a new offer and has to be accepted (or rejected) by the first person.

Consideration. The price involved is called *consideration.* Consideration may be in the form of an object of value, money, a promise, or a performed act. If one person is to receive something but give nothing in return, the contract is not enforceable. The idea of consideration is that each party to the agreement receives something of value. When you buy a pair of shoes, you get the shoes and the store gets your money. The shoes and the money are items of consideration.

Consideration is something of value.

Competent Parties. *Competent parties* are persons who are legally able to give sane and intelligent assent. Those who are unable to protect themselves because of mental deficiency or illness, or who are otherwise incapable of understanding the consequences of their actions, cannot be held to contracts. They are protected from entering into agreements that may prove to be against their best interests. Minors are not considered competent parties and therefore cannot be held to contracts, with exceptions. Generally, any person 18 or older who is not mentally deficient is considered competent. Married persons under age 18 are also considered competent to enter into agreements. Furthermore, all persons 18 or older are considered to be legally competent unless they are declared incompetent by a court of law.

Minors are not considered competent parties.

Lawful Objective. The purpose of a legally enforceable contract must be of a lawful nature. A court of law will not require a person to perform an agreed upon act if it is illegal. Without a lawful objective, the agreement has no binding effect on any person.

Agreed Upon Period of Time. Within the contract, there must be a stated length of time for which the contract is to exist. For example, if the contract is to purchase a home, the agreed upon period of time is so long as money remains due and owing. When the last payment is made, then the contract is considered fulfilled.

Legal Format. State laws provide that contracts must contain the necessary information to be enforceable. The contract may be a printed form, drawn up by attorneys, or it may be in some other readable and understandable form. It must state the date, duration of contract, persons involved, consideration, terms of agreement, and other necessary information to explain the purpose and intentions of the persons entering into the contract. In some cases, the contract, or a memorandum of contract, must be *recorded.* When a contract is recorded it is made a public record, and a

Contracts must be in proper format.

photocopy is stored by the county recorder. Before a document can be recorded, it must meet specific requirements that are set out by state law.

Void and Voidable Contracts

There are basically three types of contracts: valid, void, and voidable.

Valid Contracts. *Valid contracts* are those that contain all of the essential elements—mutual assent, consideration, competent parties, lawful objective, agreed upon period of time, and legal format. They are legally enforceable.

Void Contracts. *Void Contracts* are those that are missing one or more of the essential elements. These contracts are null and void, and are not enforceable in a court of law. An example of a void contract is one that will require doing something illegal. In other words, if you enter into an agreement and later learn that you will be doing something against the law, you cannot be forced to fulfill your part of the contract.

An illegal purpose causes a void contract.

Voidable Contracts. *Voidable contracts* contain an element within them that makes them void. If that element is not acted upon by the innocent party, the contract will become valid. An example of a voidable contract is an agreement entered into by a minor. A minor may declare the voidable contract void because contracts with minors do not meet the competent party test of a legally binding contract. However, if the minor continues to make payments on the contract after reaching age 18, he or she has made that contract valid and is legally responsible for fulfilling the contract.

Certain actions can make a voidable contract valid.

Consumer Responsibilities in Agreements

As a consumer, you have the following responsibilities regarding the contracts and agreements you enter into:

1. Understand all clauses and terms contained in the agreement. Do not sign it until you have read it. By signing, you are acknowledging that you have read and understand the contract.
2. Keep a copy of the agreement. Put it in a safe place. You may need it at a future date.
3. Be sure the agreement is correctly dated.
4. Be sure all blank spaces are filled in or marked out and that no changes have been made after your signature. Your initials at the bottom of each page will prevent subsitution of pages when there is more than one page.

Check a contract carefully before signing.

5. Be sure all provisions agreed upon are clearly written. Because interpretation may vary, vague phrases are often not enforceable.
6. Be sure all dates, amounts, and other numbers are correct and clearly written.
7. Be sure proper disclosure is made by the seller. The buyer is entitled to proper and complete information about the rate of interest, total finance charges, cash payment price, etc.
8. Be sure all cancellations and adjustments are made in accordance with the contract.

Although consumers are protected by numerous consumer protection laws, occasionally specific legal services are required. Legal services, in one form or other, are available to every citizen. But your best protection is to guard yourself in advance by understanding the agreement.

Protect yourself in the beginning.

Negotiable Instruments

The word *negotiable* means legally collectible. A *negotiable instrument* is a document that contains promises to pay moneys and is legally collectible. The kinds of negotiable instruments most people are likely to use are checks (discussed in Chapter 6) and promissory notes. A negotiable instrument is legally collectible if the following conditions are met:

Checks are negotiable instruments.

1. It must be in writing and be signed by the maker (not oral).
2. It must contain an unconditional promise to pay a definite amount of money.
3. It must be payable on demand or on a fixed or determinable future date.
4. It must be payable to the order of a particular person or to the holder of the note.
5. It must be delivered to the payee.

If any one of the above conditions is missing, the document is not a negotiable instrument; it is no longer legally collectible.

A *promissory note* is a written promise to pay a certain sum of money to another person or to the holder of the note on a specified date. A promissory note is a legal document, and payment can be enforced by law. An example of a promissory note is found in Figure 5–6.

The person who creates and signs the promissory note, agreeing to pay it on a certain date, is called the *maker*. The person to whom the note is made payable is known as the *payee*. A promissory note is normally used when borrowing a large sum of money from a financial institution.

In some cases creditors (those extending credit) will require cosigners as additional security for repayment of a note. A *cosigner* is a person who is established (has a good credit rating) and who promises to pay the note

FIGURE 5–6
Promissory Note

PROMISSORY NOTE

$ _400.00_   _January 15_   , 19_-_

I (we) _Marilyn Huykamp_   , jointly and severally,
do agree and promise to pay to _Emerald Furniture Co._
the sum of _Four hundred and °%/100_   dollars
with interest at the rate of _18_ % from _January 15, 19——_ , payable in
monthly installments of $ _72.67_ beginning _February 1_ , 19_-_
and on a like day each month until paid in full, the last payment
due _July 1_   , 19_-_. Said payment shall include interest.
In the event of default, the maker hereof agrees to pay attorneys'
fees and court costs in collection of this note.

Marilyn Huykamp
Maker

Cosigners make pay-
ments when the debtor
fails.

if the maker fails to pay. The cosigner's signature is also on a note. Young
people and persons who have not established a credit rating are often
asked to provide a cosigner for their first loan.

Warranties

A *warranty*, also called a guarantee, is an assurance of product quality
or of responsibility of the seller. The warranty may be in writing or
assumed to exist by the nature of the product. However, a warranty is not
a safeguard against a poor buying decision.

All products contain implied warranties, and some have written guarantees as well, expressing responsibilities that the manufacturer will
strictly enforce. A product is supposed to do that which it is made to do,
whether or not standards are expressed in writing. For example, a tennis
ball must bounce. If it does not bounce, it is dead. You can return the
defective ball, even if there is no written warranty.

Specific written warranties often guarantee that a product will perform to your satisfaction for a certain period of time. Many written war-
Read warranties before
you buy.
ranties state that you may return a product for repair or replacement if it
ceases to work because of a defect. Warranties will not protect against
normal wear and tear of the product.

Figure 5–7 illustrates a limited warranty that might be found when
purchasing a home product. Read it carefully to determine what the manufacturer is and is not guaranteeing.

FIGURE 5–7
Warranty

12 Y 845

Limited Warranty

This product is guaranteed for one year from the date of purchase to be free of mechanical and electrical defects in material and workmanship. The manufacturer's obligations hereunder are limited to repair of such defects during the warranty period, provided such product is returned to the address below within the warranty period.

This guarantee does not cover normal wear of parts or damages resulting from negligent use or misuse of the product. In addition, this guarantee is void if the purchaser breaks the seal and disassembles, repairs, or alters the product in any way.

The warranty period begins on the date of purchase. The card below must be received by the manufacturer within 30 days of purchase or receipt of said merchandise. Fill out the card completely and return it to the address shown.

Owner's Name: _____

Address: _____

City, State, ZIP: _____

Date of Purchase: _____

Store Where Purchased: _____

Return to: ALCOVE ELECTRICAL, INC.
42 West Cabana
Arlington, VA 23445-2909

Serial No. **12 Y 845**

VOCABULARY

Directions: Can you find the definition for each of the following terms used in Chapter 5?

financial planning
disposable income

liabilities
maker

financial resources   mutual assent
budgeting   consideration
payee   negotiable instrument
audit   cosigner
proof   warranty
assets   implied agreement
recorded

1. Agreement by two or more persons to the terms of a contract.

2. An unwritten statement that nevertheless exists.

3. Evidence that backs up or supports information.

4. Sources of income and money on which you base a budget.

5. A price to be paid, or a promise to pay, or to do something or not do something.

6. Things of value that a person owns.

7. A person who promises to pay a note if the maker fails to pay.

8. An assurance of product quality or of responsibility of the seller.

9. An orderly program for spending, saving, and investing your income.

10. An organized plan of matching income and expenses.

11. Amounts of money that you owe to others, known as debts.

12. Pieces of paper containing written promises to pay.

13. One who signs a note and agrees to pay it on a certain date.

14. One to whom a note is made payable and who will receive its proceeds.

15. An examination of your tax records by the Internal Revenue Service.

16. The money you have left over after required deductions, which you can spend or save as you wish.

17. Made a document, such as a contract, a matter of public record.

ITEMS FOR DISCUSSION

1. Why should consumers prepare a budget and be concerned about financial planning?

2. What is the difference between fixed and variable expenses?

3. Which are the four types of personal records all consumers should prepare and keep in a safe place?

4. Why is it important to maintain these four types of personal records?

5. Besides the obvious use for obtaining credit, what is another good reason for preparing a personal property inventory?

6. Why should taxpayers save copies of their tax returns and supporting receipts and evidence?

7. How is an implied contract different from an express contract?

8. In order to be enforceable in a court of law, contracts must contain six elements. Briefly define each.

9. Give three examples of contracts that must be in writing in order to be enforceable in a court of law.

10. What is the difference between a void contract and a voidable contract?

11. What is the most commonly used form of negotiable instrument.?

12. List the five conditions of negotiable instruments that make them legally collectible.

13. List five consumer responsiblities when entering into contracts.

APPLICATIONS

1. Using Figure 5–1 as a model, prepare a simple budget for yourself, listing expected income, savings, and expenses for a month. How much will you set aside for savings?

2. How will your budget change in the next few years? (What are your short-term and intermediate goals?)

3. Using Figure 5–3 as a model, prepare a net worth statement, listing as assets those items of value you possess and any debts for which you are responsible. Compute your net worth. How can you use this information?

4. Using Figure 5–4 as a model, prepare a personal property inventory, listing items of personal property in your room at home. Why should you and your family keep a record such as this?

5. After examining Form 5–5 (credit application), list the kinds of information requested by a retail store. Why do you think a store needs or wants this type of information?

6. Following the example of Figure 5–6, write out in longhand form a promissory note from you to John Doe, payable in one year of monthly payments, in the amount of $50 with interest at 15 percent and monthly payments of $4.79. Are you the maker or the payee?

7. Bring to class an express warranty from a product you or your family recently purchased. What does the warranty specifically promise to do? List any restrictions (exceptions) that the manufacturer has placed in the warranty.

CASE PROBLEMS AND ACTIVITIES

1. Based on the information given, prepare a monthly and yearly budget for Paul and Peg Jacobsen. Use Figure 5–2 as a model.
   INCOME: Net paychecks total $1,800 monthly.

EXPENSES:			
Rent payment $350		Savings $150
Utilities 100		Car payment 110
Gasoline 100		Car repairs 30
Insurance 90		Telephone 30
Groceries 200		Entertainment 100
Clothing 100		Vacation fund 100
Investment fund . . . 140		Miscellaneous 200

2. Paul Jacobsen has decided to return to college for two years to obtain his degree. He will work part-time instead of full-time, thereby reducing the Jacobsen's take-home pay by $600 a month. Tuition will be $400 each term ($1,200/year); books will cost $300 a year. Revise the Jacobsens' monthly budget.

3. Based on the information given, prepare a monthly and yearly budget for Margarite Brown. Follow Figure 5–2.
   INCOME: Net monthly paycheck is $1,200.

EXPENSES:			
Rent payment $210		Savings $120
Insurance 60		Telephone 15
Utilities 50		Car payment 150
Gasoline 60		Car repairs 20
Clothing 60		Groceries 150
Entertainment 150		Miscellaneous 155

4. Revise Margarite's budget when she agrees to share her apartment with a friend. Some expenses can be shared; but the car payment, insurance, and car repairs remain fixed. You will need to adjust her other expenses accordingly. What will you have her do with the added funds?

5. Based on the information given, prepare a net worth statement for Bob Engle. Follow Figure 5–3.
   Bob owns a car worth about $3,000, but owes $1,500 to the bank. He has $500 in savings and $100 in checking. His personal property totals $3,000, and he also owes $90 to the credit union.

6. Based on the information given, prepare a personal property inventory for Bob Engle. Follow Figure 5–4.
   Bob has these furnishings in his apartment: JWA stereo system, Model 252, SN 975923, bought last year for $500; still worth $500; sofa, present worth about $800; Bright alarm clock (SN 630AM) and Blare radio (Model 2602, SN 413T) bought years ago, total worth about $200. Bob also has the following personal items: miscellaneous clothing and jewelry, present worth about $800; Quantex wrist watch, present worth about $100; coin collection, valued last year at $600. Bob has photographs of these items.

CHAPTER 6

CHECKING ACCOUNTS AND MISCELLANEOUS BANKING SERVICES

CHAPTER OBJECTIVES

After studying this chapter and completing the activities, you will be able to:

1. Understand and prepare checks, deposit slips, checkbook registers, and bank reconciliations.
2. Define terms used in connection with checking accounts, banking services, and check endorsements.
3. Compare the advantages and disadvantages of the different types of banking services available.

PURPOSE OF A CHECKING ACCOUNT

Financial institutions such as banks, credit unions, and savings and loan associations offer a number of different services. A *checking account* is a banking service wherein you deposit money into an account and write checks, or *drafts*, to withdraw money as needed. This type of account is also known as a *demand deposit*, because you can demand portions of your deposited funds at will. Financial institutions usually charge a fee for checking services, or require that a minimum balance be kept in the account.

Checking accounts are safer than cash.

A checking account can be a useful and convenient tool. Writing a check is often safer than using cash, especially when making major purchases in person, or when paying bills or ordering merchandise through the mail. *Canceled checks* (checks the bank has processed) can be used as proofs of purchase or payment in the event a dispute arises.

Checking accounts also have built-in record keeping systems to help you keep track of money received and spent; thus, they are a great help in personal budgeting and record keeping. Finally, as a checking account customer, you have access to other banking services, such as instant loans and traveler's checks.

In exchange for the convenience of using a checking account, you must accept certain responsibilities. First, you must write checks carefully and keep an accurate record of checks written and deposits made. Second, you must reconcile your account with your bank statement promptly each month. Third, you must keep canceled checks as proofs of purchase or payment and for income tax records. Canceled checks should be kept in a safe place, such as a safe-deposit box.

Safeguard your canceled checks.

In addition, you must not overdraw your account or float a check. An *overdraft* occurs when you, the depositor or *drawer*, write a check that cannot be covered by the funds in your account. The check will bounce— go to your bank and come back to you for payment. *Floating a check* occurs when you realize your account contains insufficient funds, but write a check anyway in the hope that you can make a deposit before the

Intentional overdrafts are unlawful.

check is cashed. Overdrawing your account and floating a check are illegal practices in most states. In most cases, these acts are felonies that can result in a fine, imprisonment, or both. In addition, the bank will charge a fee of $5 to $15 for each ***NSF*** (not sufficient funds) ***check*** written.

OPENING YOUR CHECKING ACCOUNT

To open a checking (or savings) account, a depositor must fill out and sign a signature card, such as the one shown in Figure 6-1. The signature card provides the bank with important information and an official signature to compare with subsequent checks written.

FIGURE 6-1
Signature Card

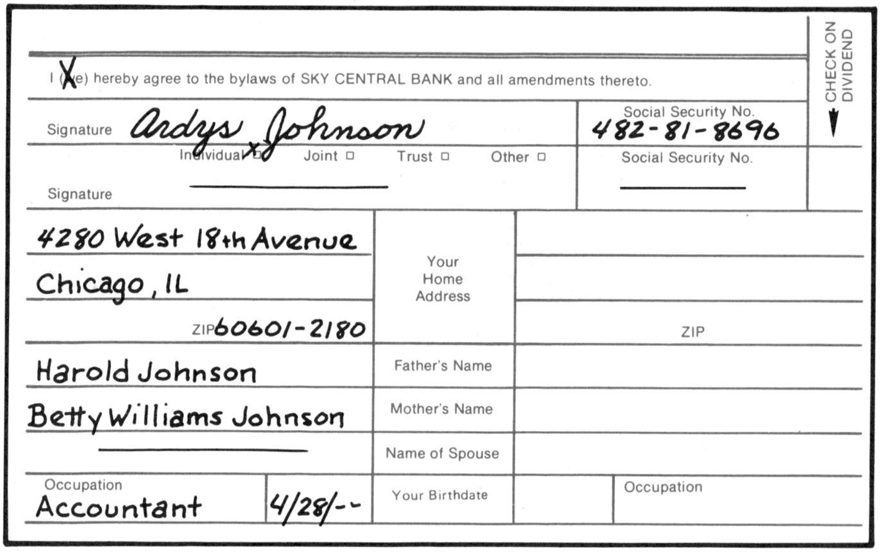
I (X) hereby agree to the bylaws of SKY CENTRAL BANK and all amendments thereto.

Signature Ardys Johnson — Social Security No. 482-81-8696

Individual ☒ Joint ☐ Trust ☐ Other ☐ — Social Security No.

Signature

CHECK ON DIVIDEND

	Your Home Address	
4280 West 18th Avenue		
Chicago, IL		
ZIP 60601-2180		ZIP
Harold Johnson	Father's Name	
Betty Williams Johnson	Mother's Name	
	Name of Spouse	
Occupation Accountant / 4/28/--	Your Birthdate	/ Occupation

In Figure 6-1, Ardys Johnson completed and signed the left side of the card. The right side is for a joint account holder. Ardys also listed her mother's full name (including maiden name) for use in identification. Anyone forging Ardys's signature is not likely to know her mother's maiden name when questioned by a teller.

USING YOUR CHECKING ACCOUNT

Checking accounts can help you to manage your personal finances—but only if you use them correctly. Careless or improper use of a checking account can result in financial losses. Some tips on using a checking account follow.

Parts of a Check

A check consists of ten parts. Figure 6-2 illustrates these parts.

FIGURE 6-2
Check

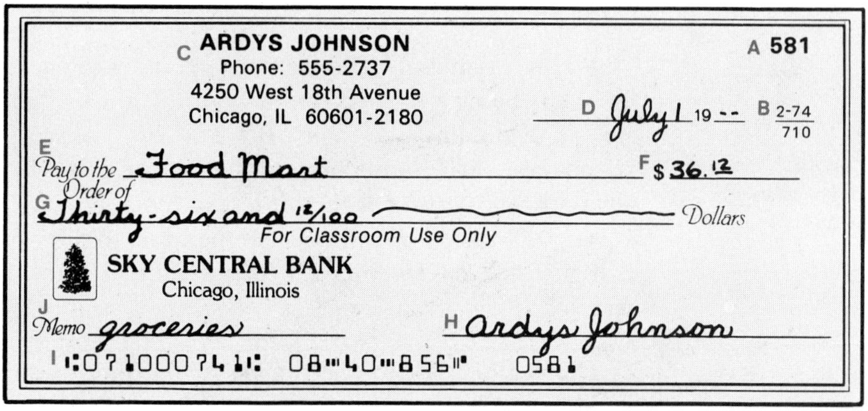

Check Number. Checks are numbered for easy identification. In Figure 6-2, Check 581 has been prenumbered by the bank (see Part A).

ABA Number. The *American Bankers Association number* appears in fraction form in the upper right corner of each check (see Figure 6-2, Part B). The top half of the fraction identifies the location and district of the bank from which the check is drawn. The number on the bottom half of the fraction helps in routing the check to the specific area and bank on which it is drawn.

Maker's Preprinted Name and Address. Most checking account owners prefer to have their name, address, and telephone number preprinted on the top left of each check (see Figure 6-2, Part C). Many stores are reluctant to accept a check unless it is preprinted with this information.

Date. The first item to be filled in is the date on which the check is written (see Figure 6-2, Part D). Do not *postdate* checks; that is, do not write in a future date. Most banks process checks when they are presented, or charge a fee for holding them. Checks over six months old may not be honored by the bank.

Postdated checks are not held by banks.

Payee. The *payee* is the person or company to whom a check is made payable. Food Mart is the payee in Figure 6-2 (see Part E).

Numeric Amount. The numeric amount is the amount of dollars and cents being paid, written in figures (see Figure 6-2, Part F). The amount should be neatly and clearly written, placed as close as possible to the dollar sign, with the dollars and cents distinctly readable. Many people raise the cents above the line of writing, as shown in Figure 6-2, and insert a decimal point between the dollar and cent amounts.

Written Amount. The written amount shows the amount of dollars and cents being paid, written in words. The word *dollars* is preprinted at the end of the line (see Figure 6-2, Part G). The word *and* is handwritten to separate dollar amounts from cents; it replaces the decimal point. Always begin writing at the far left of the line, leaving no space between words, and draw a wavy line from the cents to the word *dollars*, as shown. In Figure 6-2, the fraction *12/100* means that 12 cents out of 100 is to be paid.

The decimal point separates dollars from cents.

Drawer or Maker. The drawer or maker is the person authorized to write checks on the account. Ardys Johnson is the maker of the check in Figure 6-2 (see Part H), because she is the person who opened the checking account and who deposits funds to it. The bank has a copy of Ardys's signature on file so that they can stop someone attempting to forge Ardys's name to one of her checks.

Account Number. The account number appears in bank coding at the bottom of each check. In Figure 6-2 (see Part I), Ardys's checking account number is 08 40 856. The number *581* refers to the preprinted check number at the top of the check.

Memo. A Memo line is provided at the bottom left of each check so that the maker can write the purpose of the check (see Figure 6-2, Part J). This line does not have to be filled in; it is provided for the account holder's convenience.

Writing Checks

When writing checks, remember to follow these important guidelines in addition to the hints already given:

Write checks in dark ink.

1. Always use a pen, preferably one with dark ink that does not skip or blot.
2. Write legibly. Keep numbers and letters clear and distinct, without any extra space before, between, or after them.
3. Sign your name exactly as it appears on the check and on the signature card (see Figure 6-1) you signed when you opened the account.
4. Avoid mistakes. When you make a mistake, you should *void* (cancel) the check and write a new one. To cancel a check, write the word

Save your voided
checks.

VOID in large capital letters across the check face. Save the voided check for your records.

5. Be certain adequate funds have been deposited in your account to cover each check that you write. A check is a negotiable instrument that contains your written promise to pay a certain amount to the payee when the check is cashed.

Making Deposits

Just as you need a form to withdraw money from your checking account, you need to complete a form each time you deposit money to the account. Figure 6-3 illustrates this form, which is called a *deposit slip*.

FIGURE 6-3
Deposit Slip

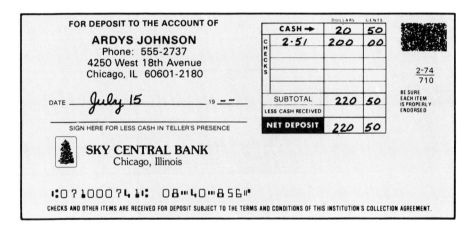

To prepare a deposit slip, follow these guidelines:

1. Insert the date of the transaction.
2. Write in the amount of **currency** (paper money) and coin to be deposited.
3. If any checks are being deposited, write in the amount of each check, together with the ABA check number.
4. Total the currency, coin, and check amounts. Write this figure on the Subtotal line.
5. If you wish to receive some cash at the time of your deposit, you should fill in the desired amount on the Less Cash Received line. Subtract this amount from the currency, coin, and check total. Write your signature on the line above the words *Sign here for less cash in teller's presence.*

Sign for cash in the
teller's presence.

6. Write the final amount of the deposit on the Net Deposit line.
7. Keep one copy of this deposit slip as proof of the amount of your deposit. Financial institutions have been known to make errors in crediting an account.

Carefully total your
deposit slip.

When writing deposit slips, you should carefully count the currency and coins you are depositing and should recheck all addition and subtraction. Make sure all checks being deposited are properly endorsed (see pages 95-97). Hand the deposit slip to the teller with the currency, coins, and checks you are depositing. Deposits can also be made at automatic teller machines (see pages 100-101).

Using a Checkbook Register

A *checkbook register* is a record of deposits to and withdrawals from a checking account. Figure 6-4 depicts a page from the checkbook register of Ardys Johnson. Through use of her checkbook register, Ardys can keep track of all checks written, service fees paid, interest earned, and deposits made. She can tell at a glance what her present account balance is and whether she needs to make a deposit to her account.

FIGURE 6-4
Checkbook
Register

ITEM NO.	DATE	PAYMENT ISSUED TO OR DESCRIPTION OF DEPOSIT	AMOUNT OF PAYMENT	✓	(-) CHECK FEE (IF ANY)	AMOUNT OF DEPOSIT	BALANCE FORWARD	
								800 00
581	7/1	To *Food Mart* For *Groceries*	36 12		.20		Payment or Deposit	- 36 32
							Balance	763 68
/	7/15	To *Deposit* For *Paycheck*				220 50	Payment or Deposit	+220 50
							Balance	984 18
/	7/16	To *Withdrawal* For *Automatic Teller*	20 00				Payment or Deposit	- 20 00
							Balance	964 18
/	7/31	To *Service Charge* For *Mth. of July*	5 00				Payment or Deposit	- 5 00
							Balance	959 18
		To For					Payment or Deposit Balance	
		To For					Payment or Deposit Balance	

PLEASE BE SURE TO DEDUCT ANY PER ITEM CHARGES OR SERVICE CHARGES THAT MAY APPLY TO YOUR ACCOUNT.

To fill out a checkbook register, follow these simple guidelines:

1. Write the preprinted check number in the first column. If you are not writing a check, draw a diagonal slash in this column, or use another distinctive notation.
2. Write the month and day of the transaction in the Date column.
3. Enter the name of the payee on the first line of the Description section. On the second line, if one is provided, write the purpose of the check.
4. Enter the amount of the check, service charge, or other withdrawal in the column headed by a minus sign. If the transaction is a deposit, write this amount in the column headed by a plus sign.
5. Transfer the amount deposited or withdrawn to the top line of the Balance column. Add this amount to or subtract it from the previous

Keep the balance col-
umn in your checkbook
register up-to-date.

balance, then write the new balance on the second line of the column.

6. The column headed by a check mark is provided so that you can check off each transaction when it appears on your monthly bank statement. The check mark shows that the transaction has been cleared by the bank and is no longer outstanding.

Always keep your checkbook register handy so that you can write down the necessary information at the time each transaction is made. Prompt and correct notations will help you keep track of your personal finances.

RECONCILING YOUR CHECKING ACCOUNT

Statements are pro-
vided to check your
account.

Financial institutions that offer checking accounts provide customers with a regular (usually monthly) *statement of account*. This statement lists checks received and processed by the bank, plus all other withdrawals and deposits made, service charges, and interest earned.

Most financial institutions return your canceled checks with your bank statement. Canceled checks serve as records of purchases and as proofs of payment. *Check safekeeping* refers to the practice of some financial institutions of not returning canceled checks to the customer. Microcopies are made of the processed checks; the checks themselves are then destroyed by the bank. If necessary, copies of canceled checks may be made from the microform for a small fee.

Reconciling is the pro-
cess of matching.

The process of matching your checkbook register with the bank statement is known as *reconciliation*. The back of the bank statement is usually printed with a form to aid you in reconciling your account. Figure 6-5 represents both sides of a typical bank statement.

On the left in Figure 6-5 is a simple statement of the bank's record of activity in the checking account. Canceled checks and other types of withdrawals are listed and are subtracted from the balance. Deposits are listed and are added to the balance. Bank service charges are subtracted from the balance, and an ending account balance is given.

It is likely that the balance your checkbook register shows will not be identical to the ending balance shown on the bank statement. In this case, you can reconcile your account by following these guidelines:

Follow the directions
on the back of the
statement.

1. Use the reconciliation form printed on the back of your bank statement, or prepare your own form.
2. Write the ending balance as shown on the front of the statement.
3. List any deposits made that do not appear on the bank statement (they should be listed in your checkbook register).

Bank Statement	Bank Reconciliation

Bank Statement
SKY CENTRAL BANK

Ardys Johnson
4250 West 18th Avenue
Chicago, IL 60601-2180

For month ended July 31, 19--:

Checks		Deposits	Balance
	7/1		800.00
32.00	7/1		768.00
36.12	7/5		731.88
22.00	7/8		709.88
	7/15	220.50	930.38
40.00	7/20		890.38
10.00	7/25	400.00	1280.38
1.00 SC*			1279.38

| Ending balance | | | 1279.38 |

*Service charge of 20 cents per check
processed

Other charges and deductions: none

Bank Reconciliation

1. Write ending balance as
shown on bank statement: *1,279.38*

2. Add credits or deposits
made that do not appear on
statement: *100.00*

3. Total lines 1 and 2: *1,379.38*

4. Write total checks outstanding (not processed): *139.90*

Check No.	Amount	
586	14	—
591	30	—
602	85	90
604	10	—

5. Subtract line 4 from line 3 and
write balance (should agree with
checkbook balance): *1,239.48*

FIGURE 6-5 Bank Reconciliation

4. Add the ending bank balance to the deposits made but not yet entered. Write down this subtotal.
5. List all checks you wrote or other withdrawals you made that do not appear on the bank statement.
6. Subtract the total checks outstanding from the subtotal. This should be the same as the balance shown in your checkbook register.

If your attempt at reconciliation is unsuccessful, check your addition and subtraction. Next, go through your checkbook register and check all addition and subtraction for the period covered by the statement. Finally, make certain that you have deducted service charges from your register balance. If you still cannot reconcile your account, report to the bank for help in discovering where the error lies.

Reconciliation must be done immediately upon receipt of the bank statement. Any errors or differences should be reported to the bank as soon as possible. Occasionally the bank does make an error, which it will be happy to correct if you report the error immediately.

ENDORSEMENTS

It is necessary to endorse a check before cashing it.

A check cannot be cashed until it has been endorsed. To *endorse* a check, the payee named on the face of the check simply signs the back of the check across its left end. There are four types of endorsements: the blank endorsement, the special endorsement, the restrictive endorsement, and the joint endorsement.

Blank Endorsement

A *blank endorsement* is simply the signature of the payee written exactly as his or her name appears on the front of the check.

(Note: If Donald's name had been written incorrectly on the face of the check, he would correct the mistake by endorsing the check with the misspelled version first, then with the correct version of his name.)

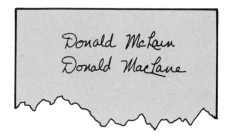

Special Endorsement

A *special endorsement*, or an endorsement in full, is written when the payee signs over a check to a third person. In the following illustration, for example, Donald MacLane uses a check written to him to pay a debt owed to Diana Jones. By using a special endorsement, Donald avoids having to cash the check before repaying Diana. The purpose of the special endorsement, then, is to specifically name the next payee who shall be entitled to cash the check.

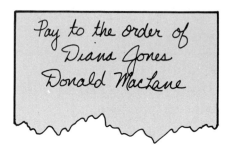

Restrictive Endorsement

A *restrictive endorsement* restricts or limits the use of a check. For example, a check endorsed with the words *For Deposit Only* above the payee's signature can be deposited only to the account specified.

The restrictive endorsement is safer than the blank endorsement for use in mailing deposits, in night deposit systems, or in other circumstances that may result in loss of a check. If a check with a restrictive endorsement is lost, it cannot be cashed by the finder.

Joint Endorsement

A *joint endorsement* is necessary when there is more than one person named as payee on the face of the check. Each payee must endorse the check before it can be cashed.

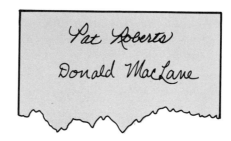

TYPES OF CHECKING ACCOUNTS

There are many types of accounts—both checking and savings—available at banks, savings and loan associations, and credit unions. Savings accounts are discussed in Chapter 8.

At most financial institutions, you will have a choice between several types of checking accounts. You should carefully study the options, because a wise choice can save you a lot of money. Some current options are the special account, the standard account, the joint account, the interest (NOW) account, the free account, and the share draft account.

Choose your account wisely; costs do vary.

Special Accounts

Most banks offer a *special checking account* to customers who will write only a small number of checks each month. No minimum balance is required for this type of account. Service fees may be charged at a low flat rate per month with an additional fee for each check written. These customers also may be charged service fees only when the number of checks written in a month exceeds a set limit. If you write only a few checks each month, this plan might be for you.

Standard Accounts

A *standard account* usually has a set monthly service fee of between $5 and $8, but no per-check fee. Often, if you are able to maintain a minimum balance, you can avoid service fees entirely. Many banks give extra services for this type of account, such as free traveler's checks, a teller machine card, or a free safe-deposit box.

Joint Accounts

A *joint account* is opened by two or more persons. Such an account is called a *survivorship account* because any person who signs on the account has the right to the entire amount deposited. If one person using

A joint account is a survivorship account.

the account dies, the other (the survivor) then becomes the sole owner of the funds in the account. All of the accounts discussed in Chapter 6 can be joint accounts.

Interest (NOW) Accounts

Most financial institutions offer what are called *interest checking accounts*. With these accounts, interest is paid if you maintain a certain minimum balance. Minimum amounts may vary greatly among different institutions.

NOW (Negotiable Order of Withdrawal) *accounts* are designed to provide the convenience of a checking account with short-term savings gains. With a NOW account, there are pluses and minuses. This type of account may not be for everyone. While you do receive interest on money deposited in a NOW account, you must put up with certain disadvantages. Minimum balance requirements may be as high as $2,500 or more, for example. If you fall below the minimum balance at any time during the month, you are automatically charged the full service fee, which may be higher than that charged for a standard account. Also, not only are you charged a service fee when your account drops below the minimum balance, but most likely you will not receive any interest for that month.

To earn interest, you need a minimum balance.

Interest rates on NOW accounts, set at 5 1/4 percent when the accounts first began, are likely to rise in the near future. Keeping money in a low-interest account can cost you money in interest lost because you could have invested elsewhere. NOW accounts vary a great deal among financial institutions; check the options carefully before selecting one.

Free Accounts

Most banks still offer *free checking* (no service fees) if you maintain a minimum balance. These minimum balances may be lower than for NOW accounts, because the bank pays no interest on deposits to free accounts. Free checking is available to senior citizens and to others during special bank promotions, such as the opening of a new bank or branch.

Free accounts are available but limited.

Share Draft Accounts

Most credit unions offer *share draft accounts*. These are checking accounts with no minimum balance requirements, no service fees, and interest payments based on your lowest monthly balance. If you are eligible for credit union membership, this type of account may be the least expensive and most convenient checking method for you.

BANKING SERVICES AND FEES

Many services are available to depositors.

A *full-service bank* is one that offers every possible kind of service, from checking accounts to credit cards, 24-hour banking machines, safe-deposit boxes, loans, and electronic funds transfers. Some other services commonly offered are certified checks, cashier's checks, money orders, and debit cards. One service that most banks offer is FDIC (Federal Deposit Insurance Corporation) insurance, which protects customers' deposits against loss up to $100,000 per account.

Certified Checks

A *certified check* is a personal check that the bank guarantees or certifies to be good. In effect, the bank puts a hold on that amount in the drawer's account so that the money will be there when the certified check is presented for payment.

Cashier's Checks

A *cashier's check* is a check written by a bank on its own funds. You can pay for a cashier's check through a withdrawal from your savings or checking account, or in cash.

Cashier's checks do not reveal the identity of the maker.

Cashier's checks are generally used to pay a person or firm when a cash payment is not desirable. A cashier's check might also be requested instead of a personal check if the payee questions your credit standing. A cashier's check can also be used for transactions in which you wish to remain anonymous, because the bank is listed as the maker of the check, and your identity is not revealed.

Money Orders

Banks sell *money orders* to those who do not wish to use cash or cannot use a check for a transaction. A money order is used like a check, except that it can never bounce. There is a charge for purchasing a money order. This charge ranges from 50 cents to $5 or more, depending on the size of the order.

Debit Cards

Debit cards allow immediate deductions from a checking account to pay for purchases. The debit card is presented at the time of purchase. When the merchant presents the debit card receipt to the bank, the

Debit cards are like checks—deducted immediately.

amount of the purchase is immediately deducted from the customer's checking account and paid the merchant. The debit card transaction is similar to writing a check to pay for purchases. The issuing bank may charge an annual fee for the card or a fee for each transaction.

Safe-Deposit Boxes

Guard your valuable documents in a safe-deposit box.

Safe-deposit boxes are available at most financial institutions for a yearly fee that is based on the size of the box. Rental fees may be between $8 and $10 for a small box to $25 or more for a large box. The customer is given two keys for the box and is allowed to store valuables and documents in the box. Private rooms are available for customers to use when opening boxes to add or take away items. Documents commonly kept in safe-deposit boxes are birth certificates, marriage and death certificates, deeds and mortgages, stocks and bonds, contracts, tax returns and receipts, and insurance policies. Jewelry, coin collections, and other small valuables are also commonly stored in safe-deposit boxes. Keeping important papers and other items in a safe-deposit box insures that the items won't be stolen, lost, or destroyed.

Loans and Trusts

Financial institutions also make loans to finance the purchase of cars, homes, vacations, home improvements, and other items. Large banks have loan departments that assist with loans, as well as provide advice for planning estates and trusts. Banks also act as trustees of estates for minors and others.

Bank Credit Cards

You can apply to a full-service bank for a *bank credit card* such as VISA or MasterCard. If you meet the requirements, the card you are issued can be used instead of cash at any business that will accept it. Banks offering national credit cards usually charge an annual fee for use of the card, as well as charge interest on the unpaid account balance.

Electronic Funds Transfers

Cash withdrawals can be done electronically.

Certain transactions, such as the paying of bills, can be made through an *electronic funds transfer*, using an automated teller machine and an automated teller card. Customers may make cash withdrawals from any of their accounts; make cash advances from their bank's VISA or Master-Card account; make deposits to any of their accounts; make payments on loans; and transfer funds from their accounts to pay their credit card, utility, and retail store account bills. With a Touch-Tone telephone, customers can check balances and pay bills from their homes or offices.

Stop Payment Orders

A ***stop payment order*** is a request that the bank not cash or process a specific check. The usual reasons for stopping payment are that the check has been lost or stolen. By issuing a stop payment order, the drawer can safely write a new check, knowing that the original check cannot be cashed if it is presented to the bank. Most banks charge a fee (usually $5 or more) for stopping payment on a check.

Bank Fees

Banks make loans from customers' deposits.

Customers' savings and deposits are the bank's primary sources of money for loans. Bank assets also come from demand deposits, from stockholders' investments, and from investments made by the bank. In addition, banks charge fees to their customers to cover costs of operation. For example, when you apply for a loan and it is granted, you are charged a loan fee. When a bank acts as a trustee, it charges a fee for this service.

Banks also charge noncustomers for services such as check cashing. If you want to cash a check at a bank where you do not have an account, the bank may charge you a fee for this service. Nondepositors pay for other services that may be free to depositors, such as traveler's checks, certified checks, and notary services.

VOCABULARY

Directions: Can you find the definition for each of the following terms used in Chapter 6?

reconciliation
blank endorsement
restrictive endorsement
payee
drawer, maker
checking account

NSF check (overdraft)
checkbook register
canceled checks
special endorsement (endorsement in full)
stop payment order

floating a check   certified check
drafts   demand deposit

1. The person to whom a check is made payable.

2. A banking term to designate that there are insufficient funds to cover a check that has been written.

3. To have payment stopped on a check after the check is lost.

4. To compare your checkbook register with the bank statement each month.

5. Checks that have been processed by the bank and returned to you.

6. An endorsement that consists only of the payee's signature.

7. An endorsement, such as the words *For Deposit Only*, that restricts use of the check.

8. Your personal record of checking account transactions.

9. The person who writes a check, paying money to another person.

10. An endorsement signing a check over to a third party.

11. A check guaranteed by the bank to be good.

12. A type of bank account that allows you to withdraw your money at will.

13. A banking service in which money is deposited and checks written.

14. A form of check for withdrawing money from a demand account.

15. Writing a check on an account that doesn't have enough money in it at the time you write the check.

ITEMS FOR DISCUSSION

1. What are reasons for having a checking account?

2. What responsibilities do customers (depositors) have when using a checking account?

3. Why is a checking account called a demand deposit?

4. Explain what is meant by the phrase *floating a check*.

5. What is a canceled check, and why is it important to a depositor?

6. Why do you need to reconcile your checking account promptly when you receive the monthly bank statement?

7. List at least four banking services provided by financial institutions.

8. Why would you be asked your mother's maiden name when opening a bank account?

9. What is a survivorship checking account?

APPLICATIONS

1. List the names, addresses, and telephone numbers of five financial institutions in your geographic location, and list the services provided by each.

2. Using Figure 6-2 (check) as an example and following the rules on pages 89-90, write these checks:
   (a) Check No. 12 to Dennis Apply for $34.44, written today
   (b) Check No. 322 to Save-Now Stores for $18.01, written today
   (c) Check No. 484 to A. P. Smith for $91.10, written today

3. Using Figure 6-3 (deposit slip) as an example and following the rules on page 91, prepare these deposit slips:
   (a) Today's date; currency $40.00; coins $1.44; Check No. 18-88 for $51.00; no cash retained
   (b) Today's date; Check No. 40-22 for $300.00 and Check No. 24-12 for $32.00; $20.00 cash retained

4. Determine your ending reconciled checkbook balance if all of the following six conditions exist:
   (a) Your ending checkbook balance is $311.40 (before the service fee is deducted).
   (b) You made an error, resulting in $30.00 less showing in your account than should be.
   (c) The service fee is $6.00.
   (d) The ending bank balance is $402.00.
   (e) Outstanding deposits total $100.00.
   (f) Outstanding checks total $166.60.

5. Determine your ending reconciled checkbook balance if all of the following six conditions exist:
   (a) Your checkbook ending balance is $800.40 (before the service fee is deducted).
   (b) The service fee is $3.00.
   (c) The ending bank balance is $1,100.00.
   (d) Outstanding deposits total $50.00.
   (e) Outstanding checks total $352.60.

6. List four types of endorsements and give a written example of each.

7. Write out on plain paper the appropriate information needed for a signature card, as shown in Figure 6-1.

8. List the banking services you would like to have when you open a checking account.

9. Which type of account will you choose? Why?

CASE PROBLEMS AND ACTIVITIES

1. Complete the given bank reconciliation form by first finishing the checkbook register and entering the service charge and then computing balances.

BANK STATEMENT
Hometown Bank

For month ended March 31, 19--

Beginning balance $100.00

Checks cashed		Deposits	Date	Balance
$24.75			3/7	$75.25
13.00		$30.00	3/8	92.25
10.00	$3.80		3/11	78.45
1.20 SC				77.25
Ending balance...$77.25				

BANK RECONCILIATION

Ending balance as shown on bank statement $_____

Add deposits not shown on bank statement $_____

_____   _____

Subtract checks written but not shown
on bank statement   _____

_____   _____

Adjusted balance (should be same as
ending balance in checkbook) $_____

		PLEASE BE SURE TO <u>DEDUCT</u> ANY PER ITEM CHARGES OR SERVICE CHARGES THAT MAY APPLY TO YOUR ACCOUNT.								
ITEM NO.	DATE	PAYMENT ISSUED TO OR DESCRIPTION OF DEPOSIT	AMOUNT OF PAYMENT		√	(-) CHECK FEE (IF ANY)	AMOUNT OF DEPOSIT		BALANCE FORWARD	
									100	00
101	3/1	To Grocery Mart / For Groceries	24	75					Payment or Deposit 24 75 / Balance 75 25	
102	3/3	To Independent Phone Co / For Tel. charges	13	00					Payment or Deposit 13 00 / Balance	
	3/5	To Deposit / For					30	00	Payment or Deposit 30 00 / Balance	
103	3/8	To Local High School / For Band donation	10	00					Payment or Deposit 10 00 / Balance	
104	3/10	To Alan's Bakery / For Bread	3	80					Payment or Deposit 3 80 / Balance	
105	3/15	To Grocery Mart / For Groceries	18	20					Payment or Deposit 18 20 / Balance	
	3/18	To Deposit / For					42	00	Payment or Deposit 42 00 / Balance	
106	3/20	To Acme Hardware / For Hammer	4	18					Payment or Deposit 4 18 / Balance	
		To / For							Payment or Deposit / Balance	
		To / For							Payment or Deposit / Balance	
									Payment or Deposit	

2. Find the errors in the following check:

RICHARD McGUIRE 518
Phone: 555-3095
2802 Saratoga Street
Ogden, UT 79393-4081

June 1 19 -- 97-145 / 1243

PAY TO THE ORDER OF _Best Buys_ $ *3500*

Thirty five and 00/100 — DOLLARS

For Classroom Use Only

🏔 **PEAK BANK & TRUST**
OGDEN, UTAH

MEMO _____ *Rick McGuire*

⑈1243014152⑈ 0518 024ᵐ90759⑆

CHAPTER 7

INCOME TAX

CHAPTER OBJECTIVES

After studying this chapter and completing the activities, you will be able to:

1. Understand the purpose of taxes, different types of taxes, and the history of taxes in the United States.
2. Define and show a working knowledge of exemptions, dependents, and taxable and nontaxable income when preparing tax returns.
3. Prepare Forms 1040EZ and 1040A U.S. Individual Income Tax Returns.

OUR TAX SYSTEM

In the democratic, free enterprise society found in the United States, money is collected by the government from citizens and companies in the form of taxes. This money, or *revenue*, is redistributed according to needs and priorities determined by Congress. The largest source of government revenue is income taxes. Other taxes providing government revenue include social security tax, unemployment insurance tax, inheritance and estate tax, automobile license tax, driver's license fees, motel and hotel room tax, long-distance telephone call excise tax, business license tax, import duties, gasoline tax, liquor and tobacco tax, utility tax, and personal property tax.

There are three basic types of taxes in the United States. *Progressive taxes* are those that increase in proportion to income. Income taxes are progressive taxes. *Regressive taxes* are those that decrease in proportion to income increases. Sales taxes are regressive taxes, because those who

Income taxes are the largest source of government revenue.

Income taxes are progressive taxes.

can least afford to pay the tax (the poor) are assessed the greatest amount in proportion to their income. ***Proportional taxes*** are those for which the tax rate remains constant, regardless of the amount of income. Property taxes (called ad valorem taxes) are proportional taxes, because all those owning property of a certain value pay the same tax.

Taxes collected are used to provide services such as education; parks and recreation; streets and roads; and police, fire, and health departments on a local level. On a national level taxes provide salaries for Congress and funds for national defense, highways, parks, welfare, foreign aid, and other services. Most of the services (local, state, and national) are provided for the general welfare of all citizens, although individual citizens may not benefit directly. For instance, through national student loan and grant programs, the entire country benefits because many of its citizens are able to obtain college educations, which increase the quality of the country's work force.

Taxes provide services for everyone.

HISTORY OF TAXES

For many years the United States operated without an income tax. Many of the new inhabitants came to America to avoid taxation, and the new society was careful to avoid it. While our country was a colony of England, the British government imposed certain taxes. However, when the Revolutionary War brought independence, there was no direct income tax imposed on citizens. The Constitution drawn in 1787 included the option to tax, but not to tax individuals directly. Excise taxes and customs duties produced enough revenue to meet the nation's needs at that time.

But while taxes were not levied against citizens by the government, the government also did not provide services for the citizens. Such was the case until the mid-1850s.

The Revolutionary War was financed by contributions from sympathetic countries such as France. The War of 1812 brought a temporary income tax; but when the war debts were paid, the tax was dropped.

Temporary income
taxes paid for wars.

When the Civil War became an economic burden, the introduction of an income tax to finance the war became necessary. In 1862 President Lincoln signed into law a bill that provided for progressive income taxes on wages earned to pay off war debts; the tax then expired. Congress introduced the first permanent income tax in the form of the 16th Amendment to the Constitution in 1909. The amendment was ratified by three-fourths of the states by 1913. Only nominal taxes were levied as a result of the 16th Amendment.

World War I (1917) cost $35 billion, paid for by taxes. The country prospered until the Great Depression of 1929. At that time the government was providing few services, and many people suffered badly without help from the government. But President Roosevelt's New Deal again brought prosperity through taxation and redistribution of income. In 1935 the Social Security Act was signed into law, creating the *Internal Revenue Service* (IRS). The IRS was designed to collect taxes and turn them over to the government for the payment of debts, commitments, and benefits. Money withheld from wages for social security is deposited with the U.S. Department of the Treasury.

During World War II taxes were increased to finance the war. This increase set a precedent for the increasing tax rates we know today. Rates are increased to pay for the growing services and needs of the government.

The IRS

The Internal Revenue Service is an administrative agency of the Department of the Treasury. The IRS has its headquarters in Washington, D.C., with seven regional offices throughout the country. Each regional office is a major data processing center that oversees at least ten district and local offices. The main functions of the IRS are to collect income taxes and enforce tax laws.

The IRS collects taxes.

In addition to collecting income taxes, the IRS performs a number of other services. In local offices, IRS employees assist taxpayers in finding information and forms. The IRS prints brochures and pamphlets to aid taxpayers in preparing their returns. Tax information and instruction booklets are furnished free to schools and colleges by the IRS. Auditors employed by the IRS examine returns selected for audit based on a computer check procedure.

The Power to Tax

Congress has the power to raise taxes.

The power to levy taxes rests with the Congress of the United States. The Constitution provides that "all bills for raising revenue shall originate in the House of Representatives." Proposals to increase or decrease taxes may come from the president, the Department of the Treasury, or from a congressman representing the interests of a geographic group of people. The House Ways and Means Committee studies the proposals and makes recommendations to the full House. Revenue bills must pass a vote in both the House and the Senate and then be signed by the president before they become law.

The Presidential Election Campaign Fund was established by Congress so that all taxpayers could share equally in the costs of election campaigns. This method of campaign financing makes it possible for all presidential candidates to compete for votes without taking large donations from minority interests, such as large corporations, unions, or wealthy individuals. When a taxpayer wishes to contribute $1 to the Presidential Election Campaign Fund, the dollar comes from taxes already withheld. Income taxes are not increased for the individual. You can elect to contribute to the Presidential Election Campaign Fund by checking the appropriate box on your tax return.

Paying Your Fair Share

Income taxes are based on ability to pay

The ability to pay is the basic principle behind the tax laws of this country. Our income tax is a graduated rate—the more income you receive, the more income tax you pay. Tax rates range from 14 to 50 percent of net income for individuals.

Our income tax system is based on *voluntary compliance*, which means that all citizens are expected to prepare (or have prepared) and file income tax returns. Taxes owed are due on or before the deadline of April 15 of each year. Responsibility for filing a tax return and paying taxes due rests with the individual. Failure to do so can result in penalty, interest charges on the taxes owed, fine, and/or imprisonment. Willful failure to pay taxes is called *tax evasion*, which is a felony.

The Federal Debt

Government bonds are loans to the government.

In 1980 the federal government spent $60.9 billion more than it collected. **Deficit spending** occurs when the government spends more money than it collects. To pay for the deficit, the government borrows money. Corporations and individuals buy bonds (such as U.S. savings bonds) or Treasury bills, which are, in effect, loans to the government. As of May 31, 1980, the total federal debt passed the $1 trillion mark.

DEFINITION OF TERMS

Before you can understand how to prepare tax forms, you need a working knowledge of the tax vocabulary. The terms described in the following paragraphs are found on income tax returns, in IRS instruction booklets, and on forms and schedules you will work with.

Filing Status

Filing status determines which tax table is used.

There are four different ways to file a tax return: (*a*) as a single person (not married), (*b*) as a married person filing a joint return (even though only one spouse may have earned income), (*c*) as a married person filing a separate return, or (*d*) as a "head of household." (A person may qualify as a head of household whether married or single if certain conditions are met in providing a residence for persons dependent on the taxpayer.) You mark your filing status on the front of the tax form. Tax rates vary according to the status claimed (see the tax tables). A more complete description of these classifications is found in IRS instruction booklets. After you file your first tax return, you will automatically receive these information and form booklets in the mail each year for use in preparing your tax returns.

Exemptions

The amount of personal exemption changes occasionally.

An **exemption** is an allowance a taxpayer claims for each person dependent on the taxpayer's income. Each taxpayer is automatically allowed one exemption for self, an additional exemption if over age 65, and an additional exemption if blind. The same exemption allowances may be taken for spouses of taxpayers.

Each exemption claimed on the income tax form excludes a certain amount ($1,000 in 1982) from a person's taxable income. You cannot claim an exemption on your tax return for a person claimed on another tax return. For example, two children may share the expense for taking care of an aging parent. Only the child who contributes more than half for the parent's care may claim the exemption. The only exception to the rule is for a student attending school full-time, until age 22. Students may claim themselves, and the students' parents may claim them as well.

Students get a special exemption status.

Dependents other than the spouse and children in the household may include children from a previous marriage. The taxpayer claiming exemption for children from a previous marriage must have contributed more than half of the funds for their support. The parent who contributes $100 a month or more per child (or by written decree or agreement) claims the exemption. The burden is on the custodial parent to prove that he or she spent $1,200 or more a year for each child's support in order to claim the exemption.

Other persons who qualify as dependents of a taxpayer include parents, grandparents, stepchildren, or other relatives who did not have income of over $1,000 during the year. To qualify as dependents, these people must receive more than half their support from the taxpayer.

Gross Income

Gross income is all the taxable income you receive, including wages, tips, salaries, interest, dividends, unemployment compensation, alimony, and so forth. Certain types of income are not taxable and are not reported as income, such as child support, gifts, inheritances, scholarships, social security payments received, life insurance benefits, veterans benefits, and workers' compensation benefits.

Nontaxable income is not reported on a tax return.

Wages, Salaries, and Tips. These items are moneys received through employment, as shown on the Form W-2, Wage and Tax Statement supplied by the employer each year.

Interest Income. Interest earned on savings accounts, certificates of deposit, and loans to others is taxable. This income must be included on your tax return.

Dividend Income. Dividends are moneys paid from profits to stockholders of a corporation. Dividends are taxable, although on certain qualifying dividends there is an *exclusion* of $100 for single taxpayers or $200 for married taxpayers filing jointly (1982). Exclusion means the first $100 or $200 of dividends received during the year is not taxable (with certain exceptions explained in the tax instruction booklets).

Unemployment Compensation. Payments you receive while unemployed may be partly taxable. If you receive $12,000 (single status) or $18,000 (married filing jointly), which includes some unemployment com-

Unemployment compensation may be taxable.

pensation payments, you must fill out a separate schedule to compute your tax liability.

Child Support. Money paid to a former spouse for support of dependent children is called *child support*. This income is not taxable for the one receiving it, nor is child support deductible for the one paying it.

Alimony. Money paid to support a former spouse is called *alimony.* It is taxable for the person receiving it and deductible for the person paying it. (The long Form 1040 is required.)

Deductions

Keep receipts for your deductions.

Deductions are expenses the law allows the taxpayer to subtract from gross income. The full dollar amount may be deducted for medical expenses, state and local taxes, property taxes, interest on home mortgages and credit purchases, union dues, and casualty and theft losses. For contributions to charities and religious organizations, you are limited to a deduction of 25 percent of the amount given. When subtracted from gross income, deductions reduce taxable income. Personal deductions are listed on Schedule A of Form 1040. Persons who file the short Form 1040A or 1040EZ cannot itemize deductions.

Zero Bracket Amount

There are different tax forms to choose from.

The *zero bracket amount* is the minimum dollar amount of deductions you need before it is worth it to you to itemize your deductions. Single persons should not itemize unless their deductions total more than $2,300; married persons, $3,400; and married persons filing separately, $1,700. Because tax tables begin at these zero bracket amounts, the standard deduction automatically allows for these amounts. In other words, if you file a short Form 1040A or 1040EZ, these minimum deduction amounts are automatically included. Only if your deductions exceed these minimum amounts is it profitable to itemize.

PREPARING TO FILE

Once income and expense records are ready, you can rough draft your tax return. You should also study the tax booklet that accompanies the printed tax forms. The booklet gives you the latest tax information, tax laws that have passed, and new information you may need to prepare your tax return. Read the tax return carefully to be sure you are taking advantage of every possible deduction and are reporting all taxable income. A simple 1040EZ tax return may require only 15 minutes to prepare; the long form 1040 may require several days after all information has been gathered. In addition to a federal tax return, you may have to file a state income tax return.

Who Must File

You must file a tax return if:

You must file if you earn a certain amount.

1. You are single, under age 65, and earn at least $3,300. You are single, age 65 or older, and earn at least $4,300.
2. You are married, filing a joint return, both you and your spouse are under age 65, and together you earn at least $5,400.
   You are married, filing a joint return, you or your spouse is age 65 or older, and together you earn at least $6,400.
   You are married, filing a joint return, both you and your spouse are 65 or older, and together you earn at least $7,400.
3. You are married, filing a separate return, and earn at least $1,000.
4. You were claimed as a dependent on your parents' tax return, but you had dividends, interest, or other unearned income of at least $1,000.
5. You are self-employed and earn at least $400.
6. You owe taxes, such as social security, that were not withheld during the year.

Persons who did not earn enough to owe taxes, but who had taxes withheld from their paychecks, should file a return to reclaim moneys withheld. If you do not file, you will not get a refund.

When to File

You must file no later than April 15 of the year after you earned income. If April 15 falls on a weekend or holiday, your tax return is due on the next regular weekday. If you file late, you are subject to penalties and interest charges.

Short Form or Long Form

You must decide whether to fill out a short form (1040A or 1040EZ) or to itemize your deductions, using the long form (1040).

Most students use Form 1040EZ.

1. *Use Form 1040EZ* if you are single; you have only your own exemption; you have no dependents; your income is from wages, salaries, and tips; your interest income is $400 or less; you have no dividend

income; and your taxable income is less than $50,000. You can claim a partial charitable contributions deduction, but no tax credits.

2. *Use Form 1040A* if your deductions do not exceed zero bracket amounts; your income is from wages, salaries, tips, interest and dividends (no maximums), and unemployment compensation; and your taxable income is less than $50,000. You can claim a partial charitable contributions deduction, the marital deduction, partial credit for political contributions, and earned income credit. You may file under any of the four filing statuses, claim all exemptions you are entitled to, and claim all qualified dependents.

3. *Use Form 1040* if you wish to itemize deductions; you can claim adjustments to income (such as alimony or business expenses); you claim credits not available on 1040EZ or 1040A (such as child care); you have income such as capital gains, self-employment income, or other business income that cannot be listed on short forms; you need to fill out any other forms or schedules that must be attached to your return; or you have taxable income of $50,000 or more.

Form 1040 is complicated and allows many deductions.

Where to Begin

During the year, save all receipts and proofs of payment for your itemized deductions. You will need these receipts to prove the accuracy of your tax return if you are audited. Save all employee withholding records. When you receive your Form W-2, Wage and Tax Statement from each of your employers (by January 31), compare it with your records and check it for accuracy. Any discrepancy between the Form W-2 and your records should be reported immediately to the employer and corrected.

Everyone who works must pay social security taxes.

If you earned more than $32,400 in 1982 or $35,700 in 1983, your employer may have withheld more social security tax (**FICA**) than the maximum ($2,170.80 and $2,391.90, respectively). The excess amount (above $2,170.80 and $2,391.90) withheld can be added to federal taxes withheld on the 1040EZ or 1040A to increase your refund or reduce your tax liability. Social security withholding rates are scheduled to change as follows:

YEAR	MAXIMUM AMOUNT OF EARNINGS	RATE	MAXIMUM TAX
1983	$35,700.00	6.70%	$2,391.90
1984	37,500.00	7.00%	2,625.00
1985	40,500.00	7.05%	2,855.25
1986	43,800.00	7.15%	3,131.70
1987	46,800.00	7.15%	3,346.20
1988	50,100.00	7.51%	3,762.51
1989	53,400.00	7.51%	4,010.34
1990	57,000.00	7.65%	4,360.50

It is wise to prepare your tax return early—as soon as you receive your Form W-2 (Wage and Tax Statement), 1099-INT (Statement for Recipients of Interest Income) forms from banks and savings institutions, 1099-UC (Statement for Recipients of Unemployment Compensation Payments) forms, and can gather all other necessary information. If you owe additional taxes, mail your return and the amount due in sufficient time to have the envelope postmarked by April 15. If you have a refund coming, the sooner you file, the sooner you will receive it. If you wait until April, your refund may be delayed for months. You will not receive interest on refunds.

Mail your tax return no later than April 15.

Once you have gathered all your information, prepare both the short and the long form to determine whether you can save money by itemizing deductions. Read all directions carefully and fill out all schedules completely.

If you do not have enough taxes withheld during the year, and you owe the government more than $100 when taxes are due, you may be subject to a penalty and have to increase withholdings for the next year. If you receive a large refund, you should increase your exemption status to have less withheld during the year.

If you discover you made an error in a tax return after it has been filed, you may file an amended return (Form 1040X) in order to claim a refund or credit, or to pay additional tax due.

You can amend your tax return.

Save copies of the tax returns you file, together with all supporting evidence (receipts) for six years. Tax returns should be kept in a safe-deposit box, together with copies of W-2s and other supporting information.

PREPARING INCOME TAX RETURNS

The federal income tax return must be completed in ink or typed with no errors or omissions. The booklets provided by the IRS have line-by-line instructions that explain each section and type of income or deduction. The preparation of tax returns is a simple process of following directions and inserting appropriate information. An unsigned tax return will be returned to the taxpayer before a refund is issued. If a joint return is prepared, both spouses must sign it.

Form 1040EZ

Line-by-line instructions for filling out the 1982 Form 1040EZ are given on the back of the form. Highlights of the instructions are described in the following paragraphs.

Step 1: Name and Address. Fill in your name, address, and social security number. Check the Yes box if you want $1 to go to the Presidential Election Campaign Fund.

Step 2: Tax Computation. On line 1 enter your total wages, salaries, and tips, as shown on your W-2 form(s). On line 2 enter interest earned on savings accounts (cannot be more than $400). Add lines 1 and 2, and enter the total on line 3.

Line 4 is for your charitable contributions. Your deduction is limited to 25 percent of your first $100 ($150 if married filing jointly) of contributions to qualified organizations. Therefore, the amount on line 4 may not be more than $25.00 ($37.50 if married filing jointly). Line 4 is subtracted from line 3, and the difference is entered on line 5.

Your personal exemption (line 6) is $1,000 for 1982. Subtract $1,000 from the amount on line 5. The result is your taxable income (line 7).

On line 8 enter the total federal tax withheld (as shown on your W-2 forms). On line 9 enter the tax you owe based on your taxable income. Look up the amount of your taxable income and the amount of tax you owe in the tax tables.

Step 3: Refund or Amount You Owe. If the amount of federal taxes withheld (line 8) is larger than the amount of tax you owe shown on line 9, you will receive a refund. Enter the amount due you on line 10. If you owe more tax than was withheld (line 9 is greater than line 8), you must pay the difference. Enter the amount you must pay on line 11. Write a check to the Internal Revenue Service and attach it to your return.

Sign your return. Make sure your W-2 form(s) and check (if applicable) are attached to the completed return, and mail the return to the nearest regional IRS office.

Some deductions are allowed on the 1040EZ.

Tax returns must be signed.

Form 1040A

Form 1040A is printed on the front and back of one piece of paper. Line-by-line instructions for completing the 1982 1040A are available in the booklet *Instructions for Preparing Forms 1040EZ and 1040A*.

On the back of Form 1040A are instructions as to who may and may not use the form. This side of the form also contains space for listing interest income sources and amounts for taxpayers having over $400 in interest income (Part I) and space for listing dividend income sources and amounts for taxpayers who received over $400 in dividend income (Part II).

Step 1: Name and Address. This first section requires writing in the name, address, social security number, and occupation of all persons filing

Use the preprinted label.

the return. Each person filing can elect to give or not to give to the Presidential Election Campaign Fund.

Step 2: Filing Status and Exemptions. In this section, select your tax filing status (single, married filing jointly, married filing separately, or head of household). Also, supply information that applies to exemptions and dependents: taxpayer, spouse, dependent children living at home, and other dependents. In the boxes at the far right, show the total number of exemptions claimed on the tax return.

Step 3: Adjusted Gross Income. Lines 6 through 12 are for listing wages, salaries, and tips, as shown on your W-2 form(s) (line 6); interest income (line 7); dividend income minus applicable exclusions (line 8); and unemployment compensation (line 9). Add lines 6, 7, 8, and 9, and enter the result on line 10. On line 11 enter the marital deduction, if applicable. This amount is computed by completing a worksheet in the instruction booklet. The marital deduction for 1982 is 5 percent of the total pay of the spouse earning the lesser amount, or $30,000, whichever is less. The maximum marital deduction for 1982 returns is $1,500. The maximum marital deduction is 10 percent or $3,000 for 1983 and subsequent years. Subtract line 11 from line 10. The difference (called *adjusted gross income*) is entered on line 12.

Married couples get a tax break.

Step 4: Taxable Income. Lines 13 through 16 are used to calculate the amount of your taxable income. The amount of allowable charitable contributions (from completed worksheet in tax booklet) is entered on line 13, and is then subtracted from line 12. The difference is entered on line 14. The total number of exemptions claimed in Step 2 above is multiplied by $1,000 and the result is entered on line 15. The amount on line 15 is subtracted from line 14, and the difference is entered on line 16. The difference between lines 14 and 15 is your *taxable income*—the amount that determines your tax liability. The amount of taxes due from you, based on your taxable income, is your *tax liability*.

Tax liability is based on taxable income.

Step 5: Tax, Credits, and Payments. Line 17a shows the partial credit for political contributions, as completed on the booklet worksheet. Tax deductions for political contributions in 1982 are limited to $100 for married persons filing jointly, or to $50 for other statuses. You may deduct half of your political contributions, as long as this deduction does not exceed the maximum for your filing status. Most state tax laws allow you to deduct the other half of your political contributions on state tax returns, to a maximum of $200 for married persons filing jointly and $100 for other statuses. Any earned income credit, as computed on the booklet worksheet, is entered on line 17c. (Earned income credit applies to people who file jointly or as head of household, have a child, and have income under $10,000. The credit can be up to $500.) The total of lines 17a, 17b, and 17c is entered on line 18. Tax liability is reduced by this amount.

To find the amount of tax you owe to enter on line 19a, turn to the tax tables in the instruction booklet and look up the amount of your taxable income as recorded on line 16. If you received any advance earned income credit (EIC), which would be shown on your W-2 slips, that amount is entered on line 19b. The total of lines 19a and 19b is your tax liability, and this amount is entered on line 20.

Tax tables are provided in the booklet.

Step 6: Refund or Amount Due. Line 21 shows a refund due you. A refund is due when taxes withheld and credits total more than your tax liability—line 18 is larger than line 20. Line 22 shows tax owed by you, when your taxes withheld and credits are less than your tax liability—line 20 is larger than line 18.

Step 7: Signature. The taxpayer and spouse must both sign a joint return, even though only one may have earned or received income.

Sample Tax Returns

Figure 7-1 shows John Calhoun's Form W-2, Wage and Tax Statement. Figure 7-2 shows his completed Form 1040EZ tax return. Mr. Calhoun is single and claims one exemption. His wages are found on the W-2 slip, which he previously checked for accuracy. John earned $134 in interest on his savings account and gave $100 in charitable contributions.

FIGURE 7-1
Sample W-2
Wage and Tax
Statement

1 Control number	22222	OMB No. 1545-0008					
2 Employer's name, address, and ZIP code			3 Employer's identification number 93-89998488		4 Employer's State number 44-88		
Blanton School District T-31 23855 SW 85th Portland, OR 97215-4562			5 Stat. employee ☐ De-ceased ☐ Pension plan ☐ Legal rep. ☐	942 emp. ☐	Sub-total ☐	Cor-rection ☐	Void ☐
			6		7 Advance EIC payment		
8 Employee's social security number 465-84-3894	9 Federal income tax withheld $2,301.00		10 Wages, tips, other compensation $14,820.00		11 FICA tax withheld $992.94		
12 Employee's name, address, and ZIP code			13 FICA wages $14,820.00		14 FICA tips		
John F. Calhoun 285 SW 28th St. #8 Portland, OR 97214-4562			16 Employer's use				
			17 State income tax $946.00	18 State wages, tips, etc. $14,820.00	19 Name of State Oregon		
			20 Local income tax None	21 Local wages, tips, etc. None	22 Name of locality Mult. Co.		

Form **W-2 Wage and Tax Statement 1982** Copy B To be filed with employee's FEDERAL tax return. This information is being furnished to the Internal Revenue Service. Department of the Treasury Internal Revenue Service

On the tax tables, John locates $13,929 (taxable income—line 7) in the Single column. His tax liability, based on his taxable income, is $2,083. When John's tax liability is subtracted from taxes withheld (line 8), the difference is $218. The amount of tax withheld is greater by $218 than John's tax liability; so he should receive a refund for that amount.

Department of the Treasury — Internal Revenue Service

Form 1040EZ Income Tax Return for Single filers with no dependents

1982

Instructions are on the back of this form.
Tax Table is in the 1040EZ and 1040A Tax Package.

Name and address

Use the IRS mailing label. If you don't have a label, print or type:

Name (first, initial, last)   John F. Calhoun
Social security number   465-84-3894

Present home address   285 SW 28th St. APT 8

City, town or post office, State, and ZIP code   Portland, OR 97214-4562

Presidential Election Campaign Fund
Check this box ☐ if you want $1 of your tax to go to this fund.

Figure your tax

Attach Copy B of Forms W-2 here

1 Wages, salaries, and tips. Attach your W-2 form(s).	1	14,820.00
2 Interest income of $400 or less. If more than $400, you cannot use Form 1040EZ.	2	134.00
3 Add line 1 and line 2. This is your **adjusted gross income**.	3	14,954.00
4 Allowable part of your charitable contributions. Complete the worksheet on page 18. Do not write more than $25.	4	25.00
5 Subtract line 4 from line 3.	5	14,929.00
6 Amount of your personal exemption.	6	1,000.00
7 Subtract line 6 from line 5. This is your **taxable income**.	7	13,929.00
8 Enter your Federal income tax withheld. This is shown on your W-2 form(s).	8	2,301.00
9 Use the tax table on pages 26-31 to find the **tax** on your taxable income on line 7.	9	2,083.00

Refund or amount you owe

Attach tax payment here

10 If line 8 is larger than line 9, subtract line 9 from line 8. Enter the amount of your refund.	10	218.00
11 If line 9 is larger than line 8, subtract line 8 from line 9. Enter the **amount you owe**. Attach check or money order for the full amount payable to "Internal Revenue Service."	11	— . —

Sign your return

I have read this return. Under penalties of perjury, I declare that to the best of my knowledge and belief, the return is correct and complete.

Your signature   x John F. Calhoun
Date   4/15/——

For Privacy Act and Paperwork Reduction Act Notice, see page 34.

FIGURE 7-2   Sample 1040EZ Return

Married persons filing jointly may also choose to file the short Form 1040EZ or the Form 1040A. Figures 7-3A and 7-3B show the Wage and Tax Statements for Michael J. and Melissa B. Anderson. Figure 7-4 is their joint return (1040A). The Andersons could not file 1040EZ because they had dividend income and contributions to political candidates to declare.

FIGURE 7–3A
Sample W-2
Wage and Tax
Statement,
Melissa
Anderson

1 Control number	22222	OMB No. 1545-0008		
2 Employer's name, address, and ZIP code		3 Employer's identification number 92-186848		4 Employer's State number 33-261
A & W Welding Supply 85 West Bensington Blvd Chicago, IL 60615-2358		5 Stat. employee / Deceased / Pension plan / Legal rep. □ □ □ □	942 emp. □	Sub-total □ / Cor-rection □ / Void □
		6		7 Advance EIC payment
8 Employee's social security number 411-86-3214	9 Federal income tax withheld $1,611.00	10 Wages, tips, other compensation $12,811.40		11 FICA tax withheld $858.38
12 Employee's name, address, and ZIP code		13 FICA wages $12,811.40		14 FICA tips
Melissa B. Anderson 312 East 34th Street Chicago, IL 60604-5214		16 Employer's use		
		17 State income tax	18 State wages, tips, etc.	19 Name of State
		20 Local income tax	21 Local wages, tips, etc.	22 Name of locality

Form **W-2 Wage and Tax Statement 1982**   Copy B To be filed with employee's FEDERAL tax return   Department of the Treasury
This information is being furnished to the Internal Revenue Service.   Internal Revenue Service

FIGURE 7–3B
Sample W-2
Wage and Tax
Statement,
Michael
Anderson

1 Control number	22222	OMB No. 1545-0008		
2 Employer's name, address, and ZIP code		3 Employer's identification number 91-4813141		4 Employer's State number 33-261
A Art Studios 48 East 11th Street Des Plaines, IL 60601-3132		5 Stat. employee / Deceased / Pension plan / Legal rep. □ □ □ □	942 emp. □	Sub-total □ / Cor-rection □ / Void □
		6		7 Advance EIC payment
8 Employee's social security number 323-40-6128	9 Federal income tax withheld $1,591.00	10 Wages, tips, other compensation $11,028.60		11 FICA tax withheld $738.92
12 Employee's name, address, and ZIP code		13 FICA wages $11,028.60		14 FICA tips
Michael J. Anderson 312 East 34th Street Chicago, IL 60604-5214		16 Employer's use		
		17 State income tax	18 State wages, tips, etc.	19 Name of State
		20 Local income tax	21 Local wages, tips, etc.	22 Name of locality

Form **W-2 Wage and Tax Statement 1982**   Copy B To be filed with employee's FEDERAL tax return   Department of the Treasury
This information is being furnished to the Internal Revenue Service.   Internal Revenue Service

To claim the marital deduction on line 11, Melissa and Michael Anderson had to complete Schedule W (see Figure 7-5) and attach it to their tax return. The marital deduction allows the couple to deduct 5 percent of the lesser of the two incomes. The lesser income may not exceed $30,000.

1982

Department of the Treasury — Internal Revenue Service

Form 1040A US Individual Income Tax Return

OMB No. 1545-0085

Step 1
Name and address
Use the IRS mailing label. Otherwise, print or type.

Your first name and initial (if joint return, also give spouse's name and initial)   Last name   Your social security no.

Melissa B. and Michael J. Anderson   411-86-3214

Present home address   Spouse's social security no.

312 East 34th. Street   323-40-6128

City, town or post office, State, and ZIP code   Your occupation Welder

Chicago, IL 60604-5214   Spouse's occupation Photographer

Presidential Election Campaign Fund

Do you want $1 to go to this fund? .... ☑ Yes ☐ No

If joint return, does your spouse want $1 to go to this fund? ☑ Yes ☐ No

Step 2
Filing status
(Check only one)
and Exemptions

1 ☐ Single (See if you can use Form 1040EZ.)

2 ☑ Married filing joint return (even if only one had income)

3 ☐ Married filing separate return. Enter spouse's social security no. above and full name here. _____

4 ☐ Head of household (with qualifying person). If the qualifying person is your unmarried child but not your dependent, write this child's name here. _____

Always check the exemption box labeled Yourself. Check other boxes if they apply.

5a ☑ Yourself   ☐ 65 or over   ☐ Blind   Write number of boxes checked on 5a and b   [2]

b ☑ Spouse   ☐ 65 or over   ☐ Blind

c First names of your dependent children who lived with you Amy _____   Write number of children listed on 5c   [1]

Attach Copy B of Forms W-2 here

d Other dependents:

(1) Name	(2) Relationship	(3) Number of months lived in your home.	(4) Did dependent have income of $1,000 or more?	(5) Did you provide more than one-half of dependent's support?
Billy	son	1	no	yes

Write number of other dependents listed on 5d   [1]

e Total number of exemptions claimed   Add numbers entered in boxes above   [4]

Step 3
Adjusted gross income

6 Wages, salaries, tips, etc. (Attach Forms W-2) .... 6 $ 23,840.00

7 Interest income (Complete page 2 if over $400 or you have any All-Savers interest) 7   284.00

8a Dividends $ 368.00 (Complete page 2 if over $400) 8b Exclusion $ 200.00 Subtract line 8b from 8a   8c   168.00

9a Unemployment compensation (insurance). Total from Form(s) 1099-UC _____

b Taxable amount, if any, from worksheet on page 16 of Instructions .... 9b   —0.—

10 Add lines 6, 7, 8c, and 9b. This is your total income. 10   24,292.00

11 Deduction for a married couple when both work. Complete the worksheet on page 17. .. 11   551.43

12 Subtract line 11 from line 10. This is your adjusted gross income. 12   23,740.57

Step 4
Taxable Income

13 Allowable part of your charitable contributions. Complete the worksheet on page 18. 13   25.00

14 Subtract line 13 from line 12 14   23,715.57

15 Multiply $1,000 by the total number of exemptions claimed in box 5e 15   4,000.00

16 Subtract line 15 from line 14. This is your taxable income. .... 16 $ 19,715.57

Step 5
Tax, credits, and payments

Attach check or money order here

17a Partial credit for political contributions. See page 19. .... ■17a $ 75.00

b Total Federal income tax withheld, from W-2 form(s). (If line 6 is more than $32,400, see page 19.)   17b $ 3202.00

Stop Here and Sign Below If You Want IRS to Figure Your Tax

c Earned income credit, from worksheet on page 21 .... 17c

18 Add lines 17a, b, and c. These are your total credits and payments. .... 18 $ 3,277.00

19a Find tax on amount on line 16. Use tax table, pages 26-31. ...... 19a $ 2,833.00

b Advance EIC payment (from W-2 form(s)) .... 19b   —0.—

20 Add lines 19a and 19b. This is your total tax. .... 20 $ 2,833.00

Step 6
Refund or amount you owe

21 If line 18 is larger than line 20, subtract line 20 from line 18. Enter the amount to be **refunded to you** .... 21 $ 444.00

22 If line 20 is larger than line 18, subtract line 18 from line 20. Enter the **amount you owe.** Attach payment for full amount payable to "Internal Revenue Service." 22

Step 7
Sign your return

I have read this return and any attachments filed with it. Under penalties of perjury, I declare that to the best of my knowledge and belief, the return and attachments are correct and complete.

Melissa B. Anderson 2/15/—   Michael J. Anderson

Your signature   Date   Spouse's signature (If filing jointly, BOTH must sign)

Paid preparer's signature	Date	Check if self-employed ☐	Preparer's social security no.

Firm's name (or yours, if self-employed) _____   E.I. no.

Address and Zip code

For **Privacy Act and Paperwork Reduction Act Notice,** see page 34.

FIGURE 7-4   Sample 1040A Return

The Andersons' charitable contribution deduction of $25 is entered on line 13. Michael and Melissa gave $150 in political contributions; $75 is entered on line 17a.

Schedule W
(Form 1040)
Department of the Treasury
Internal Revenue Service

Deduction for a Married Couple When Both Work
▶ Attach to Form 1040. ▶ For Paperwork Reduction Act Notice, see Form 1040 Instructions.

OMB No. 1545-0074

19~~~~**82**
37

Names as shown on Form 1040

Melissa B. and Michael J. Anderson

Your social security number

411 86 3214

Purpose.—Use this schedule to claim a deduction if:

• you are married filing a joint return,
• both you and your spouse have Qualified Earned Income, and
• you do not exclude income earned abroad or in U.S. possessions or claim the foreign housing deduction.

Generally, earned income is income you receive for services you provide such as wages, salaries, tips, and commissions. It also includes income earned from self-

employment. It does not include items such as interest, dividends, pensions, annuities, non-taxable income, distributions from an IRA, or deferred compensation.

Caution: Do not consider community property laws in figuring your earned income.

Adjustments.—Your earned income must be reduced by certain deductions that apply to it to figure Qualified Earned Income. Enter in the proper column of line 4 below, the amounts from Form 1040:
• line 24—Employee Business Expenses,
• line 25—Payments to an IRA,

• line 26—Payments to a Keogh plan, &
• line 31—Repayment of supplemental unemployment benefits (Sub-pay).

Example.—You earn a salary of $20,000 and have $6,000 of employee business expenses on line 24 of Form 1040. Your spouse earns $17,000 and puts $2,000 into an IRA (line 25 of Form 1040). Your Qualified Earned Income is $14,000 and your spouse's is $15,000. Therefore, on your joint return you can take a deduction of $700 (.05 × $14,000).

		(a) You		(b) Your spouse	
1	Wages, salaries, tips, etc., from line 7 of Form 1040. (Do not include any amount your spouse pays you.)	**1**	$ 12,811	40	$ 11,028	60
2	Net profit or (loss) from self-employment (from Schedule C or F (Form 1040), Form 1065 (Schedule K-1), and any other taxable self-employment income) .	**2**	—0	—	— 0	—
3	Combine lines 1 and 2. This is your total earned income	**3**	12,811	40	11,028	60
4	Adjustments from Form 1040, lines 24, 25, 26, and any repayment of Sub-pay written in on line 31 (see instructions above)	**4**	— 0	—	— 0	—
5	Subtract line 4 from line 3. This is your Qualified Earned Income	**5**	12,811	40	11,028	60
6	Write in the amount from line 5(a) or 5(b), whichever is smaller, BUT DO NOT WRITE MORE THAN $30,000	**6**			11,028	60
7	Multiply line 6 by 5% (.05)	**7**			× .05	
8	Write in the answer here and on Form 1040, line 29	**8**			551	43

FIGURE 7-5   Sample Schedule W (Marital Deduction)

The Andersons' tax liability is smaller than taxes withheld by $444. They are due a refund in that amount.

Federal tax tables, which taxpayers use to determine the amount of their income tax, are shown in Figure 7-6, pages 123-125.

Vocabulary, Items for Discussion, Applications, and Case Problems and Activities exercises for Chapter 7 are on pages 126-129.

1982 Tax Table — Based on Taxable Income

For persons with taxable incomes of less than $50,000.

Example: Mr. and Mrs. Green are filing a joint return. Their taxable income on line 16 of Form 1040A is $23,270. First, they find the $23,250–23,300 income line. Next, they find the column for married filing jointly and read down the column. The amount shown where the income line and filing status column meet is $3,706. This is the tax amount they must write on line 19a of Form 1040A.

If 1040A, line 16, OR 1040EZ, line 7 is—		Single	Married filing jointly	Married filing separately	Head of a household
At least	But less than				
23,250	23,300	4,767	3,706	5,894	4,379
23,300	23,350	4,783	3,718	5,916	4,393
23,350	23,400	4,798	3,731	5,938	4,407

FIGURE 7-6　Selected 1982 Tax Tables

1982 Tax Table (Continued)

Tax table for taxable income at least $16,000 but less than $24,000, with columns for Single, Married filing jointly, Married filing separately, and Head of a household.

1982 Tax Table (Continued)

Tax table for taxable income at least $24,000 but less than $32,000, with columns for Single, Married filing jointly, Married filing separately, and Head of a household.

FIGURE 7-6 (continued)

1982 Tax Table (Continued)

If 1040A, line 16, OR 1040EZ, line 7 is— At least	But less than	And you are— Single	Married filing jointly	Married filing separately	Head of a household
		Your tax is—			
32,750	32,800	8,282	6,523	10,212	7,649
32,800	32,850	8,302	6,539	10,237	7,668
32,850	32,900	8,322	6,556	10,261	7,687
32,900	32,950	8,342	6,572	10,286	7,706
32,950	33,000	8,362	6,589	10,310	7,725
33,000					
33,000	33,050	8,382	6,605	10,335	7,744
33,050	33,100	8,402	6,622	10,359	7,763
33,100	33,150	8,422	6,638	10,384	7,782
33,150	33,200	8,442	6,655	10,408	7,801
33,200	33,250	8,462	6,671	10,433	7,820
33,250	33,300	8,482	6,688	10,457	7,839
33,300	33,350	8,502	6,704	10,482	7,858
33,350	33,400	8,522	6,721	10,506	7,877
33,400	33,450	8,542	6,737	10,531	7,896
33,450	33,500	8,562	6,754	10,555	7,915
33,500	33,550	8,582	6,770	10,580	7,934
33,550	33,600	8,602	6,787	10,604	7,953
33,600	33,650	8,622	6,803	10,629	7,972
33,650	33,700	8,642	6,820	10,653	7,991
33,700	33,750	8,662	6,836	10,678	8,010
33,750	33,800	8,682	6,853	10,702	8,029
33,800	33,850	8,702	6,869	10,727	8,048
33,850	33,900	8,722	6,886	10,751	8,067
33,900	33,950	8,742	6,902	10,776	8,086
33,950	34,000	8,762	6,919	10,800	8,105
34,000					
34,000	34,050	8,782	6,935	10,825	8,124
34,050	34,100	8,802	6,952	10,849	8,143
34,100	34,150	8,823	6,968	10,874	8,162
34,150	34,200	8,845	6,985	10,898	8,183
34,200	34,250	8,867	7,001	10,923	8,203
34,250	34,300	8,889	7,018	10,947	8,224
34,300	34,350	8,911	7,034	10,972	8,244
34,350	34,400	8,933	7,051	10,996	8,265
34,400	34,450	8,955	7,067	11,021	8,285
34,450	34,500	8,977	7,084	11,045	8,306
34,500	34,550	8,999	7,100	11,070	8,326
34,550	34,600	9,021	7,117	11,094	8,347
34,600	34,650	9,043	7,133	11,119	8,367
34,650	34,700	9,065	7,150	11,143	8,388
34,700	34,750	9,087	7,166	11,168	8,408
34,750	34,800	9,109	7,183	11,192	8,429
34,800	34,850	9,131	7,199	11,217	8,449
34,850	34,900	9,153	7,216	11,241	8,470
34,900	34,950	9,175	7,232	11,266	8,490
34,950	35,000	9,197	7,249	11,290	8,511
35,000					
35,000	35,050	9,219	7,265	11,315	8,531
35,050	35,100	9,241	7,282	11,339	8,552
35,100	35,150	9,263	7,298	11,364	8,572
35,150	35,200	9,285	7,315	11,388	8,593
35,200	35,250	9,307	7,333	11,413	8,613
35,250	35,300	9,329	7,352	11,437	8,634
35,300	35,350	9,351	7,372	11,462	8,654
35,350	35,400	9,373	7,391	11,486	8,675
35,400	35,450	9,395	7,411	11,511	8,695
35,450	35,500	9,417	7,430	11,535	8,716
35,500	35,550	9,439	7,450	11,560	8,736
35,550	35,600	9,461	7,469	11,584	8,757
35,600	35,650	9,483	7,489	11,609	8,777
35,650	35,700	9,505	7,508	11,633	8,798
35,700	35,750	9,527	7,528	11,658	8,818
35,750	35,800	9,549	7,547	11,682	8,839
35,800	35,850	9,571	7,567	11,707	8,859
35,850	35,900	9,593	7,586	11,731	8,880
35,900	35,950	9,615	7,606	11,756	8,900
35,950	36,000	9,637	*7,625	11,780	8,921
36,000					
36,000	36,050	9,659	7,645	11,805	8,941
36,050	36,100	9,681	7,664	11,829	8,962
36,100	36,150	9,703	7,684	11,854	8,982
36,150	36,200	9,725	7,703	11,878	9,003
36,200	36,250	9,747	7,723	11,903	9,023
36,250	36,300	9,769	7,742	11,927	9,044
36,300	36,350	9,791	7,762	11,952	9,064
36,350	36,400	9,813	7,781	11,976	9,085
36,400	36,450	9,835	7,801	12,001	9,105
36,450	36,500	9,857	7,820	12,025	9,126
36,500	36,550	9,879	7,840	12,050	9,146
36,550	36,600	9,901	7,859	12,074	9,167
36,600	36,650	9,923	7,879	12,099	9,187
36,650	36,700	9,945	7,898	12,123	9,208
36,700	36,750	9,967	7,918	12,148	9,228
36,750	36,800	9,989	7,937	12,172	9,249
36,800	36,850	10,011	7,957	12,197	9,269
36,850	36,900	10,033	7,976	12,221	9,290
36,900	36,950	10,055	7,996	12,246	9,310
36,950	37,000	10,077	8,015	12,270	9,331
37,000					
37,000	37,050	10,099	8,035	12,295	9,351
37,050	37,100	10,121	8,054	12,319	9,372
37,100	37,150	10,143	8,074	12,344	9,392
37,150	37,200	10,165	8,093	12,368	9,413
37,200	37,250	10,187	8,113	12,393	9,433
37,250	37,300	10,209	8,132	12,417	9,454
37,300	37,350	10,231	8,152	12,442	9,474
37,350	37,400	10,253	8,171	12,466	9,495
37,400	37,450	10,275	8,191	12,491	9,515
37,450	37,500	10,297	8,210	12,515	9,536
37,500	37,550	10,319	8,230	12,540	9,556
37,550	37,600	10,341	8,249	12,564	9,577
37,600	37,650	10,363	8,269	12,589	9,597
37,650	37,700	10,385	8,288	12,613	9,618
37,700	37,750	10,407	8,308	12,638	9,638
37,750	37,800	10,429	8,327	12,662	9,659
37,800	37,850	10,451	8,347	12,687	9,679
37,850	37,900	10,473	8,366	12,711	9,700
37,900	37,950	10,495	8,386	12,736	9,720
37,950	38,000	10,517	8,405	12,760	9,741
38,000					
38,000	38,050	10,539	8,425	12,785	9,761
38,050	38,100	10,561	8,444	12,809	9,782
38,100	38,150	10,583	8,464	12,834	9,802
38,150	38,200	10,605	8,483	12,858	9,823
38,200	38,250	10,627	8,503	12,883	9,843
38,250	38,300	10,649	8,522	12,907	9,864
38,300	38,350	10,671	8,542	12,932	9,884
38,350	38,400	10,693	8,561	12,956	9,905
38,400	38,450	10,715	8,581	12,981	9,925
38,450	38,500	10,737	8,600	13,005	9,946
38,500	38,550	10,759	8,620	13,030	9,966
38,550	38,600	10,781	8,639	13,054	9,987
38,600	38,650	10,803	8,659	13,079	10,007
38,650	38,700	10,825	8,678	13,103	10,028
38,700	38,750	10,847	8,698	13,128	10,048
38,750	38,800	10,869	8,717	13,152	10,069
38,800	38,850	10,891	8,737	13,177	10,089
38,850	38,900	10,913	8,756	13,201	10,110
38,900	38,950	10,935	8,776	13,226	10,130
38,950	39,000	10,957	8,795	13,250	10,151
39,000					
39,000	39,050	10,979	8,815	13,275	10,171
39,050	39,100	11,001	8,834	13,299	10,192
39,100	39,150	11,023	8,854	13,324	10,212
39,150	39,200	11,045	8,873	13,348	10,233
39,200	39,250	11,067	8,893	13,373	10,253
39,250	39,300	11,089	8,912	13,397	10,274
39,300	39,350	11,111	8,932	13,422	10,294
39,350	39,400	11,133	8,951	13,446	10,315
39,400	39,450	11,155	8,971	13,471	10,335
39,450	39,500	11,177	8,990	13,495	10,356
39,500	39,550	11,199	9,010	13,520	10,376
39,550	39,600	11,221	9,029	13,544	10,397
39,600	39,650	11,243	9,049	13,569	10,417
39,650	39,700	11,265	9,068	13,593	10,438
39,700	39,750	11,287	9,088	13,618	10,458
39,750	39,800	11,309	9,107	13,642	10,479
39,800	39,850	11,331	9,127	13,667	10,499
39,850	39,900	11,353	9,146	13,691	10,520
39,900	39,950	11,375	9,166	13,716	10,540
39,950	40,000	11,397	9,185	13,740	10,561
40,000					
40,000	40,050	11,419	9,205	13,765	10,581
40,050	40,100	11,441	9,224	13,789	10,602
40,100	40,150	11,463	9,244	13,814	10,622
40,150	40,200	11,485	9,263	13,838	10,643
40,200	40,250	11,507	9,283	13,863	10,663
40,250	40,300	11,529	9,302	13,887	10,684
40,300	40,350	11,551	9,322	13,912	10,704
40,350	40,400	11,573	9,341	13,936	10,725
40,400	40,450	11,595	9,361	13,961	10,745
40,450	40,500	11,617	9,380	13,985	10,766
40,500	40,550	11,639	9,400	14,010	10,786
40,550	40,600	11,661	9,419	14,034	10,807
40,600	40,650	11,683	9,439	14,059	10,827
40,650	40,700	11,705	9,458	14,083	10,848
40,700	40,750	11,727	9,478	14,108	10,868
40,750	40,800	11,749	9,497	14,132	10,889
40,800	40,850	11,771	9,517	14,157	10,909
40,850	40,900	11,793	9,536	14,181	10,930
40,900	40,950	11,815	9,556	14,206	10,950
40,950	41,000	11,837	9,575	14,230	10,971

1982 Tax Table (Continued)

If 1040A, line 16, OR 1040EZ, line 7 is— At least	But less than	And you are— Single	Married filing jointly	Married filing separately	Head of a household
		Your tax is—			
41,000					
41,000	41,050	11,859	9,595	14,255	10,991
41,050	41,100	11,881	9,614	14,279	11,012
41,100	41,150	11,903	9,634	14,304	11,032
41,150	41,200	11,925	9,653	14,328	11,053
41,200	41,250	11,947	9,673	14,353	11,073
41,250	41,300	11,969	9,692	14,377	11,094
41,300	41,350	11,991	9,712	14,402	11,114
41,350	41,400	12,013	9,731	14,426	11,135
41,400	41,450	12,035	9,751	14,451	11,155
41,450	41,500	12,057	9,770	14,475	11,176
41,500	41,550	12,081	9,790	14,500	11,196
41,550	41,600	12,106	9,809	14,524	11,217
41,600	41,650	12,131	9,829	14,549	11,237
41,650	41,700	12,156	9,848	14,573	11,258
41,700	41,750	12,181	9,868	14,598	11,278
41,750	41,800	12,206	9,887	14,622	11,299
41,800	41,850	12,231	9,907	14,647	11,319
41,850	41,900	12,256	9,926	14,671	11,340
41,900	41,950	12,281	9,946	14,696	11,360
41,950	42,000	12,306	9,965	14,720	11,381
42,000					
42,000	42,050	12,331	9,985	14,745	11,401
42,050	42,100	12,356	10,004	14,769	11,422
42,100	42,150	12,381	10,024	14,794	11,442
42,150	42,200	12,406	10,043	14,818	11,463
42,200	42,250	12,431	10,063	14,843	11,483
42,250	42,300	12,456	10,082	14,867	11,504
42,300	42,350	12,481	10,102	14,892	11,524
42,350	42,400	12,506	10,121	14,916	11,545
42,400	42,450	12,531	10,141	14,941	11,565
42,450	42,500	12,556	10,160	14,965	11,586
42,500	42,550	12,581	10,180	14,990	11,606
42,550	42,600	12,606	10,199	15,014	11,627
42,600	42,650	12,631	10,219	15,039	11,647
42,650	42,700	12,656	10,238	15,063	11,668
42,700	42,750	12,681	10,258	15,088	11,688
42,750	42,800	12,706	10,277	15,112	11,709
42,800	42,850	12,731	10,297	15,137	11,729
42,850	42,900	12,756	10,316	15,162	11,750
42,900	42,950	12,781	10,336	15,187	11,770
42,950	43,000	12,806	10,355	15,212	11,791
43,000					
43,000	43,050	12,831	10,375	15,237	11,811
43,050	43,100	12,856	10,394	15,262	11,832
43,100	43,150	12,881	10,414	15,287	11,852
43,150	43,200	12,906	10,433	15,312	11,873
43,200	43,250	12,931	10,453	15,337	11,893
43,250	43,300	12,956	10,472	15,362	11,914
43,300	43,350	12,981	10,492	15,387	11,934
43,350	43,400	13,006	10,511	15,412	11,955
43,400	43,450	13,031	10,531	15,437	11,975
43,450	43,500	13,056	10,550	15,462	11,996
43,500	43,550	13,081	10,570	15,487	12,016
43,550	43,600	13,106	10,589	15,512	12,037
43,600	43,650	13,131	10,609	15,537	12,057
43,650	43,700	13,156	10,628	15,562	12,078
43,700	43,750	13,181	10,648	15,587	12,098
43,750	43,800	13,206	10,667	15,612	12,119
43,800	43,850	13,231	10,687	15,637	12,139
43,850	43,900	13,256	10,706	15,662	12,160
43,900	43,950	13,281	10,726	15,687	12,180
43,950	44,000	13,306	10,745	15,712	12,201
44,000					
44,000	44,050	13,331	10,765	15,737	12,221
44,050	44,100	13,356	10,784	15,762	12,242
44,100	44,150	13,381	10,804	15,787	12,262
44,150	44,200	13,406	10,823	15,812	12,283
44,200	44,250	13,431	10,843	15,837	12,303
44,250	44,300	13,456	10,862	15,862	12,324
44,300	44,350	13,481	10,882	15,887	12,344
44,350	44,400	13,506	10,901	15,912	12,365
44,400	44,450	13,531	10,921	15,937	12,385
44,450	44,500	13,556	10,940	15,962	12,406
44,500	44,550	13,581	10,960	15,987	12,426
44,550	44,600	13,606	10,979	16,012	12,447
44,600	44,650	13,631	10,999	16,037	12,467
44,650	44,700	13,656	11,018	16,062	12,488
44,700	44,750	13,681	11,038	16,087	12,510
44,750	44,800	13,706	11,057	16,112	12,535
44,800	44,850	13,731	11,077	16,137	12,559
44,850	44,900	13,756	11,096	16,162	12,584
44,900	44,950	13,781	11,116	16,187	12,608
44,950	45,000	13,806	11,135	16,212	12,633
45,000					
45,000	45,050	13,831	11,155	16,237	12,657
45,050	45,100	13,856	11,174	16,262	12,682
45,100	45,150	13,881	11,194	16,287	12,706
45,150	45,200	13,906	11,213	16,312	12,731
45,200	45,250	13,931	11,233	16,337	12,755
45,250	45,300	13,956	11,252	16,362	12,780
45,300	45,350	13,981	11,272	16,387	12,804
45,350	45,400	14,006	11,291	16,412	12,829
45,400	45,450	14,031	11,311	16,437	12,853
45,450	45,500	14,056	11,330	16,462	12,878
45,500	45,550	14,081	11,350	16,487	12,902
45,550	45,600	14,106	11,369	16,512	12,927
45,600	45,650	14,131	11,389	16,537	12,951
45,650	45,700	14,156	11,408	16,562	12,976
45,700	45,750	14,181	11,428	16,587	13,000
45,750	45,800	14,206	11,447	16,612	13,025
45,800	45,850	14,231	11,468	16,637	13,049
45,850	45,900	14,256	11,490	16,662	13,074
45,900	45,950	14,281	11,512	16,687	13,098
45,950	46,000	14,306	11,534	16,712	13,123
46,000					
46,000	46,050	14,331	11,556	16,737	13,147
46,050	46,100	14,356	11,578	16,762	13,172
46,100	46,150	14,381	11,600	16,787	13,196
46,150	46,200	14,406	11,622	16,812	13,221
46,200	46,250	14,431	11,644	16,837	13,245
46,250	46,300	14,456	11,666	16,862	13,270
46,300	46,350	14,481	11,688	16,887	13,294
46,350	46,400	14,506	11,710	16,912	13,319
46,400	46,450	14,531	11,732	16,937	13,343
46,450	46,500	14,556	11,754	16,962	13,368
46,500	46,550	14,581	11,776	16,987	13,392
46,550	46,600	14,606	11,798	17,012	13,417
46,600	46,650	14,631	11,820	17,037	13,441
46,650	46,700	14,656	11,842	17,062	13,466
46,700	46,750	14,681	11,864	17,087	13,490
46,750	46,800	14,706	11,886	17,112	13,515
46,800	46,850	14,731	11,908	17,137	13,539
46,850	46,900	14,756	11,930	17,162	13,564
46,900	46,950	14,781	11,952	17,187	13,588
46,950	47,000	14,806	11,974	17,212	13,613
47,000					
47,000	47,050	14,831	11,996	17,237	13,637
47,050	47,100	14,856	12,018	17,262	13,662
47,100	47,150	14,881	12,040	17,287	13,686
47,150	47,200	14,906	12,062	17,312	13,711
47,200	47,250	14,931	12,084	17,337	13,735
47,250	47,300	14,956	12,106	17,362	13,760
47,300	47,350	14,981	12,128	17,387	13,784
47,350	47,400	15,006	12,150	17,412	13,809
47,400	47,450	15,031	12,172	17,437	13,833
47,450	47,500	15,056	12,194	17,462	13,858
47,500	47,550	15,081	12,216	17,487	13,882
47,550	47,600	15,106	12,238	17,512	13,907
47,600	47,650	15,131	12,260	17,537	13,931
47,650	47,700	15,156	12,282	17,562	13,956
47,700	47,750	15,181	12,304	17,587	13,980
47,750	47,800	15,206	12,326	17,612	14,005
47,800	47,850	15,231	12,348	17,637	14,029
47,850	47,900	15,256	12,370	17,662	14,054
47,900	47,950	15,281	12,392	17,687	14,078
47,950	48,000	15,306	12,414	17,712	14,103
48,000					
48,000	48,050	15,331	12,436	17,737	14,127
48,050	48,100	15,356	12,458	17,762	14,152
48,100	48,150	15,381	12,480	17,787	14,176
48,150	48,200	15,406	12,502	17,812	14,201
48,200	48,250	15,431	12,524	17,837	14,225
48,250	48,300	15,456	12,546	17,862	14,250
48,300	48,350	15,481	12,568	17,887	14,274
48,350	48,400	15,506	12,590	17,912	14,299
48,400	48,450	15,531	12,612	17,937	14,323
48,450	48,500	15,556	12,634	17,962	14,348
48,500	48,550	15,581	12,656	17,987	14,372
48,550	48,600	15,606	12,678	18,012	14,397
48,600	48,650	15,631	12,700	18,037	14,421
48,650	48,700	15,656	12,722	18,062	14,446
48,700	48,750	15,681	12,744	18,087	14,470
48,750	48,800	15,706	12,766	18,112	14,495
48,800	48,850	15,731	12,788	18,137	14,519
48,850	48,900	15,756	12,810	18,162	14,544
48,900	48,950	15,781	12,832	18,187	14,568
48,950	49,000	15,806	12,854	18,212	14,593
49,000					
49,000	49,050	15,831	12,876	18,237	14,617
49,050	49,100	15,856	12,898	18,262	14,642
49,100	49,150	15,881	12,920	18,287	14,666
49,150	49,200	15,906	12,942	18,312	14,691
49,200	49,250	15,931	12,964	18,337	14,715
49,250	49,300	15,956	12,986	18,362	14,740
49,300	49,350	15,981	13,008	18,387	14,764
49,350	49,400	16,006	13,030	18,412	14,789
49,400	49,450	16,031	13,052	18,437	14,813
49,450	49,500	16,056	13,074	18,462	14,838
49,500	49,550	16,081	13,096	18,487	14,862
49,550	49,600	16,106	13,118	18,512	14,887
49,600	49,650	16,131	13,140	18,537	14,911
49,650	49,700	16,156	13,162	18,562	14,936
49,700	49,750	16,181	13,184	18,587	14,960
49,750	49,800	16,206	13,206	18,612	14,985
49,800	49,850	16,231	13,228	18,637	15,009
49,850	49,900	16,256	13,250	18,662	15,034
49,900	49,950	16,281	13,272	18,687	15,058
49,950	50,000	16,306	13,294	18,712	15,083

FIGURE 7-6 Tax Table (concluded)

VOCABULARY

Directions: Can you find the definition for each of the following terms used in Chapter 7?

revenue
progressive
regressive
proportional
Internal Revenue Service
child support
deductions
taxable income
tax liability

voluntary compliance
deficit spending
exemption
gross income
exclusion
alimony
zero bracket amount
tax evasion

1. Money collected by the government through taxes.

2. A tax based on the more income earned, the more tax paid.

3. A tax wherein the rate remains constant, regardless of the amount of your income.

4. A tax that decreases in proportion to income increases.

5. An agency of the U.S. Department of the Treasury charged with collecting federal income taxes.

6. A system whereby citizens are expected to prepare and file appropriate tax returns.

7. Willful failure to pay taxes.

8. A condition wherein the government spends more money than it collects.

9. An allowance for each person dependent on the taxpayer's income.

10. All the taxable income received during the year, including wages, tips, salaries, interest, dividends, alimony, and unemployment compensation.

11. Money that is exempt from taxation.

12. Money paid to a former spouse to support dependent children of a previous marriage.

13. Money paid to support a former spouse.

14. Expenses allowed by law that are subtracted from gross income to obtain the amount of taxable income.

15. The minimum amount of deductions needed before a taxpayer can itemize deductions.

16. The amount remaining when deductions have been subtracted from adjusted gross income.

17. The actual or total amount of taxes due, based on taxable income.

ITEMS FOR DISCUSSION

1. What is the United States government's largest source of revenue?

2. List the three types of taxes and define each.

3. List five other taxes besides the three listed in No. 2.

4. List at least five services the government provides for all citizens from taxes collected.

5. When was the first permanent income tax ratified?

6. When was the Internal Revenue Service created?

7. List three services provided by the IRS.

8. Who has the ability to levy taxes on the citizens of the United States?

9. What is meant by a tax system based on voluntary compliance?

10. What can happen to you if you deliberately do not file your tax return and pay taxes due?

11. What type of dependent can be claimed on two tax returns?

12. List five types of income that are taxable.

13. List five types of income that are not taxable.

14. How is child support different from alimony in terms of taxation?

15. Explain the zero bracket amount.

16. When must you file your federal tax return? Why?

17. What should you do if you discover an error after you have filed your tax return?

18. Under what circumstances would you file the long Form 1040 tax return?

19. Why should you file your tax return early when you expect a refund?

20. Explain the purpose of the Presidential Election Campaign Fund. If you check the Yes box on your return, does it increase your taxes by $1?

APPLICATIONS

1. Explain the need for taxes in this country. How does everyone benefit from taxes?

2. Summarize how taxing income came about in this country. Do you think that the time will ever come when taxation will no longer be needed? Explain.

3. Explain how new federal taxes are imposed.

4. How does your filing status affect the amount of taxes you will pay?

5. How does the number of exemptions claimed affect the amount of taxes you will pay?

6. What are deductible expenses?

7. When should you file the short Form 1040EZ? 1040A?

8. How many exemptions would you have if you were over 65, married, and your spouse were legally blind?

9. What is the maximum credit for a donation to a candidate for public office made by a single person? by married persons filing jointly?

10. What should you do if more than $2,391.90 in FICA taxes was withheld from your paychecks in 1983?

CASE PROBLEMS AND ACTIVITIES

1. Using Figure 7-4, Form 1040A, and the tax tables given on pages 123-125, compute the 1982 tax liability of Tony Martin. Tony's adjusted gross income was $14,000. He gave $150 to candidates for public office and had $2,004 in federal taxes withheld from his wages. He is single and is entitled to one exemption. Based on this information, how much does Tony owe, or how much is his refund?

2. Using Figure 7-4 (Form 1040A) and the tax tables (Figure 7-6), compute the 1982 tax liability of Angela Olinger. Angela's wages totaled $16,201; interest income, $190; and dividends, $200 ($100 can be excluded). She gave $75 to candidates for public office, and had $2,408 in federal taxes withheld from her wages. She is single and is entitled to one exemption. How much does Angela owe in taxes, or how much is her refund?

3. Using Figure 7-2, Form 1040EZ, prepare a 1982 tax return for Brian Reid on plain paper. Use the following information:

Brian Reid (541-33-9892)
54 Center Street
San Francisco, CA 96214-3627

Brian is a carpenter. He wants $1 to go to the Presidential Election Campaign Fund. He is single and claims only himself as an exemption. Brian's salary is $14,200, plus interest of $155. He gave $150 to charitable organizations and had $2,186 in federal taxes withheld from his paychecks.

4. Using Figure 7-4 (Form 1040A) and Figure 7-5, (Schedule W), prepare a 1982 joint tax return and Schedule W for Alex and Marilyn Harris on plain paper.

Alex K. and Marilyn J. Harris
(895-10-9008, 485-01-9089)
2450 West 18th Avenue
Dallax, TX 75201-7242

Alex is an architect, and Marilyn is a teacher. They both want to contribute $1 to the Presidential Election Campaign Fund. Married, filing jointly, Alex and Marilyn have two dependent children, Valerie and Carole.

Alex's and Marilyn's combined incomes totaled $38,400 (the lesser is $18,400). They contributed $500 to candidates for political office and had a total tax of $7,500 withheld from their wages.

Alex and Marilyn had interest income of $1,400: First Interstate Bank, $300; private loan to J. Smith, $600; time certificate at State Savings & Loan, $500.

Dividend income amounted to $1,100: $411 from CDK stock, $621 from Investors' Mutual Fund, Inc., and $68 from I.P.Q. Manufacturing Co. These dividends are subject to exclusion.

CHAPTER 8

SAVINGS

CHAPTER OBJECTIVES

After studying this chapter and completing the activities, you will be able to:

1. Understand the need for and purpose of savings.
2. List and compare the types of savings options available and the financial institutions where they can be obtained.
3. Compute interest on savings accounts with monthly, quarterly, semiannual, and annual interest rates.

WHY YOU SHOULD SAVE

The chief reason for saving money is to provide for future needs, both expected and unexpected. When nothing is set aside for these certain-to-happen needs, families experience frustration, financial troubles, and even bankruptcy.

Short-Term Needs

Often short-term needs arise that require money above what is normally allowed for by a budget. These needs typically are paid for out of savings. Some short-term needs you might encounter include the following:

Savings provide for sudden emergencies.

1. Emergencies—such as unemployment, sickness, accident, or death in the family
2. Vacations—short weekend trips and leisure activities
3. Social events—such as weddings, family gatherings, and other potentially costly special occasions

Pace Arrow motor house produced by Fleetwood Enterprises, Inc.

4. Major purchases—such as a car, major appliances, remodeling, or other expense that becomes necessary as time goes by (Things do wear out and have to be replaced, repaired, or remodeled.)

You can probably think of other short-term needs for which you should save. If you anticipate having to pay for part of your college education, for example, a regular savings plan could make it easier when the time comes to go to school.

Long-Term Goals

Large purchases require savings plans.

Many individuals and families anticipate some major purchases in the future and save to make these purchases possible. These long-term goals include outlays for such things as home ownership, children's education, retirement, and investments.

Home Ownership. A down payment on a house amounts to thousands of dollars. The larger the down payment you can make, the smaller your monthly payments will be.

Children's Education. Many couples begin a savings plan when their children are very young. Then when the time comes for college, the necessary money is waiting.

Retirement. Most people should not depend on social security payments to be sufficient support in their old age. Other plans should be made for financial security after retirement.

Investments should be made only in addition to savings.

Investment. To provide a hedge against inflation or make money for future use, people may invest in a business, real estate, insurance, stocks, collectibles, or a number of other alternatives. Because investments are often risky in nature, they should be made only *in addition to* regular savings.

Financial Security

Probably the best reason to save is to provide peace of mind in knowing that when short-term needs arise there will be adequate money to pay for them. Another reason to save is to ensure that upon retirement enough money will be available to live comfortably. Persons who set aside money each pay period experience the security of knowing that there is money available if and when it is needed.

You must forego purchases today to save for tomorrow.

The amount of money you save will vary according to several factors: (*a*) the amount of your *discretionary income* (what you have left over when the bills are paid); (*b*) the importance you attach to savings; (*c*) your anticipated needs and wants; and (*d*) your willpower, or ability to forego present spending in order to provide for your future.

HOW YOUR MONEY GROWS

Money grows when it is saved and invested. We will examine how money grows in a savings account.

Compounding Interest

The amount of money deposited by the saver is called the *principal*. Money paid by the financial institution to the saver for the use of his or her money is called *interest*. When interest is computed on the sum of the principal plus interest already earned it is *compound interest*. Figure 8-1 illustrates how annual interest is compounded.

FIGURE 8-1
Compounding
Interest Yearly

Year	Beginning Balance	Interest Earned (5%)	Ending Balance
1	$100.00	$5.00	$105.00
2	105.00	5.25	110.25
3	110.25	5.51	115.76

To compound interest, you add interest on interest.

The more often interest is compounded, the greater your earnings. Figure 8-2 illustrates what happens when 5 percent interest is compounded quarterly (every three months) and is added to the principal before more interest is calculated. You will notice that more interest is earned if interest is compounded quarterly than if it is compounded annually.

FIGURE 8-2
Compounding Interest Quarterly

Year	Beginning Balance	First Quarter	Second Quarter	Third Quarter	Fourth Quarter	Ending Balance
1	$100.00	$1.25	$1.27	$1.28	$1.30	$105.10
2	105.10	1.31	1.33	1.35	1.36	110.45
3	110.45	1.38	1.40	1.42	1.43	116.08

True daily interest is computed on each day of deposit. Banks and financial institutions can rapidly compute the interest compounding daily with computers.

Percentage Rates

The *nominal rate* of interest is calculated on the principal amount only and does not include compounding. The *true annual percentage rate* is the effective rate you will receive when the money is compounded and you receive interest on interest earned. Often when you see advertisements for interest offered at financial institutions, you see these two different rates offered, as depicted in Figure 8-3.

The effective rate is the rate you receive when interest is compounded.

FIGURE 8-3
Interest Rates

INTEREST OFFERED

12-month time certificates
Minimum deposit of $500.00

Nominal rate: 13.89%

Effective yield: 15.58%

While some time certificates allow the interest to accumulate and compound, others require that interest earned be paid into a regular passbook account where much lower interest rates are paid. This fact is an important one to know before you buy a time certificate.

WHERE YOU CAN SAVE

The main financial institutions found in most cities include commercial banks, savings banks, savings and loan associations, credit unions, and brokerage firms.

Commercial Banks

Many people prefer to keep their checking and savings accounts in the same bank for ease in transferring funds and making deposits and withdrawals. Commercial banks offer much convenience to customers in the form of services that may go along with accounts. Services may include automatic cash transfer accounts, bank cards, use of 24-hour teller machines, overdraft protection, and other free services. Ninety-seven percent of banks are insured by the FDIC. Most large commercial banks in states where branch banking is legal have many branches for ease of deposits and withdrawals. Commercial banks may be either nationally chartered or state chartered. Large banks are able to offer more services to customers, but generally minimum deposits and fees are higher. Rates offered on savings accounts will vary among commercial banks, as well as between commercial banks and savings banks, savings and loan associations, and credit unions.

Commercial banks are very convenient.

Savings Banks

Savings banks are usually referred to as mutual savings banks. These financial institutions are few in number—about 500 of them in roughly a dozen states, mostly throughout New England and the Northeast—but they are substantial in size, having nearly $150 billion in assets. Savings banks are state chartered and are insured by FDIC. A major business of savings banks is savings plans and loans on real property, including mortgages and home-improvement loans. Because of deregulation of the banking industry (1980), savings banks also offer checking accounts and other types of consumer loans.

Savings banks are state chartered.

Savings and Loan Associations

Savings and loan associations are organized primarily to handle savings and lend money: these associations make over 80 percent of all home

Slightly better rates are available at savings and loans.

mortgage loans. Money deposited in savings accounts is loaned to people purchasing homes or making home improvements. Generally, savings and loan associations are able to offer slightly higher interest rates on savings accounts (passbook and certificate) than commercial banks. Eighty percent of all savings and loan associations are insured by **FSLIC** (Federal Savings and Loan Insurance Corporation), which, like FDIC, insures individual accounts up to $100,000.

Savings and loan associations offer many of the conveniences and services of commercial banks. NOW accounts and money market accounts are available at savings and loan associations. Some savings and loans even offer major credit cards and 24-hour teller machines. Few, however, have safe-deposit boxes, automatic cash transfers, and instant loans. It is because they specialize that savings and loans are able to offer higher interest rates than banks. Rates vary among savings and loan associations—check around before depositing your money.

Credit Unions

Credit unions are not-for-profit organizations established by groups of workers in similar occupations who pool their money. Credit unions generally offer higher interest rates on savings and lower interest rates on loans. They are insured through membership in **NCUA** (National Credit Union Administration) so that deposits are insured up to $100,000 in each account. Savings accounts at a credit union are often called *share accounts*, because deposits entitle the saver to shares of interest. Credit unions also offer IRA accounts, share draft accounts (checking accounts), consumer loans, certificates of deposit, and many other services. Credit unions are offering more diversified services and are growing rapidly in most parts of the country.

Brokerage Firms

More risk often means higher returns.

Cash management accounts or money market accounts offer less convenience and involve more risk than other types of accounts, but offer high rates of return to savers. Money you deposit is invested in your behalf, and you share in the profits earned. Generally, however, large minimum deposits are required, and your check-writing privileges are restricted. Another disadvantage of these accounts is that they often are not very liquid. Savers sometimes find it inconvenient to withdraw money and make deposits.

Brokerage investment firms do not have insurance on deposits, but they do offer the advantage of *diversification*—purchasing a variety of investments to protect against large losses and increase the rate of return.

The investment firm buys different types of securities and investments, from common stock and Treasury bills to government bonds. Consequently, brokerage firms are able to offer higher interest rates than commercial banks, savings banks, savings and loan associations, or credit unions.

SAVINGS OPTIONS

Explore the options in your area.

Once you have determined to establish a savings program for yourself or your family, you need to know about different options available to you. Money that is set aside for future needs can be deposited in a number of different savings plans. Options include regular passbook savings accounts, certificates of deposit, government savings bonds and Treasury bills, cash management accounts, and IRA accounts.

Regular Passbook Savings Accounts

Savings accounts may have minimum balance requirements.

A regular passbook savings account has a major advantage of high liquidity. *Liquidity* is the quality of being easily converted into cash. A regular passbook account is said to be liquid because you can withdraw your money at any time without penalty. However, of all savings plans, a regular passbook account probably pays the least amount of interest. Interest is money paid for the use of money: the bank pays you interest on your deposits. Once you have opened the passbook account, you are free to make withdrawals and deposits. Some financial institutions charge service fees when you make more than a maximum number of withdrawals in a certain period of time. Other institutions charge a monthly fee if your balance falls below a set minimum.

Certificates of Deposit

A certificate of deposit is less liquid.

A *certificate of deposit*, or time certificate, represents a sum of money deposited for a set length of time—for example, $500 for six months. A certificate of deposit is less liquid than a regular passbook account, and sometimes requires that a minimum amount be deposited. The rate of interest is generally higher by several percentage points than on passbook accounts. But, if you withdraw your money before the deposit time is up, you will be penalized; that is, you will receive less interest. A certificate of deposit has a set *maturity date*—the day on which you must renew the certificate, cash it in, or purchase a new certificate. Some financial institutions offer certificates of deposit that allow the interest to accumulate to maturity. Other financial institutions send you a check for the interest or deposit the interest in a separate passbook account. The interest earned is placed in a passbook account to earn interest at a lower rate; that is, you do not receive interest on the interest earned.

Government Savings Bonds and Treasury Bills

U.S. savings bonds are loans to the government.

When you buy a savings bond, you are, in effect, lending money to the United States government. A Series EE savings bond is known as a _discount bond_ because you buy it for less than its cash-in value. At maturity, you receive the full value of the bond. The difference between the purchase price and the cash-in value is considered interest earned. For example, a $50 bond may be purchased at a discount for $25. A $100 bond may be purchased for $50. The interest grows through periodic increases in redemption value and is paid at the time a bond is cashed. Interest earned is then taxable. The maturity date for Series EE bonds is ten years; but a bond may be held longer, with interest continuing to build until the bond is cashed. Interest rates on Series EE bonds are variable, but 7 1/2 percent is the minimum guaranteed five-year yield.

A Series HH savings bond pays interest semiannually at 7 1/2 annual percent (the government sends a check). The bond is purchased at face value (a $500 bond sells for $500) and is redeemed at face value. Series HH bonds may be redeemed at any time after six months, but mature in ten years.

Interest is not taxable until the bonds are cashed.

Savings bonds may be purchased over the counter or by mail at most financial institutions, and the bond certificates should be kept in a safe-deposit box. The advantage of the Series EE bond is that interest is not taxed until the bond is cashed. So if you are saving for a child's college education, there is no tax until the child cashes the bond. Your child will probably have a low income when he or she is ready to enter college and will have no tax liability. Bonds are also a good investment because they are considered very safe. Bonds can be quickly and easily converted to cash; their interest is not subject to state or local taxes (only federal taxes); and if they are lost, stolen, or destroyed they can be replaced without cost.

Treasury bills are auctioned weekly.

U.S. Treasury bills are available in denominations of $10,000, then in increments of $5,000. A Treasury bill is for one year or less; that is, the bill is usually a three-month, six-month, or one-year government obligation. Treasury bills are auctioned weekly for three- and six-month maturities, and monthly for one-year maturities. Treasury bills are purchased for individuals by investment companies, mutual funds, stock brokerage firms, cash management accounts, banks, and other agents who have a pool of money for such purchases. Rates for these sales are often used as the basis for rates paid on certificates of deposit, IRAs, money market funds, etc.

Cash Management Accounts

Offered at stock brokerage companies and investment service firms, *cash management accounts*, also called money market accounts, are available for persons wishing to invest their money at higher rates of return, but with less liquidity. The minimum balance in these types of accounts is $1,000, $5,000, or $20,000, depending on the account. Interest (often called dividends) is computed monthly, and earnings sometimes are not taxable. A person saves money and deposits it in this account, and the company invests the money in stocks and bonds. Based on the return earned by the company, a dividend is paid. The dividend is usually much higher than with other savings methods. The investor is given checks, but there are frequently minimum amounts for which the checks can be written and limitations on how often withdrawals can be made.

Risk is a disadvantage.

Cash management accounts are not insured by the FDIC or other government service. However, these accounts are safe because the securities purchased are very stable. Managers of these accounts purchase government bonds and securities issued by the United States Treasury. Therefore, the risk of losing your money is low.

IRA Accounts

An IRA (individual retirement account) is a savings plan whereby an individual (or couple) sets aside a certain amount of money (up to a specified maximum) each year for retirement. Although an individual may be enrolled in a retirement plan with his or her employer, an IRA can also be opened. The advantage of an IRA over other savings plans is that amounts put into the IRA account can be subtracted from annual taxable income. You will pay taxes on the IRA when you begin withdrawing funds and will probably be in a lower tax bracket. Interest rates paid on IRA accounts vary; some are equal to Treasury bill rates, while others are set individually by the different financial institutions holding the accounts. Most financial institutions have IRA accounts available. The disadvantage of an IRA is that you cannot remove part or all the money set aside before age 59 1/2 without severe penalty. This makes it a very illiquid savings plan.

IRAs are tax-deferred savings plans.

FACTORS IN SELECTING A SAVINGS ACCOUNT

There are a number of important factors to consider in selecting a savings account and a savings institution. These factors include (*a*) safety, (*b*) liquidity, (*c*) convenience, (*d*) purpose, (*e*) interest-earning potential, and (*f*) early withdrawal penalties.

Safety

Most financial institutions are insured.

You want your money to be safe from loss. Most financial institutions are insured by agencies such as the **_FDIC_** (Federal Deposit Insurance Corporation). Accounts protected by this insurance are <u>safe up to $100,000 per account</u>. You should check on the type of regulations and insurance the financial institution of your choice has to be certain of the safety of your deposit.

Liquidity

Liquidity, or how quickly you can get your cash when you want it, may be important to you. Some types of deposits may be obtained instantly; others may take weeks or even months to withdraw.

Convenience

People often choose their financial institution because of convenience of location and services offered. Interest rates on various savings accounts and certificates may vary only slightly. Fees charged are often very similar, while minimum deposits required may give preference to a certain type of account.

Many banks have several branches within a geographic area, which makes it convenient to do your banking after work or on the way home. If there is only one branch located several miles away, it is more expensive and inconvenient for you to bank at that financial institution. A very large bank may have branches in other states and parts of the country, giving you check-cashing privileges away from home.

Many banks offer drive-up windows that open at 7:30 A.M. on weekdays and are open for a few hours on Saturday. Day-and-night teller machines may be installed at all branches, offering an added convenience on weekends, holidays, and evenings.

Interest-Earning Potential

Little risk means little return.

Interest earnings on your deposit should be as great as possible—that is, your savings should be placed in the institution that offers the highest interest returns. Usually, the more liquid your deposit, the less interest it will earn; and the more risk you are willing to take, the higher the rate of return. The account that involves the least risk, the regular passbook account, pays the lowest interest.

Figure 8-4 is an example of interest rates being paid on June 16, 1983. As you can see from the illustration, interest earned depends both on the type of financial institution in which you choose to save your money and on the type of account you open.

FIGURE 8-4
Current Interest
Rates As
Reported Weekly

> ### INTEREST RATES FOR CONSUMERS
>
> for the week ended June 16, 1983 (Rates change each Tuesday. Treasury bills are sold Mondays.)
>
> PASSBOOK SAVINGS:
>   Commercial banks 5.25%
>   Savings and loans 5.50%
>
> MONEY MARKET CERTIFICATES:
>   3-month 8.73%
>   6-month 9.08%
>
> TREASURY SECURITIES:*
>   3-month Treasury bills 8.73%
>   6-month Treasury bills 8.83%
>
> OTHER:
>   Tax-exempt bonds 9.29%
>   Daily money market funds 8.14%
>
> HOME MORTGAGES:
>   FHA or GI 12.00%
>   Conventional 12.75%
>
> *Most variable rate accounts are based on Treasury bill rates (Treasury bills are auctioned each Monday).

Purpose

Consider how much money you can put away.

Your purpose for saving money may greatly affect your choice of financial institution. Savings for a down payment on a home might best be placed at the savings and loan association that would someday make the loan to you for the home. You would establish credit with that institution and enhance your opportunities for securing the financing at a later date.

Early Withdrawal Penalties

Early withdrawal penalties should be considered when you are choosing a savings plan. If you need to withdraw all or some of your money before the maturity or withdrawal date, you may be charged a penalty.

Regular passbook accounts have no withdrawal penalties. You may make deposits or withdrawals at your convenience.

Depositors who withdraw time certificates before the maturity date are penalized. Three months' interest is lost on a six-month certificate. Six months' interest is lost on time certificates of over six months.

Early withdrawal penalties can be substantial.

An IRA account either partially or fully withdrawn before age 59 1/2 will have an interest loss of six months, plus a 10 percent penalty. In addition, all income previously set aside in the IRA will become taxable immediately (you will recall it was subtracted from taxable income on tax returns).

Cash management and money market accounts usually do not carry early withdrawal penalties. Money may be withdrawn in full or in part at any time, provided the rules are met.

Each type of account at each institution is controlled by different rules. Before you open any account, be sure to read carefully the minimum deposit and withdrawal restrictions, and other special conditions that may exist.

THE IMPORTANCE OF SAVING REGULARLY

It is important not only that you save, but also that you save *regularly*. By saving regularly in accounts that accumulate interest and pay interest on interest, you can greatly increase your earnings. Figure 8-5 illustrates the effect of compounding when regular deposits are made to savings.

FIGURE 8-5
Compounding Interest and Making Additional Deposits

Year	Beginning Balance	Deposits	Interest Earned (5%)	Ending Balance
1	$ 0.00	$100.00	$ 5.00	$105.00
2	105.00	100.00	10.25	215.25
3	215.25	100.00	15.76	331.10
4	331.01	100.00	21.55	452.56

Obviously no savings plan is effective unless you have the willpower to set aside money—to forego purchases now in order to provide for them in the future. There are ways to make regular saving easier, however, including automatic payroll deductions, savings clubs, and automatic checking account deductions.

Automatic Payroll Deductions

Pay yourself first.

It is often possible to have money withheld from your paycheck and sent directly to your savings account. Before any other bills or expenses are paid, you "pay yourself." If the money is set aside before it reaches your checkbook, it is easier to forget about, and you can budget your expenses around the remainder with less difficulty.

Savings Clubs

Many banks and other institutions offer savings clubs, such as a Christmas club. You make regular payments into a special account and agree not to touch these funds before a specified date. In this way you are forcing yourself to save for some event or need, and when the time comes you know you will have the money. Interest paid on savings clubs may vary substantially among different financial institutions.

Automatic Checking Account Deductions

Automatic deductions are forced savings plans.

You may authorize an automatic deduction from your checking account each month. In this way you are also forcing yourself to save. You must remember to enter the automatic deduction in your checkbook register so that your checkbook will balance each month.

Figure 8-6 illustrates what a person could have saved for retirement, assuming he or she could save $2,000 a year at an average of 12 percent interest a year, beginning at age 20, 25, 30, or 35. You can see the compounding effect of saving. In addition, if the $2,000-a-year savings were placed in an IRA (individual retirement account), a tax advantage would result, because the full $2,000 could be subtracted from taxable income each year.

FIGURE 8-6
Saving for
Retirement

Beginning Age	No. of Years Saved	Amount Saved Each Year	Annual Interest Rate	Money at Retirement
20	45	$2,000	12%	$2,716,400
25	40	2,000	12%	1,534,182
30	35	2,000	12%	863,326
35	30	2,000	12%	482,665

VOCABULARY

Directions: Can you find the definition for each of the following terms used in Chapter 8?

liquidity   diversification
interest   principal
maturity date   compound interest
FDIC   true annual percentage rate
FSLIC   share account
NCUA

1. Measure of how easily a deposit can be converted into cash.

2. An ending date on which a certificate or note is due (must be renewed or otherwise dealt with).

3. Money paid for the use of money.

4. Insurance company of the federal government that insures your deposit with a savings and loan association.

5. Insurance company of the federal government that insures your deposit with a commercial bank.

6. Insurance company that insures deposits kept at credit unions.

7. The type of account offered to a saver (regular savings plan) at a credit union.

8. A feature of a cash management account whereby the brokerage company buys many different types of investments.

9. A sum of money in a savings account on which interest accrues.

10. Interest computed on the sum of the principal plus interest already earned.

11. The effective yield on a deposit when compounding of interest is considered.

ITEMS FOR DISCUSSION

√ 1. List several short-term needs that you may experience in the next few months or years.

2. List any long-term plans you may have that will require money in the next five years or more.

3. What four personal factors determine the amount of money you will save?

4. Why does a regular passbook savings account pay less interest than a certificate of deposit?

5. What are the tax advantages of owning a Series EE savings bond?

6. What is an IRA?

7. Explain how a cash management account works.

8. What things should you consider when choosing a financial institution for your savings?

9. Why might people choose to save their money in a commercial bank when they could receive higher interest rates at some other type of financial institution?

10. What is the main purpose of savings and loan associations?

11. How much is an account insured for by the FDIC?

12. What is diversification?

13. List three ways you can force yourself to save every pay period.

14. What types of penalties might you face for early withdrawal of all or part of your savings?

APPLICATIONS

1. Write out your savings plans, listing short-term and long-term goals you want to meet and how you plan to achieve those goals (how much money you will save to meet them).

2. What is discretionary income and what does it have to do with saving?

3. Which of the following is the least liquid?
   (a) regular passbook savings   (d) Treasury bill
   (b) certificate of deposit   (e) IRA account
   (c) savings bond

4. What happens if you need to withdraw all or part of your time certificate before its maturity date?

5. Why is a Series EE bond called a discount bond?

6. List a significant advantage of saving by purchasing savings bonds.

7. List one disadvantage for each of the following savings plans:

   (a) regular passbook account   (d) cash management account
   (b) certificate of deposit   (e) IRA account
   (c) savings bond

8. What major advantage is gained by saving at a commercial bank?

9. Why should you join a credit union when you have the opportunity?

10. Is it safe to invest your money with a brokerage firm in a cash management account that is not insured?

CASE PROBLEMS AND ACTIVITIES

1. Compute the interest compounded for Harriet Burke, assuming she deposits $1,000 in a time certificate that compounds interest every six months at the rate of 11 1/2 percent. It is a three-year time certificate. Use these column headings:

Year	Beginning Balance	First-Half Interest	Second-Half Interest	Total Interest	Ending Balance
1	$1,000	_____	_____	_____	_____
2		_____	_____	_____	_____
3	_____	_____	_____	_____	_____

2. Marsha Olson wishes to save $100 a month. Her bank computes interest and compounds it monthly. The current rate for a passbook account is 5 1/2 percent. Compute the interest compounded for Marsha. Use this format:

Month	Beginning Balance	Deposit	Total	Interest	Ending Balance
1	_____	_____	_____	_____	_____
2	_____	_____	_____	_____	_____
3	_____	_____	_____	_____	_____
4	_____	_____	_____	_____	_____
5	_____	_____	_____	_____	_____
6	_____	_____	_____	_____	_____
7	_____	_____	_____	_____	_____
8	_____	_____	_____	_____	_____
9	_____	_____	_____	_____	_____
10	_____	_____	_____	_____	_____
11	_____	_____	_____	_____	_____
12	_____	_____	_____	_____	_____

3. Compute the interest compounded quarterly on a deposit of $500 for three years at 12 percent. Use the following column headings:

Year	Beginning Balance	INTEREST				Total Interest	Ending Balance
		First Quarter	Second Quarter	Third Quarter	Fourth Quarter		
1	$500	___	___	___	___	___	___
2	___	___	___	___	___	___	___
3	___	___	___	___	___	___	___

4. Compute your total savings if you keep $1,000 in a regular passbook account at 5 1/4 percent, compounded quarterly, for two years and if you put $1,000 in a two-year time certificate at 11.89 percent, compounded semiannually. Use these column headings:

REGULAR PASSBOOK

Year	Beginning Balance	INTEREST				Total Interest	Ending Balance
		First Quarter	Second Quarter	Third Quarter	Fourth Quarter		
1	$1,000	___	___	___	___	___	___
2	___	___	___	___	___	___	___

TIME CERTIFICATE

Year	Beginning Balance	First-Half Interest	Second-Half Interest	Total Interest	Ending Balance
1	___	___	___	___	___
2	___	___	___	___	___

5. Suppose you need to have the money from the time certificate in No. 4 before the two years are up. What is the penalty? What is the penalty for withdrawing all or part of your passbook savings account?

CHAPTER 9

INVESTING FOR THE FUTURE

CHAPTER OBJECTIVES

After studying this chapter and completing the activities, you will be able to:

1. Understand the need for and purpose of investments and describe the criteria for choosing investments.
2. List and compare investment options available and make investment decisions.
3. Give examples of fixed- and variable-income investments and describe the advantages and disadvantages of each.

INVESTMENT ESSENTIALS

Investment is the outlay of money in the hope of realizing a profit. Money is usually invested for a long term to meet future needs and goals. Good investments provide long-term protection of income.

Good investments pro-
tect income.

There are numerous investment alternatives; some of the more common investment choices will be discussed in detail in this chapter. These alternatives include real estate, collectibles, business ventures, municipal bonds, preferred stocks, corporate bonds, common stocks, mutual funds, investment clubs, commodities, money market funds, and precious metals and gems.

The Investment Environment

Stock market is a general term that describes the securities market—the place where supply and demand for investment alternatives meet.

Edward C. Topple, N.Y.S.E. Photographer

Stocks of larger companies are listed with a specific *stock exchange*, where stocks and bonds are bought and sold. The largest organized stock exchange in the United States is the New York Stock Exchange. The smaller American Stock Exchange is also in New York City. Ten other regional exchanges are located throughout the country.

The New York Stock Exchange is a big building at the corner of Wall and Broad Streets in New York City. The trading floor (where stocks are bought and sold) is about two-thirds the size of a football field. Around the edge of the trading floor are teletype booths that are open at both ends, with room inside for a dozen or more brokers. *Brokers* do the buying and selling of stocks and bonds on the exchange. Only brokers who are members of the exchange may do business at the exchange.

Spaced at regular intervals around the trading floor are trading posts, which are horseshoe-shaped counters, each occupying about 100 square feet on the floor. Behind each counter are a dozen or more specialists and employees of the exchange. All buying and selling is done around the trading posts. About 90 different stocks are assigned to each post. Placards above each counter show which stocks are sold in each section, the last price of that stock, and whether that price represents an increase or a decrease from the previous price.

Brokers must be members to be at the exchange.

Orders received at a brokerage firm are phoned or teletyped to that firm's teletype booth at the exchange. A clerk writes out the order and hands it to the floor broker to carry out. When the transaction is completed, the clerks for the brokers who bought and sold the stock report back to their respective home offices. The buyer and seller can then be advised that the transaction has been concluded and can be told the final price. Stocks listed with the exchange may be traded only during official trading hours—10 A.M. to 4 P.M., New York time, Monday through Friday (except holidays).

Buyers and sellers make offers through brokers.

You can follow the progress of a stock by looking at the latest closing stock prices in your daily newspaper. The *Wall Street Journal*, published daily in a number of regional editions, also provides up-to-date financial and business news.

Stocks not listed with an exchange are called ***unlisted securities***. Individual brokers working directly with the corporation issuing stock may purchase and sell unlisted securities. An individual may buy and sell unlisted securities with another individual. When securities are bought and sold through brokers, but not through a stock exchange, the transaction is called an ***over-the-counter exchange***. Government and municipal bonds are traded over the counter. Generally, unlisted securities are those small companies well known locally but not nationally. Because prices for unlisted securites are not set by auctioning at a large exchange and their value is more difficult to determine, they are more risky.

Unlisted securities can be bought privately.

Reasons for Investing

There are four basic reasons to invest money: (*a*) to provide supplemental income, (*b*) to make profits, (*c*) to provide a hedge against inflation, and (*d*) to provide income for retirement.

Money should be used for investment only in addition to savings. Money invested in stocks that provide dividends can provide a person with extra income to meet monthly expenses. Because there is more risk involved in investing, there is also a possibility of making large profits. Investors must be willing to gamble—to take chances that could mean big profits or big losses.

Investments protect you from the effects of inflation.

Inflation refers to the increased cost of living. A hedge against inflation is a way to make your money earn more than the rate of inflation. For example, if the annual inflation rate is 8 percent, you would want to invest your money to make more than 8 percent. A savings account would pay 5 to 6 percent. Therefore, a regular savings account would be worth less to you because it would represent less purchasing power.

At retirement, most people need to have more income than social security payments provide. Investments provide retirement income for security when earning power is diminished, and the desire to earn money through employment is low.

INVESTMENT COUNSELORS

Suppose you have just decided that, in addition to your savings, you have some money to invest. What next? You might go to your local banker and ask advice. You would then know of some investment firms in your local area and some of your options. But your banker may also try to convince you to buy your investments through the bank—bonds or securities that are very safe, yet provide a reasonable return. You may also get investment information from your lawyer or friends who have invested their money.

Trained professionals help you with investments.

The people best qualified to advise you about investments, however, are the professional investment planners, advisers, and brokers. These people are trained to give you intelligent overall advice, based on your goals, age, net worth, occupation, investment experience, life-style, family responsibilities, and other factors. The investment planner, broker, or adviser usually receives a fee for services rendered, although some mutual fund firms do not charge a commission for investing. You can purchase directly in many cases and pay no commissions, but you may not make wise investments because you are not an expert.

If you don't know a planner, adviser, or broker, perhaps a friend, associate, lawyer, or banker can recommend one to you. You may also see advertisements for investment and brokerage firms in the paper and make your own choice. Many people hesitate to use planners, advisers, or brokers because they are embarrassed about the small amount of money they have to invest—only a few hundred dollars or less a month. In this case, a broker can advise you of your options and some good investment clubs.

Don't be embarrassed to ask questions.

Some people are well informed and know what they want to buy and sell on the stock market. For these people, there is a service available called *discount brokerage*. Discount brokers buy and sell stocks for individuals for a reduced fee. The fee can be half as much as the one ordinarily charged by a full-service stockbroker who gives competent investment advice. But the discount broker gives no service other than to buy and sell stock in behalf of the customer. Large banks and savings and loan associations now have discount brokers to perform this service for customers. In most cases, you will be required to have an account at that bank so that money can be transferred from your account to pay for any stocks and bonds you purchase. For an annual fee, the bank will also keep a brokerage account for you, keep your stock certificates in the bank, and send you monthly or quarterly statements of value (showing the current value of your securities). A phone call from you to the discount broker is all that is needed to buy and sell stocks and bonds.

FIXED-INCOME AND LOW-RISK INVESTMENTS

There are a number of relatively safe investments that provide fixed income or have other safety features. These investments include notes and debentures; corporate and municipal bonds; preferred stocks; and mutual funds, investment clubs, and money market funds. Many conservative investors think these investments provide the best return for a relatively reasonable risk.

Corporate Notes and Debentures

A *corporate note* is an investment wherein you loan money to a corporation or other business and receive a note, or written promise to repay the loan plus interest, as evidence of the debt. A corporate note may be *secured*, which means payment is guaranteed by a pledge of property or other assets. If your note is not repaid, you can then claim the property pledged and sell it. An unsecured note, or *debenture*, is an investment made on the credit of the corporation only. Because the companies and corporations that borrow your money have good credit ratings and the purposes for borrowing money are good, notes and debentures are generally considered safe investments.

Interest on corporate notes is taxable.

Interest rates and maturity dates for notes are determined at the time of purchase. You know how much you will receive on your investment and when you will receive it. Notes and debentures can be short-term (for six months or less) or long-term (for over a year).

Corporate and Municipal Bonds

Municipal bonds are issued by a government division, such as a city or county, and are guaranteed by the property owners within that tax district. Before these bonds are issued, they must be approved by voters. Municipal bonds have a major advantage: you pay no federal income tax on interest earned on them. Because they are tax free, municipal bonds do not carry a high interest rate.

Interest on municipal bonds is not taxable.

Corporate bonds may be of four types. Secured bonds are those that are guaranteed by a pledge of property or other assets. A *bond indenture* is a written proof of the debt; the bonds are secured by the pledge of corporate assets. Unsecured bonds are those issued on the general credit of a corporation, and they do not involve a pledge of property. ***Registered bonds*** are those for which the corporation keeps a record of names of bonds and their owners; a change in ownership requires a change in records. ***Coupon bonds*** have individual coupons attached for each interest payment. The coupons are in the form of a check payable to the ***bearer***, or anyone who presents them to the bank for payment on the date of the coupon (usually semiannual).

Bond coupons can be cashed by anyone.

Bonds are issued in various denominations—from $1,000 to $10,000 or more. Most bonds are considered very safe investments with little risk of loss. You know when you purchase the bond exactly how much interest will be earned and when you will receive it.

Preferred Stocks

Stocks on which dividends are paid first and whose holders are paid first in the event of company liquidation are called ***preferred stocks***. There is little risk in preferred stock because dividends are predetermined. The four different classes of preferred stock are cumulative, noncumulative, participating, and nonparticipating.

There are four classes of preferred stock.

Cumulative. Cumulative stock is the most common type of preferred stock. For this type of stock, dividends not paid the year before because there were no profits must be paid this year before common stock dividends are paid.

Noncumulative. For noncumulative preferred stock, dividends not paid in previous years will not be made up when there is a profit to be distributed.

Participating. Stockholders holding participating preferred stocks are paid a set dividend. Common stockholders then receive a share of the profits. Any additional profits are shared proportionately by the two groups of stockholders.

Nonparticipating. Those holding nonparticipating preferred stock receive only the predetermined dividend. They do not receive any dividend above that declared for the year.

A cumulative, participating preferred stock would be an expensive stock to purchase, but a very safe investment with a solid rate of return. Dividends not paid one year would be made up when profits allowed, plus any excess profits would be shared with stockholders.

Preferred stock has
less risk than common
stock.
Preferred stock is typically much more expensive than common stock because it has a high, set return of investment (interest) and involves little risk. Corporations must pay dividends to preferred stockholders before they can pay common stockholders, so dividends are virtually guaranteed.

Mutual Funds, Investment Clubs, and Money Market Funds

A *mutual fund*, also called a stock fund, is an investment wherein someone else is paid to choose and buy various stocks, bonds, money market investments, etc. Many individual investors deposit their money in a mutual fund, the money is invested by chosen experts, and a dividend is paid based on how well the investments perform.

An *investment club* is similar to a mutual fund. A group of people organize to pool their money, vote on how to spend their finances, purchase the desired investments, and share the profits made. There may be twenty people, each with $1,000 to invest. This $20,000 is used to buy selected investments that meet the overall goals of the club.

Mutual funds and investment clubs have the advantage of diversification. The investor is not dependent on the rise or fall of one or two stocks, because he or she has bought shares in a company that has invested in many different stocks, bonds, and other securities. The main advantage for you as an investor in a mutual fund is that you can invest with a relatively small amount of money. Combining your money with that of many other investors in the mutual fund company or investment club enables you to purchase stocks that you as an individual would not be able to afford, and thus increases your investment earnings. Between 1976 and

Diversification is
spreading the risk.

1981, some mutual funds advanced by more than 300 percent, for example.

For small investors, the **money market fund** has proved to be an excellent investment. Money market funds invest in short-term government, bank, and corporate notes. Interest rates on these investments have been consistently higher than on savings accounts.

Small investors should consider a money market fund.

The fund approach to investment is usually relatively safe; however, the rate of return is often low when there is less risk involved. The more aggressive the fund or club with which you invest, the more you stand to gain—or lose.

VARIABLE-INCOME AND ILLIQUID INVESTMENTS

Investments that involve greater risk also provide greater returns. However, in many cases such investments become *illiquid*, which means they are not easily converted into cash. High-risk investments are not easily sold, and the market to sell them is very small. Variable-income investments include common stocks, real estate, precious metals and gems, commodities, collectibles, and business ventures.

Common Stocks

Corporate stocks may be in the form of preferred stock, discussed earlier, or common stock. **Common stock** is a security representing a share in the ownership of a company. Common stockholders share in the profits of a corporation, elect a board of directors, vote in stockholders' meetings, and take the greatest investment risk. Common stock does not carry a fixed dividend as does preferred stock. Dividends on common stocks are based on corporate profits: the better the company does, the more common stockholders stand to make. Directors of the corporation declare a dividend out of the profits of the corporation, and common stockholders receive a dividend for each share of common stock owned.

Common stock is risky.

Real Estate

To purchase **real estate** is to purchase land and anything attached to it. The single largest real estate investment most people make during their lives is the purchase of their home.

While real estate is generally considered very illiquid, buying your own home is regarded as a safe investment. Homes are purchased by making a **down payment**, which in most cases is 10 percent or more of the purchase price of the home, and financing the balance with a mortgage or

Buying your own home is a large but relatively safe investment.

trust deed. Therefore, if you buy a home costing $60,000, your down payment would be about $6,000 or more. You would pay the rest in monthly payments for the next 30 years. At 12 percent interest, your payments would be about $690 a month. The cost of owning your own home will be discussed in detail in Chapter 19.

Both new and used homes have held their value over the past ten years, according to the National Association of Realtors. The average used home valued at $25,000 in 1970 more than doubled in value by 1980. The average new home built in 1970 increased in value 15 percent more than a used house by 1980. As you can see, homes have gained in value consistently and appear to be a stable investment.

Buying real estate other than your home can be a financial strain.

True, big investors have made fortunes in real estate. But as a general rule, real estate investment (other than investment in your own home) is not wise unless you are in the 50-percent tax bracket. Other real estate investments include apartment buildings, duplexes, commercial buildings, and rental homes. But to buy these types of real estate requires a large sum of cash and often more money annually to make repairs and keep the investment going. Real estate investments provide tax advantages for those with large incomes to shelter; others would find owning rental property a financial strain.

Precious Metals and Gems

Gold, silver, and platinum are examples of *precious metals*—tangible, beautiful, desirable substances of great value. Precious metals are said to be the best hedge against inflation; but in times of low inflation rates, values of precious metals are also low.

The price of gold fluctuates with world economic conditions. The reason for this fluctuation is that gold is rare, yet a basis for money, which is always of value and universally acceptable. Figure 9-1 shows how gold and silver prices have fluctuated in recent years.

FIGURE 9-1
Gold and Silver Prices

	June 1, 1983	June 1, 1982	June 1, 1967
Gold (troy ounce)	$437.50	$318.50	$35.00
Silver (troy ounce)	11.80	10.50	1.80

Precious metals earn no interest or dividends for their owners. The profit is realized when they are sold. Gold and silver may be purchased in

Profits on precious
metals are realized at
sale.

the form of coins, but coins present a problem of storage and safekeeping because of their bulk. Gold and silver can also be purchased in the form of a certificate that states how much gold or silver bullion is being held in storage. However, for banks to hold gold or silver in storage, a minimum investment of $1,000, a commission of 4 percent, and storage fees are usually required.

Gems are natural precious stones such as diamonds, rubies, sapphires, and emeralds. Diamond prices are high and are subject to drastic change. Prices have fluctuated rapidly in recent years. A flawless, Grade D, one-carat diamond valued at $50,000 in 1980 dropped to $27,500 in 1981. But in 1971, the same diamond could have been purchased for $1,900. Likewise, rubies, sapphires, and emeralds increased in value greatly between 1971 and 1980, but decreased by 1981. When investments such as real estate become more expensive and less profitable because of high interest rates, many investors turn to precious stones. But when economic conditions are more favorable, precious stones lose their investment value.

Precious metals and gems have their greatest value as jewelry. Stones that are one carat or more are rare and are much more valuable than smaller stones. *Semiprecious stones*, such as garnets, spinels, and opals, often are a good investment. A one-carat semiprecious stone might cost between $1,000 and $2,000. Cultured pearls, however, are a poor choice for the average investor. The demand for pearl jewelry has increased over the past several years, but so has the supply of the most popular sizes of pearls. Consequently, only perfectly round black or rose pearls of a certain diameter are rare enough to be considered good investments—and these pearls are much too expensive for the average investor to consider.

Jewelry is a risky
investment.

The biggest disadvantage of investing in metals and gems is, of course, that the market to sell them is often unpredictable. If you are eager to sell, you may face a loss. When purchasing metals and gems for investment, be aware of the markup. When buying from a jewelry store, the profit to the store is 50 to 100 percent of the actual value, so you should get several quotes before buying.

Commodities

Commodities, such as livestock, crops, or copper, are quantities of goods or interests in tangible assets. You can purchase the commodity itself or what is called a *futures contract*—a contract to buy or sell a commodity on a specified date at a specified price. You could, for example, contract to buy a certain commodity at what you consider its lowest price. You would buy on credit, putting up 8 to 10 percent of the value of the contract. You would then attempt to sell the contract for a higher

You rarely take possession of commodities.

price before the date on which delivery of the commodity must be made. Thus you can buy on paper without ever having to take possession of the actual goods. Enormous profits can be made in this way.

Unfortunately, speculation in commodities is also much more risky than speculation in stocks. More people lose money than make money. If you buy a commodity at what you think is its low price, and the price either remains the same or drops lower, you lose your original investment. For this reason, investment in the commodities market should be limited to those with a great deal of excess money, financial wisdom, and the ability to take a big risk.

If, for example, you invest in cattle futures, you are buying cattle by the pound and expecting the price to rise before you sell it. In 1981 the average price per pound for live cattle was 69 cents. That is double the price of ten years earlier, but a mere penny more than the price in 1980. Soybean prices may fluctuate by only a few cents to as much as 15 cents or more. From 1971 to 1981, soybean prices rose 140 percent. Timing is the crucial ingredient of effective investment in futures—knowing when to buy, how long to hold, and when to sell.

Collectibles

Collectibles are valuable or rare items, from antiques and coins to comic books and art pieces. They are valuable because they are old, no longer made, unusual, irreplaceable, or of historic importance.

Coins are the most common collectible.

Coins are perhaps the most commonly collected items. Coins that are silver (rather than an alloy) are worth more than 20 times their face value. For example, a fifty-cent piece dated before 1964 contained almost pure silver and is worth at least $10, depending on year and condition. A $20 gold piece, worth $50 in 1971, was worth $825 in 1980.

People like to collect favorite items and hope someday their collection will be valuable. An advantage of collectibles is that you can start small and buy in small quantities. Unfortunately, collectibles are very illiquid, as a ready buyer for your collection is often difficult to find. The trick to collecting wisely is to buy only the highest quality of anything you are fond of collecting.

Business Ventures

Many a quick and tidy profit has been made by a person or group who invests in a ***business venture***—the creation of a business to sell a specific idea, product, or service. The business venture is a riskier type of investment. If the idea, product, or service catches on, it will be very profitable;

but if it fails it can represent a large financial loss. The manufacturing and selling of the hula hoop, for example, was a risky venture in which to invest several years ago. However, the hula hoop was very popular for a few years, and the original investors made large profits before the hula hoop declined in popularity. Fortunes can, then, be made and lost through investment in a business venture. In general, the best business ventures are those that offer a service that is needed but is not otherwise available.

Investment in a business venture can be very profitable.

INVESTING WISELY

A wise investment is one that results in the greatest financial gain available for your money; a poor investment is one that results in financial loss. Investing wisely is a difficult task, as you may have gathered from your reading thus far. The hints that follow, however, may make this task easier for you.

Criteria for Choosing an Investment

Some investments rise in value at a rate higher than inflation; some do not. Some investments provide retirement income that is tax sheltered; some do not. Some investments provide for increases in value that do not show up as taxable income for many years; some do not. The ideal investment would fulfill *all* of these criteria:

Some investments are tax shelters.

1. Complete safety from loss
2. High liquidity
3. High interest return
4. Growth in value that exceeds the rise in cost of living
5. Reasonable purchase price

Obviously, you may not find all of these elements in any single investment. However, all your investments should fulfill as many of these criteria as possible. The more elements fulfilled, the more desirable the investment.

Wise Investment Practices

People commonly make one or more serious mistakes in connection with their investment practices. Some mistakes are minor and can be corrected easily; others will cause serious financial damage. If you wish to avoid investment disaster, follow the wise investment practices described below.

Mistakes cause financial damage.

Define Your Financial Goals. In Chapter 5, you were introduced to the importance of setting short- and long-term goals. If these goals are not clearly defined, you will not know which investments can best serve to meet them.

Follow Through. Putting off plans and never taking action will lead to failure in meeting your financial goals. If a goal is important, it should be worked on in the present, not put off until some never-to-come future day.

Keep Good Records. In order to be aware of your future needs and goals, you need to keep good financial records. Your personal inventory and net worth statement, plus lists of insurance policies and investments, balances and locations of bank accounts, and contents and location of your safe-deposit box, etc., are essential pieces of information. Unless you know where you have been and where you are, it is difficult to plan where you are going.

Personal records must be complete.

Seek Good Investment Advice. Many people think they can make wise investments without seeking and paying for advice from an expert. In the long run, these investments may prove expensive, because poor investments can cost a great deal. In general, it is wise to seek competent advice from a trained professional before making any investment decisions.

Keep Current Your Knowledge of Investments. You should be aware of what is new in the financial market, what is or is not a good investment, when to sell and when to buy. The economy is a major consideration in making investment decisions. Although you should seek advice before making an investment move, it is your responsibility to know when to ask questions and to make any final decisions about the handling of your investment portfolio.

Remain informed about the financial market.

Investment decisions become very complicated when even the best economists and advisers cannot agree. Nevertheless, making a thorough analysis of economic trends—past, present, and future—and carefully planning and following through on your financial goals will help you to make wise investment choices.

VOCABULARY

Directions: Can you find the definition for each of the following terms used in Chapter 9?

inflation	unlisted securities
broker	stock market
corporate note	real estate
preferred stock	precious metals
mutual fund	gems
money market funds	commodities
illiquid	futures contract
common stock	

1. Agreement to buy or sell a commodity on a specified date at a specified price.

2. The increased cost of living.

3. Livestock, crops, or copper—quantities of goods or interests in assets.

4. A person who buys and sells stocks and bonds on the exchange.

5. The written promise of a corporation to pay a debt.

6. Stock for which dividends are paid first but which confers no voting rights on the holder.

7. Many people invest their money in funds with an expert who makes the decisions.

8. A type of investment fund that purchases short-term government, bank, and corporate notes.

9. A type of stock that represents a share of ownership in a company.

10. Investments that are not easily converted to cash.

11. The place where supply and demand for investment alternatives meet.

12. Stocks that are not listed with an exchange.

13. Property such as land and buildings.

14. Natural precious stones, including diamonds, rubies, and sapphires.

15. Gold, silver, and platinum—tangible substances of great value.

ITEMS FOR DISCUSSION

1. List the basic reasons for investing.

2. What is inflation? How has inflation affected you?

3. List the characteristics of the ideal investment.

4. List the five wise investment practices.

5. List ten investment alternatives.

6. What are secured and unsecured notes?

7. What is the major advantage of purchasing municipal bonds rather than corporate bonds?

8. List the four classes of preferred stock.

9. Describe how an investment club works.

10. What are unlisted securities?

11. Give examples of precious metals.

12. Give examples of gems.

13. What are commodities?

14. What is a broker?

15. Why should you invest money (in addition to savings)?

APPLICATIONS

1. List your top five choices of investment alternatives, and give an advantage and disadvantage of each.

2. Assuming you have $5,000 to invest as you wish, describe your investment choices.

3. From the financial section of your newspaper listing stock exchange closing prices, select five stocks. Make a list of the five stocks and record their closing prices for five days. The illustration in Case Problem No. 1 explains how to read the columns.

4. Explain the difference between common stocks and preferred stocks.

5. Explain the meaning of the following statement: A buyer purchased 500 shares of cumulative, nonparticipating preferred stock.

6. Why is a mutual fund or investment club a good idea for people with small sums to invest?

7. Explain the meaning of this statement: The investment was good but very illiquid.

8. The market for precious metals and gems is described by investment experts as very volatile (subject to drastic and sudden changes). Explain why precious metals and gems are good investments and why they can be poor investments.

CASE PROBLEMS AND ACTIVITIES

1. The financial section of your newspaper generally has a listing of the closing prices of the daily stock market. The daily newspaper reports the weekday closing prices; the weekend newspaper reports a summary of the week's trading activities. The following is a clipping from the *Eugene Register-Guard* showing the closing prices for 2 P.M., April 29, 1982:

On this partial listing, there are five columns of stock listings. Beginning at the left of each column of stock listings and proceeding to the right, there are five important columns: (*a*) stock name; (*b*) price-earnings (PE) ratio; (*c*) sales; (*d*) last; and (*e*) change. Names of companies are abbreviated and listed alphabetically. The PE ratio is determined by dividing the current price of the stock by the earnings (dividends) for the past 12 months. The higher the ratio, the more desirable the stock for price increase profits. Sales indicates the number of shares sold during the day in hundreds. The last column lists the last or closing price for that day. Changes from the previous day's closing price are shown in the final column. Dividends are listed between the stock name and PE columns. Dividends listed are in relation to every $10 worth of stock owned.

In the clipping, look at the first stock listed: AAR. It is down about 12.5 cents in the day's trading, as shown by the −1/8. Closing price was 6 7/8, or $6.785 a share. One hundred shares of stock were sold that day. The price-earnings ratio is 15 (the price is 15 times last year's earnings), and possibilities of making a profit because value of the stock will go up are good. A dividend is paid, but only 44 cents for every $10 of stock owned, which is considered to be low.

Refer to the newspaper clipping above and fill in the information requested below.
(a) What is the daily change for AMD?
(b) What is the closing price of that stock?
(c) How many shares of AMD were sold that day?
(d) What is the daily change for PSA?
(e) What is the closing price of that stock?
(f) How many shares were sold that day?
(g) What is the price-earnings ratio for PSA?
(h) What is the dividend for every $10 of PSA stock owned?

6. Using the financial section of your daily newspaper, keep track of the progress of five different stocks for five consecutive days. List for each stock the closing price and net change for each day. On a piece of paper, prepare a form to record your information.

NAME OF STOCK	CLOSING PRICE					NET CHANGE				
	Day 1	2	3	4	5	Day 1	2	3	4	5
1.										
2.										
3.										
4.										
5.										

CHAPTER 10

INSURANCE

CHAPTER OBJECTIVES

After studying this chapter and completing the activities, you will be able to:

1. Identify types of insurance protection and the benefits of the major types of insurance available.
2. Understand the terms used to describe insurance policies and coverages.
3. Determine your insurance needs and make choices of insurance programs to meet various needs.

INSURANCE TERMINOLOGY

To understand insurance, you must understand the basic vocabulary. Here are some typical words that relate to insurance:

1. *Actuarial table*—a table of premium rates based on ages and life expectancies
2. *Actuary*—one who calculates insurance and annuity premiums, reserves, and dividends; a specialist on insurance statistics
3. *Agent*—a trained professional acting for the insurance company in negotiating, servicing, or writing a policy
4. *Beneficiary*—a person named on an insurance policy to receive the benefits (proceeds) of the policy
5. *Benefits*—sums of money to be paid for specific types of losses under the terms of an insurance policy
6. *Cash value*—the amount of money payable to a policyholder upon discontinuation of a life insurance policy

7. *Claim*—a demand for payment for a loss under the terms of an insurance policy
8. *Coverage*—protection provided by the terms of an insurance policy
9. *Deductible*—a specified amount subtracted from covered losses; the insurance company pays only the amount in excess of the amount subtracted
10. *Exclusions*—circumstances or losses that are not covered under the terms of an insurance policy
11. *Face amount*—the death benefit of a life insurance policy
12. *Grace period*—the period following the due date of an unpaid premium during which the policy is still in effect (usually 30 days)
13. *Insurable interest*—a condition required of the insured in nearly all insurance contracts, wherein the insured must be in a position to sustain a financial loss if the event insured against occurs
14. *Insurance*—a cooperative system of sharing the risk of financial loss
15. *Insured*—the person, partnership, or corporation protected against loss (not always the owner of the policy)
16. *Loss*—an *unexpected* reduction or disappearance of an economic value; the basis for a valid claim for repayment under the terms of an insurance policy
17. *Peril*—an exposure to the risk of loss
18. *Premium*—the sum of money the policyholder agrees to pay to an insurance company periodically (monthly, quarterly, annually, or semiannually) for an insurance policy
19. *Proof of loss*—the written verification of the amount of a loss that must be provided by the insured to the insurance company before a claim can be settled
20. *Risk*—the chance of loss
21. *Standard policy*—a contract form that has been adopted by many insurance companies, approved by state insurance departments, or prescribed by law (modifications can be made to suit the needs of the individual)
22. *Unearned premium*—the portion of the original premium that has not been earned by the insurance company and is returned to the policyholder when a policy is canceled

LIFE INSURANCE

The main reason families need life insurance is that the survival of the family usually depends on the income of one or two people. If a family wage earner dies uninsured, financial disaster could result for the remaining family members. A family that has no life insurance protection sometimes has to change its life-style drastically to survive when its primary wage earner dies—even to the point of moving from its home and giving

Insurance protects the survivors.

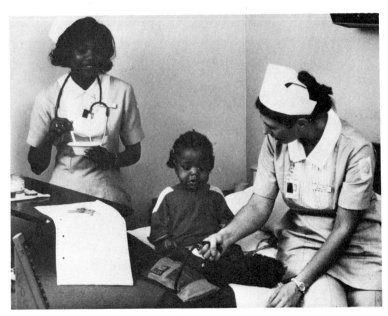

Photo courtesy of IBM Corporation

up many things. *Life insurance* protects a family from the financial disaster that might otherwise result when a primary wage earner dies.

Financial Needs for Life Insurance

There are many ongoing expenses to consider.

Life insurance needs are often hard to measure. One approach to determining the importance of life insurance coverage is to consider the financial needs that will exist for the family after the death of its primary wage earner. These needs typically include funds for last expenses, funds to support dependents, money to maintain a home, and funds for ongoing monthly expenses.

Funds for Last Expenses. Death-related costs that survivors often must pay include medical bills from a last illness, funeral expenses, and burial costs. Funeral expenses of more than $5,000 are common.

Funds to Support Dependents. If the head of a household dies, his or her dependents will still need income. In the case of small children, much insurance is needed to provide support for many years until they are able to support themselves. Insurance coverage of $100,000 or more on the life of a wage earner is common.

Money to Maintain a Home. Mortgage payments on the family home must continue each month. Otherwise, the remaining family members will be forced to sell the home and lower the family's living standard in order to reduce housing payments.

Funds for Ongoing Monthly Expenses. Outstanding debts must be paid. Food, clothing, education, utilities, and other fixed and variable expenses continue.

Term Life Insurance

One type of life insurance, known as ***term life insurance***, protects you for a set period of time—five, ten, or twenty years, or until you reach a certain age. Term insurance is death protection for a number of years only. There is no savings or cash value on a term life policy. For this reason, term insurance is the least expensive of all types of life insurance.

Term life insurance is temporary insurance only.

When a term life insurance policy is written, the insured names a beneficiary to receive the benefits of the policy if the insured dies during the term of the policy. The insured then pays the premiums, which are based on his or her approximate life expectancy as computed by an actuary. Premiums vary with the age of the insured and the amount of coverage. For example, at age 25, a person can purchase $100,000 of term insurance for about $250 a year. At age 30, the same term insurance will cost closer to $300 a year.

Decreasing Term. *Decreasing term* life insurance policies are those in which the coverage value decreases each year while the premium remains the same. A 20-year decreasing term policy, for example, decreases in value each year until the value reaches zero at the end of 20 years. If the insured dies during the first year of the policy, the policy pays $100,000. If the insured dies during the second year, death benefits decrease to $95,000. The value of the policy decreases each year thereafter.

There is no value at the end of the policy.

Level Term. *Level term* life insurance (also called renewable term) is renewable yearly, every five years, or every ten years. Evidence of insurability is not required for renewal. When a level term policy is renewed, premiums go up while the face amount of the policy remains the same. Therefore, when a $100,000 policy is first purchased, the premium may be about $240 a year. When the policy is renewed five years later, the premium may be about $280 a year. The face amount of $100,000 remains the same, however.

Premiums go up on level term insurance.

Some term insurance policies have additional features, such as optional conversion to a whole life policy, or automatic renewal. These additional features, however, raise the premiums. Also, at age 55 or 60 a term life insurance policy cannot be renewed. Therefore, term insurance is temporary protection for the wage earner while the family needs ongoing income.

Whole Life Insurance

Another major type of life insurance is *whole life insurance*, which pays the face amount to the beneficiaries on the death of the insured. The policyholder has the option of buying a straight life or a limited-payment life contract.

These policies represent permanent insurance.

Straight Life. A type of whole life policy on which premiums are paid throughout life and the face value is paid at death is called *straight life*. When a policyholder stops making payments (paying premiums), she or he may choose to receive (*a*) a cash settlement of a guaranteed amount (less than face value), (*b*) income for a period of time, (*c*) full protection for a period of time, or (*d*) continued protection at a reduced amount.

Limited-Payment Life. *Limited-payment life* is a type of whole life insurance on which premiums are higher because the payment period is limited to a specific number of years, such as 20 years, or until age 65. At the end of the established payment period, the policy is considered paid up.

Both types of whole life insurance build cash value. Money can be borrowed from the insurance company at low interest rates against policies carrying a cash value. If the loan is not repaid, that amount is subtracted from the face value of the insurance policy.

Endowment Insurance

Endowment insurance is an expensive type of life insurance policy that functions primarily as a savings contract. Premiums accumulate as a sum of money to be paid the insured on a specified date. If the insured does not die, the lump sum is paid to the policyholder at maturity of the policy. A policyholder may choose to receive a regular income after the policy matures, instead of a lump sum payment. If the insured does die before the savings plan is completed, the insurer completes the plan and pays the accumulated sum to the beneficiaries of the policy.

Endowment insurance is a savings plan.

Proceeds from life insurance policies are not taxable to a beneficiary. However, interest earned on the proceeds of life insurance policies is taxable to the policyholder.

Purchasing Life Insurance

When purchasing life insurance, keep in mind these two important facts:

Life insurance premiums are based on risk.

1. Life insurance contracts are based on the assumption that the insured is of average health and physical condition for his or her age. A person with a serious health problem, such as a heart condition, may be uninsurable (unable to get insurance).
2. Life insurance premiums are low for young people because their death risk is less.

Figure 10-1 is an actuarial table of premiums for a $10,000 term insurance policy (nonsmoker rates).

FIGURE 10-1
Actuarial Table

$10,000 Term Policy		
Age	1-Year Renewable*	10-Year Renewable
15	$ 28/year	$ 48/year
20	36	56
25	44	64
30	52	72
35	60	80
40	70	90
45	82	102
50	95	120
55	110	138
60	140	180

*Each year premiums go up by a few dollars.

Actuarial tables are based on risk. Females have lower premiums than males because the life expectancy for females is longer than for males. According to the National Center for Health Statistics (1983), a female born in 1980 can expect to live 77.7 years, while a male born the same year can expect to live only 70 years. In 1970 life expectancy was 74.7 years for females and 67.1 years for males; in 1900 it was 48.3 and 46.3, respectively.

HEALTH INSURANCE

Health care expenditures totaled $286.6 billion in 1981. Of this amount, private health insurance paid $73 billion, government (federal, state, and local) paid $122.5 billion, private individuals paid $164.1 billion, and the rest was paid by industry and donations.

In 1970, health care expenditures totaled $69.3 billion, up from $11.7 billion in 1950. In the 10 years between 1970 ($69.3 billion) and 1980 ($249 billion), health care expenses rose 259 percent.

In 1981, health services and supplies accounted for $273.5 billion. Hospital care totaled $118 billion; physicians' fees were $54.8 billion; dentists' fees were $17.3 billion; nursing home care totaled $24.2 billion; and the rest was spent on drugs, research, and construction costs.

In the last ten years medical costs in this country have skyrocketed and continue to rise sharply. It is estimated that in the 1980s every man, woman, and child in America will spend more than $1,000 a year for medical care. Much of this expense will be covered by health insurance companies.

Health insurance costs have risen sharply.

Several factors are responsible for the continued increase in costs to the public for medical care. Advances in technology and discoveries of new treatments for diseases result in a continuous need for expensive equipment and specially trained, highly paid personnel. The high cost of medical schooling, the increasing shortage of medical doctors, the increasing malpractice insurance premiums, and the rising cost of overhead and office operations are also factors that contribute to the increase in medical expenses paid by the public.

Health insurance is a plan for sharing the risk of financial loss due to accident or illness—of avoiding financial disaster in the event of large medical bills. Over 70 percent of all health insurance is issued in the form of *group health insurance* plans. Group plans provide coverage for employees or other large groups of people; all those insured have the same coverage and pay a set rate for the insurance. Pooling of resources results in greater coverage for lower premiums on group policies than could be obtained through individual policies. *Individual health* insurance plans are expensive because only a single person or household is insured under one policy. There is no pooling or grouping of financial resources to allow lowering of premiums.

Most people have group health insurance.

Medicare and Medicaid Programs

For persons over age 65, the federal government has a medical and hospital insurance program under social security called *Medicare*. A monthly premium is charged for each type of coverage (medical and hospital). Medicare hospital insurance covers hospitals and nursing home facilities. Hospital insurance pays for all covered hospital services from the first through the sixtieth day in each benefit period, except for the first $304. From the 61st through the 90th day in each pay period, hospital insurance pays for all covered services except for $76 a day.

Medicare is health insurance for the elderly.

For a monthly charge, social security recipients may add benefits to help pay costs of doctors' fees, office calls, and other medical services not covered by Medicare. For the elderly, group or individual health insurance policies supplement Medicare and offer additional coverage for retired persons. The supplemental or added coverage usually pays the deductible, or first $75 that Medicare will not pay, plus other expenses not covered by Medicare. Aged persons receive benefits under this supplementary program only if they sign up for the program and pay the monthly premium ($12.20 as of July, 1982). The plan pays for 80 percent of doctors' visits, health services, and tests, as well as physical therapy and outpatient services.

Medicaid is for those who can't pay medical expenses.

Another government program, called **Medicaid**, is provided for indigent persons, regardless of age, who do not qualify for Medicare. Medicaid benefits are paid through welfare offices and are designed for those persons who cannot pay their regular medical expenses. There is no deductible. Those who qualify to receive welfare payments generally qualify to receive Medicaid benefits as well for medical care.

Hospital and Surgical Insurance

Most hospital bills have full coverage (no deductible).

Hospital and surgical insurance benefits pay for all or part of hospital bills, surgeons' fees, and the expenses connected with certain in-hospital services such as anesthesia, laboratory work, X rays, drugs, and other care items. Usually a maximum dollar amount is allowed for each day a patient is in the hospital, for a maximum number of days. The greater the number of days and the larger the amount per day, the higher the premiums. Group policies will generally pay 100 percent of these medical costs.

Medical Expense Insurance

Medical expense insurance pays for doctors' fees for office visits and for routine services other than those connected with hospital care. Most policies have a deductible. Typically, in a group policy, the deductible is the first $100 for a single person, and $100 a person on a family policy. After the deductible is met (paid by the insured), the insurance company begins paying 80 percent of qualifying medical expenses.

Major Medical Insurance

Major medical insurance applies to both hospitalization and medical services and may be purchased as a separate policy. Most major medical policies have high limits—$250,000 to $1,000,000. Major medical insurance provides the type of coverage necessary to protect individuals and families from financial ruin as a result of prolonged hospitalization or other medical care. For example, being hospitalized for a month or longer could cost $50,000 or more, depending on services provided. Accidents or illness can happen to anyone, and large medical bills can devastate a family without adequate health insurance coverage.

Major medical protects against catastrophic illness or injury.

Disability Income Insurance

Disability income insurance helps to replace the income of a wage earner who can't work for a prolonged period of time because of an illness or injury. Benefits from disability insurance are for a maximum number of days at a maximum amount a day. Most policies have a waiting period of a week to 90 days before benefits begin; the longer the waiting period, the lower the premium. The maximum benefit is usually no more than 50 to 75 percent of an individual's regular earnings.

Dental Insurance

Most *dental insurance* is written under group insurance plans to cover such expenses as repair of damage to teeth, examinations, fillings, extractions, inlays, bridgework, dentures, oral surgery, and root canal work. Most dental insurance policies have a deductible, in addition to restrictions on the types of dental work covered and maximum amounts payable (the usual limit is 80 percent of dental bills). Orthodontic work (correction of irregularities of the teeth with braces) is rarely covered, or if it is covered, a set maximum amount is paid. The high cost of individual dental policies makes group policies most feasible.

Dental insurance has many exclusions.

A single person or a family should have adequate health insurance coverage so that unforeseen medical and dental expenses do not cause financial ruin. Although a form of national health insurance may be legislated in the United States at some future time so that all citizens have coverage (as in Canada), it is more likely that the individual family will continue to determine its own health insurance needs and provide for them.

National health insurance has been proposed many times.

AUTOMOBILE INSURANCE

In most states, automobile insurance is required for operation of a motor vehicle. Automobile insurance provides protection to owners and operators of motor vehicles. It is designed to cover the costs of damage to a motor vehicle, its owner, and any passengers. Auto insurance also covers the cost of repairs to other vehicles and medical expenses of occupants in other vehicles with which you are involved in an accident.

Automobile insurance is expensive. Premium rates are based on (*a*) driving record; (*b*) driver's education and training; (*c*) model, style, and age of car; (*d*) age and sex of driver; (*e*) location (city, county) of driver and car; (*f*) distances driven; (*g*) whether or not car is used for work; and (*h*) age and sex of other regular or part-time drivers. The driving record includes number and type of tickets received and accident record. Arrests for driving under the influence, speeding, or driving without a valid license are also part of the driving record. Driver's education courses will reduce premiums. Except for vintage models, the older the car, the less insurance required, because the car is worth less. Expensive and new cars cost more to insure because they are worth more. Sports cars, for example, are more expensive to insure than family automobiles. Young single drivers pay more for insurance than those who are over age 25 and married. Male drivers pay more than females. Certain locations are considered to be more hazardous because of narrow roads, country roads, the number of licensed drivers in the area, and the accident rate in the area: if you live in one of these locations, your rates will be higher. The farther you drive on a regular basis (such as to work), the higher your premiums. Who will be driving your car, primarily and occasionally, will also be a factor in determining insurance cost. Adding a teenage driver to a car insurance policy will increase premiums.

There are four basic types of automobile insurance. These include liability, collision, comprehensive, and personal injury protection. All four types of insurance purchased in one policy is known as *full coverage*.

Automobile insurance rates are based on many variables.

Young drivers pay more for automobile insurance.

Liability Insurance

Liability coverage is required in most states. Liability protects the insured against claims for personal injury or damage when the insured is driving his or her car or someone else's car. However, the insured receives nothing for his or her personal losses. Payments under liability coverage are for injuries and damages caused to others.

Liability insurance is required in most states.

Liability insurance coverage is described using a series of figures, such as 100/300/10. The figures mean the insurance will pay up to $100,000 for an injury to one person, $300,000 for injury to two or more persons (total), and $10,000 for property damage. Premiums charged for liability insurance vary according to amounts of coverage.

Collision Coverage

Most automobile policies provide *collision coverage*—coverage of the insured's own car in the event of an accident. *No-fault insurance* laws provide for the repair or replacement of your car by your insurance company, regardless of who is at fault at the scene of an accident. Payment for repairs is made by each insurance company to its own client. Repairs are made and paid for; then the insurance companies settle the costs later, based on which driver is at fault.

Most collision insurance has a deductible: the policyholder pays the first $50 or $100 (or any amount specified in the policy) for repairs, and the insurance company pays the rest. Because many minor traffic accidents involve minimum damage that is less than most deductibles, it is wise to have a deductible and pay low premiums. In other words, paying the first $100 for each accident is less expensive than having no deductible and paying high insurance premiums.

The higher the deductible, the lower the premium.

Comprehensive Coverage

Comprehensive insurance covers damage to your car from events other than collision or upset. Events other than collision include fire, theft, tornado, hail, water, falling objects, acts of God, accidental acts of man, and acts of vandalism. If your car is scratched while parked in a parking lot, or it receives a dent in the hood or trunk from a flying rock, your insurance will pay for all the cost of repairs. There is usually no deductible for comprehensive coverage.

Comprehensive coverage usually has no deductible.

Personal Injury Protection (PIP)

Commonly known as medical coverage, *personal injury protection* (PIP) pays for medical, hospital, and funeral costs of the insured and his or her family and passengers, regardless of fault. If the insured is injured as a pedestrian, automobile insurance personal injury protection will pay the medical expenses. Another option, sometimes called *uninsured motorist coverage*, protects you as a pedestrian when hit by a car that is uninsured.

In many states proof of insurance is required in order to obtain a current vehicle registration. Liability insurance (to protect others in the event of your negligence) is the minimum requirement. Most lenders who finance the purchase of a new or used automobile require full insurance coverage (all four types of insurance combined in one policy)

Figure 10-2 shows a comparison of coverages for automobile insurance.

FIGURE 10-2
Automobile
Insurance

AUTOMOBILE INSURANCE		
	WHO IS PROTECTED:	
	Policyholder	Other Persons
Liability insurance:		
Personal injuries	No	Yes
Property damage	No	Yes
Collision coverage:		
Damage to insured vehicle	Yes	No
No-fault provision	Yes	No
Comprehensive coverage:		
Damage to insured vehicle	Yes	No
Personal injury protection:		
Bodily injury	Yes	Yes
Uninsured motorist coverage	Yes	Yes
Medical payments	Yes	Yes
Pedestrian coverage	Yes	No

PROPERTY INSURANCE

When you rent an apartment or other space or buy a home, you will need property insurance to protect your personal possessions (contents). You will need property insurance on the structure if you own the property. An apartment or house landlord can insure the building, but cannot insure personal possessions of tenants. Therefore, tenants must insure the contents of their apartment or rented house. As a homeowner, you will want to insure the building in addition to having the added protection of liability insurance. The basic types of property insurance are fire insurance, loss or theft insurance, liability insurance, and homeowners insurance.

Tenants must insure the contents of their apartment.

Fire Insurance

More than a billion dollars is lost each year because of fires that destroy buildings and their contents. *Fire insurance* will reimburse you for fire damage to your home and possessions. Generally, insurance for contents is half the value of the building. If the building is insured for $50,000, the contents would be covered for $25,000.

Fire insurance protects the homeowner against damages that are caused by fire and lightning. Damages to a home and its contents by smoke and water as a result of the fire are also covered by fire insurance.

Overinsuring property (buying more insurance than the amount necessary to cover the value) is unwise because the insurance company will pay only the true value. Therefore, if a home valued at $40,000 with contents of $20,000 is totally destroyed, the insurance company will pay no more than $60,000, even if the owner carries $75,000 insurance. Carrying extra insurance only causes higher premiums.

The ground under the building need not be insured.

When buying fire insurance for a home, remember that the lot or land will not burn. Only the part of the structure that will burn or can be destroyed needs to be insured.

For a small additional premium, the property owner can extend coverage to add an endorsement for loss caused by windstorm, hail, riot, civil commotion, vehicles and aircraft, smoke and explosion. This is called *extended coverage* to a basic policy. Instead of adding separate coverages, the homeowner may wish to purchase a package homeowners policy, which contains all the coverages mentioned.

Loss or Theft Insurance

Loss or theft insurance coverage applies to personal property, whether it is at home or with you. Valuables are insured in the event of burglary, robbery, or damage. A *personal property floater* may also be purchased to protect certain specified items of property (such as a 35-mm camera). Under a floater policy, property is protected without regard to its location at the time of loss or damage. Rates are reasonable. For example, a camera worth $500 can be insured for about $12 a year.

Liability Insurance

Property liability insurance protects the property owner against legal claims by persons injured while on the insured's property. For instance, if a guest in your home slips and falls on your front steps, you may be held liable for medical expenses for his or her broken leg.

Homeowners need liability coverage.

All homeowners and landlords should carry liability insurance, since they are responsible for acts occurring on their property, even acts involving uninvited persons. If you own a dog, you are responsible for the acts of the dog. If the dog bites someone, your liability insurance will cover the expenses of treating the injury. Except in the case of an attractive nuisance, when someone trespasses on private property, a homeowner will not be held liable for damages, unless a trap was set with the intent to harm trespassers.

An *attractive nuisance* is a dangerous place, condition, or object that is particularly attractive to children. A swimming pool is an example of an attractive nuisance. If a child sneaks into a private pool, without permission, and is hurt, the homeowner will be held liable for damages and injuries. This is true even if steps had been taken to prevent entry into the pool.

An attractive nuisance applies to all minors.

Homeowners Insurance

Homeowners insurance combines fire, loss and theft, and liability coverage into one comprehensive policy. Generally, homeowners policies provide coverage at a lower cost than would be available if the coverages were purchased separately. A minimum amount of coverage must be purchased, but this minimum is usually an amount that will meet the needs of most people. The minimum liability for most homeowners policies is $25,000, with $50,000 or $100,000 being more common limits.

Figure 10-3 shows what coverages are included under a homeowners insurance policy.

FIGURE 10-3
Homeowners
Policy

HOMEOWNERS INSURANCE		
Properties covered:	Home	Personal property at or away from home
Perils normally covered:	Fire	Fire or lightning
	Lightning	Windstorm or hail
	Windstorm	Explosion
	Hail	Riot or civil commotion
	Explosion	Aircraft
	Riot	Vehicles
	Civil commotion	Smoke
	Aircraft	Vandalism
	Vehicles	Theft
	Smoke	Falling objects
	Vandalism and malicious mischief	Weight of ice, snow, or sleet
	Theft	Collapse of a building or any part of a building
	Breakage of glass	Accidental discharge or overflow of water or stream
		Sudden and accidental tearing asunder, cracking, burning, or bulging
		Freezing
		Artificially generated electrical current
Liability:	Bodily injury	Damage to property of others
	Cost of legal defense	Medical payments

DETERMINING INSURANCE NEEDS

It is important to have adequate insurance coverage, yet insurance premiums can be expensive. In order to manage your personal finances wisely, therefore, you must determine your insurance needs carefully to avoid paying premiums for coverage you do not require. Use the following step-by-step list as an aid in determining your insurance needs.

1. Determine your most important needs (they should be covered first).
2. Determine other types of insurance that may be needed, and list them by priority and cost.
3. Decide how much money is available in the family budget to meet these insurance needs.
4. Based on needs, shop around and ask questions. Check out the insurance companies you are considering to be sure they are sound and reputable. Discuss options and prices with agents. Take enough time to consider the options thoroughly so that you make the right decision.
5. Read and understand all policies—what is included and what is excluded—before signing and paying premiums. Know exactly what coverage you have, what is not covered, and how to file claims.
6. Periodically review your insurance program and compare it with your family's changing needs. Be sure that you and your family are adequately protected at all times.

Determine your insurance needs carefully.

VOCABULARY

Directions: Can you find the definition for each of the following terms used in Chapter 10?

agent	Medicare
beneficiary	no-fault insurance
benefits	term life insurance

coverage	proof of loss
health insurance	unearned premium
full coverage	whole life insurance
exclusions	cash value
insurance	deductible
loss	extended coverage
premium	endowment insurance

1. A feature added to a standard fire insurance policy that covers additional hazards such as windstorm, hail, riot, and other perils.

2. A type of auto insurance that eliminates the need to establish fault before payment is made to cover damages.

3. All types of automobile coverage combined into one policy.

4. The amount of damages you must pay before the insurance company begins paying.

5. A federal health insurance program for the elderly.

6. A plan of sharing the risk of financial loss due to illness or injury requiring medical treatment.

7. The most expensive type of life insurance because it combines a savings plan with insurance and pays whether or not the insured dies.

8. The amount of money paid to a policyholder if he or she elects to give up a policy and no longer make premium payments.

9. Life insurance that pays the face value to beneficiaries upon the death of the insured.

10. Life insurance that pays the face value to beneficiaries only if the insured dies during the term of the policy, while premiums are being paid.

11. A formal written statement by the insured to the insurance company to request repayment for a loss.

12. The basis of a valid claim for repayment under the terms of a policy.

13. A cooperative system of sharing the risk of a financial loss.

14. Circumstances or losses that are not covered under the terms of an insurance policy.

15. Sums to be paid for specific types of losses under the terms of an insurance policy.

16. A trained professional acting for the insurance company in negotiating, servicing, or writing an insurance policy.

17. The person named in an insurance policy to receive the proceeds (benefits) of the policy.

18. Protection provided by the terms of an insurance policy.

19. The amount of money a policyholder agrees to pay to an insurance company for an insurance policy.

20. The portion of the original premium that has not been earned by the company and is returned to the policyholder when an insurance policy is canceled.

ITEMS FOR DISCUSSION

1. Why do families need life insurance?

2. What are some of the financial needs to be considered following the death of the primary wage earner?

3. How does an insurance company determine the amount of premiums on insurance?

4. What are the three main types of life insurance?

5. Which type of life insurance is the least expensive? the most expensive?

6. Why has the cost of health insurance risen so drastically in the last several years?

7. Who is eligible to receive Medicare? Medicaid?

8. List five major types of health insurance coverage.

9. What type of automobile insurance coverage is required in most states? Who is protected under this type of insurance?

10. On what factors are the insurance premiums for automobile insurance based?

11. List the four types of automobile insurance coverage.

12. Explain the concept of no-fault insurance.

13. Why should renters have property insurance?

14. List the three major types of property insurance.

15. What type of policy protects a valuable item of personal property regardless of its location at the time of loss?

APPLICATIONS

1. What are your life insurance needs at this time in your life? What are the life insurance needs of your family?

2. Assume that you are married, have two small children, and you and your spouse have either part-time or full-time jobs. What type of life insurance should you have? How much should you have?

3. Contrast and compare these three major types of life insurance: term insurance, whole life insurance, and endowment insurance.

4. Why should families have some type of health insurance or major medical insurance coverage?

5. Why are automobile insurance premiums higher for a new car than for an older model?

6. Explain which types of coverage are included with full coverage automobile insurance.

7. Which type of automobile insurance is required to pay for damage to a car from a falling object such as a tree branch?

8. What type of automobile insurance is required in your state? How does your state ensure that this requirement is met?

9. Does your state have no-fault insurance laws? Explain the provisions of no-fault insurance in your state.

10. List several ways you can reduce the amount of your automobile insurance premiums.

11. Why should you not have more fire insurance coverage on your home than the home and its contents are actually worth?

12. Why is it necessary for homeowners to have some type of liability insurance?

CASE PROBLEMS AND ACTIVITIES

1. Judy Seubert, a friend of yours, is thinking about putting an in-ground swimming pool in her backyard. Explain to Judy the dangers of having a pool and the type of insurance coverage needed.

2. The local department store delivers a couch to your home, and your dog bites the delivery person, who demands that you pay the medical bills. You had a sign warning "Beware of Dog" posted on your

front door. What responsibilities do you have, and what type of insurance coverage do you need?

3. Interview an employee who has a group health insurance plan. Discuss what types of expenses are covered, what deductibles are applied, how much of the premium is paid by the employer and how much by the employee, and what the maximum benefits are.

4. Call a private health insurance carrier (company) and ask for information about an individual major medical insurance policy. What types of coverages are available and what are the premiums for individuals?

5. Why is it necessary for families to have life insurance on wage earners? How much coverage do you think is necessary if each wage earner makes $15,000 a year and there are children under age five?

UNIT THREE
CREDIT

CHAPTER 11

CREDIT IN AMERICA

CHAPTER OBJECTIVES

After studying this chapter and completing the activities, you will be able to:

1. Define *credit* and describe the history of credit in America.
2. List advantages and disadvantages of the use of credit by the American consumer.
3. Briefly describe the kinds and sources of credit available in the United States.

HISTORY OF CREDIT

Most purchases are made on credit.

When you borrow money or use a charge account to pay for purchases, you are taking advantage of the most commonly used method of purchase in the United States: credit. When you buy something now, but agree to pay for it later, or borrow money and promise to pay it back later, you are using *credit*. For the privilege of charging purchases or accepting a loan, you will usually pay an interest or finance charge. It is estimated that over 80 percent of all purchases made in the United States are made through the use of credit.

The need for credit arose in the United States when the country grew from a bartering and trading society to a currency exchange economy. Most historians credit this transition to the time of the Industrial Revolution. During that period items were first manufactured for sale—everyone did not produce everything for their own use any longer.

Americans began to be dependent on one another. Instead of each family being wholly self-supporting, growing its own food and providing

184

its own clothing and shelter, family heads began to work for others to earn wages. Soon the need developed for sources of credit to help families meet their financial needs. Consumer credit had begun.

One of the earliest forms of credit was the account at the local mercantile or general store. The wage earner or farmer would pick up supplies and put the amount due "on account." Accounts would accumulate for a month, for a season, or even for a year. When a paycheck was received or a crop was harvested, the account would be paid in full, and the charging process would begin again. Interest was rarely charged. But only those customers who were well known to the business owner were offered credit.

Banks loaned farmers lump sums of money as large as $500 at the start of the planting season to put in crops. The loans were repaid after the harvest. This type of credit was very expensive, however. In the 1800s, interest rates were very high, and loans were generally made only in emergency situations. Most people, including bankers, knew very little about credit and how it worked. Consequently, bankers and others making loans charged high interest rates and were very reluctant to loan large sums of money.

Early 1900s

Since 1900 interest rates have dropped. The decrease is mainly a result of a new awareness and understanding of the advantages—especially the financial rewards—of loaning money. Lending institutions

Since 1900 rates have dropped.

began to ask for security on loans (the pledging of property and income); consequently, they became more willing to make loans.

As the use of credit expanded, individual purchasing power also expanded. Because more people were willing and able to buy more goods and services, the American economy grew at a healthy pace. Conveniences as well as necessities were purchased with the help of credit, and the standard of living of the average American rose. Businesses and consumers benefited from credit. New jobs were created, and the economy grew until World War I, which created a significant debt. The war debt was paid off, however, and the United States entered the 1920s in a secure position with credit stronger than ever.

The Next 50 Years

Credit flourished after World War I.

Between 1920 and 1970, buying on credit became the American way of life. No longer was credit saved for emergencies. Many different forms of credit developed to meet changing consumer needs and wants.

In 1929 when the stock market crashed, many Americans lost their savings. Banks went bankrupt, and loans were defaulted. It took almost a decade to bring back confidence in credit and investments. But recovery was followed by war again, and World War II proved costly. The federal government went heavily into debt and was no longer able to balance its budget. However, consumer credit continued to grow and flourish. Interest rates were low, and inflation rates were stable and under 10 percent. All seemed well until the 1970s brought unusually rapid economic growth, overuse of credit, and high inflation rates.

Credit Today

Overuse of credit causes problems.

In the last 25 years, the amount of consumer credit has greatly increased. The widely accepted use of credit has created many jobs, but it has also caused problems. Many consumers at all income levels have found themselves in financial trouble with credit.

Lenders are now more willing to make loans to consumers considered high risk—those who have poor credit records or little capital to ensure their ability to repay debt. Credit cards have been generally easy to obtain for nearly all consumers who have earning ability and the desire to use credit. But the last decade has shown that, as more people borrow and use credit, the interest rates charged also rise, bringing the cost of credit to a new high.

The 1970s brought the first powerful consumer credit protection legislation. No longer was "buyer beware" the rule in credit transactions.

Consumer protection interests grew in the 1970s.

Laws were enacted to protect consumers from fraudulent practices. Both government and private agencies were formed to assist consumers with their rights and responsibilities.

The late 1970s brought a new occupation—credit counseling. Credit counselors advise others on how to use credit wisely, pay bills, and get out of trouble with credit; when to seek legal advice; and how to avoid damaging their credit ratings.

Loans on real estate purchases were at 6 percent and lower until 1970. By 1980 that rate had more than tripled. Department stores charging low consumer credit rates in the 1960s began charging 18 to 24 percent by 1981. Consumer credit reached an all-time high in the early 1980s. A corresponding record number of bankruptcies by people who could not manage credit wisely followed this growth.

CREDIT VOCABULARY

To understand credit fully, you must understand certain terms. These words are commonly used to describe credit, its availability, or its cost.

1. *Balance due*—the total amount that remains due on a loan, including both principal and interest
2. *Billing (closing) date*—the last date of the month that any purchase you made with your credit card or any payment you made on your account is recorded in the account
3. *Borrower*—the person who borrows money or uses another form of credit (When you charge something, you are, in effect, borrowing.)
4. *Capital*—the property you possess that is worth more than your debts (one of the requirements for credit)
5. *Collateral*—personal property (bonds, stocks, automobiles, livestock, proceeds from an insurance policy) pledged to a lender to secure a loan
6. *Creditor*—person to whom one owes money or goods
7. *Due date*—the date on or before which payment is due (typically 25 to 30 days after the billing date)
8. *Finance charge* (handling charge)—the interest or money charged the borrower for the use of credit
9. *Installment contract*—a written agreement to make regular payments on a specific purchase
10. *Prorate*—divide, as to divide the interest or handling charge, proportionately over a period of time
11. *Secured loan*—a loan wherein the borrower pledges property or other assets to assure the creditor of repayment
12. *Service charge* (carrying charge)—the amount charged to borrowers (customers) by merchants or banks for servicing an account or loan

ADVANTAGES OF CREDIT

Credit is handy for emergencies.

The wise consumer can gain many advantages from the use of credit. Used correctly, credit can greatly expand a family's purchasing potential and raise its standard of living in many ways.

Credit can, for example, provide emergency funds—a sudden need for cash can be solved with a credit card. Budgeting and increased buying power can be achieved through the use of credit. Major purchases may be paid for over a period of time, and establishing a good credit record by the early use of credit makes future use of credit for major purchases easier.

Credit is convenient and easy to use.

Credit is convenient. Credit customers often get better service because they can withhold payment until a problem is resolved. The proof of purchase provided by a charge slip is sometimes more descriptive than a cash register receipt and helps in making adjustments when merchandise is returned. Finally, shopping is made safer with the use of credit. Carrying a credit card or store charge card makes for faster shopping and is safer than carrying large sums of cash.

DISADVANTAGES OF CREDIT

There are many disadvantages associated with the use of credit. For instance, credit purchases generally cost more than cash purchases. An item purchased on credit and paid for with monthly payments costs more than the price marked on the tag, because interest is charged for the use of credit. An interest rate of 18 percent a year is 1 1/2 percent a month. On a $100 purchase, the interest would be $1.50 a month. The larger the purchase and the longer the period of time taken to pay the balance due, the greater the interest charges.

Credit can be expensive.

Using credit reduces the amount of comparative shopping. Many consumers shop only in stores where they have credit. Comparing prices and quality at several different stores can save money.

Credit ties up future income.

Future income is tied up when credit is used. Buying something that will require payments for several years reduces funds available for items that may be needed in the months to come. This situation can put a strain on the budget that may be discouraging.

Credit can lead to overspending. People get into trouble with credit when they buy more than they can pay back comfortably. At the end of the month, when the bills come in, they realize how much they have really spent.

Read

These disadvantages can be avoided by the wise use of credit. Consumers who start out slowly and plan their credit purchases can avoid credit problems. Credit is a privilege that must be earned and responsibly maintained—it is not a right. Use this privilege wisely and you will find credit to be a good friend.

Credit is a privilege, not a right.

KINDS OF CREDIT

There are many different credit opportunities to explore. An awareness of the kinds of credit available and sources of credit will help you to make wise choices when you make credit purchases. Most credit purchases or uses can be divided into these major categories: charge and other credit card accounts, layaway plans, installment purchase agreements, and service credit accounts.

Charge and Other Credit Card Accounts

Charge and other credit card accounts are open-ended forms of credit. ***Open-ended credit*** is credit wherein the lender places a limit on how much a qualifying customer can borrow during a given period. The borrower usually has a choice of repaying the entire balance within 30 days or repaying over a number of months or years.

Regular Charge Accounts. A regular charge account (open account) provides credit for an open period, usually 30 days. Normally, full payment is expected at the end of each period, and no interest is charged. If full payment is not made, however, a finance charge is added. A charge plate may be provided by large retailers to identify customers with valid accounts. Clothing is commonly purchased on a regular charge account.

Full payment is expected on open accounts.

Revolving Charge Accounts. A revolving charge account allows you to extend repayment of charges. There is usually a limit on the amount you can owe at one time and a minimum monthly payment that must be made. If the balance due is paid in full within 30 days or before the next billing cycle begins, finance charges are not included. If the balance due is not paid in full, a finance charge is added to the unpaid balance.

Other Credit Card Accounts. Bank credit cards such as VISA or MasterCard, oil company credit cards, and entertainment and travel credit cards operate on the same basis as the revolving charge account. The bank or other creditor charges your account for all purchases made during a month and bills you at the end of the month. Usually you do not pay a

Bank credit cards operate like a revolving charge account.

finance charge if you pay the total bill each month. However, a finance charge will be added to your bill if you pay only a portion of the unpaid balance and allow your account to accumulate. An annual fee may be charged for the use of the credit card.

Layaway Plans

Many retail businesses offer *layaway* plans. Merchandise may be laid away in your name; you make regular payments and claim the merchandise when it has been paid for in full. Most merchants require 25 percent or more of the total price as a down payment, with regular payments to be made monthly or twice monthly. A service fee, ranging from $1 to 5 percent of the purchase price, is usually charged. A coat purchased for $100 on layaway, for instance, might require a deposit of $26 (25 percent plus a $1 fee). Then three monthly payments of $25 each would pay off the balance, and you would receive the coat. You would receive a receipt when the coat is selected and as regular payments are posted to the account.

Layaways provide credit for a service.

If you change your mind about a layaway purchase, a portion of the payments already made may be forfeited. The merchant has provided a service—credit and storage of the merchandise—and is entitled to payment for that service.

Because layaway account terms vary among merchants, it is wise to compare service fees, down payment requirements, and penalties. The advantage of layaway credit is that payment can be made over a period of time. Layaway credit is available to most customers whether or not they have any other form of credit with a particular merchant.

Installment Purchase Agreements

Installment purchase agreements, also called installment loans, are contracts defining the repayment of the purchase price plus finance charges in equal regular payments (installments). For example, if an item with a purchase price of $800 is purchased on a two-year payment plan with a 15 percent annual finance charge, the total installment price of the item becomes $1,040 ($800 plus $240). Regular monthly payments of $43.34 include both principal and interest. More purchases cannot be added to an installment purchase agreement. When the balance is paid off, another agreement can be drawn up.

Installment payments include principal and interest.

Some businesses carry their own financing, and monthly payments are made directly to them. Other businesses require that customers get outside financing for installment purchases. Such financing may be obtained from a bank, credit union, or finance company. By requiring the customer to borrow money to cover the purchase, the merchant is assured of immediate payment in full. Installment payments are then made to the lender.

Installment purchase agreements generally are used for large purchases such as automobiles, appliances, furniture, or cash loans. A signed contract is usually required. The purchased item serves as collateral and will be repossessed if the agreed upon payments are not made. In the case of an automobile or mobile home, the lender retains the title until the full purchase price is paid. Large purchases such as this often require signing of a promissory note. As a consumer it is your responsibility to read and understand any contract or note before signing it.

Large purchases often require a promissory note.

Service Credit Accounts

Almost everyone uses some type of *service credit* by having a service performed and paying for it later. Your telephone and utility services are provided for a month in advance, then you are billed. Many businesses—including doctors and dentists, dry cleaners, repair shops, and others—extend service credit. Terms are set by the individual businesses. Most doctors do not charge interest on unpaid account balances, but they do expect that regular payments will be made until the bill is paid in full. Utility and telephone companies expect payment in full within a set time limit; however, they usually offer a budget plan as well, which allows you to average bills to get lower rates. Service credit accounts are usually offered by businesses whose services are considered necessary to the average consumer.

Service credit is available when needed.

SOURCES OF CREDIT

There are many sources for consumer credit. Some of the major sources are retail stores, commercial banks and credit unions, finance companies, pawnshops, and private lenders.

Retail Stores

Retail stores include department stores, drug stores, clothing stores, hardware stores, and all types of service businesses. Retailers purchase from wholesalers, who purchase from manufacturers and producers. Consumers buy directly from the retailers.

Retail stores take advantage of credit because customers like to shop where they have credit established. Most retail stores offer their own

Many retail stores have several credit plans.

accounts, both regular and revolving. Many retail stores also accept bank credit cards and other well-known national cards, such as American Express or Diners Club. Charge customers receive advance notice of special sales, discounts, and other privileges not offered to cash customers. For example, some large department stores offer a deferred billing plan for charge customers. Upon request, merchandise charged between November 1 and December 25 is not billed to the customer's account until February. No finance charges are added unless the balance is not paid by the next closing date.

Commercial Banks and Credit Unions

Banks require good reasons for loans.

Commercial banks and credit unions make loans to individuals and companies based on collateral, capital, and credit records. Interest rates vary with location or financial institution and according to what is being purchased. Good reasons for a loan, such as the need to purchase a car or home or the desire to take a vacation, are required. Banks generally charge the maximum loan interest rates allowed by law. Regular bank customers who have established credit are able to get loans at their banks more easily than noncustomers. Noncustomers may be required to open an account before a loan will be considered. Banks also offer credit cards, teller machines, and other services discussed in Chapter 6.

Credit unions make loans available to their members only. Interest rates are generally lower than those charged by banks because credit unions are nonprofit and are organized for the benefit of members. Credit unions are more willing to make loans because the members who are borrowing also have a stake in the credit union.

Finance Companies

Small loan companies take more risk than banks.

Often called *small loan companies*, finance companies usually charge high rates of interest for the use of their money. The reason for the high rates is that finance companies are willing to take risks that banks and credit unions will not take. In many cases, people who are turned down by banks and credit unions can get loans at small loan companies.

Finance companies are called small loan companies because the maximum amount that can be loaned to one person or business is set by the state. This maximum is usually small in comparison to what banks and credit unions can lend. For example, most finance companies are limited to a maximum loan amount. The loan limit may be established by the home office of the finance company or by the state in which the company is operating. It is common practice for large banks to loan over a million dollars at a time to a commercial customer.

Small loan companies take more risk than banks. Therefore, they must be more careful to protect their loans. When payment is not received when due, an officer calls the customer for an explanation. Constant contact is kept to make sure payments are made as agreed. Phone calls, letters, and personal visits are to be expected if the customer deviates even slightly from the agreed upon payment schedule. High interest rates are also another form of protection for the small loan company. In states where *usury laws* exist (laws setting maximum interest rates that may be charged), finance companies charge the maximum. Where no usury laws exist, finance companies charge as much as the customer is willing to pay. When an emergency or other extreme need arises, consumers often feel forced to pay these higher rates of interest to get the money they need.

Usury laws protect consumers from high rates of interest.

Pawnshops

A *pawnshop* is a legal business where loans are made against the value of specific personal possessions. Merchandise that is readily salable, such as guns, cameras, jewelry, radios, TVs, and coins, is usually acceptable. The customer brings in an item of value to be examined and appraised. A loan made against the property is considerably less than the appraised value of the item. Some pawnshops give only 10 to 25 percent of the value of the article; most give no more than 50 or 60 percent. For example, if you have a ring appraised at $500, you will probably be loaned between $50 and $250. You will be given a receipt for the ring and a certain length of time—from two weeks to six months—to redeem the ring by paying back the loan plus interest. If you do not pay back the loan and claim the ring, it will be sold. Merchandise taken in a pawnshop is considered collateral for the loan because it is something of value that may be sold if you fail to pay off the loan. Prices charged for the used merchandise in a pawnshop are generally lower than actual value. Sometimes you can find a bargain, and the pawnbroker still makes a profit.

Pawnshops make loans based on appraised value.

Private Lenders

The most common source of cash loans is the private lender. Private lenders include an individual's parents, other relatives, friends, etc. Interest may or may not be charged on loans made by private lenders.

Other Sources of Consumer Credit

Life insurance policies can be used as an alternate source of consumer credit. As a life insurance policy builds up a cash value, the policyholder can borrow at low rates of interest against his or her policy. The loan does

Your life insurance policy may have loan value.

not have to be paid back, but interest on the loan will be charged to the policyholder, and the amount of the loan will reduce the face value (amount) of the life insurance policy.

If you have a certificate of deposit with a bank, credit union, or savings and loan association, you can borrow money against the certificate. The certificate is used as collateral, and the interest rate charged you is usually only 2 to 5 percent above the interest rate being paid on the certificate. If you cash in the certificate, you incur interest penalties; but if you borrow money using the certificate as collateral, you get a moderate rate of interest, plus the certificate retains its full value.

VOCABULARY

Directions: Can you find the definition for each of the following terms used in Chapter 11?

balance due
revolving account
borrower
layaway
credit
service credit
creditor
retail stores
capital

finance charge (handling charge)
small loan companies
usury laws
pawnshop
prorate
service charge (carrying charge)
collateral

1. The interest or money charged the borrower for the use of credit.

2. One who lends money or the use of goods and services for payment at a later date.

3. Paying at a future date for the present use of money, goods, or services.

4. The total amount that remains due on a loan, including both principal and interest.

5. The person who borrows money or uses credit.

6. To divide proportionately over a period of time.

7. Property possessed that is worth more than debts.

8. The amount charged by merchants or other creditors to borrowers for servicing or maintaining an account.

9. An account that is not assessed a finance charge unless the balance is not paid in full by the due date.

10. Property or possessions that can be mortgaged or sold, which are used as security for payment of a debt.

11. A type of installment account that has a maximum amount of credit, and payments made include a finance charge (interest) in each regular installment.

12. Laws setting maximum interest rates that may be charged.

13. Businesses offering goods and services to consumers, including department stores, drug stores, clothing stores, etc.

14. Having a service performed and paying for it at a later date.

15. A plan whereby merchandise is set aside in a customer's name until it is paid for in full.

16. Finance companies that make relatively small loans, take more risk, and generally charge higher rates of interest.

17. A legal business where loans are made based on the value of merchandise pledged as collateral.

ITEMS FOR DISCUSSION

1. What is credit?

2. What is collateral? *something you can to back up loan*

3. When credit first began in this country, did loans have high interest rates or low rates? *High*

4. Why, when credit began, were bankers and merchants reluctant to loan money and give credit?

5. How has credit affected the American economy?

6. What kinds of jobs are created by credit?

7. List four advantages of using credit.

8. List four disadvantages of using credit.

9. What are three major kinds of credits?

10. How is a regular charge account different from a revolving charge account?

11. Explain how layaway credit operates. Why is it a good way to begin to establish credit?

12. Give three or four examples of service credit.

13. List the five major sources of credit for consumers.

14. Why do retail stores accept VISA and MasterCard in addition to their own credit cards?

15. Why do credit unions offer lower interest rates on loans than do commercial banks?

16. Why do small loan companies charge higher rates of interest on their loans?

17. Explain how a pawnshop operates.

APPLICATIONS

1. Give an example of a situation in which you would use collateral when making a purchase on credit.

2. How does your family make use of credit? Do you see credit use in your family as a good thing or a bad thing? What advantages of credit do you use?

3. List retail stores in your area that:

    (a) Extend credit by accepting credit cards.

    (b) Accept VISA, MasterCard, and other major credit cards.

    (c) Offer regular charge accounts and installment credit.

4. List several businesses in your area that offer layaway plans. Choose one such plan and list the following:

    (a) Name of store

    (b) Amount of down payment required

    (c) Layaway fee

    (d) Penalty for failure to complete payments

    (e) Maximum amount of merchandise that may be purchased on layaway

    (f) Frequency of and amount of payments needed

5. List five sources of service credit that most families use. Of these sources, do any charge a fee or interest rate if the payment is not made in full?

6. List four commercial banks and credit unions in your area. Write down their addresses and telephone numbers.

7. List four finance companies (small loan companies) in your area, together with addresses and phone numbers. (Hint: The Yellow Pages of your telephone book will list them by subject, such as under the heading "finance.")

8. List four pawnshops in your area; include addresses and phone numbers.

9. Does your state have usury laws? You can find out by consulting your library (the current *World Almanac & Book of Facts*). List some of the finance rates that states allow, including your state and neighboring states.

CASE PROBLEMS AND ACTIVITIES

1. Friends of your grandparents have never used credit. Having lived through the Great Depression, when they lost their life savings, they have never trusted others enough to pay for anything except with cash. What types of problems can result from not using credit? What would be your advice to them, knowing that they have a good income from investments and have no need to buy on credit?

2. Interview three or four adults about credit. Ask them the following questions. Prepare a short report.

    (a) How do you feel about credit in America?

    (b) Do you use credit cards, such as store credit cards or bank credit cards?

    (c) Do you think the rates of interest charged by stores and banks on unpaid balances are reasonable?

    (d) What rate of interest is charged by some creditors?

    (e) How would you advise a young person just starting out about credit?

CHAPTER 12
CREDIT RECORDS, REPORTS, AND LAWS

CHAPTER OBJECTIVES

After studying this chapter and completing the activities, you will be able to:

1. Understand the importance of credit records and summarize how and why records are compiled.
2. Explain the qualifications needed to obtain credit and list the types of questions usually asked on credit applications.
3. Outline the contents of a credit report.
4. List the provisions of the major credit laws.

CREDIT RECORDS

In determining your credit worthiness, a creditor will ask about past credit performance: were bills paid on time? were bills paid off as agreed? how much total credit was given? what is the credit that appears to be outstanding at this time? Your *credit history*, the complete record of your credit performance, will provide answers to these questions and thus help the creditor to gauge your ability to pay back new debts.

Credit File

Most people have credit files.

Every person who uses credit has a credit file. The *credit file* is a summary of a person's credit history. Each time credit is used and reported, information on the transaction will appear in the credit file.

Maintaining credit files is a big business. A company that operates for profit in the business of accumulating, storing, and distributing credit

Photo courtesy Goodyear Tire & Rubber Co.

information is called a **_credit bureau_**. There are an estimated 2,500 credit bureaus in the United States, supplying 125 to 150 million credit reports a year. TRW Credit Data, a major credit bureau, reports having files on 40 million consumers and supplying 15 million credit reports a year to 26,000 creditors.

Some credit bureaus still keep records in handwritten form and post new information by hand as it is received. Most larger bureaus, however, use computerized clearinghouses that can search and retrieve a file in seconds to give information to potential creditors. Thus, your credit file can be a folder with your name on the tab, or it can be on microfilm, or stored in a central computer. Information is stored on a local level, and when you purchase through national companies or mail-order houses you also establish a file with national bureaus. You may have a file in three or more places, depending on the sources and types of credit used.

Modern methods of storage make credit information readily available.

How Information Is Gathered

Credit bureaus gather information from creditors, called **_subscribers_**. A subscriber pays dues or an annual fee to the credit bureau. Each subscriber supplies information to the credit bureau about its accounts—

Businesses support the
credit bureaus.

names, addresses, credit balances, how payments are being handled, and so forth. Credit bureaus also gather information from many other sources. Articles about consumers found in local newspapers are clipped and added to the files. Public records are searched for information to add to a consumer's file. When someone applies for credit from a subscriber, a credit report showing all accumulated data on the applicant is requested by the subscriber. Information in the credit report is then used as the basis for granting or denying credit. Because the credit report shows the credit history of an applicant, risks to a creditor in granting credit are lowered when that creditor makes use of credit reports.

Types of Information Kept

All public information
may be included in
credit files.

Any public information becomes a part of your credit record. For instance, if you fail to pay your property taxes, file bankruptcy, file for a divorce, or apply for a marriage license, this information will be recorded in your file. Birth announcements published in newspapers, job promotions, lawsuits, and other visible activities are recorded. When you fill out a credit application, information requested such as occupation, length of employment, spouse's name and occupation, residence, length of occupancy, number of children and other dependents, and so forth is sent to the credit bureau by the subscriber. Facts supplied in this way can give future creditors sufficient information to make a wise decision about granting or denying credit to you.

FACTORS IN DETERMINING CREDIT WORTHINESS

Before potential creditors will grant credit to you, they must determine whether you are a good risk—whether you are credit worthy. If you meet certain standards that creditors feel are important, you will usually qualify for the credit you desire.

The Six Cs of Credit

Your qualifications
determine your credit
rating.

A person who is considered a good credit risk usually meets six basic qualifications. These qualifications include character, capacity, capital, conditions, collateral, and common sense.

Character. A person with a good character is one who willingly and responsibly lives up to agreements. One distinctive sign of a good character is a responsible attitude toward paying bills and meeting obligations on time.

Capacity. The ability to repay a loan or make payments on merchandise with present income is known as capacity. Creditors want to make certain that you will have enough money left over each month after other fixed expenses have been met to pay your credit debts.

Capital. Property and other assets that total more than debts are known as capital. In other words, when you add up all that you own (assets) and subtract all that you owe (liabilities), the difference (your net worth or capital) should be sufficient to ensure payment of another bill.

Conditions. All other existing debts, stability of employment, personal factors, and other factors that might affect a person's ability or desire to meet financial obligations are important conditions to be considered. For example, a person who has moved six times during the past year might not be considered a good risk because of living conditions that indicate some type of problem.

Stability is important to your credit rating.

Collateral. Property or possessions that can be mortgaged or used as security for payment of a debt are known as collateral. If a debt is not paid as agreed, the collateral is repossessed and sold to pay the debt.

Common Sense. A person's inner ability to make wise decisions is often referred to as common sense. A loan officer or credit manager would determine that you have good common sense based on how you answer questions (either orally or in writing). Good decisions are reflected in answers such as reasons for leaving employment, number and types of credit cards and balance outstanding, or references listed on an application.

Your ability to handle credit shows in your decisions.

If a credit applicant meets all six of the above qualifications, he or she is considered worthy of credit. The applicant has shown a willingness and ability to pay bills in an acceptable and responsible manner.

Credit Records and Credit Worthiness

Your credit record will reveal to a potential creditor whether you have the character, capacity, capital, conditions, collateral, and common sense necessary to gain access to additional credit. Information in your file concerning your income, payment record, employment record, and various personal factors will affect the potential creditor's decision.

Income. On an application for credit, you will be asked how much your gross or net pay is each pay period. Part-time employees who earn only a few hundred dollars a month generally will not qualify for credit.

Part-time workers may not qualify for credit.

Unless you can show that your expenses are so low that you have enough money left over to pay extra bills adequately, part-time jobs are not enough. Many credit card companies, such as American Express and VISA, require an annual income of $12,000 to $15,000 or more before they will grant credit to an applicant. Income other than regular pay may be listed, such as interest income, child support or alimony, spouse's income, or dividend income (unearned income). It is wise not to apply for credit until you are earning enough income to afford the payments.

Payment Record. Your payment record is a list of your previous credit accounts and how you paid off those debts. Based on your payment record, the credit bureau will assign you a credit rating (credit ratings will be discussed later in this chapter). If you have paid your bills on time, your credit rating will be favorable. Consequently, potential creditors will be more likely to grant you additional credit, based on the character, capacity, and common sense you have exhibited through your responsibility in paying your bills.

Paying your bills responsibly will result in more credit.

Employment Record. Many creditors require a credit applicant to have worked steadily at one job for at least six months or longer before they will extend credit. If your work history shows that you switch jobs several times a year, you will not be considered a good risk. Creditors will assume that at some future time you may be unemployed and unable to make your credit payments. You are considered stable in your employment if you have worked for a number of years for one company, or in one particular job. The longer you work consistently, the better your stability rating.

Employment history is part of your credit rating.

Personal Factors. Personal factors that are often considered by creditors include such things as occupation, geographic area, type of residence (renting or owning), age or age group, bank affiliations (types of accounts), and purpose for the credit (a good reason).

Denial of Credit

There are many legitimate reasons for which an applicant may be denied credit. Some reasons used for denying credit, however, are considered discriminatory. The Equal Credit Opportunity Act of 1975 was designed to prevent such discrimination in judgments of credit worthiness. The act provides that:

Some reasons for denying credit are discriminatory.

1. Credit may not be denied solely because you are a woman, single, married, divorced, separated, or widowed.

2. Credit may not be denied specifically because of religion, national origin, race, color, or age (except as age may affect your physical ability to perform, or your ability to enter into contracts; i.e., minors cannot be held liable for their contracts because they are not considered competent parties).

3. Credit may not be denied because you receive public assistance (welfare), unemployment, social security, or retirement benefits.

4. Credit applications may be oral or written. However, a creditor is prohibited from asking certain questions either orally or in writing.

5. A creditor may not discourage you, in writing or orally, from applying for credit for any reason prohibited by the act (such as being divorced).

In addition to these prohibitions, the act states that creditors must notify you of any action taken on your credit application within 30 days of submittal. If you are denied credit, the denial must be in writing and must list a specific reason for the denial. After a denial of credit, the creditor must keep for 25 months all information used to determine the denial and any written complaint from you regarding the denial. You have the right to appeal, and the creditor must give you the name and address of the state or federal agency that enforces credit laws for his or her type of business (there are numerous agencies).

You can appeal if credit is denied.

It is lawful and proper for creditors, in determining your credit worthiness, to ask you for the following personal information: name; age (provided it is not used as the basis for denying credit); source of income; number of dependents, their ages, and other obligations to them; obligations to pay alimony, child support, or other such payments; permanent residence and immigration status; a list of assets; amount of income; place of employment; length of employment; history of employment; outstanding debts; telephone number (or whether you have a telephone); whether you rent or own your home; length of residence at present address; residence history; savings and checking accounts in your name. A creditor may ask about your marital status only if you are making a joint application, or if your spouse will be an authorized user. If you reside in a community property state, marital status is important. (Community property states are Arizona, California, Idaho, Louisiana, Nevada, New Mexico, Texas, and Washington.) In any case, a creditor may ask only whether you are married, unmarried, or separated.

Community property states have different credit laws.

The Equal Credit Opportunity Act is a federal law. Many states also have similar laws; these laws vary widely from state to state and are changing rapidly. Many state laws are stricter than federal laws. You would be wise to be knowledgeable of those laws when applying for credit.

CREDIT RATINGS

A point system may be used to determine credit worthiness.

Many different systems are used nationwide in rating consumers' credit worthiness. In a **point system**, you are given points for employment, amount of income, length of residence, type of residence, etc. If your points total a certain number, you are given credit. But if you don't have enough points, then your personal factors don't total enough to warrant the risk of extending credit to you.

A rating system, which is fairly well accepted by most creditors, rates consumers according to how they pay back money borrowed or pay off amounts charged. Consumers may earn a rating of excellent, good, fair, or poor.

To earn an **excellent credit rating**, sometimes called an A rating, a customer must pay bills before the due date. If a payment is due on the fifth of the month, it must be received *before* the fifth. An excellent rating also means that the customer has not missed any payments and has attempted to make a larger payment than the minimum amount required.

It is important to pay your bills on time.

To earn a **good credit rating**, which is designated a B rating, a customer must pay bills on the due date or within a five-day grace period. That is, if the payment is due on the first of the month, it must be received by the fifth, but no later than the tenth, of the month. (When a bill is paid within 10 days of its due date, this is considered an automatic grace period.) A good customer pays around the due date, but never outside the grace period, and does not miss any payments.

A **fair credit rating** is earned by a customer who usually pays all bills within the grace period, but occasionally takes longer. Late charges are sometimes necessary, but normally no reminder is necessary. This person is often described as slow in paying, but fairly dependable.

A person with a **poor credit rating** is usually denied credit because payments are not regular—months are often missed in making payments, and frequent reminders must be sent. In many cases, this person has failed entirely to pay back a debt, has filed bankruptcy, or has otherwise shown that he or she is not a good credit risk.

Ratings are often determined by creditors.

In establishing a rating for a consumer, many credit bureaus ask their subscribers to rate their own customers. Then, based on other information gathered, such as total credit outstanding, job stability, and other personal factors, a composite rating is determined. Some credit bureaus merely supply credit files to their subscribers and allow the subscribers to make their own rating decisions. Because different credit bureaus use different systems of compiling information and ratings, you should check in your local area to be familiar with the system used for your credit file.

CREDIT REPORTS

A *credit report* is a written report issued by a credit bureau. This report contains relevant information about a person's credit worthiness. A separate file is kept for each person, although spouses are listed on each report. Reports are usually in the form of a computer printout, called an automated credit file. Each report is divided into sections: Identification, Summary of Information, Public Records or Other Information, Inquiries, and Trade.

Credit reports contain several types of information.

The *Identification section* is the first part of the report, and it identifies the subject. Included is such information as full name of consumer, spouse's name, how long the file has been active, last file activity date, present address, previous addresses, any nicknames, marital status, number of dependents, date of birth, social security number, and social security number of spouse.

Following the personal information is the employment information. Dates and types of employment; salary; spouse's employment, dates, and salary; and other household income sources are listed.

The *Summary of Information section* may show total credit rating points, if a point system is used; newest and oldest reporting dates; and whether public records or foreign (out-of-area) information is included. This section may also show the number of active accounts the consumer has and the credit ranges of those accounts, plus any statements added to the file by the consumer.

Active credit accounts are part of your record.

In the *Public Records and Other Information section*, there may be information about filing for bankruptcy—court and case number, liabilities, assets, exemptions, and how filed (individual, joint, or business). Also in this section is information about loan repayment or default and balance owing. Any other court proceedings against the consumer with regard to debt payment are reported in this section.

The *Inquiries section* shows the number of inquiries made by subscribers to the credit bureau within the last six months. The inquiries are listed by name, number, and date of inquiry.

Types of accounts are listed and rated.

The *Trade section* shows the consumer's present credit status. Companies reporting credit information and dates of their reports are listed. Dates accounts were opened, credit limits, amounts of monthly payments, number of years or months paying or left to pay, balances owing, and any amounts past due are listed here. Account types (joint or individual) and account numbers, number of months the accounts were late, and previous high ratings are also shown. Any out-of-area (foreign) information would be reported in this section, along with the reporting bureau, in-file date, and date given to local bureau.

All information included on the credit report is written in abbreviated form. A listing of key words and abbreviations is necessary for understanding information included on the report. Files are updated daily, and information stays in the file for seven years. In bankruptcy cases, information stays in the file for ten years.

Certain uses of credit reports are lawful.

Credit reports legally may be requested for investigations of credit applications, employment applications, and insurance matters. Anyone making unauthorized use of a credit report is liable for a $5,000 fine and/or one year in jail. You may see your own credit report, in person, for a small fee of under $10.

CREDIT LAWS

A number of credit laws have been enacted in recent years, primarily for consumer protection purposes and to provide assistance to consumers using credit. Several of these laws are summarized in the following paragraphs.

Fair Credit Reporting Act

If you are denied credit based on a credit bureau report, inaccurate information in your file may be the cause of the denial. Under the Fair Credit Reporting Act, you have a right to know what is in your file and who has seen your file. A listing of requests made for your file for credit purposes in the last six months, and for employment purposes in the last two years, must be available to you. You may see your credit file at no charge within 30 days of a credit denial. A small fee may be charged in the event you want to see your file at any other time for any reason. You have the right to have inaccurate information investigated, corrected, and deleted from your file and have a new report furnished to creditors. Or, if the information is essentially correct, you can write your own statement giving your side of the story. Your statement will be added to the file.

You can see your file for a small fee.

Fair Credit Billing Act

Under the Fair Credit Billing Act, creditors must resolve billing errors within a specified period of time. A *statement* is an itemized bill showing charges, credits, and payments posted to your account during a billing period. Suppose your monthly statement shows purchases you did not make, or that you were charged for items you returned. Perhaps you are billed for merchandise you ordered but have not received. Creditors are required to have a written policy for correction of such errors.

If you believe there is an error on your bill, you should act immediately. Do not write on the bill that has been sent to you. On a separate piece of paper, write a letter explaining what you believe the problem to be. Write clearly and give a complete explanation of why you believe there is an error. Be specific about the amount in dispute, when you noticed the error, and any details relevant to the disputed amount. For example, you might say

Write immediately when you discover an error.

> I have just received my December bill. I noticed today that there is a charge dated November 24, for Wyatt's Department Store in Calooga, Wisconsin, in the amount of $42. I have never shopped at Wyatt's, and I have never been to Calooga, Wisconsin. I have not lost my credit card, nor have I authorized anyone else to use it. Therefore, I would appreciate your looking into this matter at your earliest convenience.

Your complaint must be in writing and mailed within 60 days after you receive the statement. The error or amount disputed must be dealt with by the company in a reasonable manner and within a reasonable period of time. The creditor must acknowledge your complaint within 30 days. Within 90 days after receipt of your letter, the creditor must either correct the error or show why the bill is correct. Customers are still liable for amounts not disputed while the error dispute is being settled.

You are responsible for amounts not in dispute.

Figure 12-1 is an example of one company's written policy for handling billing errors.

Equal Credit Opportunity Act

Discrimination on the basis of sex or marital status in granting or denying credit is prohibited under the Equal Credit Opportunity Act (see also pages 202-203). According to the U.S. Department of Labor, Bureau of Labor Statistics:

More women are in the labor force.

1. Women make up over 40 percent of the labor force (1981).
2. Fifty-four percent of all women between 18 and 64 are in the labor force.
3. Thirty-two percent of mothers with children under three are working.
4. Forty percent of all working women are single, divorced, or separated and qualify for head-of-household status.
5. The employment life expectancy of a single woman is 45 years—two years longer than a man's.
6. More young single women between the ages of 18 and 24 are entering the labor force than ever before, pursuing careers that will be continued regardless of marriage and childbearing.

FIGURE 12-1
Error Policy

> IN CASE OF ERRORS OR INQUIRIES ABOUT YOUR BILL:
>
> The Fair Credit Billing Act requires prompt resolution of errors. To preserve your rights, follow these steps:
>
> 1. Do not write on the bill. On a separate piece of paper write a description as shown below. A telephone call will not preserve your rights.
>   (a) Your name and account number.
>   (b) Description of the error and your explanation of why you believe there is an error. Send copies of any receipts or supporting evidence you may have; do not send originals.
>   (c) The dollar amount of the suspected error.
>   (d) Other information that might be helpful in resolving the disputed amount.
> 2. Mail your letter as soon as possible. It must reach us within 60 days after you receive your bill.
> 3. We will acknowledge your letter within 30 days. Within 90 days of receiving your letter, we will correct the error or explain why we believe the bill is correct.
> 4. You will receive no collection letters or collection action regarding the amount in dispute; nor will it be reported to any credit bureau or collection agency.
> 5. You are still responsible for all other items on the bill and for the balance less the disputed amount.
> 6. You will not be charged a finance charge against the disputed amount, unless it is determined that there is not an error in the bill. In this event, you will be given the normal 25 days to pay your bill from the date the bill is determined to be correct.

As a result of the act, new accounts must reflect the fact that both husband and wife are responsible for payment. In this way, both spouses establish their own credit histories. Existing accounts should be changed to assure that the wife, as well as the husband, is being given credit for the payment record.

Fair Debt Collection Practices Act

The Fair Debt Collection Practices Act was designed to eliminate abusive collection practices by debt collectors. A ***debt collector*** is a person or company hired by a creditor to collect the balance due on an account. The fee charged by the debt collector is often half of the amount collected. The use of threats, obscenities, and false and misleading statements to intimidate the consumer into paying when there is a legitimate reason for nonpayment, such as an error, is prohibited. Time and fre-

Debt collectors' actions are limited.

quency of collection practices, such as telephone calls and contacts at place of employment, are restricted. Debt collectors are required to verify the accuracy of a bill and give the consumer the opportunity to clarify and dispute the bill.

Consumer Credit Protection Act

The Consumer Credit Protection Act of 1968, known as the Truth in Lending Act, requires that consumers be fully informed about the cost of a credit purchase before an agreement is signed. Regulation Z of this act provides that the creditor (lender) must disclose all of these facts, in writing, to a debtor (borrower):

You must be informed of credit charges.

1. Cash price
2. Down payment and/or trade-in price
3. Amount financed
4. Insurance costs, filing costs, and other miscellaneous added costs of any kind
5. Finance charge
6. Annual percentage rate of the finance charge
7. Deferred payment price
8. Amount(s) and date(s) of payment
9. Description of security interest (item being purchased)
10. Method of computing unearned finance charge (in case of early payoff)
11. Any other information that may be applicable or necessary

The Truth in Lending Act also limits your liability to $50 after your credit card is reported lost or stolen. There is no liability at all if the card is reported lost prior to its fraudulent use.

VOCABULARY

Directions: Can you find the definition for each of the following terms used in Chapter 12?

statement	credit bureau
credit history	Summary of Information
point system	section

Identification section	subscriber
excellent rating	good rating
credit file	poor rating
fair rating	debt collector
credit report	Trade section

1. A summary of a person's credit history that is kept at a credit bureau and from which a credit report is made.

2. Past credit performance in paying debts, amount of credit outstanding, and credit worthiness based on facts of previous credit experience.

3. A business that accumulates, stores, and distributes credit information to members.

4. A member of a credit bureau who pays fees or dues to the bureau in exchange for credit information collected and compiled into reports.

5. A credit rating based on payment of bills on the due date or within a few days (but never outside the grace period).

6. A credit rating given a person who pays during the grace period, but occasionally takes longer, incurring some late charges.

7. A credit rating earned when bills are paid before due dates and extra effort is shown in paying debts.

8. A credit rating likely to harm chances for further credit because it shows that past payments were irregular and that frequent problems arose in the credit accounts.

9. A written statement about a person's credit worthiness, issued by a credit bureau, which summarizes credit history, present indebtedness, public records, and other information available.

10. An itemized list of purchases charged, credits, and payments made on a credit account during a billing period.

11. A person or company who is hired by a creditor to collect the balance due on an account that has not been paid by a customer.

12. A type of rating used by credit bureaus in determining a person's general credit worthiness.

13. The part of a credit report that gives name, address, and other personal information.

14. The part of a credit report that gives the subject's present credit status.

15. The part of a credit report that gives the number of active accounts a subject has, with credit ranges.

ITEMS FOR DISCUSSION

1. What does a credit bureau do to earn money? Who pays for its services?

2. What is the advantage for businesses of becoming members of (subscribers to) credit bureaus?

3. What types of public records become a part of your credit record?

4. Why is it important to pay your bills when they are due, rather than a few days late?

5. Why do creditors care about how long you have worked at your present job and about how many jobs you have had?

6. List personal factors that are often considered by creditors.

7. What types of discrimination are unlawful when considering personal factors in granting or denying credit?

8. What types of personal information can lawfully be asked of credit applicants?

9. What is the name of the federal law enacted in 1975 to protect consumers from unlawful discrimination in credit?

10. How long are bankruptcy records kept in a credit file? How long are other records kept on file?

11. What is the possible penalty for unauthorized use of a credit report?

12. Do you have a right to see your own credit file?

13. What should you do if you are denied credit based on your credit file? What can you do if information in your credit file is basically correct, but damaging to you as is?

14. What is the purpose of the Fair Credit Reporting Act?

15. What should you do if there is an error on your statement from a creditor?

16. What was the purpose of the Truth in Lending Act?

APPLICATIONS

1. Go to a local credit bureau and see what type of system is being used for locating, storing, and using credit information. Write a one-page report describing the process. Be sure to include the credit

rating system used and explain how customers are rated and by whom (the creditor or the credit bureau). Before visiting the credit bureau, prepare a list of questions to ask and call first to make an appointment.

2. You have filled out an application for credit at a local department store. The store has notified you that they cannot give you credit because you have a poor credit rating. What are your rights, and what are some things you should do? You really have no bad payment records, and you have paid previous debts as agreed. Suppose there is an error; what responsibilities to you does the credit bureau have?

3. What types of personal information are likely to appear in the Information section of a credit report? Where would a credit bureau get this information?

4. Summarize the basic provisions of the following laws:

   (a) Fair Credit Reporting Act

   (b) Fair Credit Billing Act

   (c) Equal Credit Opportunity Act

   (d) Fair Debt Collection Practices Act

   (e) Consumer Credit Protection Act

5. Describe what you must do if you believe a statement you receive from a creditor contains an error. Describe the process for error correction, including your responsibilities and time limits and the responsibilities and time limits of your creditor.

6. List the five main sections contained in a credit report, and summarize the information that would be contained in each section.

7. What kinds of credit do you think you will be using in five years? How will you establish a good credit rating?

CASE PROBLEMS AND ACTIVITIES

1. Obtain a credit application form from a local merchant or national credit card company. On a separate piece of paper, list each question on the form in a column on the left. To the right of the column of questions, make another column. Indicate beside each question whether it is a(n) (a) personal question, (b) payment record question, (c) employment stability question, or (d) income question.

2. You have just received your monthly VISA bill. There is a charge on your bill of $42, but you have a receipt showing the amount should have been $24. The purchase was made at a local clothing store (you supply the name and address) one month ago. Write a letter to the bank that issued the VISA (choose a local bank) and explain the error.

CHAPTER 13
COST OF CREDIT

CHAPTER OBJECTIVES

After studying this chapter and completing the activities, you will be able to:

1. Describe the responsibilities accompanying credit use.
2. Have a working knowledge of the terminology of loans and credit costs, understand why credit can cost money, and describe how credit costs can be avoided.
3. Understand and compute simple interest.
4. Compare other methods of computing finance charges and understand the result of repaying a loan early.

RESPONSIBILITIES OF CONSUMER CREDIT

Credit must be used wisely and carefully. Failure to do so can result in having credit limited or, in some cases, withdrawn. For this reason, credit users must understand their responsibilities to their creditors and themselves, and creditors must understand their responsibilities to credit users.

User's Responsibilities to Creditors

All credit users have the responsibility to limit spending to amounts that can be repaid according to the terms of their credit agreements. By signing a credit agreement, the consumer agrees to make all payments promptly, on or before the due date.

You make many agreements to use credit.

In addition, the credit user has a responsibility to read and understand the terms of all agreements signed, including finance charges, what to do

214

in case of error, how to return items, and any other provisions of the agreement. The consumer must contact the creditor or merchant immediately when there is a problem with a bill or merchandise is discovered to be defective. In an emergency situation, when a payment cannot be made, the consumer must contact the creditor to make arrangements for payment at a later date.

User's Responsibilities to Self

Be responsibile when using credit.

　　　　　Credit users' most important responsibility is to themselves: they are responsible for using credit wisely. This responsibility includes checking out businesses and companies before making credit purchases. Better Business Bureaus and Chambers of Commerce have information about businesses and complaints that have been filed against them.

　　　　　Another important aspect of the credit user's responsibility is to do comparative shopping. A wise buyer does not make a purchase the first time an item is inspected, nor does the buyer limit his or her shopping to one store because that store offers credit. Before making a major budget expenditure, the wise buyer comparison shops and thinks about the purchase for at least 24 hours.

　　　　　To use credit privileges wisely and to best advantage, the consumer should be familiar with billing cycles, annual percentage rates, and any

added charges related to each credit account. Credit users should understand state and local laws regarding the use of credit. Finally, the credit
user must have the right attitude about borrowing and using credit. This
means entering into each transaction in good faith and with the full
expectation of meeting the obligations and upholding a good credit
reputation.

*Enter into transactions
in good faith.*

Creditor's Responsibilities to Credit Users

Creditors, including banks, retail stores, small loan companies, credit
unions, and private individuals, also have responsibilities when extending
credit to individuals and businesses. Some of these responsibilities
include:

*Creditors have well-
designed credit
policies.*

1. Assisting the consumer in making wise purchases by clearly representing goods and services, with all their advantages and
   disadvantages.
2. Informing customers about all rules, regulations, charges, fees, and
   interest rates.
3. Cooperating with established credit reporting agencies, making
   credit records available to the consumer, and promptly discussing
   and clearing mistakes in records when they occur.
4. Establishing and carrying out sound lending and credit extension
   policies that do not overburden or deceive customers. (Setting reasonable guidelines and standards for credit helps to ensure that
   more credit will not be extended to customers who cannot financially afford it.)
5. Establishing and maintaining fair and reasonable credit charges and
   methods of contacting customers who fail to meet their obligations,
   assisting whenever possible with payment schedules and other
   means for solving credit problems.

Joint Responsibilities—Credit Card Fraud

Both creditors and credit users have a responsibility to prevent credit
card fraud. The most common type of credit card fraud is the illegal use
of a lost or stolen card. While the credit card holder's liability is limited to
$50, the merchant is not protected from losses. Consequently, merchan-
dise prices must be raised to cover such losses.

*Protect your credit
cards from loss.*

It is your responsibility to protect your credit cards from loss. Carry
only the cards you need. Keep a list of credit and charge cards and their
numbers in a safe place. Notify issuers immediately when a loss occurs.
Keep a copy of all sales receipts. Put your cards in your wallet immediately after completing a credit purchase. Sign newly issued cards immediately and completely destroy (cut) expired cards.

Use your credit or charge cards carefully. Giving credit card numbers over the telephone or sending them through the mails increases the risk of fraudulent use. Know the creditor before you purchase with a credit card.

Merchants should check credit cards against lists of lost or stolen cards, make authorization calls for large purchases, and ask for identification when accepting credit cards. New cards should be sent to customers by registered mail. When creditors promptly prosecute persons who use a lost or stolen credit card, fraudulent practices are discouraged.

Expect to have your credit card number checked.

CREDIT CAN BE EXPENSIVE

To fully understand and appreciate the use of credit in your daily life, it is important to be aware of the total cost of credit. All transactions involving credit should be fully understood. Total cost, annual percentage rate, monthly payments, and all information available should be clear before a decision is made to enter into a credit agreement.

Vocabulary of Credit Costs

When you borrow money or purchase goods or services for payment at a future date, you will want to know the meaning of the terms that appear most frequently in credit agreements. Understanding the meaning of these words before entering into a credit agreement can help you to avoid problems later.

Special credit terms are widely used.

1. *Add-on interest*—interest that is added to the principal; equal payments are made each month that include both principal and interest
2. *Annual percentage rate*—the true annual rate of interest
3. *Deferred payment price*—the total amount, including principal and interest, that will be paid under a credit agreement
4. *Full disclosure*—to reveal to a purchaser (borrower), in complete detail, every possible charge or cost involved in the granting of credit
5. *Interest*—the amount paid for the use of credit
6. *Principal*—the total amount that is financed or borrowed and on which interest is computed

Why Credit Costs So Much

How much you will pay for the use of credit is determined by several factors. When each factor is considered carefully, the best possible credit agreement can be reached. These important factors include the following:

The cost of credit varies with the conditions.

1. Source of credit
2. Total amount of money borrowed

3. Length of time for which money is borrowed
4. Ability of the borrower to repay the loan
5. Type of credit selected
6. Collateral or security offered
7. Costs other than finance charges (such as delivery charges)
8. Method used in computing interest
9. Current rate of interest
10. Amount of money the lender has available to loan, and business and economic conditions that affect the lender's willingness to loan

As stated in Chapter 11, the source of credit is important; some financial institutions and lenders are able to offer lower rates of interest and better credit plans than others. The more money you borrow, and the longer you take to pay it back, the more interest you will pay. Your ability to repay the loan also affects the total cost of the loan. The greater your ability to repay and, consequently, the less risk to the lender, the better the rate of interest you will be able to get. The type of credit selected—whether a charge account, a bank loan, or a bank credit card—will vary according to the amount and rate of interest and repayment plans available. The more secure your collateral, the lower the rate of interest you will have to pay. Real estate and real property are often considered to be the most solid collateral; personal property, such as automobiles, and income are often considered unreliable. Additional costs that may be involved with credit include service or delivery fees, license or title fees, filing fees for security documents such as mortgages or liens, inspection or credit check fees, and so forth. Total cost, including principal, interest, and any other expenses involved in the purchase, is known as the deferred payment price.

Consider how long you need to pay off a debt.

Collateral will help you get a better interest rate.

To get an accurate picture of the total cost of credit, add up all the costs. Then subtract the original purchase price of the item. The difference is the dollar cost of credit.

TOTAL PRICE (including all finance charges)

— CASH PRICE (what you would have to pay if you paid in
  _____   full, in cash, at the time of purchase)
COST OF CREDIT

The current rate of interest is often affected by the ***prime rate***, which is the rate of interest lenders offer to their best commercial (business) customers. Private individuals pay more than the prime rate because the risk is greater to the lender.

Individual loans are riskier than business loans.

The ***discount rate*** is the rate of interest that banks are charged to borrow money from the Federal Reserve System. The prime rate is usually at least three percentage points above the discount rate, a difference that allows the banks to make a reasonable profit on loans. Therefore, when the discount rate is 8 percent, the prime rate is about 11 percent, and consumers can expect to pay about 14 percent for consumer loans.

When business conditions and interest rates call for tight lending policies, consumer loans become more expensive and difficult to get.

COMPUTING THE COST OF CREDIT

Easy computations can be made to determine the cost of credit, using the formula for simple interest, or the formula for calculating the total installment interest. The cost of a revolving charge account can be calculated using the previous balance method, the adjusted balance method, or the average daily balance method.

There are several methods for computing the cost of credit.

Simple Interest

Simple interest is computed on the principal only. The result is the total amount to be paid to the lender, usually in equal monthly portions for a set length of time. The formula for computing simple interest is

$$\text{Interest (I)} = \text{Principal (P)} \times \text{Rate (R)} \times \text{Time (T)}$$

Principal. The amount borrowed, or original amount of debt, is called the principal. When you ask for a loan, the principal is the amount loaned to you, before interest is added (add-on interest) or subtracted (discount interest). For example, if you borrow $5,000 to buy a car, that $5,000 is the principal, or amount of the loan.

The amount borrowed is called the principal.

Rate. The interest rate is expressed as a percentage. The higher the rate, the less desirable the loan for the consumer.

Time. The length of time the borrower will take to repay a loan is expressed as a fraction of a year—12 months, 52 weeks, or 360 days (in most business transactions, the standard practice is to use 360 as the number of days in a year). For example, if a loan is taken for six months, the time is expressed as 1/2. If money is borrowed for three months, the time would be expressed as 1/4. When a loan is for a certain number of days, such as 90, the time would be expressed as 90/360, or 1/4.

A simple interest problem is shown in Figure 13-1. In this problem, a person has borrowed $500 and will pay interest at the rate of 12 percent a year. The loan will be paid back in four months.

FIGURE 13-1
Simple Interest

$$I = P \times R \times T$$

$I = ?$
$P = \$500$
$R = 12\%$
$T = 4 \text{ months}$

To multiply by a percent, first change it to a decimal: drop the percent sign, then move the decimal point two places to the left.

$I = 500 \times .12 \times 4/12$ (Four months is 4/12 or 1/3 of a year.)
$ = 500 \times .12 \times 1/3$
$ = 60 \times .3333$
$ = \$20$

The simple interest formula can also be used to find principal, rate, or time when any one of these factors is unknown. For example, in Figure 13-2 the rate of interest is 18 percent, and the loan was repaid in 18 months. What was the principal?

FIGURE 13-2
Simple Interest
(Principal)

$$I = P \times R \times T$$

$I = \$26$
$P = ?$
$R = 18\%$
$T = 18 \text{ months}$

$26 = P \times .18 \times 18/12$
$ = P \times .18 \times 3/2 \ (1.50)$
$ = P \times .27$

$P = 26 \div .27$
$ = \$96.30$

(or change the formula to read:

$$P = \frac{I}{R \times T}$$

$$= \frac{\$26}{.18 \times 1.50}$$

$$= \frac{\$26}{.27}$$

$$= \quad \$96.30)$$

To find the missing rate, again the formula may be used. See Figure 13-3 for an illustration.

FIGURE 13–3
Simple Interest
(Rate)

$$I = P \times R \times T$$

$I = \$18$
$P = \$300$
$R = ?$
$T = 240 \text{ days}$

$18 = 300 \times R \times 240/360$
$ = 300 \times 2/3 \times R$
$ = 200 \times R$

$R = 18 \div 200$
$ = .09 \text{ or } 9\%$

(or change the formula to read:

$$R = \frac{I}{P \times T}$$

$$= \frac{18}{300 \times 2/3}$$

$$= \frac{18}{200}$$

$$= .09 \text{ or } 9\%)$$

As shown in Figures 13-2 and 13-3, you can either plug the numbers into the existing formula, or rearrange the formula. Either way, you can find the unknown amount by simple mathematics.

Installment Interest

As you have just learned, simple interest is calculated on the basis of one year of time. However, lenders may charge a monthly interest rate on unpaid balances. On installment loans, charge accounts, and credit card accounts, interest may be charged only on the amount that is unpaid at the end of each month. When you borrow money from a bank, the amount of interest is added to the principal amount. This total, or installment, price is also part of the deferred payment price.

Interest is often charged on the unpaid balance.

The down payment is often called a deposit, or amount given as security to ensure that other payments will be made. When you buy a car, the car you traded in is often considered a down payment because the older car is worth money. The down payment is part of the deferred payment price because it is part of the total amount needed to purchase the good or service desired. Many merchants require that the down payment be at least 10 percent or more of the purchase price.

The rate of interest charged on installment contracts is called the annual percentage rate (APR). By law, installment contracts must reveal the finance charge, the amount financed, and the annual percentage rate. The formula for calculating the annual percentage rate is presented in the Appendix.

The annual percentage rate must be revealed.

In Figure 13-4, the annual percentage rate is calculated on an installment purchase in which a down payment was made. The total number of payments is multiplied by the amount of each payment to determine how much, in addition to the down payment, will be paid for the merchandise. Each payment includes principal and interest. The deferred payment price is the total of all the payments added to the amount of the down

FIGURE 13-4
Annual
Percentage Rate

The Kramers are buying a new sofa. The cash price is $800. The installment terms are $100 down and the balance in 12 monthly payments of $66 each.	
1. Down payment	$100
+ Payments (12 × 66)	+ 792
= Installment price	$892
2. − Cash price	− $800
3. = Finance charge	$ 92
4. APR (divide finance charge by cash price: 92 ÷ 800 = APR)	11.5%

payment. When the cash price is subtracted from the deferred payment price, the difference is the amount of the finance charge. When the amount of the finance charge is divided by the cash price, the result is the annual percentage rate.

The finance charge is the cost of credit.

Interest on Revolving Charge Accounts

The cost of using a revolving charge account varies with the method the merchant uses to compute the finance charge. Merchants use the method that will bring the highest amount of interest. Interest is usually calculated by computer and is based on the monthly billing cycle. Purchases made up to the closing date are included in the monthly bill. Finance charges are computed on the unpaid balance after the billing date. Merchants may calculate finance charges on revolving charge accounts using the previous balance method, the adjusted balance method, or the average daily balance method.

Previous Balance Method. When the *previous balance method* is used, the finance charge is added to the previous balance. Then the payment made during the last billing period is subtracted to determine the new balance in the account. Figure 13-5 shows how a $500 balance at 18 percent interest (1 1/2 percent a month) would be computed using the previous balance method.

FIGURE 13-5
Previous
Balance Method

BALANCE	+	FIN. CHG.	=	BALANCE	−	PMT.	=	NEW BALANCE
$500.00		$ 7.50		$507.50		$50.00		$457.50
457.50		6.86		464.36		50.00		414.36
414.36		6.22		420.58		50.00		370.58
		$20.58						

To compute the finance charge, the balance is multiplied by .015 (18 percent divided by 12). The finance charge is then added to the balance before the payment is subtracted to determine the new account balance.

Adjusted Balance Method. When the *adjusted balance method* is used, the monthly payment is subtracted from the balance due before the finance charge is computed. As you can see in Figure 13-6, using $500 at 18 percent with $50 payments, the total finance charge is less than when the previous balance method is used.

FIGURE 13-6
Adjusted
Balance Method

BALANCE	−	PAYMENT	=	BALANCE	+	FIN. CHG.	=	NEW BALANCE
$500.00		$50.00		$450.00		$ 6.75		$456.75
456.75		50.00		406.75		6.10		412.85
412.85		50.00		362.85		5.44		368.29
						$18.29		

Average Daily Balance Method. Many large department stores and creditors use the *average daily balance method* of computing finance charges. The finance charge is based on the average outstanding balance during the period. This average daily balance is computed by adding together all daily balances and dividing by the number of days in the period (usually 25 or 30). Payments made during the billing cycle are used in figuring the average daily balance, as of the date received. Since payments made during the period reduce the average daily balance, the finance charge using this method is often less than when the previous balance method is used. The minimum finance charge is 50 cents to $1 if the account is not paid in full, regardless of the amount of the balance.

When an installment agreement or loan is paid off before it is actually due, the result is unearned interest. If you agree to an installment loan that will take two years to pay off, but you pay it off in less than two years, you will pay less total interest. Therefore, the sooner you pay off a loan, the more you save in interest charges. Various methods of calculation are used to determine how much interest is saved. One method, called the Rule of 78, is presented in the Appendix.

Unearned interest means less interest paid.

AVOIDING UNNECESSARY CREDIT COSTS

Credit can be very advantageous to the consumer when it is used wisely. Most credit costs can be avoided or minimized if the following simple guidelines are followed:

1. Don't accept more credit than you need. Although having credit there when you need it may seem comforting, unused credit can count against you, too. *Unused credit* is the amount of credit above what you owe that you could charge, to a maximum amount (credit limit). For example, if the maximum credit limit on your VISA account is $1,000 and you owe $200, your unused credit is $800. Other creditors may be reluctant to loan money to you because you could at any time charge that other $800, thereby reducing your ability to pay back another loan. Potential creditors, then, may view you as a bad risk because of your unused credit. Unused

Unused credit can work against you.

credit accounts are also temptations for you to use more credit than you need.

2. Don't increase credit spending when your income increases. Instead of spending or tying up that increase in income, put it into savings or invest it. This way you can avoid the trap of being totally dependent on your income. Other costs of living will rise also; therefore, that increase in pay should not be spent so readily. It is wiser to reduce existing debt or save the additional income for future use.

3. Keep credit cards to a minimum. Most credit counselors recommend carrying only two or three credit cards. The more credit cards you have, the more temptation you have to buy. A bank credit card is often good at many places, and many individual accounts are not needed.

4. Don't charge amounts under $25. If you make yourself pay cash for small purchases, you won't be surprised with a big bill at the end of the month. Having to pay cash will make you realize the extent of the purchase; consequently you will buy less, and only when you really need an item.

Pay for small purchases with cash.

5. Understand the costs of credit. You should compute for yourself the total cost, payment, length of time you will make payments, total finance charges, and so on, for any credit purchase, if this information is not provided in writing. Study the figures carefully and consider the commitment of future income you are making, and how this commitment will affect your budget in the months to come.

6. Shop for loans. The type and source of your loan will make a big difference in cost. The costs from three different sources should be compared. Decisions to make major purchases should be planned carefully—never made on the spur of the moment. Don't sit and figure costs in a lender's office. Go home, figure all costs, and consider the purchase carefully without the presence of third persons.

Major credit purchases should be planned carefully.

7. Use credit to beat inflation. With the help of credit, you can often purchase needed items on sale that you could not purchase if cash were your only payment option. In this way, you can avoid price increases and save dollars.

8. Let the money you save by using credit work for you. When you purchase on credit, rather than spending cash, you can put your cash into savings or investments that will earn you interest or dividends. Many people find it very difficult to save any money at all. But by putting aside some money in this way, you not only provide funds for later use, but you also earn more money to help pay for the cost of the credit.

9. Time your credit purchases carefully. By purchasing after the closing date of the billing cycle, you can delay your payment for two

months rather than one month. Your repayment time is usually 25 to 30 days. You can extend your time to repay for 60 days, interest free, if your timing is right. Know the closing dates and billing cycles for all your credit accounts and use them to your advantage.

Through credit, you can have use of your money longer.

10. Use service credit to the best advantage. Don't pay bills that will be covered by insurance. If your medical or dental insurance will pay for 80 percent or more of a claim, do not pay your share until the insurance company has been billed and has paid their portion. In this way, you will have full use of your money and will not over-pay a bill and have to wait for a refund. Hospitals, doctors, and others often take weeks or months to refund overpayments. Service credit, which is available to most consumers, should be used wisely.

11. Keep track of all interest paid on credit purchases. Interest you pay can be deducted from your federal income tax liability using Schedule A. Keep track of interest paid and compare your total with year-end statements provided by creditors.

VOCABULARY

Directions: Can you find the definition for each of the following terms used in Chapter 13?

simple interest
adjusted balance method
previous balance method
deferred payment price
interest
rate
discount rate
add-on interest

average daily balance method
unused credit
annual percentage rate
principal
time
full disclosure
prime rate

1. The total amount borrowed, on which interest is charged.

2. The total amount, including principal, interest, and down payment, that will be paid for merchandise in an installment purchase agreement.

3. The amount of credit available, above what you owe, up to your maximum credit limit.

4. A short and easy method of computing interest on short-term loans that have no down payment.

5. To reveal to a borrower in complete detail every possible charge or cost involved in the granting of credit.

6. An installment plan whereby interest is added to principal, then equal payments of principal and interest are made monthly until the balance is paid in full.

7. The true annual rate of interest.

8. The dollar cost of credit.

9. Stated as a percentage that represents interest.

10. Written as a fraction of a year and used to compute interest charged in payment of a loan.

11. A method of computing finance charges whereby the interest is first added to the amount due, then the amount of payment is subtracted to get the new balance.

12. A method of computing the finance charge whereby the monthly payment is first subtracted from the balance, then the finance charge is computed and added to get the new balance.

13. A method of computing the finance charge that is based on the average of balances during the month.

14. The rate of interest bank lenders offer to their best commercial (business) customers.

15. The rate of interest banks are charged to borrow money from the Federal Reserve System.

ITEMS FOR DISCUSSION

1. How is a loan with add-on interest different from a loan that has discount interest? Which is probably better, and why?

2. Describe how the cost of credit is determined.

3. List ten factors that affect the cost or rate of interest a customer will have to pay to get a loan.

4. What is the prime rate?

5. List ten things you can do to avoid unnecessary credit costs.

6. What is meant by "timing your purchases" to your advantage?

7. What is the formula for computing simple interest?

8. Why is the down payment added to the total amount of payments made to determine the deferred payment price (installment price)?

9. What is included in the deferred payment price?

10. How can unused credit work against you when you␇re applying for a new loan?

11. What is meant by the word *time* used in computing simple interest?

12. What is your liability and responsibility if your credit card is lost or stolen?

13. What kinds of things can you do to protect yourself from losing your credit cards and having large purchases made with your credit cards?

14. What kinds of things can merchants do to protect themselves from losses due to fraudulent credit card use?

APPLICATIONS

1. Using the formula for simple interest (I = PRT), solve the following problems, rounding to the nearest penny:

   (a) I = ?
   P = $500
   R = 18 percent
   T = 6 months

   (b) I = ?
   P = $1,000
   R = 13.5 percent
   T = 8 months

   (c) I = ?
   P = $108
   R = 21.6 percent
   T = 3 months

   (d) I = ?
   P = $89.50
   R = 16 percent
   T = 9 months

2. The following simple interest problems have different elements missing. Either change the formula to find the missing element, or insert the given elements into the formula and solve as shown in this chapter. Round to the nearest penny. Use the formula I = PRT.

   (a) I = $8
   P = ?
   R = 12 percent
   T = 60 days (60/360)

   (b) I = $54
   P = ?
   R = 18 percent
   T = 18 months (18/12)

   (c) I = $510
   P = $2,100
   R = ?
   T = 2 years (24/12)

   (d) I = $36
   P = $108
   R = ?
   T = 18 months (18/12)

3. Using the procedure illustrated in Figure 13-4, determine the annual percentage rates for the following problems:

   (a) The purchase of an item requiring a down payment of $60, with the balance to be paid in 12 equal payments of $60 each. The cash price is $700.

   (b) The purchase of an item that has a down payment of $100 and 24 equal payments of $90. The cash price is $2,000.

   (c) The cash price of an item is $200. The down payment is $20, and 10 equal payments of $22 each are to be made.

   (d) The cash price of an item is $895. With $95 down, the balance is payable in 15 payments of $60 each.

4. The previous balance method of computing interest is determined by first calculating interest, then subtracting the monthly payment to determine the new balance. Complete the following chart, using a calculator and rounding to the nearest penny. The interest rate is 12 percent. What is the total interest paid?

BALANCE	+	FINANCE CHARGE	=	BALANCE	– PAYMENT	=	NEW BALANCE
$100.00		_____		_____	$20.00		_____
_____		_____		_____	20.00		_____
_____		_____		_____	20.00		_____

5. With the adjusted balance method of computing interest, the monthly payment is subtracted before interest is calculated. The amount of interest is then added to get the new balance. Complete the following chart, using a calculator and rounding to the nearest penny. The interest rate is 18 percent. What is the total interest paid?

BALANCE	– PAYMENT	=	BALANCE	–	FINANCE CHARGE	=	NEW BALANCE
$500.00	$50.00		_____		_____		_____
_____	50.00		_____		_____		_____
_____	50.00		_____		_____		_____

CASE PROBLEMS AND ACTIVITIES

1. Your friend Barry is unable to determine whether he is getting a good deal on a loan of $100 for 6 months when he pays back $114. What is the simple interest rate he is paying? (Use I = PRT.)

2. You are considering buying a piano. The cash price of the piano is $600. The company selling the piano is willing to sell it to you for $50 down and 12 equal payments of $50. What is the installment price? What is the amount of interest?

3. If you were to purchase a major appliance and pay for it this year, borrowing $800 at 18 percent for 8 months, how much total interest would you pay?

4. What is the annual percentage rate when you buy a car that would sell for $8,000 cash by trading in your used car for a down payment of $2,000 and paying the balance at $195 a month for 36 months?

CHAPTER 14

BANKRUPTCY

CHAPTER OBJECTIVES

After studying this chapter and completing the activities, you will be able to:

1. List and explain the different methods of solving credit problems.
2. Outline the bankruptcy law, including exemptions, types of income excluded, and the two bankruptcy options.
3. List the major causes of bankruptcy and describe the advantages and disadvantages of declaring bankruptcy.

SOLVING CREDIT PROBLEMS

One of the major disadvantages of credit is that it can lead to over-spending. When credit is not budgeted wisely, credit problems can arise. In this chapter, we will explore some of the ways of dealing with credit-related problems.

Credit problems don't happen suddenly.

Credit problems do not happen suddenly. They usually arise after months and years of poor planning, impulse buying, and careless budgeting. If a credit problem is detected early enough, the cure is simple and easy. However, it is best to plan to use your credit wisely from the beginning, so that credit does not become a major problem.

The 20/10 Rule

Credit counselors often suggest use of the **20/10 Rule** to those beginning in credit: never borrow more each year than 20 percent of your

yearly take-home pay, and never agree to *monthly* payments that are more than 10 percent of your monthly take-home pay. The 20/10 Rule applies to credit purchases other than for housing; that is, it applies to charge account purchases. By keeping your take-home pay free from set or fixed payments, you have more control over your finances.

The 20/10 Rule applies to credit purchases.

For example, let us say that you and your spouse have yearly take-home pay of $21,000 (monthly take-home pay of $1,750). Credit borrowing should not exceed a total of $4,200 (20 percent of yearly take-home pay), and your monthly credit payments should not be more than $175. By following the 20/10 Rule, you avoid tying up future income with large credit-related debts. Thus, you maintain control of your finances. You can make reasonable house and car payments; pay insurance, utilities, and other necessary fixed expenses; and still have money left over for entertainment, clothing, and miscellaneous purchases.

Not-for-Profit Credit Counseling

Before you get into serious problems with credit, you can seek advice and counseling from one of many private or government-sponsored counseling services. Small fees are charged, usually according to your ability to pay. A counselor will help you set up a good budget and show you how to

Fees are based on your ability to pay.

make your income do the most for you. The credit plan is voluntary; you are under no legal obligation to use or to continue to use the plan. You cannot get loans from a credit-counseling service, but you can get good advice for finding a workable plan for your situation. You can find out about credit counselors by calling county or city offices and asking for consumer credit-counseling services. Private agencies and groups that assist in credit counseling are listed in the Yellow Pages of your telephone book.

Commercial Debt-Adjustment Firms

There are numerous companies operating for profit that charge a fee to help you get out of credit trouble. Services provided and fees charged vary widely (any fee charged will increase the debt you owe). Often you will be asked to turn over your checkbook, paychecks, and bills to the debt-adjustment company. A credit adviser will contact your creditors to work out repayment plans and will make payments for you. Generally services include a five-step plan. The debt-adjustment adviser will

1. Contact creditors and arrange for payments that can be made from your earnings.
2. Take your paycheck and checkbook, then make debt payments and give you an allowance until all bills have been paid off and you can be trusted to take over again. This can take two years or more if you are in deep trouble.
3. Counsel you so that you understand how you got so far into debt and how to avoid doing so in the future.
4. Work with you to create a workable budget that you can live with. Credit cards are taken away and given back slowly after the adviser is certain that you understand how to use them wisely.
5. Supervise your budget and help you make any needed changes or adjustments.

It may take two years to clear up a credit problem.

When you are desperate and cannot seem to control your purchases, you should turn yourself in for help. You may not like the strictness or discipline involved, but the training is valuable in terms of helping you to see that you do not get too deeply into debt again. Debt-adjustment companies, like credit-counseling services, are listed in your telephone book Yellow Pages and in business directories.

Consult the Yellow Pages or business directories.

Legal Recourse

When credit problems arise that cannot be solved by your own actions or through assistance, the final step for relief is bankruptcy. When you are *bankrupt*, you are legally insolvent—not capable of paying your bills.

Bankruptcy is processed through a federal court. All your assets, income, and property are turned over to the court; you are permitted some allowances (called exemptions), and the rest is divided among your creditors. The bankruptcy procedure allows you to start over by ridding you of most of your debts. In many cases, your creditors receive only a percentage of what you owe them. But, as we will see later in this chapter, there is much more to bankruptcy than meets the eye. A decision to declare bankruptcy is not an easy one, but one that involves the careful weighing of many considerations.

Creditors receive a proportional share.

THE BANKRUPTCY LAWS AND THEIR PURPOSE

Bankruptcy laws have been present in this country for many years. Their purpose has been to rescue debtors from hopeless situations and allow them to start over again. The laws have been revised to make it easier for individuals to declare bankruptcy. But many of the pitfalls still remain.

There are two basic types of bankruptcy: voluntary and involuntary. ***Involuntary bankruptcy*** occurs when creditors file a petition with the court, asking the court to declare you bankrupt—unable to meet your bills. The court then takes over your property and other assets and pays off your debts in proportional shares. Involuntary bankruptcy does not occur very often because most creditors prefer to be repaid in full over a period of time rather than settle only for a portion of your remaining assets.

The court takes over your property.

Voluntary bankruptcy, the most common kind, occurs when you file a petition with a federal court asking to be declared bankrupt. After notice of your pending bankruptcy is given in local newspapers and by letters to your creditors, creditors may file claims. The court collects your assets, sells your property as needed, and distributes the proceeds equitably among your creditors. A ***proportional share*** is a percentage based on total debt. For example, let us say that your total debt is $15,000 and your total assets are $5,000. You owe one creditor $1,500. The proportional share owed this creditor is 10 percent of your assets, or $500. The remainder of that debt is ***discharged***—meaning you no longer owe the balance after the bankruptcy. Notice, however, that some debts do continue after bankruptcy: taxes, child support, alimony, and others.

Taxes and family obligations remain.

Bankruptcy Reform Act of 1978

The federal bankruptcy code was revised by Congress in 1978, and more liberal rules took effect in October of 1979. The new act was thought of by many as a sign of the times; anticipation of the recession and economic woes of the 1980s made the revision necessary. Many businesses and creditors complain that the new code makes it necessary for them to tighten credit: it is too easy for people to give up rather than accept responsibility for their debts. Statistics seem to support this theory. In the fiscal year 1981 (July 1, 1980, through June 30, 1981), more than 450,000 people filed bankruptcy—double that of a year earlier. On the other hand, bankruptcy still casts a black shadow over an individual's credit record. Bankruptcy information remains in a credit file for as long as ten years. Further revisions of the bankruptcy laws are under consideration.

Bankruptcy casts a dark shadow on your credit record.

For individuals, there are two basic ways to file bankruptcy: Chapter 7 and Chapter 13. Other regulations apply to businesses.

Chapter 7 Bankruptcy

Commonly called a straight bankruptcy proceeding, ***Chapter 7 bankruptcy*** wipes out most, but not all, debts. Some debts must still be paid, including child support, alimony, income taxes and penalties, student loans, and court-ordered damages due to malicious acts. Once declared bankrupt, an individual cannot file for straight bankruptcy again for six years.

To get debts discharged, debtors must give up all their property except for certain exempted items. An ***exempted item*** is an item of value or a possession that the debtor is allowed to keep because it is considered necessary to survival. Federal laws allow the following items to be exempted:

Exempted items allow a debtor to start over.

1. $7,500 equity in a home
2. $1,200 interest in a motor vehicle
3. Items worth up to $200 each under the categories of household goods and furnishings, appliances, clothing and personal items, animals, crops, and musical instruments
4. $500 in jewelry
5. $750 in tools or books required for work
6. Proceeds from life insurance policies, unemployment insurance income, pension income, and veterans benefits

Thirty-two states require a debtor to use a state exemption schedule rather than the federal schedule. The remaining 18 states allow a choice of either federal or state exemptions. Some state schedules are more generous than the federal list.

Eighteen states allow a choice.

New legislation has been introduced to tighten up the code revisions of 1978. Many businesses and creditors are afraid of the liberal bank-

Bankruptcy causes tighter credit rules.

ruptcy code and are pushing for legislation that gives more rights to creditors and makes it less desirable for debtors to claim bankruptcy. When bankruptcy rules are liberal, credit becomes tighter. The only protection creditors can take is prevention through careful screening of applicants and higher requirements of income, employment, and credit stability.

Chapter 13 Bankruptcy

An alternative proceeding that avoids much of the stigma of straight bankruptcy is called Chapter 13 bankruptcy. Often referred to as the wage earner's plan, ***Chapter 13 bankruptcy*** allows creditors to get some of their money back. Debtors keep all their property and work out a compulsory, court-enforced plan to repay a portion of the debts over a period of time, usually three years. Under Chapter 13, some debts are totally discharged. But family obligations still remain for child support and alimony.

Chapter 13 bankruptcy may seem more equitable and better for the debtor in terms of reestablishing credit. However, the blemish on the debtor's credit record caused by any form of bankruptcy is hard to overcome for a number of years.

Legal Advice

You need an attorney.

A person considering bankruptcy should seek good legal advice. In most states it is possible to file for bankruptcy without an attorney. But the law is complicated, and a good bankruptcy attorney can tell you which of your assets will be protected and which exemptions you can claim. The attorney can also assist you in deciding which bankruptcy plan will work best to help you solve your credit problems. Attorneys' fees for handling bankruptcies can range from $150 to $1,500, depending on the case. But good legal advice in this situation can save you that much and more.

Reaffirmation of Debts

Reaffirmation requires a court hearing.

Creditors may ask debtors to agree to pay their debts after bankruptcy is completed. This agreement is called ***reaffirmation***. Reaffirmation requires a court hearing, and the debtor is given 30 days to change his or her mind about making a promise to repay. A creditor is prohibited from harassing the debtor to reaffirm after the court proceedings are over.

While there is little incentive for debtors to reaffirm debts, an honest and sincere person might want to choose one debt over another and try to pay back some of what he or she is not legally obligated to pay.

MAJOR CAUSES OF BANKRUPTCY

Bankruptcy is an end-of-the-road solution to credit problems. It is certainly a last resort when no other choices appear to be available. The most common reasons for claiming bankruptcy are catastrophic injury or illness, business failure, emotional spending, and failure to budget and plan.

Catastrophic Injury or Illness

Medical care costs a great deal. Insurance policies have dollar limits for major illnesses. The single largest cause of bankruptcy is large medical bills beyond the amount insurance covers. For example, a person hospitalized for six months to a year could easily owe $100,000 a month for medical care, drugs, room charges, and other fees. If there is no insurance, that person's savings can be wiped out in the first month. Often the only way to escape this type of debt is through bankruptcy.

A major illness can wipe out your savings.

Business Failure

Every year thousands of small businesses fail. People invest their life savings and more to start a business. Unfortunately, for a number of reasons—ruinous economic conditions to poor financial planning—many small businesses do not make it beyond the first year. Other small business owners borrow more money and go further into debt in order to keep afloat until times get better. Owning and operating a small business can be very risky. Success depends a great deal on luck—in addition to good financial plans, knowledge of the product or service, favorable business location, and good economic conditions.

Small businesses are very risky.

Emotional Spending

Emotional rather than rational reasons for buying lead many consumers to eventual bankruptcy. Purchases in excess of what can be comfortably paid for, income increases eaten up by inflation and soaring expenditures, money spent to impress others rather than for planned purchases—all result in *overextension* of credit. Overextension occurs when purchases exceed what can be handled comfortably with present income. Usually overextension is temporary and is not a serious problem. A job loss, a business failure, or some other disaster, however, can put sudden and great pressure on an already weak financial structure. Then, before the deficiency can be corrected, debt rises beyond the debtor's capability to pay it off. In most cases there is very little to show for the thousands of dollars spent unwisely—nothing that can be sold to pay off debt. Extensive travel,

It is easy to slip deeper into debt.

long vacations, extravagant parties and entertainment are expensive pleasures that have no resale value.

Failure to Budget and Plan

Most people who go bankrupt for none of the preceding reasons fall into another category: people who have no goals nor plans. They do not have or follow a budget. Many do not know how to set up or keep a budget and are not willing to ask for help or advice in solving their credit problems.

Bankruptcy is not limited to any class of people.

Bankruptcy is not a condition limited to poor people. Many classes of people find themselves in trouble with credit. Poor planning can occur at any income level in any financial circumstance. At whatever financial level a person may be, spending and charging must be in proportion to income. A budget and financial plan are necessary, regardless of total income. A record of income and expenses is essential to responsible use of credit for spending. While preventing or preparing for a major illness is not possible, most other causes of bankruptcy can be avoided by careful planning and forming of decisions based on good financial judgment, advice, and goals.

ADVANTAGES OF BANKRUPTCY

For those who are beyond the point of no return, bankruptcy offers a solution to credit problems. While this solution is not without a price, bankruptcy does offer a number of advantages.

Debts Are Erased

Bankruptcy gives a fresh start.

Straight bankruptcy offers a fresh start. Overwhelming bills can be reduced or eliminated, and the debtor can start over. With good financial planning and counseling, future credit problems can be avoided, and the bankruptcy will have taught many valuable lessons.

Exemptions Are Allowed

While the majority of assets must be given up in order to erase debts under straight bankruptcy, certain amounts and types of properties are not taken. With these exemptions, a new start is possible. When a husband and wife file joint bankruptcy, the cushion for a new start becomes even softer because the dollar amounts for exemptions may be doubled.

Certain Incomes Are Unaffected

Certain types of income are not included.

Bankruptcy will not affect certain types of income a debtor may have, including social security; veterans benefits; unemployment compensation; alimony; child support; disability payments; and payments from pension, profit-sharing, and annuity plans. These sources of income need not be considered, even in a Chapter 13 bankruptcy, in which a compulsory payment plan is established.

The Cost Is Small

Attorneys' fees and court costs in bankruptcy are relatively small in comparison with the amount of financial relief provided. When total debts have reached such proportion that income cannot stretch to pay them off, the relief is considerable in comparison with the costs involved. On the first visit to an attorney's office a debtor will be given total cost estimates and information about the options available in bankruptcy proceedings.

DISADVANTAGES OF BANKRUPTCY

Bankruptcy is a last resort.

While bankruptcy offers several advantages to the debtor, there is a price to be paid. Bankruptcy should be considered a last report, and then only after thorough investigation of the consequences of bankruptcy and of all the available alternatives. Some of the consequences of bankruptcy are discussed in the following paragraphs.

Credit Is Damaged

Despite the more liberal bankruptcy regulations, a bankruptcy judgment still casts a heavy cloud over an individual's credit record. The judgment cannot be wiped off credit records for ten years. Bankruptcy is a notice to creditors and others that, at one time, the debtor was not able to meet his or her responsibilities. Depending on the circumstances that caused the bankruptcy, mistrust in personal and business affairs may result and continue well beyond the ten years.

Property Is Lost

A bankrupt (a person who becomes insolvent) does not necessarily get to keep exempt items unless they are owned free and clear. When something is owned *free and clear*, no debt of any kind is owed against it.

Some property may be sold.

Consider this example. Assume you own a house worth $40,000 that has a mortgage of $25,000 against it. Your equity is $15,000. While the bankruptcy code allows you to keep the first $7,500 of equity in your home, you may be required to sell the home. You will be allowed $7,500, and the other $7,500 must be used to pay off creditors.

If you own a car valued at $3,000, and you owe $1,800 against it, your equity is $1,200. This amount is the same as the exemption allowed for a car. Thus, you will not have to sell the car. However, if you have a car valued at $8,000, with a loan of $5,000, your equity is $3,000. You are allowed only $1,200 equity, the legal limit. In this case you will probably have to sell the car and use all proceeds over $1,200 to help pay off your creditors.

Some Obligations Remain

Some debts are not erased.

Regardless of the type of bankruptcy selected, all debt is not erased. Certain obligations, such as child support and alimony, must be paid in full. Other debts also remain: income taxes and penalties, student loans, court-ordered damages in connection with intentional acts of mischief, and other debts at the discretion of the bankruptcy court.

Some Debts Can Be Reaffirmed

If a lender can prove that there was any type of false representation on the bankrupt's part in connection with a debt, the debt will not be discharged. In other cases, creditors may ask debtors to reaffirm a debt—to promise to pay it back even though it was discharged. By reaffirming old debts, the bankrupt does not get the fresh clean start that is probably needed.

Cosigners Must Pay

Cosigners are in a delicate situation.

A cosigner can be held responsible for guarantee of a debt after the borrower has been declared bankrupt. A cosigner does not have to pay if the debtor has chosen a Chapter 13 bankruptcy, however, because creditors receive an equitable share of the debtor's assets in this case, and must accept this share as full payment.

BANKRUPTCY PETITIONS

Forms for filing bankruptcy are complicated and lengthy. The first form that is filed in a bankruptcy procedure is the bankruptcy petition.

An example of a bankruptcy petition prepared and submitted by an attorney is shown in Figure 14-1. Numerous other forms requiring specific information and declarations are required to complete the filing procedure.

FIGURE 14-1
Bankruptcy
Petition

IN THE FEDERAL BANKRUPTCY COURT FOR THE <u>Eastern</u> DISTRICT OF <u>Kentucky</u>

IN THE CASE OF _____)   DEBTOR'S PETITION FOR BANKRUPTCY
)
<u>Matthew Franklin</u> _____)   Chapter 7
)
_____ , Debtor,)
)
_____)   Case No. 84-<u>202</u>_____

Petitioner, herein called debtor, appears before the Court and alleges as follows:

1. Petitioner's address is <u>513|Main Street, Biggs, KY 43721-0132</u> , and the above court has jurisdiction over this matter.

2. Petitioner has resided in this federal district for the last 180 days, or six months, prior to the filing of this petition.

3. Petitioner is entitled to the benefits of the bankruptcy laws of the United States, and files this petition as a voluntary debtor, seeking relief under Chapter 7 of the United States Bankruptcy Code.

WHEREFORE, petitioner prays for relief according to the provisions of said bankruptcy Chapter 7, and files herewith all supplemental information necessary for the court to make said determination of voluntary bankruptcy.

Patricia Van Schaik
Attorney for Petitioner

<u>5101 Third Street</u>
Address of Attorney

<u>Cincinnati, OH 45201-6735</u>

ATTESTATION:

I, <u>Matthew Franklin</u> _____ , petitioner (debtor) named in the foregoing petition, do hereby certify that I have read the foregoing petition and its documents attached thereto, and they are true and correct.

Matthew Franklin
Petitioner

STATE OF <u>Kentucky</u> _____)
) ss.
County of <u>Pike</u> _____)

On <u>May 3</u> _____ 19--___ , the petitioner, <u>Matthew Franklin</u> ___ , did appear before me and acknowledge that s/he did sign the foregoing petition of his/~~her~~ own free will.

Geoffrey Combs
Notary Public for <u>Kentucky</u> _____ (state)

My Commission Expires: <u>March 14, 19--</u>

VOCABULARY

Directions: Can you find the definition for each of the following terms used in Chapter 14?

20/10 Rule	bankrupt
involuntary bankruptcy	voluntary bankruptcy
proportional share	Chapter 7 bankruptcy
Chapter 13 bankruptcy	exempted item
reaffirmation	overextension
free and clear	discharged

1. Legally insolvent—not capable of paying bills.

2. A plan designed to prevent credit problems, which allows 20 percent of yearly take-home pay or 10 percent of monthly take-home pay to be used for paying off charge account debts.

3. A percentage of the bankrupt's total assets received by a creditor, based on how much is owed that creditor in proportion to the bankrupt's total debts.

4. A type of bankruptcy in which creditors file a petition with the court asking the court to declare a debtor bankrupt.

5. A type of bankruptcy in which the debtor files a petition with the court asking to be declared bankrupt.

6. A value or possession in which the debtor is allowed to retain a certain equity because that item is considered necessary to the debtor's fresh start.

7. A type of bankruptcy proceeding known as straight bankruptcy.

8. A type of bankruptcy that is often called the wage earner's plan.

9. Agreement to pay back a debt to a creditor after the debtor has been declared bankrupt and the debt has been discharged.

10. The use of more credit than can be paid back comfortably with income.

11. A debt that is excused by the court and, by judgment of bankruptcy, no longer has to be paid by the debtor.

12. A phrase that describes an item having no debt, loan, or other credit outstanding against it.

ITEMS FOR DISCUSSION

1. List the four commonly used plans for solving and preventing credit problems.

2. Explain the 20/10 Rule.

3. Where can you find out about the not-for-profit credit-counseling services in your local area?

4. What is the purpose of bankruptcy?

5. What are the two basic types of bankruptcy (one is initiated by creditors, the other by debtors)?

6. Which types of family obligations are not discharged by bankruptcy?

7. List six exempted items under Chapter 7 bankruptcy. Are the exemption amounts for these items doubled for married persons?

8. Once declared bankrupt, how long before you can again file bankruptcy (straight bankruptcy)? How long does a bankruptcy judgment remain on your credit records?

9. How does Chapter 13 bankruptcy differ from Chapter 7?

10. Why is it a good idea to seek advice from an attorney before filing bankruptcy?

11. How long does a debtor have to change his or her mind about reaffirmation of a debt?

12. List the four most common reasons for claiming bankruptcy.

13. List four advantages and five disadvantages of filing bankruptcy.

14. Which types of income are not subject to bankruptcy?

15. Why do creditors object to the liberal bankruptcy laws that were put into effect in 1979?

APPLICATIONS

1. Explain the difference between involuntary and voluntary bankruptcy. Why is involuntary bankruptcy uncommon?

2. Which types of debts are not discharged by bankruptcy? Why are these types of debts not eliminated so that the debtor can start fresh?

3. Which would seem to be the most favorable to the average consumer who feels responsibility for debts but just cannot go on any longer—Chapter 7 or Chapter 13 bankruptcy?

4. There is very little incentive for debtors to reaffirm debts after being declared bankrupt. Why would a debtor wish to repay a loan after the court has declared it is not necessary?

CASE PROBLEMS AND ACTIVITIES

1. Read the classified section of your newspaper continuously for one week, checking for bankruptcy notices. Cut all you can find from the legal notices section and answer these questions:

   (a) How many total bankruptcies were filed in a seven-day period?

   (b) How many of the bankruptcies were joint bankruptcies (husband and wife)?

   (c) What is the lowest amount of debt claimed?

   (d) What is the highest amount of debt claimed?

   (e) How many of those filing represented themselves? How many used an attorney?

   (f) What was the lowest amount of property claimed as exempt?

   (g) What was the highest amount of property claimed as exempt?

2. Search through the Yellow Pages of the telephone book and through business directories and make a list of the following:

   (a) Not-for-profit credit-counseling services

   (b) Commercial debt-adjustment firms

   (c) Attorneys specializing in bankruptcy

   (d) Classes or other credit-counseling services provided in the community, either free or for a fee.

3. Look up the original Bankruptcy Act in a reference book and write a report covering the following:

   (a) Provisions of the law in outline form

   (b) Exemptions allowed and types of income excluded

   (c) Procedures or steps involved

4. Look up the Bankruptcy Reform Act of 1978 and answer these questions:

   (a) How has the law changed to help consumers?

   (b) What are the new provisions not found in the old bankruptcy laws regarding exemptions and income that is excluded?

5. Does the state in which you live require you to use a state exemption schedule rather than the federal schedule?

6. Is it possible in your local area to file bankruptcy without the aid of an attorney? What is the procedure for filing a bankruptcy, with or without an attorney? (You can find out by calling your local legal aid society or by asking at a courthouse.)

UNIT FOUR
CONSUMER RIGHTS AND RESPONSIBILITIES

CHAPTER 15

ROLE OF THE CONSUMER IN THE MARKETPLACE

CHAPTER OBJECTIVES

After studying this chapter and completing the activities, you will be able to:

1. Understand the basic components of a market economy and how they create balance in a free enterprise society.
2. Understand and describe deceptive practices used to defraud consumers.
3. Use safeguards in buying, understand rights and responsibilities, and resolve problems.

CHARACTERISTICS OF THE MARKETPLACE

All countries operate by means of some type of economic system. Citizens within each country are a vital part of that system. When citizens understand their role in the marketplace, they benefit themselves and the total economic system as well.

We live in a free enterprise system.

The United States economy is a free enterprise system. We will briefly explore the basic characteristics of free enterprise and how this system affects personal financial management in this chapter. In Unit Six, "Consumer Economics," we will cover the free enterprise system in detail.

Mixed Economy

In the United States we have a *mixed economy*, which means that both producers and consumers are active and vital parts of the system.

Producers are citizens and businesses that make products and services available for others to purchase. *Consumers* are citizens and businesses that purchase and use the goods and services produced for sale. Everyone is a consumer; that is, everyone must consume at least some goods and services produced by others in order to live. Hermits—people who live in seclusion and rely on themselves for food, clothing, and shelter—are rare in our society. Many consumers are also producers; i.e., they provide goods and services for others to consume.

Everyone is a consumer.

Supply and Demand

Supply and demand are the key factors that determine what is produced, in what quantity it is produced, and at what price it is sold. *Supply* is the quantity of goods and services that producers are willing and able to manufacture. *Demand* is the willingness and ability of consumers to purchase goods and services at certain prices.

Generally if consumers demand a product (are willing and able to buy at a certain price), producers will make it. The system works in this manner: Increased demand pushes up the price of the product. The high price brings large profits to the producers. High profits attract more producers and often cause current producers to make more of the product; so the supply increases. More supply pushes the price back down. The principle

As supply increases, price decreases.

is simple—the more scarce an item is, the more expensive it becomes. The supply and demand process continues indefinitely until the market for the product attains equilibrium.

Consumer Power

Consumers have the ultimate power in a supply and demand economy; indeed, consumers determine what is produced and at what price. When consumers purchase a good or service, they are casting dollar votes for continued production of that good or service. If consumers refuse to buy a good or service, the price will drop. If the product or service still does not sell, it will no longer be produced. Producers will only supply those goods and services that people want and are able to buy. Thus, in our free enterprise system, consumers actually exercise the power to determine what will be produced and at what price. There are, of course, exceptions to this rule, as in any economy; but generally the consumer plays a vital role in the marketplace through decisions to purchase or not to purchase goods and services.

Consumers have the ultimate power.

Creating Demand

Producers also have power in a supply and demand economy because they can employ various techniques to affect consumer buying decisions. Advertising is perhaps the method most commonly used to induce consumers to want products. ***Advertising*** is the communication of product information through mass media to the consumer for the purpose of increasing the demand for a good or service. It can be informative and give important facts about quality goods and services. Sometimes, however, advertising can be false and misleading and, unfortunately, damaging to the consumer's personal financial situation. In order to manage your personal finances successfully, you must learn to understand our economic system and become a careful consumer.

Advertising creates demand.

BALANCE IN A FREE ENTERPRISE SYSTEM

Three basic components are necessary for a free enterprise economy to function smoothly. Competition, income distribution, and informed consumers work together to balance this type of economic system. If one of these components is missing or is not functioning properly, the system begins to fail. We see high prices when supply is high, inflation, and other by-products of an inefficient economy.

Competition

In order for prices to be based on supply and demand, ***competition*** is necessary. Competition occurs when there is more than one producer or supplier of a good or service. All producers must compete with each other to sell the same or similar products. When there is only one producer or supplier, a monopoly exists, and low-quality goods and services and high prices often result. When many producers compete to sell a product to the consumer, high-quality goods and services and low prices usually result.

Price fixing eliminates competition.

It is not enough, however, that competition simply exist. To be truly effective in maintaining the supply and demand system, competition must also be pure—without price fixing or other controls. ***Price fixing*** occurs when producers who are supposed to be competitors conspire to set the same prices on the same goods or services. There is no real competition because prices have been predetermined, or fixed. Price fixing violates the principles of a free enterprise system, and it is illegal. Producers found guilty of price fixing are subject to fines and imprisonment.

Income Distribution

All persons have purchasing power.

In a free market society, all consumers must have purchasing power. To have ***purchasing power*** is to have money with which to buy goods and services. In our country, most all persons have purchasing power through income distribution; for instance workers have income from their jobs. Those persons who cannot work may receive ***transfer payments*** from the government—money collected from employers and workers, which is then distributed to those who do not work. Transfer payments may be in the form of social security benefits, veterans benefits, welfare and child assistance programs, or disability payments. Children and minors have purchasing power through their parents. Basically, in this country, all persons have the ability to purchase goods and services. Income distribution gives balance in a free enterprise system where it is necessary for all citizens to participate in the marketplace.

Informed Consumers

Consumers must be informed.

The final component of a free enterprise system is informed consumers who know their rights and responsibilities in the marketplace. When consumers make wise decisions, the system works to weed out inferior products and keep prices at acceptable levels. When consumers do not act in a responsible manner, prices increase. The free enterprise triangle gains strength when each of the three parts works to its fullest potential. When one component breaks down, the others go out of control. Figure 15-1 illustrates the balance of basic components in a free enterprise system.

FIGURE 15-1
Free Enterprise
System

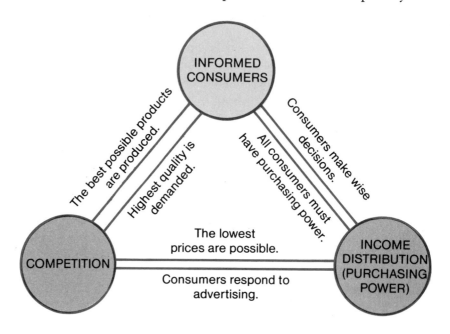

FRAUDULENT AND DECEPTIVE MARKETING PRACTICES

The marketplace can be deceptive.

The marketplace is full of deceptive and misleading ways for suppliers to increase demand for a product—ways to induce consumers to buy goods and services of inferior quality, or things they do not really need or want. Described in the following pages are a number of commonly reported fraudulent and deceptive marketing practices that all consumers should be aware of in order to protect themselves and their finances. In many cases, little can be done once the consumer has been duped into making a purchase. Dishonest sellers quickly disappear or deny wrongdoing. Therefore, consumers must prepare themselves to recognize a potential fraud before they become a victim. Prevention is still the best safeguard against financial misfortune.

Bait and Switch

Consumers are baited by spectacular bargains.

The *bait and switch* technique is an insincere offer by a merchant who baits the buyer into the store by advertising an exciting bargain. But when the customer arrives to purchase the advertised product, the merchant then switches the customer's interest to a more expensive product that will yield a higher profit. In some cases the bait is a poor-quality product and is placed next to high-quality merchandise. The poor-quality bait is advertised to be of better quality than it is, giving the customer the idea that he or she is really getting a bargain. In other cases, when customers ask for the bait merchandise, they are told that it has been sold, but that comparable merchandise is available—for more money. Or a crafty salesperson may try to convince the customer that he or she really does not want the bait item, but rather a similar product of better quality—for more money. The bait and switch technique is a crafty plan to get customers into a store to sell them more expensive merchandise than they had planned to buy.

The baited item is switched to a more expensive model.

A wise consumer knows products and prices. When a product is advertised at a special price, the consumer knows its quality and regular price. Product knowledge is gained through shopping around before making major purchases. In this way, consumers can protect themselves against the bait and switch technique.

Referral Sales

A *referral sale* means that the seller promises a money rebate, prize, or discount if the buyer can provide names of friends and acquaintances who are prospective customers. Such promises are illegal when actual payment of the rebate, prize, or discount is not made. Delaying payment pending a sale, presentation, or other event is also illegal.

In any event, referral sales techniques provide the seller with names, addresses, and telephone numbers of prospects. People on the referral list are expected to purchase the product because their friend gave the seller their names. Persons who volunteer the names and addresses of friends cannot expect appreciation from the friends who are later harassed by companies or organizations to purchase merchandise they do not want in order to help others win a prize or receive a discount or rebate. Consumers should resist providing sellers with the names and addresses of their friends and acquaintances. The end of a friendship is a high price to pay for a discount.

Do not give names and addresses of friends.

Fake Sales

Probably the most common of all consumer frauds is the *fake sale*. A merchant advertises a big sale, but items are at regular price, or the price tags are disguised to show a price reduction when there actually is none. Often prices are increased just prior to the sale, and price tags are altered to show the so-called markdowns. The only way consumers can protect themselves from fake sales is to know products and prices and to plan

Super savings may be
no savings at all.

purchases. Just because a flashy sign shouts "SUPER SAVINGS" does not mean that there are price reductions. Advertising campaigns, newspaper ads, and window signs may announce a big sale. Only a wise consumer is able to distinguish a real bargain from a fake sale.

Lo-balling

Many repair businesses engage in the deceptive practice of lo-balling. *Lo-balling* is advertising a repair service special at an unusually low price to lure customers, then attempting to persuade the consumers that additional services are needed. For example, when an appliance or implement is dismantled, other necessary repairs are discovered. The consumer is offered a special or regular rate for the additional repairs, and if the offer is refused, an extra fee is charged for reassembly.

Additional "needed
repairs" are found.

Another form of lo-balling is applying pressure, either bluntly or subtly, to convince an automobile owner that additional work is necessary for the safe maintenance of his or her car. For example, a repair shop may offer a special on brake relining. But when the brakes are inspected, several other necessary repairs are discovered. The customer may wind up with a front-end alignment, wheel balancing, and other repairs that are not really as urgent as the car owner is led to believe.

Consumers can protect themselves against this type of lo-balling by stipulating that they want no repairs other than those agreed upon. Any other than the specified repair must have authorization on receipt of an estimate by telephone or in writing. Unauthorized work should not be paid for. Before having additional work done, the consumer should get a second opinion. The matter should be checked with a spouse, a friend in the automobile business, or with someone who can offer an expert opinion. Consumers should make it clear that no extra services or repairs beyond those advertised will be paid for without prior consent.

Get a second opinion.

Pyramid Sales

Multilevel sales, called *pyramid sales*, are selling schemes, illegal in many states, in which sellers are promised a lot of money quickly and with little effort for selling a product. A cash investment of some kind is usually required. The pyramid consists of managers or dealers at the top and a lot of middle and lower workers arranging parties, recruiting new salespersons, and selling products to friends and acquaintances. Having a lot of people selling products to their friends allows a manager to make big profits with little effort. However, the consumer finds it very difficult

Pyramid sales mean
selling to your friends.

to make a profit or recover the initial cash investment because friends are unwilling to buy the product or service.

No way to lose—or is there?

Pyramid sales are often begun with a meeting in which a fast-talking and enthusiastic person convinces a group of people that they can make a fortune. They cannot lose; everyone can make it big! Unfortunately the product is often not of high quality or even comparable quality to the same or similar products sold through regular retail outlets. In a relatively short time, there is neither profit nor sales because people will not buy the product more than once. Only persons at the top of the pyramid can expect to win. The remainder, those persons at the bottom of the pyramid, are expected to continue mushrooming sales at an increasing pace. Increasing sales is not possible because the market is saturated, and sellers run out of friends who will buy the product.

Pigeon Drop

The term *pigeon drop* refers to any method used by experienced con artists to convince vulnerable people to invest in phony deposits, swampland real estate, or other swindles. People are said to be vulnerable when they are open to attack and easy to convince or persuade.

Vulnerable people fall for swindles.

The pigeon is the unsuspecting consumer. People who have few defenses or little knowledge of such scams, but do have a source of money, are most often chosen. For example, older people on fixed incomes become the targets of fast-talking "financial experts." Older people may be asked to deposit their savings in an investment fund. These funds are then to be loaned out at high interest rates. Monthly payments are promised the pigeon for the use of his or her money. In some cases the pigeon is dropped (defrauded) immediately, and the trusted adviser disappears with the money. In other cases the swindler maintains an outwardly healthy business and pays dividends to the pigeon until it is no longer advantageous to do so. Then the swindler disappears with the investments. By maintaining a supposedly legitimate business for a period of time, the swindler can gain additional victims—friends eager to get in on the deal at the recommendation of the original pigeon. New victims are also dropped.

They disappear with the investments.

The best protection against this type of swindle is the local Better Business Bureau. The Bureau is equipped to investigate questionable schemes, so-called investment experts, and unsound business firms. Consumers should insist upon credentials, prospectuses, and proof of past dealings. Trust in and trade with only ethical and established firms. Deposit your money in banks and savings and loan associations that are insured by the government.

Deal with a reputable business.

Fraudulent Representation

The name may be fraudulent.

Telephone or door-to-door sales made by persons who claim to represent well-known and reputable companies is a recent new type of swindle. Consumers buy products or services, then learn that they have been sold rebuilt, stolen, or inferior merchandise with the reputable name on it. In some cases the product or service purchased is worthless or unusable. One such scam is the sale of discount coupons to be used in numerous restaurants and businesses. The coupons sound like a wise purchase because for a very reasonable price the buyer can save hundreds of dollars. But when the coupons are presented for a discount or free merchandise, the merchant has not authorized the coupon.

Before buying a service or product from a representative claiming to represent a major company, it is smart to check with the company. One phone call can save a lot of money. Don't feel compelled to buy a product when it is demonstrated. The local Better Business Bureau is informed of questionable practices reported on the same salespeople.

Health and Medical Product Frauds

Ads claiming amazing results should be questioned.

A common type of swindle involves deceptive advertising for expensive "miracle" pills, creams, and devices to enhance the consumer's health and beauty. Advertisements promise that these products can do everything, from causing hair to grow on a bald head to causing a person to lose ten pounds a week. The advertisements are designed to appeal to the typical consumer's desire to be healthy and attractive with little or no effort. Usually deceptive health and medical advertisements carry endorsements and pictures of people who have found success using the product. Magazines, newspapers, and flashy tabloids often carry these advertisements. The manufacturers ask that you mail a sum of money to a post office address to receive one of the miracle devices or a quantity of pills or cream. Many times the money is accepted, but the product is not mailed

"Miracle" products often are totally ineffective.

to the consumer. In most cases, any product received may be totally ineffective. Pills, creams, and similar products, when analyzed, may actually be sugar or an over-the-counter medication readily available for a much lower price in local stores.

THE RESPONSIBLE CONSUMER

Knowing of the existence of various deceptive marketing tactics is the first step in consumer responsibility. To keep the economic system running efficiently and to manage your personal finances successfully, you also need to understand how to protect yourself from becoming the victim of these fraudulent and deceptive practices. Prevention is the best protection; after you once have been swindled, it is difficult to undo the financial damage you have suffered. In order to protect yourself, you can learn to identify deceptive practices, use safeguards when buying, understand your rights and responsibilities, and seek redress when necessary.

Identify Deceptive Practices

When any of the following claims are made, they should serve as warnings of possible deception. Warning signals include claims or offers made through advertising or by salespersons; for example,

Something for nothing usually has a price.

1. Something can be obtained for free.
2. You will receive a free gift for an early reply.
3. You or your home has been specially selected.
4. High earnings can be made with no experience or little effort.
5. An advertising survey or questionnaire is being taken.
6. A no-obligation demonstration is offered.
7. You must decide immediately or lose the golden opportunity.
8. An incredibly low price is offered for a high-quality product.

Use Safeguards When Buying

The following list includes several recommendations to help you make wise buying decisions:

List prices are the usual prices.

1. Be aware of regular or "list" prices of common items. Terms often used in advertising, such as *manufacturer's list price* and *suggested retail price*, and phrases such as "comparable value," "very important value," or "value $40, you pay only $35," attract your attention, but prices actually may not be reduced.
2. Shop at several stores. Comparative shopping is comparing quality, price, and guarantees for the same products at several different stores.
3. Understand sale terminology. *Sale* means that certain goods are offered at certain prices, but not necessarily at reduced prices. *Clearance* means that the merchant wants to clear out all the advertised merchandise, but not necessarily at a reduced price. *Liquidation* means that the merchant wants to sell immediately to turn the inventory into cash; again, prices may not be reduced.
4. Avoid impulse buying. Follow a list.

Avoid buying during times of stress.

5. Do not make major purchases during periods of emotional stress—at the end of a crisis, during a time of loneliness or frustration, or at any time when your judgment is impaired.

6. Compute unit prices. ***Unit pricing*** is the determination of the cost per unit of items sold in quantity. The selling price is reduced to the lowest unit price. For example, to compare the price of a 15-ounce box with the price of a 24-ounce box, divide the price of each box by the number of ounces in each box. The result is the price per ounce of each box. The lowest unit price for products of comparable quality is the best buy. Figure 15-2 shows unit price computations.

FIGURE 15-2
Unit Pricing

Which is the better buy?

   A. 24 ounces for $2.59 or 15 ounces for $1.89?

      $2.59 ÷ 24 = 10.8¢ per ounce
      $1.89 ÷ 15 = 12.6¢ per ounce

   B. 3/89¢ or 6/$1.99?

      $ .89 ÷ 3 = 29.7¢ each
      $1.99 ÷ 6 = 33.2¢ each

To determine unit pricing, divide the price by the number of ounces or units. This gives you a price per unit to compare to another price per unit.

7. Read labels. Know ingredients.
8. Check containers and packages carefully to see that they have not been opened or damaged. Report any suspicious packaging defaults to the store manager.

Ask questions to understand your rights.

9. Read and understand contracts and agreements before signing.
10. Check the total cost of an item, including delivery charges, finance fees, and other add-on costs.
11. Ask for references from representatives of companies to be sure they really do represent the company. Call the company to check.
12. Patronize businesses that have good reputations and those at which you are a well-known customer.
13. Check the validity of certifications and endorsements. Use your local Better Business Bureau.
14. Always wait at least 24 hours before making a major purchase. Be sure the purchase is not made on impulse and that you were not coerced into wanting the item.

Understand Your Rights and Responsibilities

Consumers who take precautions avoid many errors and later problems with their agreements and purchases. You are responsible for seeking information and advice to become knowledgeable of products

Know your responsibilities as a consumer.

and services before you buy. To protect yourself, you should observe the following:

1. Be familiar with sources of information on goods and services, such as *Consumer Reports*, local agencies, etc.
2. Read warranties and guarantees; ask questions so that you can fully understand performance claims. Get written guarantees and warranties whenever possible.
3. Read and understand care instructions before using a product.
4. Analyze advertisements about products before buying.
5. Insist upon enforcement of consumer protection laws—know how to get consumer redress.
6. Inform appropriate consumer protection agencies of fraudulent and unsafe performances of products and services. Do not hesitate to make your dissatisfactions known so that others may be helped, and the product or service improved.
7. Suggest, support, and be aware of consumer legislation.
8. Report wants, likes, and dislikes as well as suggested improvements and complaints to dealers and manufacturers.

State your likes and dislikes.

Seek Redress

When you have a complaint or need to solve a problem about a product or service, you have several consumer redress alternatives. *Consumer redress* is getting the action needed to resolve a problem with a product or service. Here are some suggestions for filing a complaint and obtaining adjustments for problems.

Complain first in writing to the person or company selling the product. Be specific about the problem. Produce evidence of the problem. Retain all warranties, sales slips, receipts, etc. Send photocopies of necessary information to explain and support your position. Use the firm approach; say that you are dissatisfied and why. Indicate the type of adjustment desired—refund, repair, replacement, or other action.

Use the firm approach.

If the seller refuses to make an adjustment, then write to the manufacturer or distributor and state your complaint. Indicate that you previously wrote to the original seller of the product. Be specific. Enclose a copy of your letter of complaint to the company that sold you the product or service. Send photocopies of evidence, such as sales slips, warranties, receipts, or anything else that will help you support your position. Use the firm approach and state what type of adjustment you want. Specify a reasonable time limit to resolve the problem.

Give a time limit to resolve the problem.

If the desired adjustment is still not made, file a complaint with the appropriate government agency for consumer protection. There may be more than one private or public agency to assist you in solving the problem.

Seek legal recourse when advisable. For claims of less than $1,000, small-claims court offers a much faster and less expensive process. Some states may have lower dollar limits for small-claims, but still have very effective small-claims court procedures. Because attorneys are not required for filing in a small-claims court, costs are lower. All that is required is payment of a small filing fee and appearance on the assigned court date. Small-claims courts are discussed in detail in Chapter 17.

In some cases, you may receive a judgment in your favor if a supplier has violated the federal Consumer Protection Act or a state law. You could be awarded attorneys' fees, court costs, minimum damages of $200, and punitive damages. An attorney could advise you of your chances of such a judgment. Class action suits filed on behalf of a number of consumers who have the same complaint generally take many years to settle.

VOCABULARY

Directions: Can you find the definition for each of the following terms used in Chapter 15?

mixed economy	producers
consumers	supply
demand	advertising
competition	price fixing
purchasing power	transfer payments
bait and switch	referral sale
fake sale	lo-balling
pyramid sales	pigeon drop
consumer redress	unit pricing

1. The action needed for a consumer to resolve a problem with a product or service.

2. Reducing the cost of a product to the per-unit price so it can be compared to prices of other sizes or products.

3. Deceptive marketing practice whereby consumers are supposed to get others to sell to their friends.

4. A fraudulent practice whereby con artists convince people to invest in phony deals.

5. Advertising certain repairs at unusually low prices, then urging additional repairs and more costs upon the consumer.

6. An advertised ''big sale'' that really offers merchandise at regular prices.

7. A deceptive practice whereby the seller promises money, prizes, or discounts if the buyer provides names of friends.

8. A technique in which an item is offered for sale, but customers are urged to buy a similar item at a higher price.

9. Money given to citizens that was collected from other citizens.

10. Having money with which to buy goods and services.

11. Occurs when more than one producer or supplier of a good or service exists, and each tries to get the majority of consumers to buy its product.

12. A method of communicating information to the consumer to sell goods and services.

13. Willingness and ability of consumers to purchase goods and services at certain prices.

14. The quantity of goods and services that producers are willing and able to manufacture.

15. An economic system in which both producers and consumers play an active and vital role.

16. Citizens and businesses that purchase and use goods and services.

17. Citizens and businesses that make products and services available for others to purchase.

18. Occurs when producers get together and set prices, eliminating competition.

ITEMS FOR DISCUSSION

1. Explain what is meant by this statement: Everyone is a consumer.

2. As the supply of a product increases, what happens to the price?

3. How do consumers have the power to determine what is produced and at what price?

4. What are the three basic components that provide balance in a free enterprise system?

5. How can the consumer be protected from bait and switch tactics?

6. What can you do to prevent lo-balling?

7. Con artists prey on vulnerable people. What is meant by the term *vulnerable*?

8. List five warning signals that alert consumers to the possibility of deceptive marketing practices.

9. What are some safeguards to use when buying products and services?

10. List four ways you, as a responsible consumer, can protect yourself in the marketplace.

11. What procedures should you follow to seek a solution to a problem with a product or service?

12. Why should you consider a small claims court to resolve a consumer complaint?

APPLICATIONS

1. What is the purpose of advertising?

2. Watch one hour of television in the early evening (between 7:00 and 8:00 P.M. is best) and record the number and types of commercials. What do the advertisements tell you about goods and services? Make a chart on a piece of paper, listing each commercial and describing it as shown in the following example:

TIME OF COMMERCIAL	PRODUCT ADVERTISED	LENGTH OF COMMERCIAL	PRODUCT INFORMATION FEATURED
7:08 P.M.	Toothpaste (NewBrite)	30 seconds	New flavor; old also available

3. There are three basic components that create balance in a free enterprise system: competition, income distribution (purchasing power), and informed consumers. What happens when competition is missing? purchasing power? informed consumers?

4. Search through magazines, newspapers, and other sources for advertisements offering the following:

(a) Something for nothing

(b) Bonus for early reply

    (c) Offers of gifts and prizes

    (d) Other deceptive practices

Collect the advertisements and bring them to class.

CASE PROBLEMS AND ACTIVITIES

1. Compute the following unit prices (lowest units to compare values):

    (a) 3/98¢

    (b) 4/$1.00

    (c) 24 oz./$1.98

    (d) 2 lbs./$2.19

    (e) 3 lbs. 6 oz./$6.99

    (f) 6/89¢

    (g) 3/$1.49

2. Copy the ingredients from the labels of the following products:

    (a) Aspirin

    (b) Breakfast cereal

    (c) Liquid cleaning product

    (d) Poisonous substance

Are there any warnings on any of the above labels? What type of precautions are suggested?

3. Copy the words written on a warranty or guarantee for a household product that your family has purchased. What does the manufacturer agree to do? What exceptions are stated? What actions does the manufacturer state it will not agree to do?

4. Read through a copy of *Consumer Reports* in your library and answer the following questions:

    (a) Who publishes the magazine?

    (b) Who advertises in the magazine?

    (c) In one issue, how many different types of products are tested and compared for quality?

    (d) Write a short (one paragraph) summary of an article that interested you (from the issue of *Consumer Reports* that you read).

5. Assume you bought a new hair dryer at a local department store last week. Write a letter of complaint because the hair dryer makes a strange rattling noise. Give factual information concerning the dryer and request a refund or other adjustment.

CHAPTER 16

CONSUMER PROTECTION

CHAPTER OBJECTIVES

After studying this chapter and completing the activities, you will be able to:

1. Describe the provisions of the Consumer Bill of Rights.
2. Describe the provisions of significant federal consumer legislation.
3. Identify state and national sources of consumer information and assistance.

SIGNIFICANT FEDERAL CONSUMER LEGISLATION

For many years the consumer's position in the marketplace was characterized by the phrase "buyer beware"; in other words, the consumer was given little assistance or protection against fraudulent practices. Since 1960, however, a number of major consumer-protection laws have been passed. One of the most important steps in the direction of consumer protection was the adoption of the Consumer Bill of Rights. The Consumer Bill of Rights was proposed by President Kennedy during his 1962 State of the Union Address, and later expanded by Presidents Nixon and Ford. It includes the following:

Consumer rights are outlined in the Consumer Bill of Rights.

1. The right to safety—protection against products that are hazardous to life or health.
2. The right to be informed—protection against fraudulent, deceitful, or grossly misleading practices and assurance of receiving facts necessary to make informed choices.

263

3. The right to choose—access to a variety of quality products and services offered at competitive prices.
4. The right to be heard—assurance of representation of consumer interests in formulating government policy and of fair and prompt treatment in enforcement of the laws.
5. The right to redress or remedy—assurance that buyers have ways to register their dissatisfaction and to have complaints heard.
6. The right to consumer education—assurance that consumers have necessary assistance to plan and use their resources to their maximum potential.

Specific laws have been passed to ensure that consumers get quality products and services for their hard-earned dollars. The most significant consumer laws enacted by Congress throughout our history are described in the following pages.

Food, Drug, and Cosmetic Act of 1938

The FDA enforces the Food, Drug, and Cosmetic Act of 1938.

The Food, Drug, and Cosmetic Act of 1938 requires that foods be safe, pure, and wholesome; that drugs and medical devices be safe and effective; and that cosmetics be safe. The law also provides that these products be truthfully labeled. The weight or volume of the contents and name and address of the manufacturer must be on the label. The use of containers that are misleading because of size, thickness, or false bottoms is prohibited.

Wool Products Labeling Act of 1940

Wool products must
have proper labels.

Amended in 1965, the Wool Products Labeling Act of 1940 requires proper labeling of the amount and kind of wool contained in all products made of wool, except carpeting and upholstery. Percentages of new, reused, or reprocessed wool and other fibers, care of the product, and the identity of the manufacturer must be shown on the labels of products containing 5 percent or more wool.

Flammable Fabrics Act of 1953

Children's clothing
must be flame resistant.

Amended in 1967, the Flammable Fabrics Act enabled the Consumer Product Safety Commission to set flammability standards for clothing, children's sleepwear, carpets, rugs, and mattresses. Interstate commerce of all wearing apparel made of easily ignited material is prohibited. The flammability standard for sleepwear requires that the garment will not catch fire when exposed to a match or small fire. The flame retardant finish must last for 50 washings and dryings. Proper care instructions to protect sleepwear from agents or treatments known to cause deterioration of the flame retardant finish must be on all labels.

Kefauver-Harris Drug Amendment of 1962

Brand names are more
expensive than generic
products.

As a result of the Kefauver-Harris Drug Amendment of 1962, drug manufacturers are required to file with the Food and Drug Administration (FDA) notices of all new drugs. New drugs must be tested for safety and effectiveness before being sold to consumers. This amendment also provides for the manufacture and sale of generic drugs. *Generic* is a general term used for a product having the same qualities or contents as a well-known brand-name product. A generic drug is often less expensive because it carries no trademark registration. National brand names are usually more expensive than generic products because of the added costs of advertising and marketing.

National Traffic and Motor Vehicle Safety Act of 1966

The National Traffic and Motor Vehicle Safety Act of 1966 established national safety standards for automobiles and for new and used tires. The National Highway Traffic Safety Administration of the Department of Transportation is charged with supporting and enforcing provisions of the act. Increasing public awareness of the need for safety devices, testing for safety, and inspecting vehicles for proper safety equipment are also responsibilities of the National Highway Traffic Safety Administration.

Hazardous Substances Labeling Act of 1960; Child Protection and Toy Safety Act of 1969

Labels must warn of potential dangers.

The Hazardous Substances Labeling Act, passed in 1960, requires that warning labels appear on all household products that are potentially dangerous to the consumer. As a further precaution against unfortunate accidents, the Child Protection and Toy Safety Act was passed in 1969, banning from interstate commerce those household products that are so dangerous that warning labels do not provide sufficient safeguards. This act also bans the sale of toys and children's articles containing hazardous substances and those that pose electrical, mechanical, or thermal dangers. Under either law, the FDA has the power to inspect and remove such products from the marketplace. In most cases, hazardous products are recalled. A *recall* is a procedure whereby the manufacturer stops production of a product and refunds the purchase price of items already sold. Sometimes a recalled product can be repaired so that it is no longer hazardous; it can then be returned to the consumer.

Permanent Care Labeling Rule

Read the label to know what care is needed for a garment.

Effective since 1972, the care labeling rule specifies that clothing and fabrics must be labeled permanently with laundering and care instructions. Labels must give instructions sufficient to maintain a garment's original character. By carefully reading the labels on garments you purchase, you can estimate how much time or money will be required to maintain the garment. Care labels must stay attached and be easy to read for the life of the garment.

SOURCES OF CONSUMER PROTECTION

When you need assistance with a consumer problem, you may not be sure where to look. There are numerous sources available to you. Your first choice may not be the right one, but by asking, you will be referred to the appropriate agency of the federal or state government, or to a specific private organization. The following description of federal consumer agencies available might help you select the appropriate source of information.

Federal Consumer Agencies

Numerous government agencies on the federal level provide information of interest to consumers. Some of these agencies handle consumer

Some agencies handle complaints; others do not.

complaints, and others direct complaints to agencies or sources that address consumer issues. Some well-known federal agencies are described in the following paragraphs.

Department of Agriculture. Within the Department of Agriculture, there are a number of agencies that exist to meet various consumer needs. The *Agricultural Marketing Service* inspects food to ensure wholesomeness and truthful labeling, develops official grade standards, and provides grading services. For example, eggs must meet specific standards to be classified as extra large, jumbo, large, medium, or small. The *Food and Nutrition Service* provides food assistance programs, such as the food stamp and school lunch programs, and information on diets, nutrition, and menu preparation. The *Cooperative Extension Services* provides consumer education materials (pamphlets and booklets) on such topics as budgeting, money management, food preparation and storage, gardening, credit counseling, and many more. Most of the materials are free.

Assistance is provided for school lunch programs.

Department of Commerce. The *National Bureau of Standards* is an agency within the Department of Commerce that sets measurement, product, and safety standards. All food packages must indicate whether the weight shown includes the packaging or is a *net weight*—the weight of the product without the container or package.

Department of Health and Human Services. Two of the many agencies within the Department of Health and Human Services are the Food and Drug Administration and the Office of Consumers Affairs. The *Food and Drug Administration* (FDA) is charged with enforcing laws and regulations preventing distribution of mislabeled foods, drugs, cosmetics, and medical devices. The FDA requires testing and approval of all new drugs; conducts testing of new and existing products for health and safety standards; provides standards and guidelines for poisonous substances; controls the standards for identification, quality, and fill of food containers; establishes guidelines for labels and proper identification of product contents, ingredients, nutrients, and directions for use; investigates complaints; conducts research; and issues reports, guidelines, and warnings about substances its researchers find to be dangerous or potentially hazardous to health.

All new drugs are tested before they enter the marketplace.

The *Office of Consumer Affairs* represents consumer interests in federal agency proceedings, develops consumer information materials, and assists other agencies in responding to consumer complaints. Specific consumer complaints received by the Office of Consumer Affairs are referred to the appropriate government and private agencies for further assistance.

Federal Communications Commission. The *Federal Communications Commission* (FCC) regulates radio and television broadcasting and interstate telephone and telegraph companies. In addition, the FCC establishes communications standards for and controls the quality of transmissions from radio stations, television networks, cable television networks, CB (citizens band) and ham radios, and any other transmissions through public airspace. What can or cannot be said or done over the air is regulated by the FCC. An advertisement may be discontinued or modified if the FCC determines that it is false or misleading.

Telephone and telegraph lines are controlled by the FCC.

Federal Trade Commission. The *Federal Trade Commission* (FTC) is concerned with protecting consumers from unfair methods of competition, false or deceptive advertising, deceptive product labeling, inaccurate or obsolete information on credit reports, and disclosure of the true cost of credit. Anyone can file a complaint with the FTC by sending a letter, accompanied by as much supporting evidence as possible.

Anyone can file a complaint by sending a letter.

United States Postal Service. The United States Postal Service operates the *Postal Inspection Service* to deal with the consumer problems pertaining to illegal use of the mails. The Postal Inspection Service enforces postal laws, protecting consumers from dangerous articles, contraband, fraud, and pornography. Through its Consumer Protection Program, the Postal Inspection Service resolves unsatisfactory mail-order transactions, even in cases where no fraud has occurred.

State and Local Agencies

Most states have a consumer protection agency, or the state attorney general may handle consumer affairs. Other consumer leagues and public interest research groups are also active in many states. These groups may publish newsletters, pamphlets, brochures, and handbooks on current consumer issues. A handbook published in many states addresses landlord/tenant rights and responsibilities.

There are numerous consumer research groups.

On the local level, consumers may have access to legal aid societies, newspaper and broadcast action reporters, or consumer representatives on local utility or licensing boards. Independent consumer groups focusing on specific issues, such as food prices, may operate on the local level.

The *Better Business Bureau* (BBB) functions on both state and local levels. The BBB has no legal authority, but serves as a clearinghouse of information about local businesses. Complaints against local businesses may be filed with the BBB. The merchant is given an opportunity to respond to the complaint. If the merchant does not respond to the com-

The Better Business Bureau is a clearinghouse of information.

plaint, the Better Business Bureau may advise the consumer to seek another form of redress. Information regarding the nature of complaints filed against local merchants is available upon request.

Private Organizations

Private organizations help by giving consumers advice on the purchase of various products and the performance that can be expected from these products. Two such organizations are Consumers' Research, Inc. and Consumers Union of the United States, Inc. A not-for-profit organization, Consumers' Research conducts extensive testing for quality and performance. Results of these tests are published in *Consumers' Research Magazine* along with ratings given the products tested. Also a not-for-profit organization, Consumers Union has the largest consumer testing facility in the world. Through its monthly magazine, *Consumer Reports*, Consumers Union gives test results and product ratings. To assure that all ratings are unbiased, all products tested are purchased by Consumers Union. No advertising is accepted, and no free products are accepted for testing from manufacturers. *Consumer Reports* also prints articles dealing with insurance, credit, and other items of consumer interest. An annual report of items previously published in *Consumer Reports* is also published by Consumers Union.

Products are tested and ratings are published.

Another private organization providing assistance in protecting consumer rights is the *Major Appliance Consumer Action Panel* (MACAP). MACAP is comprised of representatives of the home appliance industry and provides assistance in resolving or minimizing consumer problems in the purchase and use of home appliances.

Consumers may also seek the support of a *consumer advocate*—one who promotes or protects the causes or interests of consumers. Ralph Nader is the most well-known consumer advocate. When Ralph Nader finds, through research and investigation, that an injustice or dangerous condition exists, he pursues it in behalf of all consumers. Ralph Nader may file lawsuits against companies or organizations to force them to meet safety standards, correct inequitable situations, or properly inform of dangers in the use of their products.

A consumer advocate helps to protect consumers in the marketplace.

Many other consumer groups are active in assisting consumers in finding solutions to problems in the marketplace. Names and addresses of these groups may be obtained from sources such as Better Business Bureaus, the Consumers Federation of America, and the Consumer Information Center in Pueblo, Colorado. Information about other agencies and their purposes, consumer rights and responsibilities, and sources of consumer assistance, both governmental and nongovernmental, is available in most public libraries.

STATE AND FEDERAL NUMBERS

Many consumers are unaware of complaint-handling resources available through their own state governments. Each of the 34 states listed below maintains a toll-free 800 number for consumers to use in making inquiries or registering complaints. Some offices handle complaints on almost any subject; others specify their area of interest. Hours of operation are listed for local time zones. Figure 16-1 is a list prepared by the

Many states have toll-free numbers to call for assistance.

FIGURE 16-1
State Consumer
Toll-Free
Numbers

ALABAMA (Montgomery)
Hours: 8:00-5:00
1 800 392-5658
In state only. Advice given over the phone. Complaints must be submitted in writing for action.

ARIZONA (Phoenix)
Hours: 8:00-5:00
1 800 352-8431
In state only. Handles complaints concerning possible fraud.

ARKANSAS (Little Rock)
Hours: 8:00-5:00
1 800 482-8982
In state only. Handles complaints concerning possible fraud or false advertising and will answer general inquiries.

CALIFORNIA (Sacramento)
Hours: 8:00-5:00
1 800 952-5210
In state only. Handles complaints concerning auto repair jobs.

1 800 952-5567
In state only. Information regarding solar energy uses/insulation.

Hours: 9:00-12:00; 1:00-4:00
1 800 952-5225
In state only. Takes general complaints.

COLORADO (Denver)
Hours: 8:00-5:00
1 800 332-2071
In state only. Handles complaints concerning possible price fixing or other antitrust matters.

CONNECTICUT (Hartford)
Hours: 8:30-4:30
1 800 842-2649
In state only. Handles all types of complaints and inquiries.

FLORIDA (Tallahassee)
Hours: 7:45-4:30 (recording after hours)
1 800 342-2176
In state only. Handles most types of complaints and inquiries.

GEORGIA (Atlanta)
Hours: 8:00-5:00
1 800 282-4900
In state only. Handles general complaints and inquiries.

ILLINOIS (Chicago)
Hours: 8:30-5:00
1 800 252-8972
In state only. Handles complaints and inquiries related to state tax, senior citizens relief tax and other matters.

ILLINOIS (cont.)
1 800 252-8980
In state only. Handles complaints and inquiries on used car problems.

1 800 252-8903
In state only. Handles complaints and inquiries on public aid fraud.

INDIANA (Indianapolis)
Hours: 8:15-4:45
1 800 382-5516
In state only. Handles general consumer complaints and inquiries.

KANSAS (Topeka)
Hours: 8:00-5:00
1 800 432-2310
In state only. Handles general complaints and inquiries.

KENTUCKY (Frankfort)
Hours: 8:30-5:00
1 800 432-9257
In state only. Advice given over the phone. Will send complaint forms or refer.

LOUISANA (Baton Rouge)
Hours: 8:30-5:00
1 800 272-9868
In state only. Handles general complaints and inquiries.

MASSACHUSETTS (Boston)
Hours: 9:00-5:00
1 800 632-8026
In state only. Handles energy related complaints and concerns.

1 800 392-6066
In state only. Handles public utility complaints and inquiries.

MICHIGAN (Lansing)
Hours: 8:30-5:00
1 800 292-4204 (Bureau of Automotive Regulation) In state only. Handles auto complaints.

1 800 292-5943 (Commissioner of Insurance) In state only. Handles insurance related complaints.

1 800 292-9555 (Public Service Commission) In state only. Handles utility related complaints.

MISSISSIPPI (Jackson)
Hours: 8:00-5:00
1 800 222-7622 (Governor's Hotline)
In state only. Consumer complaints are referred.

MISSOURI (Jefferson City)
Hours: 8:15-4:45
1 800 392-8222
In state only. Handles complaints involving fraud and misrepresentation in the sale of goods.

U.S. Government and available free of charge from the Consumer Information Center, Pueblo, Colorado.

For information and help with your questions about the federal government, use the toll-free information numbers given in Figure 16-2. These numbers will allow you to contact the nearest Federal Information Center (part of the U.S. General Services Administration). You can contact a center toll free if you live in any of the cities listed in Figure 16-2, or in a state with an 800 number shown.

FIGURE 16-1
(continued)

MONTANA (Helena) Hours: 8:00-5:00 (answering service after hours) 1 800 332-2272 In state only. Refers complaints and inquiries to the proper state office.	**OHIO** (Columbus) Hours: 8:00-5:00 (recording after hours) 1 800 282-0515 In state only. Handles general complaints and inquiries.
NEVADA (Carson City) Hours: 8:00-5:00 1 800 992-0900 In state only. Operator connects consumer with state agencies. Consumer must know which agency to request.	**OKLAHOMA** (Oklahoma City) Hours: 8:00-5:00 1 800 522-8555 (Capitol Straight Line) In state only. Handles general complaints and inquiries.
NEW HAMPSHIRE (Concord) Hours: 8:00-4:00 1 800 852-3456 (Governor's Office of Citizens Services) In state only. Handles complaints and inquiries concerning energy. 1 800 852-3311 (State Council on Aging) In state only. Information about and for the elderly.	**OREGON** (Portland) Hours: 8:00-5:00 1 800 452-7813 In state only. Will link caller to appropriate state agency. **SOUTH CAROLINA** (Columbia) Hours: 8:00-5:00 1 800 992-1594 In state only. Handles general complaints and inquiries.
NEW JERSEY (Trenton) Hours: 9:00-5:00 (recording after hours) 1 800 792-8600 In state only. Refers complaints and inquiries to the proper agency.	**SOUTH DAKOTA** (Pierre) Hours: 8:00-5:00 1 800 592-1865 In state only. Tie line. Must ask for specific division.
NEW YORK (Albany) Hours: 7:30-4:30 1 800 342-3736 In state only. Handles consumer inquiries on all types of insurance coverage. Hours: 9:00-5:00 1 800 522-8707 In state only. Refers consumer inquiries on utilities to the proper public service/utility. Hours: 7:30-4:30 1 800 342-3823 In state only. Handles complaints concerning auto repairs performed within the last 90 days. Hours: 9:00-4:00 1 800 342-3722 (recording after hours) In state only. Answers inquiries about energy programs, conservation and regulations.	**TENNESSEE** (Nashville) Hours: 8:00-4:30 1 800 342-8385 In state only. Handles general complaints and inquiries. **VERMONT** (Montpelier) Hours: 8:00-4:30 1 800 642-5149 In state only. Handles general complaints and inquiries. **VIRGINIA** (Richmond) Hours: 8:30-5:00 1 800 552-9963 In state only. Handles general complaints and inquiries.
NORTH CAROLINA (Raleigh) Hours: 8:00-5:00 1 800 662-7777 In state only. Receives inquiries about insurance coverage.	**WASHINGTON** (Seattle) Hours: 1:00-5:00 1 800 552-0700 In state only. Will mail out complaint forms or make referrals.
NORTH DAKOTA (Bismark) Hours: 8:00-5:00 1 800 472-2600 In state only. Investigates allegations of consumer fraud. Hours: 8:00-5:00 1 800 472-2927 In state only. Handles general consumer complaints.	**WISCONSIN** (Madison) Hours: 8:00-4:45 1 800 362-3020 In state only. Handles general complaints and inquiries.

ALABAMA
Birmingham 205 322-8591
Mobile 205 438-1421
ALASKA
Anchorage 907 271-3650
ARIZONA
Phoenix 602 261-3313
Tucson 602 622-1511
ARKANSAS
Little Rock 501 378-6177
CALIFORNIA
Los Angeles 213 688-3800
Sacramento 916 440-3344
San Diego 714 293-6030
San Francisco 415 556-6600
San Jose 408 275-7422
Santa Ana 714 836 2386
COLORADO
Colorado Springs 303 471-9491
Denver 303 837-3602
Pueblo 303 544-9523
CONNECTICUT
Hartford 203 527-2617
New Haven 203 624-4720
FLORIDA
Fort Lauderdale 305 522-8531
Jacksonville 904 354-4756
Miami 305 350-4155
Orlando 305 422-1800
St. Petersburg 813 893-3495
Tampa 813 229-7911
West Palm Beach 305 833-7566
Northern Florida 1 800 282-8556
   (Sarasota, Manatee, Polk, Osceola, Orange, Seminole,
   and Volusia counties and north)
Southern Florida 1 800 432-6668
   (Charlotte, DeSoto, Hardee, Highlands, Okeechobee,
   Indian River and Brevard counties and south)
GEORGIA
Atlanta 404 221-6891
HAWAII
Honolulu 808 546-8620
ILLINOIS
Chicago 312 353-4242
INDIANA
Gary/Hammond 219 883-4110
Indianapolis 317 269-7373
IOWA
Des Moines 515 284-4448
Other locations 1 800 532-1556
KANSAS
Topeka 913 295-2866
Other locations 1 800 432-2934
KENTUCKY
Louisville 502 582-6261
LOUISIANA
New Orleans 504 589-6696
MARYLAND
Baltimore 301 962-4980
MASSACHUSETTS
Boston 617 223-7121
MICHIGAN
Detroit 313 226-7016
Grand Rapids 616 451-2628

MINNESOTA
Minneapolis 612 349-5333
MISSOURI
Kansas City 816 374-2466
St. Louis 314 425-4106
Other locations within area code 314 1 800 392-7711
Other locations within area codes 816 & 417 1 800 892-5808
NEBRASKA
Omaha 402 221-3353
Other locations 1 800 642-8383
NEW JERSEY
Newark 201 645-3600
Paterson/Passaic 201 523-0717
Trenton 609 396-4400
NEW MEXICO
Albuquerque 505 766-3091
Santa Fe 505 983-7743
NEW YORK
Albany 518 463-4421
Buffalo 716 846-4010
New York 212 264-4464
Rochester 716 546-5075
Syracuse 315 476-8545
NORTH CAROLINA
Charlotte 704 376-3600
OHIO
Akron 216 375-5638
Cincinnati 513 684-2801
Cleveland 216 522-4040
Columbus 614 221-1014
Dayton 513 223-7377
Toledo 419 241-3223
OKLAHOMA
Oklahoma City 405 231-4868
Tulsa 918 584-4193
OREGON
Portland 503 221-2222
PENNSYLVANIA
Allentown/Bethlehem 215 821-7785
Philadelphia 215 597-7042
Pittsburgh 412 644-3456
Scranton 717 346-7081
RHODE ISLAND
Providence 401 331-5565
TENNESSEE
Chattanooga 615 265-8231
Memphis 901 521-3285
Nashville 615 242-5056
TEXAS
Austin 512 472-5494
Dallas 214 767-8585
Fort Worth 817 334-3624
Houston 713 226-5711
San Antonio 512 224-4471
UTAH
Ogden 801 399-1347
Salt Lake City 801 524-5353
VIRGINIA
Newport News 804 244-0480
Norfolk 804 441-3101
Richmond 804 643-4928
Roanoke 703 982-8591
WASHINGTON
Seattle 206 442-0570
Tacoma 206 383-5230
WISCONSIN
Milwaukee 414 271-2273

FIGURE 16-2 Federal Toll-Free Information Numbers

CONTACTING THOSE WHO REPRESENT YOU

National elected officials include the president and the vice-president of the United States, serving four-year terms; United States senators, serving six-year terms; and the members of the United States House of Representatives, serving two-year terms. Governors of states usually are elected to four-year terms. Other state elected officials include the secretary of state, state treasurer, and state attorney general; superintendent of public instruction; labor commissioner; state senators and state representatives.

Each court (federal, state, and local) has at least one judge, and several clerks of the court to assist in filing and information gathering. County officials (elected) include the county administrator, district attorney, sheriff, and tax assessor, plus a number of commissioners. Other elected local officials include the mayor, city council members, and city manager. These officials are available at county and city office buildings and meet regularly or are available to the public by appointment. The phone book lists various officials separately by state and by county, with each department listed alphabetically.

If you desire to communicate with an elected official, there are several ways to do so:

Public officials are available for appointments, telephone calls, and correspondence.

1. In person. Appointments can be made during regular office hours as well as at meetings of government bodies, which are generally open to the public (except for executive sessions). There are opportunities to speak at almost all hearings.

2. By phone. Brief calls at reasonable hours are generally effective. Your state may have a Wide Area Telecommunications Service (WATS) line, which enables citizens to call elected officials toll free. You can leave a message, and your call will be returned. When calling Washington, D.C., remember time zone differences.

3. By wire. Personal Opinion Messages may be sent to the president, vice-president, U.S. senators and representatives, your governor, and the state legislators. The cost is $3.50 for 20 words, excluding your name and address, unless there are additional signatures. You can call 1-800-648-4100 to place a message.

You can write to elected officials.

4. By letter. An effective letter written to the appropriate representative states clearly the purpose of the letter; identifies a bill by proper name and number; refers to only one issue; and arrives while the issue is current. Give reasons for your position and avoid emotionalism. Ask for specific relief—what you want the elected official to do.

In almost all cases, your contact will be answered by an elected official. Telephone calls are generally returned within one or two working days. Letters are answered within a week or two.

VOCABULARY

Directions: Can you find the definition for each of the following terms used in Chapter 16?

generic
recall
net weight
Federal Communications
    Commission
Postal Inspection Service
consumer advocate
Agricultural Marketing Service

National Bureau of Standards
Food and Drug Administration
Office of Consumer Affairs
Federal Trade Commission
Better Business Bureau
Major Appliance Consumer
    Action Panel

1. The administrative agency that regulates radio and television broadcasting and interstate telephone and telegraph companies.

2. A local and state agency with no legal authority that is a clearinghouse of information about local businesses.

3. A general term used for a product having the same qualities or contents as a well-known brand name.

4. The procedure whereby a manufacturer stops production and refunds the purchase price of items already sold.

5. The weight of a product without the container or package.

6. An agency that inspects food to ensure wholesomeness and truthful labeling.

7. This group represents consumer interests in federal agency proceedings, develops consumer information materials, and assists with consumer complaints.

8. An agency that sets measurement, product, and safety standards for food packages.

9. An agency concerned with protecting consumers from unfair methods of competition, false or deceptive advertising, and other deceptive practices.

10. An agency charged with enforcing laws and regulations preventing distribution of mislabeled foods, drugs, cosmetics, and medical devices.

11. A division of the U.S. Postal Service that deals with consumer problems pertaining to illegal use of the mail.

12. One who promotes or seeks to protect the causes or interests of consumers.

13. A group comprised of representatives of the home appliance industry, which provides assistance in resolving and minimizing consumer problems in the purchase and use of home appliances.

ITEMS FOR DISCUSSION

1. What consumer protection action was proposed by President Kennedy in 1962?

2. List the six major items in the Consumer Bill of Rights.

3. What was the purpose of the Food, Drug, and Cosmetic Act of 1938?

4. How long must a flame retardant finish last in clothing, as provided by the Flammable Fabrics Act of 1953?

5. Who tests all new drugs that are produced for sale in the marketplace?

6. What are the functions of the National Highway Safety Administration?

7. What was the major purpose of the care labeling rule (1972)?

8. Which two major agencies are within the Department of Health and Human Services?

9. What types of communications, in addition to radio and television broadcasting, are controlled by the FCC?

10. What do the letters *BBB* stand for?

11. Who publishes a monthly magazine known as *Consumer Reports*?

12. List and describe the four ways to communicate with an elected official.

APPLICATIONS

1. Why are consumers encouraged to ask for generic products rather than brand-name products?

2. What types of information are included in monthly issues of *Consumer Reports*? Who advertises in this magazine?

3. Does your state have a toll-free number to call for consumer inquiries or to register complaints? If so, what types of assistance are available?

4. What is the federal toll-free information number nearest you?

5. In your state, who holds each of the following elected offices?

   (a) Governor

   (b) Secretary of state

   (c) State treasurer

   (d) Attorney general

   (e) Superintendent of public instruction

   (f) Labor commissioner

   (g) State senators

   (h) State representatives

6. For your city and county, list the names of the following elected officials:

   (a) Sheriff

   (b) District attorney

   (c) Mayor

   (d) City council members

   (e) City manager

   (f) Tax assessor

CASE PROBLEMS AND ACTIVITIES

1. Select any garment that you are wearing. Read the care label and write down its entire message.

2. Cut the labels from three or four food products, such as soup, cereal, snacks, and processed foods. List the different types of information—such as quantity per serving, ingredients, vitamin and mineral content, etc.—you find on the label. Are there ingredients you do not recognize? Is the nutritional value what you expected?

3. List your state and local sources of consumer assistance, such as the consumer protection, private, and governmental agencies that could assist you with a consumer complaint.

4. Consult the last annual report of the *Consumer Reports*. Summarize three articles in this paperback book that are of interest to you.

5. Read a current issue of *Consumer Reports*. Summarize an article of interest to you, including the kinds of information found about the items being compared and rated. List the other items also reported in that issue.

6. Your local library contains much information about consumer problems and assistance. Visit the library and list in outline form what types of information are available for consumers who need information.

7. Attend a public hearing on a local issue—land use, zoning, etc.—and write a report on who was present, what was discussed, and the conclusion reached. Hearings are held in city hall or county buildings and are open to the public for testimony and input.

CHAPTER 17

LEGAL PROTECTION

CHAPTER OBJECTIVES

After studying this chapter and completing the activities, you will be able to:

1. Describe the organization of the legal system in the United States at federal, state, and local levels.
2. Explain the procedures involved from the time a complaint is filed until a judgment is entered by a court.
3. Define remedies available to consumers—from self-help through negotiating, to filing a lawsuit and seeking government assistance.

THE LEGAL SYSTEM

At the base of our legal system are the courts. A *court* is a tribunal established by government to hear and decide matters properly brought before it, to give redress to the injured or enforce punishment against wrongdoers, and to prevent wrongs. Each court is empowered to decide certain types or classes of cases. This power is called *jurisdiction*, which is the legal right and authority of the court to hear and decide a case. A court may have original or appellate jurisdiction, or both. The court of original jurisdiction is the trial court. A *trial court* has the authority to hear a dispute when it is first brought into court. A court having appellate jurisdiction is the appellate court. An *appellate court* has the authority to review the judgment of a lower court.

Courts are also classified in terms of the nature of their jurisdiction. A *civil court* has the authority to hear disputes involving the violation of the

> Certain courts have power to hear certain types of cases.

278

private legal rights of individuals. Disputes between private citizens, private groups, companies, and corporations are heard in civil courts. In addition, both disputes against a branch of the government (local, state, or federal) and consumer complaints are heard in civil courts. A *criminal court* is for the trial of crimes regarded as violations of certain duties to society and disturbances of public peace and order. The government, representing all the people, prosecutes the alleged wrongdoer. Appeals can be made by the losing party in civil or criminal matters, if it appears that an error or injustice has been committed.

The government represents the people in criminal cases.

Court Personnel

The assistance of many people is required for the efficient operation of our court systems, federal and state. Included are persons in the direct employ of the courts, officers of the court, and sometimes a jury.

The judge is the presiding officer.

Judge. The judge is the presiding officer in the court and is either elected or appointed. Attorneys are usually selected by the parties in the dispute, but are sometimes selected by the judge, to present the issue in the case to the court.

Clerk. The duties of the clerk of the court are to enter cases upon the court calendar; to keep an accurate record of the proceedings; to accept, label, and provide safekeeping for all items of evidence; to administer the oath to witnesses and jurors; and sometimes to approve bail bonds and compute the costs involved.

Reporter. The court reporter keeps a word-by-word record of the trial, usually through the use of a special recording machine. These records of the proceedings are available to each of the attorneys and are necessary for appeals.

Bailiff. Deputy sheriffs serve as sergeants at arms during court proceedings. Bailiffs maintain order in the courtroom at the instruction of the judge.

Jurors are selected from lists of local citizens.

Jury. The *jury* is a body of citizens sworn by a court to hear the facts submitted to them during a trial and to render a verdict. A trial jury consists of not more than twelve persons. A juror must be over age 21 and under age 70, a resident of the county, and able to see and hear. Jurors are chosen from a list of local citizens—usually from tax or voter rolls.

Federal Courts System

The bases of federal jurisdiction are the United States Constitution and the laws enacted by Congress. The federal courts hear only matters that concern the nation as a whole—matters pertaining to constitutional rights, civil rights, interstate commerce, patents and copyrights, internal revenue, currency, and foreign relations. Other areas, such as crimes, contracts, and divorces, are left to the states in which the acts are committed. The federal courts may hear matters between citizens of two different states, but only if the dispute involves $10,000 or more.

The U.S. Supreme Court chooses cases it will hear.

United States Supreme Court. The Supreme Court is the top court of the federal court system and is located in Washington, D.C. The Supreme Court is the only federal court expressly established by the Constitution. Appeals from federal appellate courts and from state supreme courts that pertain to federal issues are heard by the Supreme Court. The Supreme Court chooses which cases it will hear. The Court sets its own *docket*, or schedule of cases, dates, and times for issues to be heard. Only cases of the greatest importance and national consequence are accepted. Thousands of actions are appealed every year; but the Supreme Court accepts only about 125 for consideration. There are nine Supreme Court justices, including a chief justice, who are named to their positions for life. No federal judge may be dismissed or impeached for any reason other than gross misconduct.

Courts of Appeal. The United States, including the District of Columbia, is divided into twelve judicial circuits. Each of the circuits has a court of appeals. Each appellate court has from five to nine judges, who review final decisions of the district courts. The decisions of the courts of appeals are final in most cases.

There are 90 federal courts.

District Courts. Geographically, the United States is divided into ninety areas, or federal districts, with a court assigned to each. Each district covers a state or a portion of a state. Some states may have more than one federal district court, while none may be located in other states. Each district court is a trial court, also divided into civil or criminal divisions. District courts are staffed by judges who hear cases individually, not as a panel.

Special Federal Courts. Additional special courts have been established by Congress to hear only cases of a special nature. These special federal courts include the Court of Claims, Customs Court, Court of International Trade, Tax Court, Court of Military Appeals, and the territorial courts.

State Courts System

The greatest share of legal matters is handled in state court systems. This is not only because state systems outnumber the federal system by 50 to 1, but also because there are limits placed on the federal system by the Constitution. The Tenth Amendment to the United States Constitution grants each state the sovereign power to enact and enforce state laws.

A state's laws are found in its constitution.

A state's laws are contained in its constitution and enacted by its own legislature. These laws are binding upon the citizens of a state and must not violate the U.S. Constitution. Each state has the power to run its own court system to decide issues that involve state laws. Each state establishes its own set of court procedures, determines court names, divides areas of responsibility among the various courts, and sets limits of authority among the state courts.

Cases may be appealed to higher courts.

State Supreme Court. In most states the highest court is the state supreme court, sometimes called the Court of Final Appeal. Ordinarily, the state supreme court has appellate jurisdiction. The decision of a state supreme court is final, except in cases involving the federal Constitution, laws, and treaties. In many states, there are appellate courts and one supreme court.

District and Circuit Courts. General trial courts, often called state district courts, circuit courts, or superior courts, decide matters beyond local courts. These courts hear civil cases involving large sums of money, criminal matters with major penalties, and cases that are appealed from local courts whose decisions are questionable. Judges at this level are usually appointed by the state governor, although some may be elected for terms of four to six years. Decisions from district courts may be reviewed by the highest state court.

County and City Courts. The lowest state court levels are found at the city or county level. These courts may also be called municipal or justice courts. Courts at this level have authority limited by geographic boundaries. Civil and criminal cases are heard at the local level. However, civil cases must be for small amounts only. In some states, the maximum amount in dispute in a civil case is $500. At the local level, disputes usually are heard and decided by judges, not by juries. In very small areas, a judge may be called a justice of the peace, who is an appointed, part-time official. Justices of the peace in other areas are elected officials. Special courts at the local level may be called police courts, traffic courts, small-claims courts, and justice-of-the-peace courts.

Many disputes are heard by judges.

Court Procedure

The filing of a lawsuit involves many steps, costs, and outcomes. You will need an attorney who will advise you of your chances of winning your case, laws pertaining to your case, and what you need to do to prepare for trial. The services of a competent attorney will cost from $50 to $100 an hour, or more in some areas. Some attorneys will work on a contingency fee basis, which means they receive fees only if you win the case. Your state bar association can supply names of attorneys who specialize in the area of your complaint. Your attorney will appear in court in your behalf and represent your interests. In all states there is a ***Statute of Limitations***, which restricts the length of time in which court action may be taken on various complaints. For example, in many states personal injury lawsuits must be filed within two years from the date of the injury. A lawsuit filed after the two-year limit will be dismissed.

You have a time limit within which to file.

Generally, a lawsuit involves the following steps: a complaint is filed; the defendant is served; the defendant appears; the case is tried; a judgment is entered; and costs are awarded.

Plaintiff Files Complaint. The person filing the complaint is known as the *plaintiff*. The plaintiff sees an attorney and discusses the facts of the case. The attorney considers the matter, conducts extensive research on similar cases, and advises the client of the prospect of winning the lawsuit. If the client (plaintiff) wishes to pursue the matter, the attorney draws up the necessary papers, which the plaintiff signs. Action is begun by filing the complaint with the clerk of the appropriate court. A filing fee of $75 to $200 is usually required. Generally, the complaint consists of a description of the acts complained of by the plaintiff and a request for relief.

A filing fee is required if you wish to appear in court.

Defendant Is Served. A certified copy of the complaint is served upon the defendant named in the lawsuit. The *defendant* is the person against whom the plaintiff is making a complaint. The local sheriff's department or a private service company may be used to serve the defendant. Usually, several days are required to serve the defendant, who must be presented with the papers personally. A reasonable time in which to appear (file a response to the complaint) is then allowed the defendant. Ten days are allowed if the defendant is served in the same county; if in the same state, 30 days; outside the state, 60 days or more. The defendant must decide whether to default—not answer and automatically lose—or answer the complaint. If the defendant does not answer, the plaintiff will receive the requested relief by default judgment.

Attorneys prepare papers to file in court.

The defendant must first obtain the services of an attorney and discuss the case. Then the defendant's attorney prepares and files the answer. A counterclaim asserting the plaintiff's guilt, and therefore liability in the matter, could be filed by the defendant. A *counterclaim* states that the defendant believes the plaintiff to be at fault and demands damages as a result of the plaintiff's actions. At this point, the defendant may also file a motion to dismiss (called a demurrer), which states that even if the plaintiff's complaint is true, the plaintiff is still not entitled to any relief. The defendant may also allege that there is insufficient evidence, improper jurisdiction, or other legal reasons why the matter should not be set for trial.

Defendant Appears. After the defendant's attorney has filed an answer with the appropriate court, a date is set for the trial. The trial date is set several months before the matter can be heard. During the time before trial, much work must be done by the plaintiff and defendant, and by their attorneys. Attorneys gather information, talk to witnesses, prepare legal arguments, take depositions, hire investigators, examine reports, and negotiate with the opposing party. *Depositions* are written,

Written statements are taken to preserve memory of an event.

sworn statements of witnesses taken before court appearances in order to preserve the memory of the issues. Many cases are settled before going to trial because both parties realize the risk involved in a trial. If a settlement can be reached, a formal agreement is signed, and the case is dropped.

You can ask for a jury trial.

Trial Takes Place. All defendants are entitled to request a jury trial in state courts. For a jury trial, several days may be necessary to question and choose a panel of jurors. Attorneys are careful to eliminate anyone who appears prejudiced, knows any person who will be present at the trial, or who for any reason might not be able to reach an unbiased decision. Once the jury is seated, the trial begins.

The plaintiff's case is presented first. Any evidence and witnesses to support the case are included in the presentation. The defendant then presents evidence and witnesses in defense against the plaintiff's allegations. Then the attorneys for both sides make closing arguments and the jury deliberates. A decision is reached and announced to the court.

Judgment Is Entered and Costs Are Awarded. Based on the decision of the jury or the judge, a judgment is entered. The losing party has a limited time in which to appeal. A case heard in a state district court may be appealed to a circuit court. After the circuit court, the case may go to the state appeals court, and then to the state supreme court. Any matters involving national interests may be appealed to the United States Supreme Court, which may or may not choose to hear the issue.

Court costs are awarded to the winning party.

Costs awarded to the winning party include the costs of filing papers with the court, the cost of having the sheriff or other officers of the court take official action, fees paid to witnesses, jury fees, and the cost of printing the record of the trial. Sometimes a reasonable attorney's fee may be awarded.

In addition to monetary damages, the plaintiff may seek what is known as equitable relief. *Equitable relief* is a legal action that allows a previous order to be rescinded, requires a situation to be restored to its previous state, or provides for the performance of a specific act. For example, you could ask the judge to allow you to withdraw from a legal contract. A judge may, in some situations, deny monetary damages to a plaintiff if the defendant will restore certain items to their rightful owner—the plaintiff. Equitable relief is often granted when a monetary judgment would not adequately serve to compensate an innocent or damaged party for injuries caused by the actions of the defendant. An action or restraint from action (equitable relief) may be more appropriate than monetary damages.

FINDING A REMEDY

Review your courses of action.

If you are a victim of a consumer problem, you may want to review the courses of action available to you. Self-help, small-claims court, a private or class action lawsuit, or help from a government or private agency to stop the practices and help you get your money back are your alternatives for redress.

Self-Help Remedy

After you have carefully analyzed the problem and believe you are entitled to some type of relief, you can proceed to seek redress. Negotiating and withholding payment are two self-help techniques you may find effective.

Negotiating. A negotiated settlement is one voluntarily entered into by both sides. The buyer must be willing to give up some things in return for the seller's changing his or her position. In most cases, when consumers complain and want some type of settlement, the seller is willing to discuss the issues to reach some type of agreement so that the goodwill of the customer can be maintained. Negotiating is a process that requires tact and precision. You must know the problem, what you want done about it, and what you are willing to do to make a settlement. Negative emotions and statements will not facilitate an agreement.

Legal action is more expensive than other alternatives.

A customer who has purchased a product that is faulty or otherwise unsatisfactory should seek an agreeable remedy with the merchant before pursuing legal remedies. Once the merchant is alienated from (unfriendly toward) the customer because of the customer's actions, the possibility of a negotiated settlement is reduced. Negotiated settlements are often much less expensive and easier to achieve than seeking legal relief. It is essential that the consumer follow up immediately after the damage has occurred. A long wait before seeking a remedy can sometimes result in no relief for damages.

When two parties in a dispute cannot reach an agreement, arbitration may be used. The arbitrator is usually chosen by both parties, and both parties agree to accept the decision of the arbitrator. In some cases a panel is chosen—one arbitrator representing each party, and the two arbitrators choosing a third panel member. Arbitration services are expensive, but much less expensive than court action.

There are many alternatives to settling disputes in the courts. The Yellow Pages of your telephone book has listings for mediation and arbitration services. In addition, Figure 17-1 lists sources of information and assistance that you can contact by writing or calling.

FIGURE 17-1
Sources of
Assistance

Arbitration	The American Arbitration Association (headquarters) 140 W. 51st Street New York, NY 10020 Call: 212-484-4000 Has offices in 25 cities (see your local telephone book).
Bar Referral	The American Bar Association can give the name and address of the nearest dispute resolution center. Write: American Bar Association's Special Committee on Alternative Dispute Resolution 1800 M Street NW Washington, D.C. 20036 Call: 202-331-2258 You will receive a list of 200 centers for $10.
Business Disputes	For free publications for businesses on saving money on legal disputes through use of a panel of dispute resolvers, write: Center for Public Resources 680 Fifth Avenue New York, NY 10019 Call: 202-541-9830
Divorce Mediation	Divorce Mediation Research Project 1720 Emerson Street Denver, CO 80218 Send $10 to receive a partial list of mediators who specialize in divorce. Endispute Suite 803 11 Dupont Circle NW Washington, D.C. 20036 Call: 202-232-5368 Offices also in Chicago, Los Angeles, and San Francisco. West Coast affiliate: Judicial Arbitration & Mediation Service P.O. Box 10333 Santa Ana, CA 92711 Call: 714-972-1616
Lawyer Tips	For tips on dealing with lawyers, write: HALT Americans for Legal Reform Suite 309 201 Massachusetts Avenue NE Washington, D.C. 20002 Call: 202-546-4258

Withholding Payment. As a consumer you have rights when there is a credit dispute. You must put your complaint in writing and explain clearly the reason why you are withholding payment on the disputed amount. The seller is compelled to respond to your complaint and has time limits in which to resolve the matter. You should pay all other amounts due as

Pay amounts not in dispute.

agreed. Do not withhold payment on amounts not in question, as this will weaken your position. Your credit cannot be damaged if you follow the proper procedures for questioning credit charges.

When merchandise is purchased with credit, you have more leverage than if you pay cash, because the merchant is motivated to get payment for the merchandise that is already in your possession. Again, diplomacy is required.

Small-Claims Court

Attorneys are not allowed in small-claims court.

If the amount is relatively small, you might consider small-claims court. The matter will be heard quickly, but the decision is final. Fees are small. You must represent yourself—no attorneys are allowed—and there is no jury. The matter is decided by a judge. A request for a jury would remove the matter to a district or circuit court. Most states have a maximum amount of $500 to $1,000 in damages that can be recovered in a small-claims court.

Small-claims courts are usually easy to use. An instruction sheet that explains how to file a small claim is available at your county courthouse. You must know the name and address of the person with whom you have a problem. You must know the amount in controversy and make a short statement of why you are entitled to the money.

Once your claim is filed, a copy of it is served upon the defendant. The defendant has ten days to appear. If the defendant contests the claim, a hearing date is set. The hearing lasts about a half hour. The plaintiff presents his or her side of the case; the defendant presents his or her side. You may bring in written statements or evidence, as well as witnesses. You should summarize your position on one page and present it to the judge.

No permanent record is kept.

No record is made of the small-claims court hearing. It cannot be appealed—the judge's decision is final. The benefit of taking your dispute to small-claims court is the saving of money. You pay no attorney fees. Court filing fees are small—$5 to $20 is common. The case is heard in a few weeks at most, giving you speedy relief. If the defendant does not appear, you win by default. The judge proclaims a judgment and the losing party is required to pay damages.

It is important in a small-claims court hearing that you be organized, calm, and specific about your complaint. If you are asking for $500 in damages, you must be prepared to show why you deserve that sum. The judge will ask questions of the plaintiff and defendant. Usually the judge will make an immediate decision, or will take a 15-minute break and return with the decision.

Many people are experts at appearing in small-claims court. Collection agencies, for example, appear often in small-claims court and know exactly what will happen. If it is your first appearance, you may be nervous and unable to explain your position. Therefore, it is important to prepare yourself by outlining what you will say, gathering evidence you want to present, and summarizing your position. You may read your statement and give a copy to the judge.

Under the Unlawful Trade Practices Act, a person who purchases goods or services and suffers a loss of money or property as a result of the willful practices performed by another person may bring an action to recover actual damages or $200, whichever is greater. In other words, if you bought a piece of merchandise valued at $15 that caused you great harm, and it was the willful act of the seller to sell you that defective merchandise, you can collect $200 rather than the value of the merchandise. You, the buyer, must prove loss. For example, if the $15 item exploded and caused you to break your glasses and see the doctor to be treated for burns, then you have actual loss.

Willful acts by sellers can cost $200 in damages.

The Truth in Lending Act provides that if the lender willfully fails to disclose those things required, the buyer is entitled to actual damages sustained, or twice the finance charge under the contract, but not less than $100 or more than $1,000.

In any small-claims action, the plaintiff must prove that the defendant's act was willful—in other words, that the defendant intended to defraud and knowingly and willingly proceeded to do so. The plaintiff must also prove that a loss was sustained as a result of the defendant's willful actions.

You must prove the acts were intentional.

Private or Class Action

You may wish to consider filing a private lawsuit. If others are affected as you are, a class action lawsuit may be appropriate. In either event, lawsuits can be very costly and take several years to resolve. Be sure you are willing to take the risk and invest the time to resolve the matter in court.

A private lawsuit is filed to resolve a dispute between an individual (or a business) and others. The lawsuit is called a civil case and is resolved by compromise or formal court trial. Many lawsuits are settled between parties before going to trial.

When more than one person is damaged because of the acts of another, a class action lawsuit may be filed. In this case, a person sues another in behalf of himself or herself and all others who may have been affected by the defendant's actions in the same way.

In a class action, the maximum recovery allowed against creditors is $100,000 or 1 percent of the net worth of the creditor, whichever is less. Consumers suing creditors through class action are not given the double recovery or minimum $100 damages that are normally awarded in private lawsuits. In a class action suit, there could be a million consumers represented; setting a limit on damages awarded prevents an unreasonable recovery amount.

Maximum recovery protects from an unreasonable penalty.

In a class action, the size of the attorneys' fees ordered by the court (the losing party pays the attorneys' fees for the winner) and the court costs are at the discretion of the judge. For example, if the creditor loses the suit, the judge considers the size of damages awarded, frequency of complaints and severity of damages, the failure of the creditor to meet his or her responsibilities to the public, the resources of the creditor, and the number of persons adversely affected by the creditor's actions.

Anyone can file a lawsuit.

Anyone can file a lawsuit. The advantages and disadvantages of filing a lawsuit should be weighed carefully before you decide. Because of the courts' busy schedules, you may wait from one to three years after you have filed the complaint to appear in court. After a court renders a decision, the losing party may file an appeal. You cannot collect a judgment until the appeal is resolved. Therefore, it could be many years before you actually receive any monetary benefits from a lawsuit.

One can never be sure of winning a lawsuit. There may be unknown facts or conditions that will affect the outcome of the action. Therefore, you should enter a lawsuit only if you can afford to lose the money you invest in it, and only if you believe there is much more involved than the money you stand to gain.

Consumer groups help you if your rights are violated.

In some cases, you can convince a consumer protection group to file a lawsuit in your behalf. For example, the American Civil Liberties Union files lawsuits to protect the rights of masses of citizens. The ACLU collects money from donations to pay the fees and costs involved. Many individuals cannot afford to pursue legal remedies without the help of such groups, because of the cost involved.

Governmental Assistance

Government agencies will give information and assist with a complaint.

In addition to the sources of consumer assistance listed in Chapter 16, you may wish to seek help from a government agency to help stop the practices and get your money back. In many cases, the cost to you is small, while the benefit to all consumers is great. Government agencies that have information and can assist you with a consumer complaint include the following:

AUTOMOBILES

National Highway Traffic Safety
Administration

COLLECTION, CREDIT

State Consumer Protection Division
(at your state capitol)

DRUGS/FOODS

Food and Drug Administration

HOUSEHOLD

Consumer Product Safety Commission

INVESTMENT FRAUD

Federal Trade Commission

Securities and Exchange Commission

MEDICAL/DENTAL

State Board of Medical Examiners

State Department of Commerce

State Board of Dental Examiners

State Health Division

State Board of Pharmacy

MEDICARE

Social Security Administration

MISREPRESENTATION/FRAUD

State Consumer Protection Division

Local District Attorney

Local Better Business Bureau

TRANSPORTATION

Interstate Commerce Commission

WARRANTIES

Federal Trade Commission

VOCABULARY

Directions: Can you find the definition for each of the following terms used in Chapter 17?

court
trial court
civil court
jury
Statute of Limitations
defendant
depositions

jurisdiction
appellate court
criminal court
docket
plaintiff
counterclaim
equitable relief

1. A legal action that allows a previous order to be rescinded, restoration of a previous state, or the performance of a specific act.

2. A tribunal to hear and settle matters brought before it.

3. A tribunal for the trial of crimes regarded as violations of duties to society.

4. A tribunal having authority to hear disputes involving private individuals.

5. The legal right and authority to hear and decide a case.

6. A body of citizens sworn by a court to hear issues of fact and render a verdict.

7. A schedule of cases, dates, and times of issues to be heard by the court.

8. The original court that hears a dispute first brought into court.

9. The person who files a complaint and brings an issue before a court.

10. A tribunal having authority to review the judgment of a lower court.

11. A law that controls the length of time in which a court action must be taken or else the grievance must be forgotten.

12. The person against whom a complaint is made.

13. Written, sworn statements of witnesses, records of which are used in court at a later date.

14. An assertion by a defendant that the plaintiff is at fault.

ITEMS FOR DISCUSSION

1. Describe what types of matters are heard before these courts:
   (a) Trial court
   (b) Appellate court
   (c) Civil court
   (d) Criminal court

2. List and briefly describe the officers of the court.

3. On what bases is the federal court system operating?

4. What is the top court of the federal court system?

5. How many districts are there for federal district courts in the United States?

6. List several courts that are considered special federal courts.

7. What is the top court in the state court system?

8. What are the lowest state courts? Give two examples.

9. List the six steps that occur when a court action is filed and carried through trial to a decision of a judge or jury.

APPLICATIONS

1. Why are small-claims courts easy to use and, in some cases, more advantageous?

2. A lawsuit is filed by the plaintiff. Explain what happens until a judgment is entered for the plaintiff.

3. A case that involves a dispute in a city is filed with the circuit court of a county in the same state. When the case is heard in a trial court, where can the case be appealed?

4. As a store customer, you are dissatisfied with a product purchased. Explain your self-help remedies and actions to consider in resolving the dispute.

5. List six government agencies that have information and can assist you in a consumer complaint. Also identify the type of complaint to take to the agencies listed.

CASE PROBLEMS AND ACTIVITIES

1. Name the present justices of the U.S. Supreme Court, with their terms of office. Put a star by the name of the chief justice.

2. Spend a half day at a local county courthouse. Make arrangements to observe a case being tried. You will not be allowed to leave the room until the court adjourns, nor will you be allowed to enter while court is in session. You may observe a civil or criminal matter. Write a report on what you observe.

3. Visit your local law library located at the county courthouse or at a law school if you have a university with a law school in your area. List five types of references available. Look up the Statute of Limitations for filing lawsuits in your state and tell how long you have to file actions in the following situations:

   (a) Wrongful death or injury

   (b) Real property infringement

   (c) Civil action where you are the injured party of a contract

   Also in your law library, you will find books that summarize cases tried and decided in your state. Find a case that interests you and summarize the issues of the case, the court's decision, and your reactions.

UNIT FIVE
PURCHASING GOODS AND SERVICES

CHAPTER 18
CONSUMER DECISION MAKING

CHAPTER OBJECTIVES

After studying this chapter and completing the activities, you will be able to:

1. Demonstrate an understanding of the decision-making process by applying it to a real or hypothetical problem.
2. List and describe factors that influence consumer decision making.
3. Analyze and compare advertising gimmicks and promotional devices used to induce consumer spending.

THE CONSUMER DECISION-MAKING PROCESS

Decisions should be carefully planned.

Buying decisions play an important role in your efforts to manage your personal finances. Good decisions can save you money; bad decisions can be expensive. For this reason, your decision to purchase a product or service should always be based on careful consideration of available information and alternatives. The five-step consumer decision-making process presented in this chapter is a logical plan to use in solving problems caused by wants, needs, and goals. By following this process, you can make wise and economical buying decisions.

Define the Problem

First, you must define the problem.

The first step in the consumer decision-making process is simple: define the need or want to be satisfied and state it in a short, concise sentence. Then when your want or need has been pinpointed, you can proceed to the goal of satisfying the need or want in a manner that fits your

financial resources. For example, you and your roommate have just moved into an apartment complex that offers no laundry facilities. Your problem is that you want and need clean clothes; your goal is to find a way to satisfy this need in an economical fashion. The problem, when solved, will achieve your goal of finding laundry facilities and will satisfy the need for clean clothes in a way that will give you the most value for the money you spend. This first step in the consumer decision-making process is an important one, because it is at the problem level of satisfying needs and wants that you make decisions concerning the purchase of products and services.

Obtain Accurate Information

Once you have determined the problem, you must then gather information relating to your problem. List all alternative solutions to the problem and the cost of each. In the laundry problem example, there are three basic solutions:

List all possible solutions to the problem.

1. Use a laundromat.
2. Buy a new washer and dryer.
3. Buy a used washer and dryer.

In order to make a wise decision regarding your problem of obtaining clean clothes, you will need to know what products and services are available and how much it will cost you to use or purchase them. For instance, you will need to know where laundry facilities are located. The cost of use will include the price for each washer and dryer load as well as mileage for driving to and from the laundry and the time involved. For the possible purchase of new appliances, you will need to list desired features and then visit various appliance stores, department stores, and discount stores for the purpose of comparative shopping. At each location, you should list the brands available, features available, costs, and warranties. The classified ads are a good source for used washers and dryers.

Comparison shopping provides alternatives.

Whenever possible, keep a written record of the information you collect on choices of products and services. By doing so, you can make comparisons of alternatives and costs more easily. Figure 18-1 shows information collected for comparison in the laundry problem.

Compare Alternatives

When comparing total costs, you must consider time and convenience factors as well as dollar amounts. In some cases, convenience may be more important than cost, as long as the cost is reasonable. Using the previous example, you may decide that the convenience of having a washer and dryer in your apartment is worth the extra dollar cost. You may also decide to buy a new washer and dryer, even though the cost will be greater, because you prefer to avoid the expense of possible repairs. Purchasing used rather than new appliances results in greater risks because previous owners may or may not have cared for and maintained the appliances properly.

Convenience may be more important than cost.

On the other hand, if your housing situation is temporary, and you and your roommate anticipate that you will share the apartment for less than a year, going to the nearest laundromat and sharing the expenses may be the best choice. These are just a few of the factors you must consider in this step of the consumer decision-making process.

Consider how long you will live in the apartment.

Select an Alternative

If you follow the steps outlined in the preceding paragraphs, the decision you make will be based on a careful analysis of the problem, thorough information gathering, and analysis of that information. In our example, the decision is to determine whether to use a laundromat or to buy a washer and dryer. The cost is the price you will pay for what you decide to do. All choices have prices, because to choose one thing is not to choose another. The wise decision in this or in any situation is the one that is within your budget and that gives you the most value for your dollar investment.

You should be satisfied with your decision.

FIGURE 18-1
Information for
Comparison

COST COMPARISON	Per Month	Per Year
Option 1: Use a Laundromat		
Time: about 4 to 6 hours each weekend spent at laundromat	20 hrs.	250 hrs.
Gasoline: 6 miles round trip, once each weekend, 52/year	$ 3.00	$ 36.00
Washer, 75 cents each load, 6 loads a weekend	18.00	216.00
Dryer, 50 cents each load, 6 loads each weekend	12.00	144.00
	$35.00	$396.00
Option 2: Buy New Machines		
Average quality machines, on sale (washer/dryer)	$600.00 one-time cost	
Monthly payments (2 years to pay off, 13 percent interest)	$26.63	$319.50
Costs of repair, upkeep, service contract, etc., are additional. There is no time expense, because other things can be done while machines are running. Machines should last 5 to 10 years.		
Option 3: Buy Used Machines		
Average quality used washer/dryer at garage sale	$300.00 one-time cost	
Monthly payments (usually have to pay cash; borrow money from bank for 1 year at 13 percent interest)	$28.25	$339.00
Costs of repair and upkeep are additional. Machines should last 3 to 5 years.		

Take Action

After you have selected the best alternative, you must take action to accomplish the goal of satisfying your need. Because you have made a thorough analysis of information necessary to solve your problem, you can be sure that you have made a wise decision.

PERSONAL FACTORS THAT INFLUENCE SPENDING DECISIONS

There are many personal factors that influence consumer spending decisions. *Personal factors* are those influences in a person's or family's life that determine spending patterns, preferences, and choices. Some persons and families may be influenced greatly by one or more of the following factors: personal resources; position in life; customs, background, and religion; and values and goals.

Personal Resources

Your personal resources affect your choices.

Your *personal resources* include your time, money, energy, skills and abilities, and available credit. The greater the quantity and the higher the quality of any one of these factors, the greater your purchasing power. Generally speaking, the more resources you have available to you, the greater your earning potential and the greater your buying capacity.

Position in Life

Your position in life includes such factors as age, marital status, sex, employment status, and life-style. At different times in your life, your needs and wants are different. Within each of life's stages, your spending patterns will also vary. Spending patterns of single people are different from those of married couples and families. Spending patterns at age 40 are different from those at age 30. Right now your spending patterns are probably different from those of your parents, and your parents' patterns differ from your grandparents' patterns because of age differences alone. If you have been working for 20 years, your spending patterns are different from the person who just started working three months ago.

Customs, Background, and Religion

A *custom* is a long-established practice that may be considered an unwritten law. Families may be dedicated to traditions that have been followed for generations. This is particularly true of religious groups or of cultures in which strict rules and policies are followed. Persons in these religious or cultural groups may observe special holidays and occasions

Customs can be strong motivating influences.

that are not observed nationally. Buying patterns of these groups are greatly influenced by the values and priorities in their lives. In many cases, custom overshadows all other buying preferences.

Values and Goals

Values are expressed through choices.

Values, which lie at the base of all our purchasing decisions, are slow to change. Goals change often. You accomplish goals and move on to others. Your total value system may change as your goals in life are met, or not met. Individual and family values and goals are expressed through choices of entertainment, literature, sports, luxuries, and so on. These choices are reflected in decisions to purchase goods and services, use of time and energy, and attitudes toward possessions and their accumulation.

OUTSIDE FACTORS THAT INFLUENCE SPENDING DECISIONS

To understand how the world in which you live plays a role in your decision-making process, you must consider the following: the economy, technological advances, the environment, and social pressures.

The Economy

Inflation causes loss of purchasing power.

The *economy* is the system or structure of economic life in a country. This term describes the financial well-being of the nation as measured by economists. As you will learn in Unit 6, the general condition of the economy affects every one of us, and we react to it accordingly. For example, in a period of high inflation, when prices are rising rapidly, people tend to buy more and save less. Prices rise so rapidly that money purchases less each day. There is little incentive to save because the rate of interest on savings is much less than the rate of inflation, and to save money is to lose money. When the rate of inflation is low, the economy is slow, and interest rates are high. When interest rates on automobile loans are high, fewer people are able to buy new cars. Consequently, older cars are kept longer. In these times, people save more and buy less (or buy less expensive items) because they do not want to pay the high rates of interest, but they do want high interest rates paid on their savings accounts.

Technological Advances

You may be fascinated or even obsessed with new electronic games. Or you may be interested in the world's first water-powered automobile.

Perhaps you want to add a new solar heating device to your home to make it more energy efficient. In America, a high value is placed on new technological advances. Many people want to have the newest, most convenient, modern, and interesting gadgets. As new goods and services are created to increase our level of comfort and standard of living, we willingly purchase them. These types of purchases, whether large or small, are important to the emotional well-being of the consumer who needs to have the latest gimmick to feel a part of what is going on in the world.

Faster, better ways of doing things are important to us.

The Environment

Concern for the environment can affect consumer buying decisions to a great extent. The physical environment and quality of life are very real concerns today. Our natural resources are scarce and are disappearing rapidly. Air quality, of vital importance to our health and well-being, is a problem individuals and the government spend much time and money to solve. In addition, millions of dollars are spent each year to help preserve the natural beauty, landscape, waterways, wildlife, and other natural resources of our country. Citizens find themselves concerned with home projects, community activities, and statewide programs to beautify and preserve, recycle, and protect existing resources and environment. Thus, this interest in the environment affects consumers' actions and also their product preferences because products purchased must be ecologically safe and biodegradable (or otherwise recyclable) to meet present and future environmental standards.

Conservation is a high priority in America.

Social Pressures

Social pressures often induce consumers to buy goods and services beyond their real wants and needs. People can be influenced to make purchases by their friends, relatives, and co-workers. The media (radio, television, newspapers) also act as sources of social pressure for consumers. Through advertising, the media convince consumers to buy goods and services designed to keep them young, good looking, healthy, and appealing to the opposite sex. America is a country obsessed with youth, beauty, physical fitness, and material comforts. We are easily enticed into buying merchandise we do not need—status symbols, such as a second car or designer clothes that are beyond our budget, rather than necessities. The list is endless. Understanding how outside factors such as the economy, technological advances, the environment, and social pressures influence our spending patterns can help us to make wise consumer decisions.

Advertising appeals to hidden fears and desires.

MARKETING STRATEGIES THAT INFLUENCE SPENDING DECISIONS

Marketing strategies are designed to sell products.

Numerous marketing strategies lure us into stores to buy goods and services. Many of these strategies are subtle, and we are often unaware of their impact on our buying patterns. Some frequently used marketing strategies explained in this chapter are advertising, pricing, sales, and promotional techniques.

Advertising

The primary goal of all advertising is to create within the consumer the desire to purchase a product or service. Some advertising is false and misleading; other advertising is informational and valuable.

A variety of media are available for advertising—billboards, television, radio, newspapers, magazines, leaflets, balloons, and T-shirts—all carefully coordinated to reach specific consumer groups. Advertising agencies create colorful and attractive campaigns: They compose jingles and catchy tunes, develop slogans and trademarks, design colorful logos, and choose mascots to identify their products. There are three basic types of advertising: product, company, and industry.

Product Advertising. Advertising to convince consumers to buy a specific good or service is called ***product advertising***. The name of the advertised product is repeated several times during radio and television commercials. Testimonials from people who have used the product, giveaways, promotional gimmicks, and other clever and catchy methods are used to persuade consumers to purchase products and services. Advertisements are carefully planned to appeal to specific types of consumers. A ***target audience*** is a specific consumer group to which the advertisements for a product are directed. Research has revealed specific characteristics of people who will probably be interested in a given product or service. Day of the week, time of day, and type of program are taken into consideration by television advertisers. All these factors are important when trying to reach a target audience. Products advertised during football games differ from products advertised during daytime television because the target audiences are different.

Advertising is directed to a target audience.

Companies advertise to promote a good image.

Company Advertising. Advertising to promote the image of a store, company, or retail chain is known as ***company advertising***. Usually price is not a consideration, and specific products are not mentioned. Emphasis is placed on the quality of the products or services the company sells, warranties and/or guarantees offered, or social and environmental concerns of the company. In a store advertisement, you may hear or read about the company's friendly employees, its wide selection of products or services, or its claim that you can find everything you want in one place. These advertisements are designed to prompt a favorable attitude toward the company so that you develop a loyalty to the store and will not shop anywhere else. Company advertisements may be accompanied by catchy slogans and tunes, happy cartoons, or pleasant scenes to which products of this company make a contribution.

Industry Advertising. Advertising to promote a general product group, without regard to where these products are purchased, is called *industry advertising*. For example, the dairy industry emphasizes the nutritional value of milk and other natural dairy products. Consequently, the whole dairy industry benefits when people drink more milk and eat more dairy products. Oil industry advertisements stress concern about energy conservation, environmental protection, and the search for new alternative forms of fuels. The automobile industry gives safe-driving tips and reasons for buying American-made cars. General health and safety advertisements are often presented in industry advertising campaigns, such as the Smokey the Bear fire safety commercials and the stop-smoking ads.

Industry advertising is general and many retailers benefit.

Pricing

The price of merchandise depends on several factors. Supply and demand determine what will be produced and the general price range. The cost of raw materials and labor, competitive pressures, and the seller's need to make a reasonable profit are some of the factors that determine the price of a product. But there is more to pricing than adding up the production costs and including a profit. Retailers understand the psychological aspects of selling goods and services and use pricing devices to persuade consumers to buy. For example, if buyers believe they are getting a bargain, or are paying a lower price, they are more inclined to buy a product or service. ***Odd-number pricing*** is the practice of putting odd numbers on price tags—99 cents instead of $1.00. Because the price is under a dollar, it appears to be a bargain. By paying $5.98 instead of $6.00 the customer is happy because he found a sound buy; the retailer is happy because she has made a profitable sale.

There are psychological aspects of selling products.

Discounts or low unit prices are often available for buying in large sizes or quantities. However, you cannot assume that because you are buying the large economy size you are actually paying less per ounce than if you bought a small size. Compare unit prices on all sizes.

Sales

Stores advertise end-of-month sales, anniversary sales, clearance sales, inventory sales, holiday sales, preseason sales, and so on. Merchandise may be marked down substantially, slightly, or not at all. In order to be sure that you are actually saving money by buying sale items, you must do comparative shopping and know the usual prices. When an advertisement states that everything in the store is marked down, check carefully for items that only appear to be marked down in price.

Know product prices when shopping sales.

A *loss leader* is an item of merchandise marked down to an unusually low price, sometimes below the store's actual cost. The store may actually lose money on every sale of this item because the cost of producing the item is higher than the retail price. However, the loss leader is used to get customers into the store to buy other products as well. Sales on other items are expected to make up for the loss sustained on the loss leader. There is nothing illegal or unethical about a loss leader as long as the product advertised is available to the customer on demand. A customer who buys only loss leaders and super sale items is called a *cherry picker*. Retailers rely on customers to buy other products to make up for the loss caused by sales of the loss leader. Consequently, cherry pickers are not highly favored by retailers.

Loss leaders are used to draw you in to buy other things, too.

Promotional Techniques

In order to get customers into stores, retailers may use one or more promotional techniques: displays, contests and games, trading stamps, coupons, packaging, and sampling.

Displays. Retail stores often use window displays, special racks of new items, or sampling promotions to entice customers. Products are arranged attractively, and the promotion may carry a theme centered around the nearest holiday—Halloween, Thanksgiving, Christmas, Valentine's Day, Mother's Day, Father's Day, or the Fourth of July. Color schemes, decorations, music, and special effects often set off the products being offered to appeal to consumers' ego needs.

Contests and Games. Grocery stores, department stores, fast food restaurants, and other retail stores that depend on repeat customers often use contests and games to bring customers into the store. Individual product packages, such as cereal boxes, may contain game cards. The possibility of winning something or getting something for nothing appeals to

Contests and games lure in new customers and keep old ones interested.

many people. Large and small prizes are offered with the intention of getting customers to come back and buy more so that they can get more game cards, have more chances to win, and receive some of the minor prizes. Careful reading of the rules on the reverse side of the game card or other token reveals the customer's chances of winning. Usually, the chances of winning a major prize are small.

Trading Stamps. The trading stamp is a promotional gimmick that is still popular in some parts of the country. Some stores give trading stamps based on the total dollar amount of individual purchases. These stamps are collected and redeemed for prizes, reduced prices on special purchases, or other types of rewards. This type of promotion is designed to maintain customer loyalty—the more customers shop in the same store, the more stamps they can collect. Many customers think that they are getting more for their money or are getting something for nothing when they receive trading stamps.

Trading stamps are still popular in some areas.

Coupons. Manufacturer coupons offer cents off on specifically described products from a specific manufacturer and may be redeemed wherever the product is sold. Store coupons offer discounts on specific products, usually for a short period of time, and only at a specific store. Manufacturer and store coupons may be inside a package, on the outside of the package, in newspapers or magazines, or on a store shelf. Coupons may not be redeemed for cash, but may be used to give cents off on the product promoted on the coupon. The effect of the coupon is to lower the price of the product in an attempt to lure customers to choose that product or the store offering the bargain over its competitors. Stores that accept manufacturer coupons return the coupons to the manufacturer for a refund in the amount given to the customer. Figure 18-2 shows coupons issued by a manufacturer and a store.

Coupons offer discounts on merchandise.

Packaging. Packages are designed to appeal to the eye with the necessary information correctly and attractively arranged. Distinctively designed packages are used to attract the customer's attention away from competitive products. Company logos, brightly colored designs, pictures of people promoting or using the product, and other attention getters may appear on product boxes. Special features are emphasized, such as: sugar free, no saccharin, fortified with eight vitamins and minerals, new and improved, safe for children, and many others. Manufacturers know that the package or container must be attractive because it plays such an important role in inducing purchases. Size and shape of packages are significant. Containers that appear to hold more of the product and contain-

FIGURE 18-2A Manufacturer Coupon   **FIGURE 18-2B** Store Coupon

ers that are reusable as storage devices also attract consumers. Often, a game or prize inside the box is also shown on the outside, or coupons are contained inside the package or on the package. A cents-off price means that the price on the package is reduced by a discount amount usually shown in big letters.

Sampling. Many companies use direct advertising of their products through sampling. Small sample-size free packages of a product may be sent directly to households. Or company representatives may give out samples, free drinks, or tastes of products in selected stores, in shopping centers, or on street corners. Usually when a new product is first introduced into the marketplace, sampling allows potential customers to try the new product. Some companies advertise in magazines and newspapers, with offers for free samples by mail. All you have to do is fill out the coupon with your name and address and mail it in. In addition to a sample of the product, you may receive a coupon to be used on future purchases of the new product.

VOCABULARY

Directions: Can you find the definition for each of the following terms used in Chapter 18?

define the problem	custom
personal resources	economy
target audience	product advertising

industry advertising   company advertising
loss leader   odd-number pricing
personal factors   cherry picker

1. To state what specific want or need must be satisfied.

2. A customer who buys only loss leaders and super sale items.

3. An item of merchandise marked down to a very low price, often below actual cost.

4. The practice of putting uneven price numbers on merchandise to make the price appear low.

5. Factors present in one's life that influence spending patterns.

6. Time, money, energy, skills, abilities, and credit—the more you have, the more you can spend.

7. A long-established practice that is the same as an unwritten law.

8. A system or structure of life in a country that describes its financial well-being.

9. Advertising that attempts to convince you to buy a certain good or service.

10. Technique used to promote and maintain customer loyalty.

11. A specific consumer group.

12. A type of promotion that attempts to sell a general product group, without regard to where it is purchased.

ITEMS FOR DISCUSSION

1. List the five steps in the consumer decision-making process. Briefly describe each.

2. What are some personal factors that influence a person's or a family's spending patterns?

3. What are some outside factors that determine a person's or family's spending patterns?

4. List six different advertising media. Which one(s) do you see most frequently?

5. What is a target audience?

6. What is odd-number pricing? Is it used frequently in the advertising that you see most often?

7. Why don't retailers like to see cherry pickers?

8. On what theme do promotional displays often center?

9. What types of businesses often offer contests and games to attract customers?

10. What types of trading stamps are available in your community?

11. What is a store coupon?

12. What is a manufacturer coupon?

APPLICATIONS

1. Using the steps in the consumer decision-making process, make a decision that will satisfy your need for a piano.

2. How do your spending patterns differ from those of your parents? What things do you buy that your parents also purchase? Can you trace any of these purchases to strong family custom, background, or religion?

3. How are you or the members of your family affected when interest rates are very high? Do you benefit, or are you hurt? How? Can you think of anyone who is affected in an opposite way from you? Why is this so?

4. What community-centered and national environmental concerns do you have? What can you do as a single concerned citizen to help preserve the quality of the environment?

5. Spend an evening viewing television or listening to the radio. List the jingles, tunes, key words, phrases, and slogans used in each commercial. How many commercials can you automatically sing along with?

CASE PROBLEMS AND ACTIVITIES

1. Watch a television program for one hour any time during the day. Determine the target audience (teenagers, children, homemakers, sports fans, families, adults only) of the program. Pay close attention to all commercials shown during the hour. Write your answers to the following questions on a separate piece of paper.

(a) List all the commercials. Categorize them as either product, company, or industry advertising. (Public service advertisements and political campaigns are industry advertisements.)

(b) Rate each commercial as good, fair, or poor, depending upon how well it is directed to the television program's target market.

(c) Rate each commercial according to tastefulness (either good taste or poor taste). Do you find it offensive, degrading, insulting? Explain why you liked or disliked the commercial.

2. Bring to class an advertisement insert from a newspaper. It should be from a department store, local discount store, or grocery store. Write your answers to these questions on a separate piece of paper:

(a) How many advertisements show odd-number pricing?

(b) How many individual advertisements mention how much money will be saved or what the regular price is?

(c) Are there any coupons or references to coupons?

(d) Are trading stamps, games, or special incentives mentioned in the advertisement?

(e) Is the advertisement insert attractively arranged?

(f) Is the insert in color or black and white?

(g) Rate the advertisement insert as to quality, attractiveness, and readability.

(h) Do you see any loss leaders or super buys?

Attach the advertisement insert to your paper. On the insert, write comments next to items to identify them as examples of loss leaders, odd-number pricing, etc.

3. Describe a store display built around the theme of the most recent major holiday. Describe colors used, products displayed, product arrangement, location in the store, etc. Were there any actual price reductions?

4. List any stores in your area that use one or more of the following promotional techniques. Beside each store name, describe the specific techniques used.

(a) Contests and games   (d) Sampling

(b) Trading stamps   (e) Other

(c) Coupons

CHAPTER 19

HOUSING

CHAPTER OBJECTIVES

After studying this chapter and completing the activities, you will be able to:

1. Describe the various housing alternatives and potential living arrangements you can anticipate.
2. List the advantages and disadvantages of renting a residence, complete a rental application, and understand a lease and an inventory.
3. Discuss landlord/tenant obligations, considerations of home ownership (positive and negative) and describe the process of buying a home, moving costs, and installation charges.

HOUSING ALTERNATIVES

Housing choices depend on needs.

Most people spend half or more of their time at their place of residence. For this reason, it is important to give careful thought and planning to selecting the best housing alternative for you at a given period in your life. Making wise housing decisions will provide you with comfort, convenience, affordability, and utility. Alternatives for housing discussed in this chapter include dormitories, apartments, duplexes, condominiums, and houses.

Dormitories

Many college-bound young people prefer to live in a dormitory on campus. Dormitories provide a convenient location, plus eating facilities,

with the meals included in the cost. Although individual rooms are small, with limited space for a bed, study area, and closet, the cost per school term may be less than for other available private housing.

Apartments

An apartment is typically the preferred choice for the first residence away from the parents' home. Because the amount of rent paid on an apartment is based on the size of the apartment and facilities provided, finding an apartment for the amount you can afford to pay is fairly easy.

Efficiency apartments are usually least expensive.

Efficiency apartments provide the least amount of living space, but are also the least expensive. In an efficiency, there is only one large room serving as the kitchen, living room, and bedroom. Larger one-, two- and three bedroom apartments with separate living and dining areas are available in a variety of floor plans, including two-story models, called townhouses.

Apartments are usually located in multi-unit buildings in which the number of units may be as few as two or as many as several hundred. Facilities provided may include a laundry room, storage area, swimming pool, tennis courts, and clubhouse. In addition, all or part of the utilities may be included in the rent payment.

Duplexes

Duplexes offer more privacy than apartments.

A duplex is a two-family house. Usually both halves of the house are exactly the same, but there are separate entrances for each. Generally located in quiet residential areas, duplexes offer more space than apartments.

Condominiums

A condominium is an individually owned unit in a multi-unit structure. The condominium owner, upon purchase of a unit, becomes a member of the owners' association, which is responsible for the property management. A monthly fee is paid by each owner to cover the cost of maintaining the common areas and the outside portion of the units. The individual owners are responsible for maintaining the interior of the units. Common areas may include a variety of athletic and recreational facilities.

Houses

A house is a single-family detached home. Houses are built in many sizes and in many different styles. Generally houses are either single story, two story, or split-level and may be new or an existing structure. Both rental costs and purchase prices of houses vary with size, facilities, and location.

LIVING ARRANGEMENTS

Make living decisions before leaving home.

Major decisions to determine your living arrangements must be reached before moving out of your parents' home. With whom to live, where to live, what to take, when to move—all are considerations that must be given careful thought.

With Whom to Live

Choosing a roommate is sometimes a difficult task. Is there someone, or ones, among your friends and acquaintances with whom you would enjoy living? Some people do not get along well with others for many reasons. Be sure you are compatible with your potential roommate(s) before you move in together. Discuss possible areas of disagreement that may cause trouble if not settled in advance. Some questions that should be answered before making a commitment to share living quarters include these:

1. Do you smoke or drink? How do you feel about others who do?
2. Do you like a clean living area at all times, or are you easygoing and casual about your environment?
3. Do you have steady employment or another source of income to ensure that you can be depended on to pay your share of the common expenses?
4. What are some of your goals? Do you want to continue your education, work full-time, travel, etc.?
5. What are your leisure activities? What activities can you share with your roommate(s)?
6. What type of transportation do you and your roommate(s) have? What is the approximate cost? Will you share expenses? If so, how will you divide them?

Share your feelings with potential roommates.

You might want to consider having more than one roommate. The more personalities involved, however, the more difficult it becomes to have problem-free relationships. Matching similar personality types will increase the chances for a successful living arrangement.

Get to know your room-mate(s) well before moving in.

The more you know about each potential roommate, the better you will be able to get along and work out problems. It is a good idea to get to know each person before moving in together. Spend time together at school, after school, in the evenings, and on weekends participating in school, family, and other group activities. In this way, you can see what interests you have in common, how each of you interacts with the other(s) and in groups, and what personality traits are strongest. It is not necessary that roommates be completely alike in order to get along. However, they do need to be aware of, and be able to accept, each other's qualities and traits.

Where to Live

Off-campus housing needs careful planning.

The decision of where to live will depend largely on finances. For students attending college and choosing on-campus housing, many of the decisions discussed in this chapter will be predetermined. Off-campus housing involves more planning and careful consideration. Those who will not attend college or who choose an off-campus residence must begin their housing plan with a solid financial analysis: What is a realistic amount to pay for rent or mortgage payments? You must determine how much you can comfortably pay. Then you can begin shopping around for the best housing plan to meet your needs. Some costs to consider when deciding where to live include the following:

1. Deposits and fees to rent or purchase a residence. A *deposit* is a pledge or down payment.
2. Deposits for and average monthly costs of utilities. A *utility* is a service such as light, power, or water provided by a public utility company.
3. Length of time you plan to live in the residence.
4. Distance from place of work or school.
5. Distance from laundry, shopping facilities, and other frequently used services.
6. Costs of maintenance or upkeep expected of you.

Car and gasoline expenses are a big consideration.

Most financial experts advise allotting between 15 and 30 percent of your total budget for housing. Houses should cost no more than two and a half times your gross income.

What to Take

If you are buying a home, you will need to plan to furnish it completely yourself. Rental residences, however, come furnished or unfurnished. *Furnished* means that the basic furnishings are provided—bed and dresser; sofa, chairs, and lamps; dining table and chairs; and essential appliances. An *unfurnished* rental residence may or may not include basic kitchen appliances such as stove and refrigerator. Usually the fewer the items furnished, the lower the rent. If you have enough items or can acquire the essentials for an unfurnished residence, the savings in rent payments can be considerable.

You will pay lower rent by providing your own furniture.

Home furnishings can be purchased or rented. Purchase and rental payments should be carefully compared before any decision is made. Renting furnishings can be very expensive. Many furniture rental companies offer a *lease option*. With a lease option, each rent payment applies toward the purchase. Your option may be for a specified period of time, at the end of which you will have paid for the furniture entirely. An alternative is that at the end of the one-year rental period, you have the option to buy the furniture at a price reduced by a part of each rental payment made during that year.

Make a list of needed items for living independently.

Basic household and personal items necessary for setting up housekeeping include the following:

1. Towels, sheets, tablecloths, and cleaning cloths
2. Cleaning supplies (including mops, brooms, buckets, vacuum cleaner, detergent, and cleansers)
3. Personal items (including shampoo, cosmetics, soap, lotions, medicines, and other personal hygiene items)
4. Clothing, shoes, and other apparel

5. Dishes, silverware, pots, pans
6. Lamps, clothes hangers, clocks, radio, television, plants, and other decorations.

Carpeting is usually provided. But you may need to supply such items as throw rugs, draperies, a shower curtain, and mirrors. Some of these items may be contributed by one roommate or the other; some may be purchased jointly. A list of things to be purchased jointly should be made before the move is made. Each roommate should have available his or her share of the expenses prior to making the purchases. If you purchase some things jointly and one of you decides to move, you must then divide the purchases. At the time of purchase, each person should agree to take some items and give up other items. To avoid arguments later, keep a written record of these agreements.

Some expenses are shared with roommate(s).

When to Move

The timing of your move can be an important factor in its initial success or failure. At least six months before you actually plan to move, you should begin making preparations. Others who have experienced a similar move can be of great help to you with advice and contributions of household items.

At the time you are ready to move from your present home, you should make these preparations:

1. Set aside money in savings to cover cleaning deposits, first and last months' rent, fees, and initial expenses and purchases. In most cases $500 or more may be necessary. If you have a pet, an additional deposit or fee may be charged. Most deposits are refundable, if you meet your obligations. Fees are not refundable.

You need to be able to pay your rent on time.

2. Have a steady and reliable source of income with which you can pay the obligations you agree to pay, such as rental agreements, utility bills, and shared expenses.

3. Accumulate what you need to have in order to live alone, such as clothing, towels, sheets and other bed items, small appliances, dishes, etc. You may have been accumulating these things through the years. If so, you will have to purchase few items when you move.

4. Discuss with your roommate(s) all options, requirements, expenses, and other concerns. Decide if you are prepared financially and emotionally to meet the challenges. Be aware of each other's strengths and weaknesses and decide if you are willing to make changes to meet each other's needs.

5. Plan the move with your career goals in mind. If it is your goal to finish college, then your plan should work in harmony with that goal

A well-planned move can save you unnecessary expense and effort.

and help you to achieve-it. For example, if you are planning to go to college in September and live on campus, it would probably not be wise to go out on your own for the three summer months. The expenses would be too high, and you would be better off saving your money to help meet college expenses. Your goals and those of your roommate(s) should be discussed in detail.

6. Make arrangements for transporting furnishings.

A good way to organize your preparations is to make a needs inventory, such as the one shown in Figure 19-1. You and your roommate(s) will decide what will be needed and check off each item when it is acquired or accomplished.

FIGURE 19-1
Needs Inventory

	What Is Needed	Date Needed	Cost	Date Completed
1.	Dishes/towels	Oct. 1	$100	_____
2.	First and last months' rent	Oct. 1	700	_____
3.	Cleaning deposit	Oct. 1	100	_____
4.	Car (one to share)	Sept. 1	100/mth.	_____
5.	Radio/television	Oct. 1	300	_____
6.	Job for roommate	Aug. 1	——	_____
7.	Household Budget	Sept. 1	——	_____
8.	Discussion with roommate(s)	June 1	——	_____
9.	Discussion with parents	June 1	——	_____

GROUP FINANCIAL DECISIONS

Plan to pay your share of joint expenses.

All roommates will have a responsibility to meet the obligations they agree upon. Rent is an example of a joint obligation; each person must pay his or her share so that the total rent is paid on time. Utilities probably will be shared equally, as will garbage service, cable TV, monthly telephone charges, and group activity expenses. Long-distance telephone calls should be paid for individually. But expenses such as gasoline or groceries might be divided according to percentage of use. Laundry services usually are an individual expense.

Group budgeting allows for the careful allocation of expenses, so that each person pays his or her share. The budget should be prepared and put into writing following a good discussion. Figure 19-2 is an example of a group budget.

FIGURE 19-2
Group Budget

Expense	Monthly Cost	Cost Per Roommate		
		Robin	Helen	Arlene
Rent	$300	$100	$100	$100
Utilities (avg.)	60	20	20	20
Gasoline	60	30	20	10
Groceries	150	50	50	50
Household supplies	12	4	4	4
	$582	$204	$194	$184

A joint account can be used to pay some expenses.

A method of paying these expenses is for each person to have a separate account for individual expenses, and for the group to have a joint account from which shared expenses are paid. Each person is required to deposit a certain amount into the joint account by the first of each month. Then checks are written from the joint account to pay for rent, utilities, and other expenses incurred throughout the month. Individual expenses are paid individually.

Any plan for taking care of expenses should be agreed upon by all roommates, so that everyone is satisfied. Each will know how group expenses will be paid and how individual expenses will be paid.

RENTING YOUR RESIDENCE

Renting may cause some inconveniences.

A *tenant* is one who rents or leases from a landlord. A *landlord* is the owner of the property that is rented or leased to another person. The variety of rental housing provided by landlords emphasizes the advantages of renting. However, the lack of many conveniences and facilities provided by landlords adds to the disadvantages of renting your residence.

Advantages of Renting

Rental living is the most popular choice among singles and young married couples. Renting provides a number of advantages, such as mobility, convenience, social life, and lower living expenses.

Mobility. Many single persons prefer to rent because of the ease and speed with which they can move when a good job opportunity comes along. One of the advantages of renting is that the living arrangement need not be permanent. If you plan to work or go to school for only a few months, renting your residence for that short period is wise.

Convenience. Many landlords prove a number of conveniences for their tenants. For example, some rental properties have laundry facilities in each unit; others have laundry facilities located in a central area for all tenants. Extra storage space may also be provided for the convenience of the tenant. Recreational facilities are an important addition to many rental properties. Finally, many apartment or condominium complexes are conveniently located near major shopping areas, downtown areas, or important industrial and professional business centers.

Many apartments have recreational facilities.

Social Life. Apartments located in multi-unit buildings of any size offer the opportunity to meet others and socialize on an informal basis. You are not isolated, without neighbors and other people nearby, when living in a rental complex. In addition, recreational facilities at many large complexes provide numerous opportunities to socialize regularly.

Socializing is easier in a multi-unit building.

Lower Living Expenses. Apartments usually are less expensive to rent than houses. But the most important factor in lowering individual living expenses is provided by sharing expenses with roommates.

Disadvantages of Renting

Anyone who has lived in apartments or other rental properties can list numerous disadvantages. Noise, lack of privacy, small quarters, lack of storage space, lack of parking space, and expense are frequently mentioned disadvantages of renting.

Noise. Those who live in dormitories, apartments, duplexes, or condominiums share common walls with neighbors above, below, or beside them. Consequently, music, conversations, and other activities of neighbors can be overheard. Late hours or unusual habits of neighbors can be very irritating.

Close living creates noise problems.

Lack of Privacy. Because conversations and other activities can be overheard through common walls, tenants often feel that their neighbors know too much about their private lives. Problems associated with too many shared facilities—laundry, recreation, etc.—also become very annoying to some tenants after a time.

Small Quarters. The typical apartment is smaller than some other housing alternatives. Five hundred to 1,000 square feet of living space is average for an apartment. A house may have 1,200 or more square feet of living space.

Lack of Storage Area. The small size of most dormitory rooms and apartments adds to the problem of adequate cabinet and closet space. The smaller the rental unit, the less cabinet and closet space available, and the larger the amount of open space. Also, few rental properties offer more than a small amount of additional storage space for rarely used items.

You may not have all the storage space you need.

Lack of Parking Space. Many rental properties do not provide garages or off-street parking. Tenants' automobiles are subjected to the hazards of the weather as well as hazards associated with parking on busy streets. In those complexes that provide parking lots, visitor parking is often very limited.

Expense. Generally the larger and nicer the rental property, the higher the rent. The more extras provided, such as pool, laundry, and other facilities, the higher the rent. An apartment with a garage is also more expensive.

Rental Application

Whenever you rent a residence, you may be expected to fill out an application. The purpose of the application is to allow the landlord to check out your employment (income), previous rental experience, credit rating, and so on. This type of checking is done to assure the landlord that you are a good risk—that you pay your bills and will be a good tenant. A landlord may deny rental because of past rental experience, employment record, and credit rating. However, rental may not be denied solely on the basis of race, religion, national origin, sex, or marital status. Some states have passed laws to prohibit denial of rental to tenants with small children. Figure 19-3 is an example of a rental application.

Landlords often check references.

Leases and Month-to-Month Tenancy Agreements

Basically there are two types of agreements used when renting: leases, sometimes called rental agreements, and month-to-month tenancy agreements. A *lease* is a written agreement to rent certain property at a certain price for a specified time period. You may sign a lease for six months, one year, two years, or any period agreed upon. Rent will not be raised until the lease expires. But if you decide to move before the lease expires, you

A lease is a written contract.

FIGURE 19-3
Rental
Application

Rental Application

Name _____   Date _____

Address _____   Phone _____

Name(s) of other person(s) to be living here _____

_____

Previous Address _____

_____   How Long? _____

Employer _____   Phone _____

Address _____   How Long? _____

Bank _____Savings _____   Checking _____

Credit References

Name _____   Address _____

Name _____   Address _____

are still responsible for the remaining rent payments. At least 30 days prior to the end of your lease, the landlord should inform you of the rent increase. If you do not wish to stay longer than the time of your lease, you must notify the landlord in writing at least 30 days prior to departure. See Figure 19-4.

A *month-to-month tenancy agreement* is an agreement, oral or written, to rent certain property at a set price on a month-to-month basis; that is, with 30 days' notice, a tenant may move out and not be held responsible for additional rent payments. The ease of moving in and out is an advantage. But, because the length of time of the agreement is not specified, the rent may be raised at any time. You can also be asked to leave at any time.

A lease and a month-to-month tenancy agreement will include provisions for deposits and their return, termination of rental, rent payments, tenant and landlord responsibilities, and various other matters. If you do not understand any part of the lease or agreement, ask the landlord about it. If the answer is not satisfactory, get a legal interpretation or refuse to sign the agreement. Both a lease and a month-to-month tenancy agreement are legally binding documents when you have placed your signature on them. Therefore, it is very important that you fully understand the lease or agreement before signing it.

Understand the lease before you sign it.

FIGURE 19-4
Lease

RESIDENTIAL LEASE AGREEMENT
AND SECURITY DEPOSIT RECEIPT

THIS INDENTURE, made this _____29th_____ day of _____October_____ , 19¨ , between

_____Brendan Martin_____ , hereinafter designated the Lessor

or Landlord, and _____Teresa Thomas_____ , hereinafter designated the Lessee,

WITNESSETH: That the said Lessor/Landlord does by these presents lease and demise the residence

situated at _____614 Dundas Street_____ in _____Cincinnati_____ City,

_____Hamilton_____ County, _____Ohio_____ State,

of which the real estate is described as follows:

614 Dundas Street, Cincinnati, Ohio,

upon the following terms and conditions:

1. **Term:** The premises are leased for a term of one (1) years, commencing the 1st day of November , 19¨, and terminating the 30th day of November , 19¨.

2. **Rent:** The Lessee shall pay rent in the amount of $ 400.00 per month for the above premises on the 1st day of each month in advance to Landlord.

3. **Utilities:** Lessee shall pay for service and utilities supplied to the premises, except None which will be furnished by Landlord.

4. **Sublet:** The Lessee agrees not to sublet said premises nor assign this agreement nor any part thereof without the prior written consent of Landlord.

5. **Inspection of Premises:** Lessee agrees that he has made inspection of the premises and accepts the condition of the premises in its present state, and that there are no repairs, changes, or modifications to said premises to be made by the Landlord other than as listed herein.

6. **Lessee Agrees:**
   (1) To keep said premises in a clean and sanitary condition;
   (2) To properly dispose of rubbish, garbage and waste in a clean and sanitary manner at reasonable and regular intervals and to assume all costs of extermination and fumigation for infestation caused by Lessee;
   (3) To properly use and operate all electrical, gas, heating, plumbing facilities, fixtures and appliances;
   (4) To not intentionally or negligently destroy, deface, damage, impair or remove any part of the premises, their appurtenances, facilities, equipment, furniture, furnishings, and appliances, nor to permit any member of his family, invitee, licensee or other person acting under his control to do so;
   (5) Not to permit a nuisance or common waste.

7. **Maintenance of Premises:** Lessee agrees to mow and water the grass and lawn, and keep the grass, lawn, flowers and shrubbery thereon in good order and condition, and to keep the sidewalk surrounding said premises free and clear of all obstructions; to replace in a neat and workmanlike manner all glass and doors broken during occupancy thereof; to use due precaution against freezing of water or waste pipes and stoppage of same in and about said premises and that in case water or waste pipes are frozen or become clogged by reason of neglect of Lessee, the Lessee shall repair the same at his own expense as well as all damage caused thereby.

8. **Alterations:** Lessee agrees not to make alterations or do or cause to be done any painting or wallpapering to said premises without the prior written consent of Landlord.

9. **Use of Premises:** Lessee shall not use said premises for any purpose other than that of a residence and shall not use said premises or any part thereof for any illegal purpose. Lessee agrees to conform to municipal, county and state codes, statutes, ordinances and regulations concerning the use and occupation of said premises.

10. **Pets and Animals:** Lessee shall not maintain any pets or animals upon the premises without the prior written consent of Landlord.

11. **Access:** Landlord shall have the right to place and maintain "for rent" signs in a conspicuous place on said premises for thirty days prior to the vacation of said premises. Landlord reserves the right of access to the premises for the purpose of:
    (a) Inspection;
    (b) Repairs, alterations or improvements;
    (c) To supply services; or
    (d) To exhibit or display the premises to prospective or actual purchasers, mortgagees, tenants, workmen, or contractors.
    Access shall be at reasonable times except in case of emergency or abandonment.

12. **Surrender of Premises:** In the event of default in payment of any installation of rent or at the expiration of said term of this lease, Lessee will quit and surrender the said premises to Landlord.

13. **Security Deposit:** The Lessee has deposited the sum of $ 400.00 , receipt of which is hereby acknowledged, which sum shall be deposited by Landlord in a trust account with Citizens bank, savings and loan association or licensed escrow, Cincinnati branch, whose address is 201 Main Street, Cincinnati, Ohio.

All or a portion of such deposit may be retained by Landlord and a refund of any portion of such deposit is conditioned as follows:
   (1) Lessee shall fully perform obligations hereunder and those pursuant to Chapter 207, Laws of 1973, 1st Ex Session or as may be subsequently amended;
   (2) Lessee shall occupy said premises for one (1) months or longer from date hereof;
   (3) Lessee shall clean and restore said residence and return the same to Landlord in its initial condition, except for reasonable wear and tear, upon the termination of this tenancy and vacation of apartment;
   (4) Lessee shall have remedied or repaired any damage to apartment premises;
   (5) Lessee shall surrender to Landlord the keys to premises;
Any refund from security deposit, as by itemized statement shown to be due to Lessee, shall be returned to Lessee within fourteen (14) days after termination of this tenancy and vacation of the premises.

IN WITNESS WHEREOF, the Lessee has hereunto set his hand and seal the day and year first above written. /s/ Brendan Martin   /s/ Teresa Thomas

LANDLORD   LESSEE
610 Dundas Street

Cincinnati, Ohio

ADDRESS

(Acknowledgment)

Source: *Real Estate Principles & Practices,* Maurice A. Unger and George R. Karvel, Seventh Ed., South-Western Publishing Co., 1983.

Inventory

If you reside in a rental property, you are expected to leave the property as you found it. Normal wear and tear is expected and accepted. However, anything broken or misplaced is not acceptable. Therefore, to assure that you are not accused of such acts as breaking, damaging, or taking furnishings, take an inventory of the premises at the time you move in. The inventory should list and describe the conditions of the property. You will note broken windows, missing window screens, holes in walls, torn carpeting, plumbing problems, appliance damage or problems, etc. This inventory should be taken with the landlord, and a copy made for each of you. When you move out, you and your landlord should once again take an inventory. Figure 19-5 shows an inventory and condition report that can be used in a variety of rental situations.

Take an inventory when you move in.

LANDLORD/TENANT RESPONSIBILITIES

Although most states have passed landlord/tenant laws, there are no national laws. However, landlord/tenant laws for residential rental units generally include similarly worded landlord and tenant obligations.

Landlord Obligations

Housing laws in most states require that landlords provide a dwelling place that is habitable (livable) at all times. A dwelling place is considered habitable if the following conditions are met:

Landlords have responsibilities to tenants.

1. The exterior (including roof, walls, doors, and windows) is weatherproof and waterproof.
2. Floors, walls, ceilings, stairs, and railings are in good repair.
3. Elevators, halls, and stairwells meet fire and safety regulations. (Smoke detectors are required in each unit in most states. Tenants are responsible for testing the alarms, replacing batteries, and reporting any defects.)
4. Adequate locks are provided for all outside doors, working latches are provided for all windows, and exits meet fire and safety regulations.
5. Plumbing facilities comply with local and state laws and are in good working condition.
6. Water supply provided is adequate.
7. Lighting, wiring, heating, air conditioning, and appliances are in good condition and comply with local and state building and safety codes.

Safety standards must be met in rental units.

FIGURE 19-5
Inventory and
Condition
Report

INVENTORY AND CONDITION REPORT

Use this report to record the contents and condition of your unit when you move in and before moving out. If you mark anything as being either dirty or damaged, describe it fully on an additional sheet. Use the blank before each item to indicate how many there are. Ask the landlord to sign your copy.

LIVING ROOM		Dirty Yes* No	Damaged Yes* No			Dirty Yes* No	Damaged Yes* No
___ Couch	1	☐ ☐	☐ ☐	___ Oven racks	43	☐ ☐	☐ ☐
___ Chair	2	☐ ☐	☐ ☐	___ Broiler pan	44	☐ ☐	☐ ☐
___ End table	3	☐ ☐	☐ ☐	___ Working refrigerator	45	☐ ☐	☐ ☐
___ Easy chair	4	☐ ☐	☐ ☐	___ Ice trays	46	☐ ☐	☐ ☐
___ Floor lamp	5	☐ ☐	☐ ☐	___ Working sink	47	☐ ☐	☐ ☐
___ Table lamp	6	☐ ☐	☐ ☐	___ Working garbage disposal	48	☐ ☐	☐ ☐
___ Coffee table	7	☐ ☐	☐ ☐	___ Counter tops	49	☐ ☐	☐ ☐
___ Light fixture	8	☐ ☐	☐ ☐	___ Range hood with working fan	50	☐ ☐	☐ ☐
___ Rug or carpet	9	☐ ☐	☐ ☐	___ Working dishwasher	51	☐ ☐	☐ ☐
Floor	10	☐ ☐	☐ ☐	___ Hot and cold running water	52	☐ ☐	☐ ☐
Walls	11	☐ ☐	☐ ☐	___ Drawers	53	☐ ☐	☐ ☐
Ceiling	12	☐ ☐	☐ ☐	___ Dinette table	54	☐ ☐	☐ ☐
				___ Dinette chairs	55	☐ ☐	☐ ☐
BEDROOM				___ Light fixture	56	☐ ☐	☐ ☐
___ Bed frame(s)	13	☐ ☐	☐ ☐	Floor	57	☐ ☐	☐ ☐
___ Headboard(s)	14	☐ ☐	☐ ☐	Walls	58	☐ ☐	☐ ☐
___ Mattress	15	☐ ☐	☐ ☐	Ceiling	59	☐ ☐	☐ ☐
___ Mattress cover	16	☐ ☐	☐ ☐				
Bed springs	17	☐ ☐	☐ ☐	**BATHROOM**			
___ Dresser	18	☐ ☐	☐ ☐	___ Towel racks	60	☐ ☐	☐ ☐
___ Nightstand	19	☐ ☐	☐ ☐	___ Tissue holder	61	☐ ☐	☐ ☐
___ Drapes or curtains	20	☐ ☐	☐ ☐	___ Mirror	62	☐ ☐	☐ ☐
___ Mirror	21	☐ ☐	☐ ☐	___ Medicine cabinet	63	☐ ☐	☐ ☐
___ Light fixture	22	☐ ☐	☐ ☐	___ Counter top	64	☐ ☐	☐ ☐
___ Rug or carpet	23	☐ ☐	☐ ☐	___ Working sink	65	☐ ☐	☐ ☐
Floor	24	☐ ☐	☐ ☐	___ Working tub	66	☐ ☐	☐ ☐
Walls	25	☐ ☐	☐ ☐	___ Working shower	67	☐ ☐	☐ ☐
Ceiling	26	☐ ☐	☐ ☐	___ Working toilet	68	☐ ☐	☐ ☐
				___ Toilet seat	69	☐ ☐	☐ ☐
BEDROOM				___ Shower curtain	70	☐ ☐	☐ ☐
___ Bed frame(s)	27	☐ ☐	☐ ☐	___ Cabinet	71	☐ ☐	☐ ☐
___ Headboard(s)	28	☐ ☐	☐ ☐	___ Light fixture	72	☐ ☐	☐ ☐
___ Mattress	29	☐ ☐	☐ ☐	___ Hot and cold running water	73	☐ ☐	☐ ☐
___ Mattress cover	30	☐ ☐	☐ ☐	Floor	74	☐ ☐	☐ ☐
___ Bed springs	31	☐ ☐	☐ ☐	Walls	75	☐ ☐	☐ ☐
___ Dresser	32	☐ ☐	☐ ☐	Ceiling	76	☐ ☐	☐ ☐
___ Nightstand	33	☐ ☐	☐ ☐				
___ Drapes or curtains	34	☐ ☐	☐ ☐	**MISCELLANEOUS**			
___ Mirror	35	☐ ☐	☐ ☐	___ Door key	77	☐ ☐	☐ ☐
___ Light fixture	36	☐ ☐	☐ ☐	___ Windows	78	☐ ☐	☐ ☐
___ Rug or carpet	37	☐ ☐	☐ ☐	___ Window screens	79	☐ ☐	☐ ☐
Floor	38	☐ ☐	☐ ☐	___ Mailbox	80	☐ ☐	☐ ☐
Walls	39	☐ ☐	☐ ☐	___ Mailbox key	81	☐ ☐	☐ ☐
Ceiling	40	☐ ☐	☐ ☐	___ Thermostat	82	☐ ☐	☐ ☐
				___ Other	83	☐ ☐	☐ ☐
KITCHEN				___	84	☐ ☐	☐ ☐
___ Working stove	41	☐ ☐	☐ ☐	Do all the windows work?			
___ Working oven	42	☐ ☐	☐ ☐	Does the heat work properly?			

_____ Tenant

_____ Witness

_____ Date

_____ Landlord

_____ Date

* Describe fully on an additional sheet.

Source: Oregon Student Public Interest Research Group (OSPIRG)

8. Buildings and grounds are clean and sanitary; garbage receptacles are adequate. (Tenants may be responsible for garbage removal charges.)

Tenant Obligations

Tenant obligations usually are stated specifically in the lease or month-to-month agreement. If tenant obligations are not stated, the following obligations and responsibilities are implied:

1. To read, understand, and abide by the terms of any lease or month-to-month agreement signed.

2. To pay the rent on or before the due date. Failure to make a rent payment as stated in the lease or rental agreement may result in late fees, termination of the lease or agreement, or eviction. Through *eviction*, a landlord may legally demand that a tenant move from the premises.

You must give notice of your intent to vacate.

3. To give 30 to 60 days' notice of intent to move. This notice will prevent the forfeiture of deposits and allow the landlord time to rent the unit before you move. See Figure 19-6.

4. To keep the premises in good, clean condition and to prevent unnecessary wear and tear or damage to the unit.

Use landlord's property with care and consideration.

5. To use a dwelling unit only for the purposes for which it is intended. For example, you should treat appliances and other furnishings in a reasonable manner. If the landlord pays for any or all utilities, use them in a reasonable manner. If a washer and dryer are provided in individual living units, any commercial usage is prohibited.

FIGURE 19-6
Notice to Landlord

Date_____

Dear _____:
      Landlord's Name

I will vacate the premises located at _____
Apt. _____, on _____. This letter constitutes
30 days' notice as required in my lease.

Attached is a copy of the Inventory and Condition Report that I completed
when I moved in. You will note the items for which I am not responsible. I
believe the premises will be left in the condition in which they were found,
with these exceptions:

for which I know I am responsible. Other than those listed, I know of no
other damages to the premises, and I believe I am entitled to a refund of
$_____ of my original deposit of $_____, made when
I moved in.

My new address will be _____

_____
Please mail my deposit check to the address within 30 days of vacancy.

               Yours truly,

            _____
               Tenant(s) Name(s)

6. To allow the landlord access to the living unit to make repairs and/ or improvements.
7. To obey the rules of the apartment complex or other community living area covering quiet hours, use of recreational facilities, use of laundry facilities, parking regulations, etc.

BUYING YOUR RESIDENCE

Home ownership provides financial advantages.

Many people reach a point in their lives when they must decide whether to buy a house or continue to rent. Because the purchase of a home is probably the most important and most expensive decision people make, the advantages and disadvantages should be weighed carefully. Although many single people own their own homes, marriage and family usually create the greatest needs for home ownership. To provide more space and room for expansion, hobbies, and recreation for children are often the reasons given for buying a home.

Advantages of Home Ownership

Some of the more important advantages that home ownership provides are the savings in taxes, an increase in equity with each payment, and increased privacy and personal freedom. Home ownership likewise provides a sense of security, permanence, and belonging to a neighborhood or city. The personal values that cause a desire for home ownership are hard to describe, but nevertheless they are important factors in the decision to buy a home.

Tax Savings. Interest paid on your mortgage and real estate property taxes are deductible from state and federal income taxes. The effect of these deductions is to lower the cost of home ownership. Renters cannot deduct any part of their rent payments from their income taxes.

Equity Increases. *Equity* is the difference between the appraised value of your home and what you owe on your home. For example, if you purchase a home valued at $75,000 with a mortgage of $50,000, your equity is $25,000. With each mortgage payment, you decrease the amount of debt but increase the amount of equity. When you sell the home for more than you paid for it, you will make money because you will have the amount of your equity and a profit returned to you.

Privacy and Personal Freedom. Home ownership offers privacy and personal freedom not available to renters. In your own home you make all the decisions and have free use of all facilities. Owning a home also provides a feeling of security and independence. Knowing that the roof over your head is yours to do with as you wish and when you wish can be very satisfying. With home ownership comes the freedom to have as many pets as you want, a backyard to work and play in at any time, and possibly an opportunity to plant a garden.

Disadvantages of Home Ownership

Most of the disadvantages of home ownership relate to cost. In addition to a monthly mortgage payment, other costs generally not found in renting are necessary for homeowners. Some of the costs involved are the down payment, mortgage, closing, property taxes, insurance, utilities, and maintenance and repairs.

Down Payment. Most conventional (not government backed) loans require a 10 to 30 percent down payment. For example, if you are purchasing a home for $50,000, you will need $5,000 (10 percent) to $15,000 (30 percent) for the down payment. For many singles and young married couples, saving enough money for the down payment takes a number of years.

Mortgage. The balance of the purchase price, after the down payment, is usually borrowed from a bank or other financial institution. You will sign a note, which is secured by a 20- to 30-year mortgage. The larger your down payment, the lower your monthly mortgage payments. Property taxes and insurance premiums are often included in the mortgage payments.

Closing. Closing costs may add another $1,000 to $5,000 to the purchase of your home. The purchaser usually pays for a title search to have the abstract on the property updated. The *abstract* is a summary of all previous transactions involving the property you wish to buy. Additional costs that the purchaser may pay are for a personal credit report, loan fees, assumption fees (to assume someone else's mortgage loan), closing fees, recording fees, tax and interest prorations, and fire insurance.

Property Taxes. Homeowners pay property taxes based on the market value of their home. The *market value* is the highest price a property will bring in a competitive and open market. The local taxing authority determines a taxable value for your home that is close to the market value. A tax rate is determined based on a county budget. If the property tax rate is $24 a thousand, and you own a $50,000 home, you will pay 50 times

$24, or $1,200 a year, in property taxes. The total amount of property taxes paid annually is deductible on Schedule A of your tax return.

Insurance. A homeowner must have insurance covering the structure as well as the contents. A more detailed explanation of homeowners insurance is presented in Chapter 10.

Utilities. Because most homes are larger than apartments or other rental units, the utility bills are usually larger, too. The homeowner pays for all utilities and garbage services, whereas a renter may pay for some but not all these items. In addition, when any repairs are needed to water or sewer lines, the homeowner is fully responsible for the costs involved.

Some bills are higher for houses than apartments.

Maintenance and Repairs. Maintenance and repairs, inside and outside the home, are the responsibility of the owner. These responsibilities include painting, mowing, trimming, landscaping, fertilizing, pulling weeds, spraying for insects, etc. Roofs are generally good for 15 to 25 years. If you have purchased an existing (not new) home, you may have to replace the roof after only a few years. The amount of insulation necessary to keep the house warm in winter and cool in summer may need to be increased. Energy-saving improvements, such as adding insulation, are deductible on your income tax return.

The owner makes all improvements and repairs.

The Process of Buying Your Home

If after you consider carefully all the costs involved, you decide to own a house, you begin the process of purchasing a home. This process can take many weeks or even months. Generally, the procedure can be summarized as in the following paragraphs.

Searching for your home can take several months.

Selection. In order to find the house you want to buy, you will need to see many houses. You can look by yourself or work with a real estate salesperson, who is trained to know the market, help you find the right home, and assist you in the purchase, financing, and closing. There is no charge to you, the purchaser, for these services. Either way, you will visit many homes listed with the real estate agency, advertised for sale in the newspaper, or that you drive past and want to see. In the newspaper classified ads, homes are listed by area of town or geographic location. Some are for sale by the owner; others are listed with real estate offices.

Real estate offices that belong to a multiple listing service offer a valuable service to homeowners: wide exposure to persons in the business of selling homes. Most metropolitan, urban, and suburban areas have many real estate sales offices located within their boundaries. When these real estate offices form an organization called a ***multiple listing service***, all listings from each office are combined into one book. All salespeople within that geographic area have access to all real estate listings and can sell any one of them to a buyer. Thus, when you list your house for sale with one real estate salesperson, you really have all the salespeople in the area working for you as well. The person who lists your house could receive half of the sales commission; the person who sells your house would receive the other half. The cost to you is the same, yet your exposure to the sales market is much greater when you list your home with a person or company that is a member of a multiple listing service.

All salespeople have access to multiple listings.

Persons seeking to buy a home in a specific area also have greater exposure to available homes because they can see many listings in all parts of the city. The cost to the buyer is the same; real estate commissions are included in the sale price of a home. Most multiple listing books come out twice a month. Homes are listed according to value and location. The less expensive homes are listed first in each section. For example, one section of town might be called South Hills, and the lowest priced home in South Hills might be $45,000. All homes in South Hills would be listed in a group, from $45,000 homes to the most expensive.

After you have viewed many homes in the area you prefer, you may decide you want to buy one of them. Before you can take possession of the house, you must complete the formal buying process, which may take several weeks or months.

Earnest Money Offer. To let the seller (owner) know you want to buy his or her home, you sign an agreement called an ***earnest money offer***. It is a formal, written offer to buy the home. The offer explains the terms of the purchase—the down payment; the mortgage you will assume or get on your own; when you will pay what is due, take possession, and close the deal. This agreement is called an earnest money offer because with it you will pay a certain amount of money—the earnest money, usually $1,000 to $5,000, depending on the selling price—to show the seller that you are serious and that the home can be removed from the market. If you fail to meet the terms of the agreement, you will have damaged the seller because the house was held off the market for awhile and could not be sold to anyone else. Therefore, you may forfeit your earnest money to the seller if you do not buy the home according to the agreement. One way to avoid losing your money is to write into the offer that the sale is contingent on finding financing.

Protect yourself from losing an earnest money offer.

When the seller accepts your offer exactly as it is stated, this is called an ***acceptance***. You may withdraw your offer at any time until the seller

You can withdraw an
offer before it is
accepted.
accepts it. If any conditions of the offer are changed, the seller makes what is known as a ***counteroffer***. You have the choice of accepting or rejecting the counteroffer. For example, the seller may want a different date of possession or a larger cash down payment.

Escrow. After both parties have reached an agreement, a neutral third party is chosen to prepare the transaction for closing. The process whereby a neutral third party holds the deed and works through the details of a transaction for the purchase of a home is known as ***escrow***. The escrow agent accepts the earnest money offer and the amount of money paid, which is kept in a trust account. Then the escrow agent orders a title search, which lists all the facts about the property being purchased: name(s) of title owner(s), liens against the property, easements and assessments, property taxes, and so forth. Loan papers are ordered from lending institutions, and all necessary papers are prepared. If any
Problems sometimes
arise during the escrow
process.
problems arise, the buyer and seller are notified so that the problems can be resolved. Inspections, such as termite examinations, are carried out. Credit reports are ordered. Proper prorations are computed, and closing documents are prepared.

Closing. When the escrow process is completed, the seller and buyer are notified of a closing date. The buyer brings in the amount of money needed and signs necessary papers. Then the seller signs necessary papers. The escrow agent records necessary papers for transfer of title
The buyer takes pos-
session after closing.
and pays the money to the seller. Finally, the buyer can take possession of the property. The buyer of the house gets papers, such as title insurance policy and mortgage release, held in escrow when he or she makes the last mortgage payment. Until then, he or she holds only the mortgage papers.

MAKING THE MOVE

Several costs are involved in the actual, physical change of your residence. Two costs you will need to be prepared for are moving costs and installation charges.

Moving Costs

Moving costs may involve time and money in careful packing, storing, transporting, loading and unloading, and unpacking. The distance you move is an important factor. The greater the distance you move, the greater the expenditure of time, energy, and money. A move across town

The greater the distance, the higher the cost.

is much less expensive and demanding in terms of time and money than a cross-country move. If you have your own automobile, the problem is eased somewhat. Still, careful planning and packing are essential to be sure you move the items that you really need and will use.

In order to move your possessions to another residence, you may need to rent a truck or trailer; borrow a van or pickup; have friends or family help; or send some items by mail, freight, bus, or other available carrier. You may also decide to store some items because you have no immediate need for them, and because they would take up valuable space.

If you rent a truck or trailer, you may find a local rental agency that will rent one that you can leave in the city to which you are moving. One-way truck and trailer rental fees are based on a flat rate, plus mileage and gasoline. The rates vary and should be compared to get the best price. A typical rate is $100 a day, plus 20 cents a mile and gasoline. In addition, you may be charged a deposit of $300 or more that will be refunded when you return the truck to the designated location.

Rental rates vary.

Trucks, vans, pickups, and trailers may also be rented for local moves. The charges are similar, except that you will not pay as much per mile because you will not drive as far.

Figure 19-7 shows the truck rental charge to drive a one-way truck 100 miles. You will use about 10 gallons of gasoline, assuming you average 10 miles a gallon with the truck.

FIGURE 19-7
One-Way Truck Rental Charges

Refundable deposit (you may use credit card in lieu of cash)	$300.00*
Rental fee ($100 for 24 hours)	100.00
Mileage (100 miles at 20 cents a mile).	20.00
Gasoline (10 gallons at $1.35 a gallon)	13.50
Insurance (liability, collision, comprehensive, medical— required unless you have your own coverage to protect you)	20.00
Total.	$453.50

*$300.00 is refundable when the truck is returned in same condition as when rented.

Of course, if you hire a moving company to move your possessions to your new residence, the charges will be considerably more because you will pay for labor as well. By renting a truck, pickup, van, or trailer and using your own labor for loading, driving, and unloading, you save money. But you also accept the responsibility involved in using the equipment of others.

Installation Charges

As a new occupant of a house or rental unit, you will pay some installation charges. Although fees vary with the type and location of the residence, there are usually charges for installation of a telephone and cable TV, and for turning on the electricity and other utilities. To obtain these services, most of which are essential, you may be required to show your ability to meet your financial obligations. Many utility companies charge a deposit, which is refundable after a year or two, when you have proved your ability to pay your bills.

Hook-up charges can be costly.

FIGURE 19-8
Telephone Services and Charges

Security deposit (For someone who has not established credit. Deposit is held for one year, then refunded with interest as a credit on monthly bill.)	$60.00
Installation (New service; no existing wall jacks) $2.40 per jack, plus labor at a minimum of $25.00 for the first 15 minutes. For every 15 minutes thereafter, add $9.00.	$35.55
Moving from one residence to another within the same city	$35.55
Monthly service Standard wall phone Touch-Tone service Private line Two-party line Two-party limited line (limited to 35 calls a month; additional calls, 12 cents each)	$ 2.75 $ 1.00 $14.00 $10.94 $ 7.25
Standard mounting cord, (from wall) 7 or 14 feet	N/C
Standard handset cord, 6 or 12 feet (Longer cords may be purchased at varying lengths and prices.)	N/C
Call Forwarding $2.75 both for $5.75 Call Waiting (must be private line) $3.50	

Connection charge $6.10
                                                                   no extra charge
                                                                   for both services
Disconnect one service $6.10	

Unlisted number requested at time service begins	N/C
Unlisted number requested later (requires number change)	$25.25
Unlisted number (monthly)	$ 1.55
Extension phones One-time connection charge Monthly rental (varies with type of telephone)	$ 5.00 $2.75 – $4.00

Other companies, such as the telephone company, charge a one-time fee that is not refundable. You may be charged a fee of $60 to $100, depending on your city, to have a telephone installed. The installation charge is added onto the first bill you receive. Then monthly service rates continue according to the type and number of phones you choose, kinds of services selected, and other factors. For example, you pay more if you have a private line, or if you have Touch-Tone service. You also pay more to have an *unlisted telephone number*. If your telephone number is unlisted, it is not listed in the telephone directory and cannot be obtained through directory assistance. An unlisted number assures privacy and prevents many unwanted calls.

Monthly service charges rise as options increase.

A chart showing telephone services and charges is given in Figure 19-8. Charges for installation, line, equipment rental, and other services will vary with geographic areas and within various parts of large cities. Monthly telephone bills will include charges for long-distance calls and federal and state taxes, which will cause the amounts to vary each month.

VOCABULARY

Directions: Can you find the definition for each of the following terms used in Chapter 19?

utility	landlord
deposit	lease
tenant	acceptance
furnished	escrow
unlisted telephone number	market value
unfurnished	eviction
equity	month-to-month tenancy
earnest money offer	agreement
counteroffer	abstract
lease option	

1. A landlord's legal remedy for removing someone from a rental unit.

2. A condition of a rental unit when nothing is provided—no chairs, tables, beds, etc.

3. A service, such as light, power, water, or gas, which is provided by public companies or corporations.

4. The difference between the value of your home and what you owe on your home.

5. A pledge or a down payment.

6. An agreement whereby each rent payment applies toward the purchase of an item.

7. A rental unit, with furnishings, such as living room furniture, bed, table, and chairs, provided by the landlord.

8. One who rents or leases from a landlord.

9. A summary of all previous transactions involving a certain property.

10. The highest price a property will bring in a competitive and open market.

11. When the seller accepts a buyer's offer exactly as it is stated.

12. A telephone number that is not listed in the telephone directory and cannot be obtained through directory assistance.

13. The owner of the property rented or leased to another person.

14. A written agreement to rent property at a certain price for a specified time period.

15. A change by the seller of any of the conditions of the original offer.

16. A written agreement letting the seller know that you want to buy the house.

17. A written agreement to rent certain property at a set price on a month-to-month basis.

18. A neutral third party who is used to prepare the real estate transaction for closing.

ITEMS FOR DISCUSSION

1. How soon before a move should you begin making plans?

2. List four advantages of renting a residence.

3. List four disadvantages of renting a residence.

4. What is the difference between a furnished and an unfurnished residence?

5. How does a condominium differ from an apartment?

6. What is the purpose of a rental application?

7. How does a lease differ from a month-to-month tenancy agreement?

8. Why should you complete and have a landlord sign an inventory when you move into a rental unit?

9. List five tenant obligations when renting.

10. List six conditions a landlord must meet in order to make rental property habitable.

11. What are some advantages of owning your home?

12. What would be the typical down payment on a $50,000 home?

13. What is the market value of a home?

APPLICATIONS

1. Ask two persons each of the questions below. Based on the answers, determine if the three of you would be a compatible living group.

   (a) Do you smoke or drink? How do you feel about persons who do?

   (b) Are you a clean, fussy housekeeper or easygoing, casual, and relaxed about your surroundings? How often do you clean?

   (c) Do you work steadily, part-time or full-time? How would you pay your share of the rent and other shared expenses?

   (d) What are some of your goals regarding college, your job, recreation?

   (e) What do you like to do in your spare time? What are your group activities? your individual activities?

   (f) What type of transportation do you have or plan to have? What are the costs involved? Which costs will be shared?

2. What have you accumulated that you would want to take with you to a new residence? (Examples: radio, television, towels, furniture, cleaning items, dishes.)

3. What would you have to buy that is essential to living independently?

4. Make a list of things you should do before considering moving out on your own.

5. In order to move your possessions from your present home to a new residence, what types of transportation are available to you? What is the best and least expensive for you?

CASE PROBLEMS AND ACTIVITIES

1. Prepare a report comparing the rental prices and availability of apartments, duplexes, condominiums, and houses in your area. To compare prices, living conditions must be comparable; you must compare two-bedroom unfurnished apartments to two-bedroom unfurnished duplexes, etc. Also note how many are available in each category at the present time, the high and low prices, and the average rental prices.

2. Study the listings of homes for sale in the classified ads of your newspaper. Answer these questions:

   (a) What is the lowest sale price you can find?

   (b) Describe the house with the lowest sale price.

   (c) What is the highest sale price you can find?

   (d) Describe the house with the highest sale price.

   (e) How many houses are for sale in one day's newspaper ads? What is the name and date of the newspaper?

   (f) How many homes are listed for sale by owner?

   (g) Describe the house that you would choose to own; include size, price, features, location, etc.

3. Using the community resources in your area, find out the hookup or installation deposits and fees for the following services:

   (a) Telephone

   (b) Electricity

   (c) Cable TV

   (d) Water or garbage services

   Are any of these fees partially or fully refundable? If so, under what conditions?

4. Find out the monthly rates for the following telephone services in your area:

(a) Standard phone

(b) Touch-Tone service

(c) Colored phone

(d) Special model

(e) Private line

(f) Call Forwarding

(g) Call Waiting

(h) Unlisted telephone number

(i) Additional phones

CHAPTER 20

FAMILY DECISIONS

CHAPTER OBJECTIVES

After studying this chapter and completing the activities, you will be able to:

1. Describe the costs and planning involved in getting married.
2. Outline the steps needed in planning a successful vacation.
3. Discuss the planning and costs involved in having a baby.

MARRIAGE

An important decision usually made in the early adult years is about the family. Will you get married in the near future? Will you and your spouse both work? What are your desires about raising children? What are some joint family goals you want to plan? When you decide to begin your own family, these decisions need careful consideration.

Marriage is an important decision.

Couples planning a life together will make a number of decisions and choices. When planning for their marriage, a couple will discuss in detail the engagement, premarital counseling, ceremony costs and plans, and the honeymoon.

Engagement

When two people decide that they wish to be married, they become engaged. If an engagement ring is chosen, it is worn on the third finger of the left hand of the prospective bride. The choice of style, size, and kind of stone and setting will determine the price to be paid. The price of an engagement ring may range from a few hundred to a few thousand dollars or more. Jewelers generally counsel that it is wise to invest approximately two months' income in the engagement ring. Some couples prefer matching wedding bands, in which case an engagement ring often is not worn.

An engagement period of six months to a year is customary in this country. Once the engagement is announced, then begins the careful planning of the many steps to ensure a smooth and memorable wedding.

Premarital Counseling

In order to have a wedding in some churches, counseling sessions are often required. The couple meets with a member of the clergy or other counselor, together and separately, to discuss issues that will be vital to the success of the marriage and later family life. The sessions may be a predetermined number, such as four or six. Or the number of sessions may vary according to how well prepared for marriage the counselor or cleric thinks the couple is. Topics most often discussed include money and budgeting, the meaning of the marriage commitment, in-laws and other potential problems, and religious aspects of marriage that are unique to each faith and each house of worship. The counseling sessions should be planned early so that they are taken care of well before final preparations are being made for the wedding.

Premarital counseling often answers important questions.

Ceremony Costs and Plans

Planning for the wedding ceremony should begin at least six months in advance. Figure 20-1 is a bride's budget worksheet, which shows the many preparations to consider. This worksheet should be completed in rough draft form as the wedding planning progresses. The cost of each item will vary according to style, quantity, and preferences. As costs begin to add up, the bride and groom may decide to eliminate, expand, or reduce some of the expenses involved.

Guest lists are prepared by the bride and groom and by each set of parents; these lists are then combined. Guests may include relatives and friends of the couple. The number of guests being invited and the size of the wedding party will determine the number of invitations needed, size of the church, cost of the reception, and so forth. The ***wedding party*** consists of the persons who are active participants in the wedding ceremony: the bride and groom, best man, maid or matron of honor, bridesmaids, ushers, flower girl, and so on.

Guest lists are prepared by the bride and groom.

Traditionally, almost all wedding expenses have gone to the bride's family. This custom is changing. Now, the groom's family usually picks up

FIGURE 20-1
Bride's Budget
Worksheet

ENGAGEMENT PARTY	BRIDESMAIDS' LUNCHEON	RECEPTION
Invitations............. $____	Invitations and	Hall rental.............. $____
Food................... ____	place cards .... $____	Decorations............ ____
Beverages .... ____	Food................... ____	Music.................. ____
Music.................. ____	Beverages .... ____	Food................... ____
Rental fees .... ____	Rental fees .... ____	Beverages .... ____
Decorations........... ____	Decorations........... : ____	Wedding cake.......... ____
Professional	Professional	Favors .... ____
services .... ____	services .... ____	Professional
Gratuities.............. ____	*Gratuities.............. ____	services .... ____
		*Gratuities.............. ____
Total.................. $____	Total.................. $____	
		Total.................. $____
STATIONERY	**PHOTOGRAPHS**	
		OTHER
Invitations............. $____	Engagement	
Announcements .... ____	portrait.............. $____	Bridal consultant
At-home cards .... ____	Wedding	fees................. $____
Personal	portrait .... ____	Accommodations
stationery........... ____	Formal photos .... ____	for out-of-town
Stamps .... ____	Reprints .... ____	attendants .... ____
		*Security guard .... ____
Total.................. $____	Total.................. $____	Sound recording
		of ceremony .... ____
CLOTHING	**WEDDING CEREMONY**	*Insurance for
		wedding gifts .... ____
Wedding dress........ $____	Sanctuary rental .... $____	Bride's
Headpiece/veil........ ____	Music.................. ____	blood test
Shoes.................. ____	Decorations........... ____	(if required) .... ____
Accessories............ ____	Flowers for	Groom's ring .... ____
Personal	attendants .... ____	Gift for groom .... ____
trousseau........... ____	Aisle runner........... ____	Gift for
	Transportation	attendants .... ____
Total.................. $____	to/from ceremony... ____	Special effects......... ____
	*Gratuities .... ____	Other fees .... ____
* Denotes expenses usually	Miscellaneous .... ____	____
shared by both families		____
	Total.................. $____	
		Total.................. $____
GRAND TOTAL.. $____		

Wedding costs can be
shared.

some of the expenses—such as rehearsal dinner or reception—or splits the expenses with the bride's family. Generally, however, the following expenses belong solely to the groom:

1. Bride's ring(s)
2. Marriage license
3. Wedding gift for the bride
4. Gifts for the best man, groomsmen, and ring bearer
5. The bride's bouquet and going away corsage, corsages for mothers and grandmothers, and boutonnieres for the men in the wedding party
6. Cleric's or judge's fee
7. Bachelor dinner (unless given and paid for by the best man)
8. Lodging (if necessary) for out-of-town groomsmen

9. Groom's special clothing, including clothing for rehearsal dinner, wedding, honeymoon
10. Expenses in sending wedding presents to new home
11. Honeymoon costs (which may be shared equally between bride and groom if the bride is working)

The planning of the wedding is usually done jointly by the bride and groom, with much consideration given to cost. The size of the wedding, the time of day, the location, and the formality of the bride's dress are what determine the style of the wedding. A *formal wedding* may be held in the daytime or in the evening, and all guests and participants wear formal attire (which, for evening, includes long gowns and tuxedos). A *semi-formal wedding* usually is held during the afternoon or early evening, with less formal wear required of guests. While the wedding party may still dress as formally or informally as they choose, guests generally wear suits and dresses normally chosen for special occasions. An *informal wedding* may be held outside, in a church, or almost anywhere. No special clothing is required for the wedding party or for the guests.

Other types of wedding ceremonies are preferred by some couples. A civil ceremony is performed by a public official, such as a judge or justice of the peace. This type of ceremony is quick, inexpensive, and requires the presence of two witnesses in most states.

Honeymoon

Most honeymoons are out of town.

Immediately following the wedding reception, the newly married couple usually takes a honeymoon trip. Most couples plan a trip out of town. Resort areas and places that provide different types of entertainment are popular. A honeymoon may last from several days to several weeks, and cost as much as several thousand dollars. A couple generally plans the honeymoon together, carefully considering preferences and costs involved. Honeymoons may be inexpensive automobile trips, elaborate cruises, or flights to exotic islands. The length and type of honeymoon will depend on time available, cost, and desires of the couple. More elaborate plans usually involve using travel agencies and other sources of travel information. Travel options are discussed thoroughly in the vacations section of this chapter.

FAMILY LIVING DECISIONS

When two people unite in marriage, they form a new family unit. Thereafter, decisions are made by the couple, based on each person's

Families must set goals for the future, too.

needs and wants, and joint needs for the future. Ideally, joint decisions regarding family goals, the family budget, and division of responsibilities must be open to discussion at all times.

Family Goals

Just as individuals make plans and goals, the family unit must examine needs and priorities and set goals for the future. Plans for major purchases, vacations, leisure activities, hobbies, club and group memberships, and special events should be thoroughly discussed.

Budgeting will help goals become a reality.

The couple must look also at short-term goals, such as where to live; whether both partners will work; what major purchases to make this year and next; and what activities the couple will participate in, jointly and separately.

Intermediate goals include what will happen in the next five or ten years—whether children are wanted; where the couple will live, geographically; when to purchase a home; and the employment outlook and stability for each spouse.

More than half of all American wives choose to work or must work, even after children are born. Two incomes allow couples to purchase more goods and services because they have more disposable income; they can afford higher housing payments and qualify for more credit. The career goals of each spouse should be discussed, understood, and agreed upon by the couple. How long the wife will work, when and if the couple wants children, when the wife will return to work, if the husband will take leave from work for child care—all are important decisions.

Some couples may need to survive on one income temporarily while the other spouse finishes education, training, or job preparation. Because it takes five to ten years to become financially secure, many couples choose to work longer before having children. Other couples choose to keep two incomes and not have children.

Long-term goals include plans for children's education (savings and investments), special events, retirement, and vacations for leisure time.

To define each of the above types of goals is a time-consuming but necessary activity. This activity is important because it serves to outline the family's future expectations so that plans can be drawn to meet them.

Family Budget

A family budget should allow for savings and investments to meet future goals. Joint decisions are often complicated and difficult to reach because there are more variables to consider. Nevertheless, family budgeting is an essential part of a successful marriage. Financial security is an

Financial security helps
marriages.

important element in a successful relationship. And financial security can be attained by careful planning and budgeting.

Financial plans ensure that mutual goals will be met. The family budget makes provisions for short-term, intermediate, and long-term goals. A two-income family is able to set aside extra money for expected and unexpected events.

There are tax advantages to be considered in financial planning. For married couples, the total tax on combined earnings is lower. With planning, a couple can avoid taxes while setting aside money for future needs. A *tax shelter* is a legal method of avoiding paying taxes on present earnings. Couples whose combined incomes total $40,000 or more a year often seek tax shelters to avoid paying large amounts of taxes.

Working couples look
for tax shelters.

A *tax-deferred annuity* is a contract wherein you agree to set aside a certain amount of money each month and defer paying taxes on the earnings until a later date. The advantage of a tax-deferred annuity is that when you retire you will be earning less, and your total tax payments will be less.

Dividing Responsibilities

Two-income families will probably have different divisions of duties than one-income families. Because both spouses work, household responsibilities need to be divided appropriately so that each spouse bears an equal share of the burden. In addition to household chores and duties, the couple also needs to divide other responsibilities. For example, individual and joint checking accounts may be desirable. If there is only one checking account, it makes balancing the account much easier when only one person writes checks on that account. But who will carry the checkbook and be responsible for paying the bills? Many couples choose to have individual checking accounts, where each spouse is responsible for part of the income and part of the bills. For example, the wife may choose to pay utilities, groceries and household expenses, and her car payment. The husband may choose to pay the rent or house payment, entertainment, insurance, and miscellaneous expenses. Then each spouse is responsible to balance his or her checking account each month and meet his or her part of the budget.

Household
responsibilities differ
for working couples.

Separate accounts are
often desirable for
working couples.

Perhaps one spouse is in charge of collecting, storing, and retrieving tax information for the preparation of tax returns. The other spouse might be responsible for making vacation arrangements, reservations, and itineraries. By dividing and sharing the responsibilities of the household, goals can be achieved in an orderly manner with each spouse contributing equally.

VACATIONS

Vacations are an important part of our lives. Planned vacations maximize the time available for fun and enjoyment. Vacation decisions include determining the kind of vacation, making plans and reservations, at-home preparations, and covering last-minute details.

Kind of Vacation

The first decision is to determine the type of vacation you want: relaxation, excitement, travel, adventure, special events, visiting relatives, or any combination. The vacation plans for any type of vacation also depend on how long you have, including travel time, and how much total money you will have to spend.

The type of vacation determines other plans.

Based on type of vacation desired and time and money available, you can list your alternatives, as shown in Figure 20-2. Then you can discuss and weigh the alternatives and make a final decision.

FIGURE 20-2
Vacation
Analysis

$100 or less	$150-$500 to spend	$1,000 or more
Camping	Longer trip (total time)	Car or plane trip
Visiting relatives	Car trip	Amusement parks
Short trips	Sports (skiing, other	Motel/hotel
Sports events	adventure)	Varied entertain-
Tours/group travel	Entertainment/eating	ment options
Three days or less	out	Five days or more
	Three to five days	

The more money available, the longer and more expensive the vacation possible. Your choices may be different from those listed above. Each family needs to decide what type of vacation is desired, budget income to allow money to meet that need, and plan the vacation accordingly. While a camping trip may be very attractive to one family unit, it may be totally undesirable for another. Having a successful vacation depends on properly defining the type of vacation desired, having the money to spend on it, and planning it carefully.

Plans and Reservations

To make maximum use of time available for vacationing, it is a good idea to write out what will happen, when, at what cost, and what needs to be done. An *itinerary* is a detailed schedule of events, times, and places.

An itinerary lists your
plans in detail.

You can make your own for the entire trip, listing each day's activities. An example of a vacation trip itinerary is found in Figure 20-3.

All the different places you plan to go and things you plan to do should be listed on the itinerary. You may want to list the time it takes to do certain activities, distances to get to and from activities, methods of transportation, costs of entry, and special notes, such as "bring camera."

FIGURE 20-3
Itinerary

ITINERARY		
Date	Time	Activity
Monday	8:00 A.M.	Arrive at airport (Flight 739 leaves at 9:05 A.M.).
	10:00 A.M.	Arrive at Los Angeles airport. Take hotel shuttle service; arrive at hotel by 10:45 A.M.
	12:00 Noon	Lunch at hotel restaurant.
	1:30 P.M.	Disneyland for remainder of day. Dinner at Disneyland.
Tuesday	8:00 A.M.	Breakfast at Howard Johnson's.
	9:00 A.M.	Knott's Berry Farm (20 minute ride by tour bus). Spend day there; eat lunch there.
	7:00 P.M.	Leave Knott's Berry Farm; go to dinner at Bob's Big Boy.
	8:00 P.M.	Return to hotel.
Wednesday	8:00 A.M.	Breakfast at Pancake House.
	9:00 A.M.	Universal Studios. Tour begins at 10:00, lasts until noon.
	12:00 Noon	Lunch at nearby restaurant. Catch tour bus at 1:30 to return to hotel.

When designing your itinerary, be sure to leave enough time to do the planned activities in comfort and relaxation. Check on seasonal adjustments that may change operating days, amounts of fees, and opening or closing times.

Reservations are
recommended.

Reservations should be made whenever possible. A *reservation* is an advance commitment whereby you are assured of receiving a service. A room reservation guarantees that when you arrive at the hotel/motel, a room will be waiting for you. Hotels and motels may be booked up, or full, well in advance of your vacation date; therefore, reservations should be made early—a month or more before your vacation is not too soon.

Reservations should also be made for airlines, buses, trains, boats, or car rentals. If boarding passes are needed, you can get a reservation. Some airlines will give discounts for making and paying for reservations more than seven days before the flight.

At-Home Preparations

Stop your newspapers
while you are away.

Before leaving on your vacation, you should take care of many things at home. Ask a neighbor to pick up your newspaper, or have the paper stopped if the vacation is longer than a few days. Mail delivery should be stopped, also; have your mail held at the post office. This can be done by filling out a form at the post office that notifies them of the dates to hold your mail, and when it can be delivered again. When this is done, mail and papers will not gather in your mailbox, leaving evidence that you are away from home. Arrange for the feeding of pets, caring of plants, mowing of the lawn, and other normal duties around your home. It is a good idea to use an automatic timer for lights so that they come on in the evening and go off a few hours later. Soft music is often recommended. All doors and windows should be locked securely, and curtains and drapes closed, except for small windows with sheer curtains through which visibility is impaired from the outside. It is a good idea to ask a neighboring family to keep an eye on things, and let them know when you are leaving and returning. It is also common to alert the local police so that they can drive by your home once in awhile while you are gone to check for intruders.

Last-Minute Details

Careful packing of clothing and supplies is necessary. Make a list of things you will need, including cameras, special clothing, shoes, and personal items. Take only what you need, in the smallest possible containers. Be sure to pack enough clothing to last the entire vacation without laundering (unless it is a very long vacation). Any rented equipment should be obtained as early as is convenient without incurring additional cost. All bottles and other containers should be closed tightly to avoid leakage. Do not forget any prescriptions or other medications frequently needed.

You may wish to take major credit cards. However, leave at home in a safe place all those cards you do not need. Take enough cash to pay those expenses that require cash only; others can be charged on a bank card or paid for by traveler's checks. Traveler's checks may be purchased at any bank or other financial institution in denominations of $10, $20, $50, etc. The smaller denominations are usually easier to cash. There is usually a

Traveler's checks can be replaced if lost or stolen.

small fee for traveler's checks, depending on the dollar amount. If traveler's checks are lost or stolen, they will be replaced if you produce the list of check numbers. Always keep the list separate from the checks.

Reservations may need to be confirmed (checked) because flights are often canceled or changed. You should check at least 24 hours in advance to be sure your flight is confirmed. You may choose to use a *travel agency*, which is an authorized agent for all airlines to issue tickets and make reservations and confirmations in your behalf. There is no fee for services of a travel agent. Because travel agents do not work for any specific airline, they can find flight connections that will result in less waiting time between flights, lower air fares, and better departure times. Sometimes, however, you may have to change planes more often to get a lower rate or better flight time.

There is no charge to you for use of a travel agency's services.

Arrive early to avoid being a victim of overbooking.

Plan to arrive at the airport at least an hour before your flight's departure time. This gives you time to check in, get a seat assignment, and go through the appropriate steps for boarding. Often, flights are *overbooked*, which means that the airline has sold tickets for more seats than there are available. Airline ticket agents sometimes do this because many people book more than one reservation and do not show up for the less-preferred flight. Should you be a victim of overbooking, the airline will offer from $100 to $300 to any passengers willing to take a later flight. The money will help pay for your vacation, but you will also be off your time schedule. By arriving early to check in, you can avoid an overbooking problem.

Be sure that appliances are turned off (stove, iron, curling iron). As a precaution, do not use any appliances the morning of your departure. In the excitement of preparing to leave, you could easily forget to turn off or unplug them. A last check before leaving will reassure you that nothing has been left on. Leave a copy of your itinerary with a neighbor or friend in case of emergency.

HAVING A BABY

Having a baby may be one of the family unit's decisions. Some of the costs to be considered are prenatal expenses, delivery costs, and first-year needs.

Prenatal Expenses

A *prenatal expense* is a cost that is incurred before the baby is born. When pregnancy is first discovered, there are many initial expenses that continue until the birth of the baby.

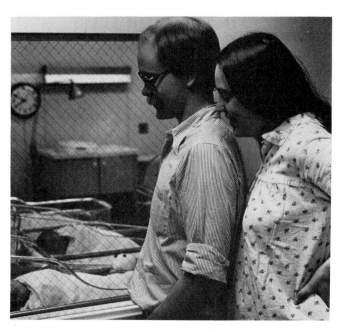

© Dale G. Folstad, 1983

Prenatal Medical Care. During the first trimester (three months) of pregnancy, visits to the doctor occur about once a month. Routine blood tests and special vitamins for proper nourishment of the baby are usually required.

Prenatal expenses start right away.

In most cases, the doctor will expect payment for services to begin immediately. Even when the patient has insurance, most medical offices expect the patient to make regular payments, since insurance companies do not pay their share of costs until after the baby is delivered. These costs are usually a package deal that includes doctor visits and delivery fees. For example, a doctor may charge a flat fee of $950. Charges for blood tests, laboratory services, special tests or extra services, or hospital charges are not included in the doctor's fee.

During the next six months of pregnancy, doctor visits will be more frequent. During the last month, doctor visits are weekly, hospital arrangements are made, and the delivery is planned for a set date.

Maternity Clothing. The expectant mother will need special clothes. After the third or fourth month, everyday clothes become tight and are no longer comfortable. Specially designed maternity clothes allow for expansion and comfort. Usually, five or six changes of clothing are desirable. The maternity wardrobe will include tops and slacks, a dress or two, special underclothing and nylons, and comfortable shoes with low heels.

Special maternity clothing is required.

Furniture and Supplies. Before the baby arrives in the home, some essential pieces of furniture must be acquired. Furniture used the most during the first few months includes a crib, dresser, and a dressing table. In the baby's crib are blankets and sheets, a mobile, and bumper guards to protect the baby from the crib rails. Within a short time, parents will also need to provide additional furniture, such as a high chair, playpen, walker, and stroller. A car seat is required in many states. All of these items are relatively expensive, and purchases should be planned well in advance of the time they will be needed.

Additional furniture is needed.

The baby will also need diapers and personal care products. If a diaper service is not used, several dozen cloth or disposable diapers are needed, as well as baby bottles, powder, lotion, and other items that parents may choose or doctors may recommend. Many babies are fed a milk formula until six months of age or older. The formula may be liquid in cans or bottles, or a powder mixture. All these things need to be ready and waiting when the baby comes home from the hospital.

Many babies drink a formula for six months.

Delivery Costs

In addition to the doctor's charge for delivery, other costs at delivery include anesthesia or any type of pain reliever. Additional doctors necessary during delivery and the pediatrician will also submit their charges for payment. A *pediatrician* is a doctor who specializes in the care and treatment of diseases of small children. Immediately upon delivery, the pediatrician takes the baby to be checked, weighed, and prepared for the nursery. The pediatrician will then remain the child's physician until approximately twelve years of age.

Many costs at delivery are in addition to the package deal.

The usual hospital stay for a normal delivery is one or two days. A Caesarean (surgical) delivery usually requires a hospital stay of three to five days. While they are in the hospital, there is a daily charge for both mother and child. In addition, all services rendered carry a charge.

First-Year Needs

The new family member has many needs, and many new expenses are incurred during the first year. Some of those needs are food, postnatal visits, clothing, personal care supplies, toys, and babysitters.

Food. In a few months, the baby will begin eating cereals, baby foods (strained fruits and vegetables), and soft solids. Special vitamins and fluoride are often prescribed, since the child begins cutting teeth around six months of age.

A baby needs special care in feeding the first year.

Postnatal visits. The baby will need to be examined by a pediatrician regularly during the first year. These visits are called ***well-baby visits.*** The baby is not ill, but the doctor checks for proper growth and gives necessary immunizations. Because there is no illness, insurance coverage usually does not provide benefits for these visits or the immunizations. These visits usually occur at four months, six months, one year, one and one-half years, and again before the child starts school. Shots and pills are administered to protect the baby from diphtheria, polio, measles, tetanus, whooping cough, and other childhood diseases that could be very harmful to a small baby.

Well-baby visits are not covered by insurance.

Clothing. Baby and toddler clothing is expensive. The baby grows rapidly and clothes are soon too small. First-year clothing requirements for babies include underclothes, socks, shoes, sleepers, pants and shirts, jackets and coats, hats, and gloves. Many different changes of clothing are usually needed.

Babies soon outgrow their clothes.

Personal Care Supplies. Personal products specifically for the baby—diaper rash creams, powders, shampoos and soaps, baby aspirin and other over-the-counter medicines, thermometers, and special prescriptions are necessary during the first year. Care should be taken to keep these products out of reach of a crawling baby or a toddler.

Toys. As the child grows physically, it has the need to explore the world and learn about its shapes, colors, and parts. Toys and gadgets aid in the development of coordination and stimulate mental growth. Crib toys, such as mobiles, aid the development of visual acuity and hand and finger dexterity. Many parents also provide tub toys, teddy bears, teething rings, building blocks, and an assortment of other carefully selected products that are safe and suited to the age of the child.

Toys stimulate a child's mental development.

Babysitters. The baby cannot go everywhere with the parents. Careful selection of a competent and trustworthy babysitter to care for the baby properly when the parents are absent is essential. Babysitting fees vary, but are usually under minimum wage.

Babysitters should be carefully selected.

VOCABULARY

Directions: Can you find the definition for each of the following terms used in Chapter 20?

wedding party
semiformal wedding
tax shelter
itinerary
overbooked
well-baby visits
formal wedding

informal wedding
tax-deferred annuity
reservation
travel agency
prenatal expense
pediatrician

1. A legal way to avoid paying taxes on present earnings.

2. A contractual savings program wherein taxes are postponed until payments are received at retirement.

3. An advance commitment whereby a traveler is assured of a plane seat or a motel room.

4. A cost incurred before a baby is born.

5. Doctor visits that are not covered by insurance because the baby is not ill.

6. A doctor who specializes in the treatment of medical needs and diseases of small children.

7. Persons who participate in the wedding ceremony: bride and groom, best man, maid of honor, bridesmaids, ushers, flower girl, ring bearer, candle lighters, etc.

8. A type of wedding in which everyone, including guests, wears formal attire.

9. A type of wedding in which only the wedding party is dressed formally.

10. A type of wedding that is usually held outdoors and has no clothing requirements for wedding party or guests.

11. A detailed list of events, times, and places planned for a trip or vacation.

12. An agent who is authorized to write and sell airline tickets.

13. The result when an airline sells more tickets for a flight than it has seats available.

ITEMS FOR DISCUSSION

1. What is the purpose of premarital counseling?

2. How long before the wedding should a couple begin making preparations?

3. List some responsibilities (expenses) that are traditionally accepted by the bride and her family.

4. List some responsibilities (expenses) that are traditionally accepted by the groom and his family.

5. Who is included in the wedding party?

6. What is the difference between a formal wedding and a semiformal wedding?

7. What are some advantages and disadvantages to couples who work for several years before having children?

8. What types of vacation options are available from which to choose?

9. What types of things are listed on a vacation itinerary?

10. How soon should you make hotel reservations before taking a vacation trip?

11. List some preparations that you need to make before leaving on vacation. Include those preparations designed to keep people from realizing that you are gone.

12. What is the purpose of using traveler's checks instead of carrying cash?

13. How much does a travel agency charge a customer for making reservations and issuing airline tickets?

14. List three prenatal expenses.

15. What are some of the costs involved in child delivery?

16. List some expenses that will be incurred by a couple during the first year of a child's life.

APPLICATIONS

1. Describe a wedding that you have attended in the last year or two (include wedding party, dress, flowers, reception, etc.).

2. Describe the wedding of your choice, including setting, type of ceremony, wedding party, total cost, number of guests, honeymoon plans, etc.

3. Why do working couples need to find tax shelters and annuities?

4. How does a family's budget differ from an individual's budget?

5. Design a three-day itinerary for a plane trip to a resort area within about a thousand miles of where you live. Include all necessary information.

CASE PROBLEMS AND ACTIVITIES

1. Write a report describing different engagement ring options:

   (a) Diamond solitaire with matching bands. Compare costs of different size diamonds.

   (b) Gold and silver bands. Compare quality, width, and costs.

   (c) Costs of stones other than diamonds: rubies, emeralds, sapphires. Compare different sizes of each.

   (d) Financing plans available to young couples.

2. Gary Tautkus and Joan McPhearson will be married in a month. Both are working and plan to work at least five years before having children. They have asked for your opinion on how household duties should be divided, since both of them work eight hours a day, five days a week. Devise a plan for dividing duties and responsibilities; include checkbook balancing and financial planning.

3. You and a friend have decided to take a trip. Based on the following three hypothetical cases, describe the kinds of trips you would take and list all of the costs that would be involved in each.

   (a) You each have $75 to contribute and could get away for a three- or four-day weekend. You have one automobile that does not need maintenance or repairs.

   (b) You each have $500 to spend and could get away for three to five days.

   (c) You each have $1,500 to spend and could be away for ten days.

CHAPTER 21
CONTINGENCY PLANNING

CHAPTER OBJECTIVES

After studying this chapter and completing the activities, you will be able to:

1. Identify emergency situations that can be prevented and list safety precautions.
2. Explain what is involved in automobile purchase and maintenance.
3. Define the costs and steps of divorce.
4. Discuss why a person needs a will and identify the costs involved in last illness and death.

EMERGENCIES

Misfortune strikes everybody. Although it may not be possible to avoid certain emergency situations, others can be minimized as far as damages suffered. Emergency situations can be divided into these general categories: household accidents, vehicular accidents, work-related injuries, and other accidents and injuries.

Household Accidents

Thousands of injuries occur each year in the home, many of them serious. Household injuries can be avoided, however, through use of certain commonsense preventative measures.

The kitchen, with cupboards, shelves, drawers and storage areas, food, and appliances, is an especially attractive area for small children. Cleansers, detergents, and other products that are *toxic* (poisonous) can cause

Poisonous substances should be kept out of reach.

serious injury or death. Cooking ingredients should be placed in high cupboards, out of the reach of small children. Poisonous products should always be stored in their original containers: a soda bottle should not be used to store cleaning fluid. Any product containing a questionable substance should be stored away from food. The kitchen is a good place to display emergency information about what to do and whom to call in case of poisoning, choking, drowning, electric shock, bleeding cuts, fractures, burns, shock, and head injuries. A complete first aid kit (with instructions on use) should be handy at all times. (See Figure 21-1.)

Keep a first aid kit handy at all times.

The bathroom is a potentially *lethal*—deadly or dangerous—play area for small children. The toilet lid should always be kept down when a toddler or infant is in the house. If a small child falls headfirst into the toilet,

---

WHAT TO DO IN CASE OF:

BLEEDING CUTS

The first concern is to stop the bleeding. Use gauze or a clean cloth; apply pressure directly to the wound. Once the bleeding has stopped, clean the wound, using *hydrogen peroxide*. Wash the entire area with soap and water; bandage.

Call a doctor if:
1. Blood is spurting.
2. You cannot stop the bleeding with direct pressure.
3. There is a deep puncture wound.
4. There is glass or another substance in the wound.
5. There is a large and gaping wound.

FRACTURES

Broken bones always require medical attention. Do not try to realign a fractured limb. Splint the arm or leg in order to transport the victim without jarring the injury. If you suspect a broken neck or back, do not move the victim; call an ambulance immediately.

HEAD INJURIES

Hard blows to the head can cause internal bleeding.

Call a doctor if:
1. The person loses consciousness at the time of the accident.
2. A child is confused or disoriented, or is drowsy and hard to arouse.
3. There is vomiting.
4. There is bleeding from the nose or ears.

SHOCK

Serious injury, bleeding, or severe blow can cause shock. The victim will look very pale, with cold clammy skin. The pulse will be weak and rapid. This is serious; call an ambulance or get the person to the hospital immediately. Keep the person warm, lying flat with legs elevated.

BURNS

Soak the burned area in cold water for 30 minutes or so. This will cool the burn, prevent further damage, and diminish the pain and swelling. Do not use ointments or oils. If the burn is severe, however, do not apply anything. Do not remove clothing if it is sticking to the burn. Transport the victim to a hospital immediately.

NOSEBLEED

Twist small pieces of cotton into shapes to be inserted into nostrils. Pinch the nose firmly and hold for several minutes. Remove the cotton when the bleeding stops. Have the person lie down. Call a doctor if bleeding has not stopped after 20 minutes.

CHOKING

If the victim is a child, hold him or her upside down across the knees and give blows to the back between the shoulder blades. On an adult, use the Heimlich maneuver: Approach from behind. Make a fist with one hand, thumb side against the victim's abdomen, below the rib cage. Press into the victim's abdomen with a quick upward motion. Repeat if choking continues. You must force air around the lodged object. Try artificial respiration until help arrives.

DROWNING

Mouth-to-mouth resuscitation must be started immediately. Because of water swallowed, vomiting often follows. Push against the victim's stomach to get water out. Get air into the victim's lungs. Seek medical help immediately. Water in the lungs can result in pneumonia.

ELECTRIC SHOCK

Do not touch the victim until the source of power is removed. Turn off the current; give mouth-to-mouth resuscitation. Call for medical help.

POISONING

Call the nearest poison control center immediately, or take the victim to the emergency room of the nearest hospital. You can make the person vomit or you can neutralize the substance in the stomach. Corrosive poisons burn the mouth and inner parts; do not induce vomiting.

FIGURE 21-1 Emergency Information

he or she can drown in the small amount of water it contains. Children should never be left unattended while bathing, swimming, or otherwise in or near water. Appliances such as hair dryers should be unplugged and kept away from sinks and tubs. Personal care items should be kept out of reach of children.

Because of lack of space, many families store items not frequently used in attics, garages, high cupboards, and basements. Retrieval of stored items can be dangerous. Ladders should be placed firmly with a second person holding the legs for support. Falling is a common household accident that can be avoided with care and thought.

Weapons should be locked away securely.

Weapons, including guns and knives, should be locked away with ammunition locked in a separate place. Tools and power devices stored in garages and work areas should be kept out of reach of children. Chemicals, fertilizers, oil, gasoline, and other such products should be stored securely, following rules of storage safety for combustible and flammable products. Fire hazards are created by cleaning rags, papers, and cluttered possessions. Unused refrigerators or other storage containers should have the doors removed so that children cannot become trapped in them.

Vehicular Accidents

The National Highway Traffic Safety Commission estimates that every person will be involved in one automobile accident during their lifetime, on the average. The commission also estimates that one in three persons will be involved in a major accident that will injure them and send them to the hospital for treatment. The leading cause of death of persons under age 35 is the automobile accident, which can injure, cripple, or kill without warning. Careful driving, along with using seat belts and keeping your car in good running condition, helps to reduce risks. Tires need to be

Tire pressure is important to mileage and safety.

maintained at the correct pressure and replaced when the tread becomes too thin for driving safety. The engine should be serviced regularly, the belts and hoses inspected, and the water and fluid levels (brakes, transmission, battery) checked. Most serious accidents happen after dark and within 25 miles of home. ***Defensive driving*** is watching for the bad driving decisions of others and involves tactics such as slowing down, yielding right-of-way, maintaining safe distances between cars (one car length for every 10 mph), and using headlights on two-way roads and whenever visibility is impaired.

Work-Related Injuries

Each year there are injuries and illnesses that are employment related. Many work-related injuries are caused by carelessness and employee

Photri

error. Others are caused by unsafe working conditions. High levels of chemicals or toxins in the air, noise that damages hearing after a number of years, or fumes that damage lung tissue are examples of unsafe working conditions. On-the-job injuries can be reduced by carefully observing safety rules, wearing proper clothing or other protective equipment, and being constantly aware of possible dangers. The nature of the work can cause symptoms to develop many years later. For instance, black lung is developed by coal miners after years of working in the mines with insufficient oxygen. Noxious gases and fumes circulate in the air while the workers are digging. Persons who work with radioactive substances and agents known to cause cancer may not develop cancer until several years later. Some cases of exposure to radiation do not result in incurable cancer for as long as 20 years. Yet the cancer can be traced back to the direct exposure or risk taken in the past. Developing an awareness of the types of potential hazards of an occupation should be a priority for today's worker.

Other Accidents

Other types of accidents and injuries also occur daily. Most are the result of some human error or mechanical failure. Examples include drowning accidents, plane and train accidents, injuries due to extreme weather conditions, and bicycle mishaps. Broken bones, torn ligaments, and other injuries occur when people participate in sports and athletic activities.

While you cannot prevent injuries and accidents entirely, you can prepare yourself in several ways to survive them: (*a*) insure against the risk of loss, (*b*) reduce the risk of loss, or (*c*) avoid the circumstance that could lead to loss. For example, you may be considering a ski trip to the mountains. Risks include icy roads that may cause automobile damage and personal injury, and skiing accidents. Health insurance can protect against body damage losses; automobile insurance can protect against car damage losses; taking chains and preparing your vehicle for snow and ice can reduce driving risks; and not taking the trip at all will avoid any loss.

You can prepare for emergencies.

AUTOMOBILE PURCHASE AND CARE

Expenses of automobile ownership only begin with the purchase. One must also consider the contingency costs of maintenance and the possibility of loss due to theft of a vehicle.

Buying a Car

Whether you want a new or used car, as a wise consumer you should shop around, compare prices, and take your time in selecting such a large purchase. Before looking, make a list of features that are important to you, such as power steering, power brakes, automatic transmission, or air conditioning. While such features can be added later, it is more convenient to buy the car equipped. Stick to your list and know what you want. Test drive many different cars and ask questions. A price **markup** on a new car includes any additions to the basic price of a delivered car. Additional preparations for sale, such as undercoating, paint touch-ups, and the dealer profit, are included in the markup. Markups usually begin at about 10 percent of the basic car price and go as high as customers will pay. Several sources are available to consumers for determining the dealer's cost and suggested retail prices for new cars and factory-installed optional equipment. One source for new car prices is a paperback book called *Edmund's New Car Prices*. Another source is *Consumer Reports* magazine.

Added features increase your car's value.

When you buy a new car, you can pay cash for the car or trade in your old car. A **trade-in** is an older vehicle of some type used to reduce the price of the new car by the amount of money the dealer will give you on your old vehicle. Since the dealer will try to make a profit from the sale

A trade-in will reduce the price of a new car.

of your old car, you should try to get as much for your old car as possible. Sometimes you can advertise and sell your old car and get more for it than a dealer would give you on a trade-in. Because you are not trading in an old car that the dealer may have to repair before reselling, the dealer will usually offer a lower price on the new car.

Before selling or trading your old car, find out what a realistic selling price is for your car. Used car values are listed in the ***NADA*** (National Automobile Dealers Association) ***Blue Book***, which lists a low book value for a basic car for six years. Additional features of your car, such as automatic transmission, power steering, air conditioning, low mileage, etc., will add to its value. When these features are added, your car is said to meet high book value. The ***high book value*** of a used car includes the low book value plus the value of its added features. Know the book values for your used car as well as for any used car you plan to purchase to assure that you pay or receive a realistic price.

Probably the most important thing to remember in purchasing a car is patience. A car is a large purchase that deserves the time and attention of a careful choice. Avoid high-pressure sales tactics. Take your time in making the decision, since a car purchase will result in monthly payments for three or four years.

There are approximately 29,000 franchised new car dealers in the United States. The U.S. Better Business Bureau reports that less than 10 percent of complaints about car purchases are against new car dealers. The National Automobile Dealers Association issues a code of ethics for its members—the franchised new car dealers. If you feel you have been treated unfairly by a new or used car dealer, you can complain to the growing network of Automotive Consumer Action Programs (called AUTOCAPs). There are more than 40 AUTOCAPs in the U.S. that mediate disputes between consumers and car dealers. AUTOCAP panels include dealers and nondealers, state and local consumer protection agency members, and representatives from district attorneys' offices. The local automobile dealers association listed in the Yellow Pages of the telephone book can give you the address of the nearest AUTOCAP.

New car dealers have a code of ethics.

Automobile Maintenance

The monthly car payment is only the beginning of the costs of owning a car. Your budget must include a monthly provision for regular car maintenance and repairs. While the car is new—first 12,000 miles or whatever is covered by a warranty—you may be relieved of some maintenance and repair costs. But the car will still need regular servicing, such as oil changes, which include a new oil filter and lubrication. Oil changes and lubrications are recommended every 3,000 to 5,000 miles or every three months. Engine tune-ups are needed every 12,000 to 20,000 miles or once a year. Checking and replacement of belts and hoses, wiper blades, fuses, lights, and tires are needed regularly. Occasionally, a major repair is needed. For example, a water pump may need replacing, brakes may become worn after a few years, and other repairs under the car and in the engine may be needed. Mufflers may need replacement or repair, wheels may need to be balanced, and front-end alignments are needed regularly, too.

Many costly repairs can be avoided or minimized by careful driving habits and regular maintenance. Caution is needed when having your car repaired, however. An estimated $125 a year for each car in the United States is spent on unnecessary repairs. A vast majority of auto repair shops do not charge for labor by the clock hour. They charge for the amount of time allowed for a repair in a flat-rate manual. Flat-rate manuals allow no time for road tests after repairs are made. Therefore, the mechanic has incentive to do the job as quickly as possible and to sell extra parts. Choose your repair shop carefully. An authorized automobile dealership is not always the best choice for servicing and making repairs on your car. Check with the Better Business Bureau about service and repair shops in your area. Ask for recommendations from friends and neighbors. When you find a shop to service your car, become a steady customer. The more you know about your own car, the more protection you have against repair fraud. Read the manual that came with your car and ask questions.

Maintenance costs also include protecting your car's paint. Keep the car clean and have a good coat of wax on it. Use a cleaning compound to remove tar and scratches and then apply wax at least once a year. If your car is parked outside during all kinds of weather, the paint has less protection and can *oxidize*—permanently lose its shine due to exposure to weather and sun.

Repair shops use flat-rate manuals.

Cars need frequent washing and waxing.

Car Theft

Nearly a million motor vehicles are stolen each year in the United States. About a third are never recovered. While theft is covered under comprehensive automobile insurance, the insurance company only pays the value of the car at the time of the theft—not the price you paid for it.

Expensive automobile models (those costing $12,000 or more) are the main targets for car theft. Some cars are stolen for parts, or only parts are

Expensive cars are stolen most often.

stolen, because manufacturers do not stock all the parts needed for older, used cars. Let's look at some ways you can protect yourself against automobile theft.

Shopping centers are popular places for car thieves. Make sure your car is locked and parked in a well-lighted area, as close to stores and traffic as possible. Less than 45 seconds are required to enter a car, cross the distributor wires, and start it. Approximately 40 percent of cars stolen are taken by tow trucks in broad daylight. A tow truck without a name on it, or with a name not listed in local telephone books, signals something is wrong.

You can slow down car thieves.

Persons living in highly populated urban areas are most often car theft victims. Professional car thieves cannot be stopped, but they can be slowed down. The best protection against theft is an ignition-kill system, which interrupts the voltage needed to start a car. A second switch must be turned on with a second key before the car will start. An ignition-kill system costs about $60 installed. A factory-installed system can also ward off thieves. One of the best precautions against theft of older used cars is the removal of the standard door lock buttons and installation of tapered buttons. Tapered lock buttons are very difficult to pull up with any type of device inserted through the doors or windows. New cars usually come with tapered locks and are more difficult to enter.

Remove tape decks at night.

Never leave packages, purses, or other valuables in plain sight in the car. Valuables in plain sight are an invitation for a break-in. Keep these items in the trunk or well covered. Also, home-installed tape systems and speakers are easily removed by thieves. If your car is parked outside at night, these valuables should be removed.

DIVORCE

In all but a few states, a divorce is now called a ***dissolution of marriage***, which means that irreconcilable differences have led to the breakdown of the marriage. Furthermore, one partner does not have to prove fault by the other partner to be granted a divorce. If one partner wants the marriage to be dissolved, it can be done. The only time fault is considered is when the issue of child custody arises.

Cost of Divorce

Expenses involved in divorce are high. Attorneys' fees (one attorney for each party), court costs and filing fees, child support and alimony, division of property, and settlement costs may be included. The more

Divorce expenses are
high.

issues there are to settle, the higher the attorneys' fees will be. When child custody is an issue and a court hearing is necessary, the fees are even higher. Often parties can agree outside of court and enter into a property settlement agreement. The ***property settlement agreement*** is a document specifying the division of property and assets agreed to by both parties and entered into court for the judge's approval. The more that can be settled outside of court, the less the costs of divorce proceedings.

In most cases, the parent who is granted custody of the children will receive child support from the other parent. The amount of child support is based on the income and ability of the parties, on the assumption that both parties are responsible for supporting the children to the best of their abilities. Alimony is awarded in some cases when one spouse has been dependent on the other for a number of years and has little means of self-support. Most alimony awards are for a limited number of years, or may be based upon a former spouse completing education or training for

Child support is at the
judge's discretion.

employment. Child support and alimony are at the discretion of the judge and become binding on the parties under the divorce decree. Amounts of child support and alimony can only be modified by another court order.

Steps in Divorce

Dissolving a marriage is often a lengthy and unpleasant matter. Usually the papers are not actually filed until the couple has been separated for some time and it appears to be in everyone's best interest to pursue a legal dissolution of marriage. One party goes to an attorney, and the attorney prepares the documents, which are filed with the court. The other party is served with copies of the papers, called Petition for Dissolution of Marriage, and given a short time to appear (file papers) if there is a disagreement with the proposals set forth in the petition. The petition sets forth how the first party proposes to divide property and award custody, amounts desired for child support, visitation rights, and so on. If the sec-

A default is a failure to
appear in court.

ond party fails to appear (defaults) then the first party is awarded whatever is asked in the petition. In most cases, the second party does appear and a court date is set to decide the issues that cannot be settled between the parties. Often it takes many months, even a year or more, for the case to be heard in court. Consequently, a temporary hearing will be held to establish temporary custody, child support, visitation rights of the noncustodial parent, and other matters. Many of the temporary provisions tend to become permanent. That is, often both parties agree in writing to property settlement and other matters prior to the court date. When the judge approves the agreement, it is entered as part of the ***decree***, which is a

A decree is final and binding on all parties.

final statement of the dissolution decisions. A decree is final and binding on both parties until modified by the court.

If the parties cannot agree on a settlement, the case then goes to court. There is no jury in divorce cases. Both parties testify and present their cases. Witnesses may be called in the issue of child custody to determine which parent would be the better custodial parent. The judge's decision is based entirely on the best benefit for the child or children of the marriage. All other matters—property, alimony, amount of child support, visitation rights—are also decided in court. The court hearing may last several days. Once the decree is entered, a waiting period of 60 to 90 days before either party may remarry is usually imposed.

DEATH

Aging and death are parts of living and need planning and attention. Preparations are not only for those who are about to die; they should be considered by all responsible adults.

Writing a Will

You need a will if you have children or property.

Many people do not understand the need for a will. A will expresses a person's wishes for disposal of property after his or her death. A will only passes title to property that does not otherwise pass. For example, if you own a car jointly with another person, on your death the car will go to that other person. The car need not be mentioned in the will. A *testator* is the person who makes a will. When you die, if you do not have a will, but own property that will not automatically pass to another person, you are said to be *intestate*, and the state in which you live will determine to whom your property will go. In most states, if you die without a will and are married, your property will go to your spouse. If you have a spouse and children, the spouse will get half and the children will divide the other half. Each state has its laws about how property and money will be divided. If you want things to be otherwise, you need a will.

Anyone who has reached the age of majority (18 years of age in most states) and is of sound mind can make a valid will. Couples with children need to have a will in order to name guardians to provide care for their children in the event of their deaths. Anyone previously married needs a will to be sure property will be divided as he or she wishes.

A *simple will* is a short one- or two-page document that lists spouse and children and provides how each shall inherit. Most wills are prepared by attorneys. Simple wills for a husband and wife take a short time to prepare and usually cost less than $150. A will must be witnessed by two persons not mentioned in the will. Witnesses must be 18 or older, not related, and able to attest to the mental competency of the person making a will at the time the will is written. An example of a will is shown in Figure 21-2.

A *holographic will* is one written in a person's own handwriting. A handwritten will is legally valid in nineteen states and should be witnessed just as one typed and prepared by a lawyer. Because a handwritten will is often easier to contest (question), a typed will is recommended.

A *trust will* is a very complicated will, most always prepared by a lawyer. A trust is many pages long and lists specific provisions for holding property, assets, and money for minor children or others. A trustee is named to manage the money, and all duties and powers are described. The trustee may be a bank, a financial institution, or a person. The testator lists all persons who may have a claim to his or her estate, specifies all bequests of property to other persons, and lists any specific needs and how they shall be fulfilled.

In any will, all issue (children) must be mentioned, whether or not they shall inherit money or property. When a child is left out, a question arises as to the intent of the testator. Children not born when a will is drawn are presumed to inherit along with other children. Because of the complexities of inheritance laws and taxes, it is advisable for all couples with children and assets to consult a lawyer to draw up wills to dispose of their property as they wish.

Wills should be kept in a safe-deposit box, with a copy of the will and location of important documents listed in the home. Less than 25 percent of all people are prepared for death. This preparation involves writing a will, leaving burial instructions, listing the location of important papers and all accounts, and making specific bequests of personal property.

Survivors' Benefits

Surviving spouse and children are usually provided with some kind of death benefits. Life insurance benefits are not taxable to the recipients. Benefits from a life insurance policy can be obtained by mailing a copy of the death certificate, the original life insurance policy, and a claim form to the life insurance company. Social security pays a one-time lump-sum benefit of about $255 to help cover funeral expenses. The social security benefit is paid to the estate of any person who was collecting social security retirement benefits or who was eligible to collect benefits. If this benefit is not received soon after death, it must be applied for. The Veterans

A simple will is inexpensive.

A trustee acts in behalf of the testator to carry out provisions of a will.

Survivors are entitled to benefits but may have to apply.

LAST WILL AND TESTAMENT OF ANTHONY JOHN HINTON

I, Anthony John Hinton, of the City of Dayton and State of Ohio, do make, publish, and declare this to be my Last Will and Testament in manner following:

FIRST: I direct that all my just debts, funeral expenses, and the cost of administering my estate be paid by my executrix hereinafter named.

SECOND: I give, devise, and bequeath to my beloved daughter, Carol Hinton Campbell, now residing in Englewood, New Jersey, that certain piece of real estate, with all improvements thereon, situated in the same city and at the corner of Hudson Avenue and Tenafly Road.

THIRD: All the remainder and residue of my property, real, personal, and mixed, I give to my beloved wife, Kimberly Sue Hinton, executrix of this, my Last Will and Testament, and I direct that she not be required to give bond or security for the performance of her duties as such.

LASTLY: I hereby revoke any and all former wills by me made.

IN WITNESS WHEREOF, I have hereunto set my hand this tenth day of October, in the year nineteen hundred --.

Anthony John Hinton
Anthony John Hinton

We, the undersigned, certify that the foregoing instrument was, on the date thereof, signed and declared by Anthony John Hinton as his Last Will and Testament, in the presence of us who, in his presence and in the presence of each other, have, at his request, hereunto signed our names as witnesses of the execution thereof, this tenth day of October, 19--; and we hereby certify that we believe the said Anthony John Hinton to be of sound mind and memory.

William Schoenborn	residing at	251 Wonderly Avenue Dayton, Ohio 45419-2521
Samuel Vance	residing at	3024 James Hill Road Kettering, Ohio 45429-2454
Irene Vasilkova	residing at	423 Goldengate Drive Centerville, Ohio 45459-2459

FIGURE 21-2 Last Will and Testament

Administration pays another stipend to survivors of veterans. The benefit may include a grave marker, funeral services, and cash of $400 or more, depending on type and length of service and branch of armed forces. Children of veterans may also be entitled to scholarships and educational grant benefits. Many employer pension plans pay lump-sum or monthly benefits to widows and families. Employer-paid benefits may not be automatic, and the widow(er) may have to apply to receive these benefits. Survivors need to check thoroughly to see what policies, retirement plans, and other benefits have accrued through the years.

Last Expenses

Final expenses require planning.

The costs involved when a person dies can range from a few hundred dollars to several thousand dollars. These expenses include final medical and hospital charges, funeral expenses and casket, and burial. By preparing instructions and making provisions for these costs in advance, you spare survivors the emotional decision-making process that may be capitalized on by others. Survivors who are grieving the loss of a loved one often are unprepared to make the many decisions involved in planning a funeral and burial. At such an emotional time, a family may incur elaborate final expenses that they or the estate cannot afford.

Cremation is less expensive than burial.

Cremation is a process of reducing a body to ashes in a high-temperature oven. The ashes are placed in an urn that is presented to the family or placed in a vault. Cremation is a less-expensive alternative to burial, but there are special requirements. When a body is not cremated within a certain time span, usually two days, it must be embalmed or otherwise prepared for burial. These costs must be paid even though cremation is later chosen.

Funeral services, which usually last a half hour, may be performed in a church or in a funeral home. The cost can be as much as $1,500, which includes embalming, preparations, music, printed remembrances, and newspaper notices. All decisions about these matters must be made in a relatively short period of time.

A prepaid funeral plan saves survivors emotional stress.

Many funeral homes have prearranged plans available at guaranteed costs. Money for the funeral is placed into an account that is insured by the FDIC or FSLIC and earns interest. Although the money is for the funeral, it can be withdrawn in an emergency. Written instructions will save the family from overspending at the time of death, save emotional and financial distress, and assure the family that the type and cost of the funeral is as desired by the loved one.

Typical funeral home charges include moving the body (to funeral home, to cemetery); embalming and preparation; casket; use of facilities;

funeral director's and staff fees; hearse; family limousine; pallbearers' car; flower car; escort to cemetery; obituary (newspaper death notice); funeral notice in newspaper; printed memorial folders, memorial book, and thank-you cards; death certificate; and all necessary permits. The cost of a burial plot and marker are additional expenses.

VOCABULARY

Directions: Can you find the definition for each of the following terms used in Chapter 21?

toxic	trust will
defensive driving	lethal
trade-in	markup
high book value	NADA Blue Book
dissolution of marriage	oxidize
decree	property settlement agreement
simple will	intestate
holographic will	testator

1. Watching for poor driving by others to avoid accidents.

2. An old car used as a down payment to purchase a new vehicle.

3. Dangerous and potentially deadly for small children.

4. Value resulting when value of added features is added to the low book value of an automobile.

5. Permanent loss of shine to a car's paint because of exposure to sun and weather.

6. A substance that is poisonous and causes illness or death if swallowed.

7. A form of divorce that provides that a marriage can be ended without proving fault.

8. Additions to the base price of an automobile, such as delivery costs, undercoating, and dealer profit.

9. A written agreement by husband and wife to dispose of and divide the assets of a marriage.

10. A handbook for car dealers and financial institutions that lists values of used cars for six years.

11. A final statement that settles all issues of a dissolution of marriage and is binding on the parties.

12. A long and complicated will that makes guardianship or trustee provisions.

13. To die without making a will.

14. A will that is handwritten.

15. One who makes and signs a will before two witnesses.

16. A short, one- or two-page will listing bequests by a testator.

ITEMS FOR DISCUSSION

1. What are some precautions to take in the kitchen to protect small children and toddlers from injury and accident?

2. How can you reduce the risk of automobile accident injuries?

3. What are three ways to be prepared for injuries and accidents?

4. What are some things to remember before making an automobile purchase?

5. To whom can you complain if you feel you have been treated unfairly by an automobile dealer?

6. What types of regular maintenance are needed on an automobile?

7. Why does an automobile need to be washed and waxed regularly?

8. List several ways you can help prevent your car from being stolen.

9. What are some of the costs involved in getting a divorce?

10. What is meant by the term *intestate*?

11. Where should a will be kept? What about copies?

12. What types of survivors' benefits are available when a person dies?

13. What is cremation?

APPLICATIONS

1. Make a list of potentially dangerous areas in your home. What can be done to make them safer?

2. Identify some work hazards for the occupations listed below. What can workers or the employer do to reduce some of these risks?

   (a) Mine worker

   (b) School teacher

   (c) Construction worker

   (d) Dentist

   (e) Barber

3. Make a list of features that are very important to you to have in an automobile. Describe what your ideal car would look like, inside and out.

4. Interview someone who has owned the same car for three consecutive years. Within a three-year period of time, what types of repairs and maintenance were required on the vehicle? List them, together with the cost of each.

5. What property or money do you own that is not jointly held with someone else? To whom would you like to see your property go at your death? Make a list of what you have and to whom you would like to make bequests.

CASE PROBLEMS AND ACTIVITIES

1. From library sources, locate the following information:

   (a) Number of traffic deaths in your state last year

   (b) Whether this figure represents an increase or a decrease over the previous year

   (c) Number of victims not using a safety belt

2. Have you or someone you know been involved in an accident or injury? Describe an injury or accident—how it happened, injuries sustained, and how it could have been prevented or injuries reduced.

3. A friend comes to you for advice about buying a car. What advice will you give to aid the person in making a good choice and getting the most for his or her money?

4. Determine the NADA Blue Book value for a used automobile that you might be interested in purchasing. What things will add to the

low book value? What is the range (low book value to high book value)? Check a library source, such as *Edmund's New Car Prices*, and find the dealer's cost of several new cars. List them, together with the cost of added features you would like to have on a car (air conditioning, power windows, etc.).

5. What types of divorce/dissolution laws are in effect in your state? Are they no-fault or fault laws? What are the waiting periods? Describe the procedures for dissolution.

6. Write a simple will for yourself, listing your property and to whom you want it to go. Date the will and have two witnesses sign it. If you are 18, is your will valid?

7. In your area, what would be the approximate total cost of a funeral? Visit a funeral home or get information through research about the services provided and costs.

UNIT SIX
ECONOMICS

CHAPTER 22

ECONOMICS AND YOU

CHAPTER OBJECTIVES

After studying this chapter and completing the activities, you will be able to:

1. Identify individual and societal needs and wants and define the term *economics*.
2. List the four factors of production and describe them in economic terms.
3. Outline types of production decisions that must be made and list factors contributing to those decisions.

WHY STUDY ECONOMICS?

Before we can begin our study of economics, we must understand the meaning of the word and the importance of the subject. *Economics* is the study of human efforts to solve the problem of making scarce resources meet the unlimited needs and wants of society. When we study economics, we study human behavior in producing, exchanging, and consuming material goods and services to satisfy needs and wants. Specifically, we study a diverse array of topics from balancing household budgets to labor disputes, farm surpluses and taxes, debt, inflation, and unemployment—all vital issues.

No one can escape the principles of economics—the study of scarcity. As we will discuss later, society's needs and wants are always increasing, and there is no way our existing resources could possibly meet all our present needs and wants, nor the continuing and unknown needs and wants

Well-informed
consumers know basic
economics.

of the future. As a result, consumers must make choices concerning which needs and wants to fulfill and how best to fulfill them. We study economics to learn how to make wise and responsible choices, for our individual good and for the good of society.

Benefits to Society

An informed citizen has an understanding of economics.

Consumers who are well informed and knowledgeable about economics make wise decisions that determine the courses of their own lives and contribute to the destiny of their country's economic future. By giving you a better understanding of the world in which you live, economics can help you to be a more productive, responsible, and effective citizen who is a part of the positive changes in society. One major function of an informed citizen—that of voting—depends a great deal on a good understanding of important social and economic issues.

Consumers who are knowledgeable about economics can help to conserve the country's resources. Wise economic decisions facilitate the use of resources to their maximum potential (conservation), while unwise choices lead to waste and mismanagement of scarce resources, to the detriment of society as a whole. Because natural, human, and human-made resources are limited in supply and quality, consumers have a responsibility to future generations to make good decisions now.

Personal Benefits

The study of economics is of practical value in our daily lives, both personally and professionally. As an academic subject, economics can be used as an aid in making good decisions that will allow us to enjoy effective, productive, and rewarding lives. For instance, a citizen who understands such concepts as inflation and unemployment (their causes and cures) is better able to survive personally during periods of inflation, recession, or even depression. In studying economics, we learn not only how and why such things happen, but also how to deal with such problems and bring about solutions.

Understanding economics is a personal benefit.

As a vocational subject, economics is also valuable. Many persons choose economics careers. Big businesses, labor unions, and government offices hire economic specialists, counselors, and advisors; every successful business person relies on dependable interpretation of economic indicators. Although economics may not specifically teach you how to make more money, it can give you insight into ways to make your money do more for you. Once you have a good basic understanding of economics, you will be better equipped to survive in a world that can be very threatening and unsympathetic and that is constantly changing.

ECONOMIC NEEDS AND WANTS

Our needs and wants can be divided into two groups. We have basic survival needs and other life-improving or fulfilling wants and needs.

Basic Needs

Basic survival needs include (*a*) food and water, (*b*) shelter, and (*c*) clothing. As you can see, ***basic needs*** are those ingredients necessary for maintaining physical life. Some authors would add safety and security to this list, because until these basic needs are met, there is little necessity for any of the other things life has to offer. Many people do not have these basic needs met in their lives. Daily they struggle to remain alive in the midst of war and conflicts, and they have little concern for other needs besides safety and food.

Basic needs must be met first.

Other Needs and Wants

Life-improving or fulfilling wants and needs include the following:

1. Food, clothing, and shelter beyond what is necessary for biological survival.

2. Medical care to improve the quality and length of life.
3. Education to achieve personal goals, both social and economic.
4. Travel, vacations, and recreation to improve personal enjoyment of life.
5. Gadgetry or extra items to make life more fun and give it extra excitement, challenge, or meaning.

You may have decided that many of the life-improving needs and wants are necessary for your happiness. But you must admit, they are not absolutely necessary to your physical survival—you may simply have become used to them and, therefore, expect to have them.

Two important concepts can be drawn from this information: (*a*) material wants and needs are virtually unlimited, and (*b*) economic resources to meet those needs and wants are limited (scarce). Humanity's material desires for goods and services cannot be satisfied; we always want more than we can have! It can safely be said that at any point in time, society has unfulfilled wants and needs—biological needs (food, clothing, shelter) plus other wants and needs that are socially oriented or involve learned responses (cars, vacations, luxuries).

Our needs and wants are unlimited.

Individual Needs and Wants

What each of us decides we need and want depends on a number of individually unique factors. These factors are different among individuals and different among societies. All factors may change at different points in our lives. Individual factors include personal style, income, education, security level, and leisure time.

Personal Style. Each person has his or her own set of values and personal preferences. Personal taste may be formal or informal, flashy or subdued, dominating or easygoing. One person may prefer dark colors; another may choose pastels. One person may enjoy a weekend alone in the mountains hiking, while another would choose a visit to Disneyland. Based on those personal tastes, style, and preferences, we make choices; we fulfill our wants and needs according to those personal values.

Our choices are based on our tastes and styles.

Income. What a person is able to earn and spend will greatly influence the type of consumer choices she or he can make. The more disposable income—money left over after expenses are paid, which you can spend as you wish—the higher the quality and quantity of your selections. Whether or not a person can afford to buy goods and services to fulfill the wants and needs she or he considers important will affect his or her satisfaction or dissatisfaction with employment, personal life, goals, and other

Your career meets or fails to meet your wants and needs.

personal factors such as self-worth or self-esteem. Figure 22-1 is a comparison of 1981 incomes showing where a given income would fall in relation to other incomes. The median family income in 1981 was $22,388. The *median* income is the statistical middle of this list of figures. In a list of statistics, the same number of statistics are positioned above the median as are positioned below the median.

FIGURE 22-1
Median Incomes

HOW YOUR PAY RANKS*

If family income is:	You are in this range:
More than $75,000	Top 2%
$50,000 or more	Top 9%
$25,000 or more	Top 44%
$20,000 or less	Bottom 43%
$15,000 or less	Bottom 31%
$10,000 or less	Bottom 17%
$5,000 or less	Bottom 6%

*Based on median income in 1981

Reprinted from *U.S. News & World Report*
Copyright, 1982, U.S. News & World Report, Inc.

From the chart above, you can see that if you earn $25,000 or more you would be in the top 44 percent income range. But if your total income is $15,000 or less, you are in the lower 31 percent income range.

You can evaluate the career you are considering from the standpoint of income it provides. For example, you might be considering a career as a systems analyst. By researching the average earnings of a person in this type of work, you might find that in your area the level of pay you could expect is about $23,000. In this position you would be in about the middle of the wage scale and would find that about half of the labor force would be earning more than you, and half would be earning less. You need to evalute how well the $23,000 salary will be able to meet your needs and wants as well as fulfill your status attainment, social standing, and prestige requirements. If purchasing power and social status are important considerations for you, you might want to reconsider your career choice and prepare yourself for a career that would fall in the top 44 percent of median incomes or higher.

Education. *Formal education* is knowledge gained through attending formal institutions of learning. The end result is a diploma or degree, which is evidence that the recipient has accomplished a certain educational goal and has met the standards required for graduation. The level of education achieved will influence a person's needs and wants and his or her methods of fulfilling them because it will affect income. A person who has earned a college degree is likely to make different choices (based on greater earning power) than a person who dropped out of high school at age 16. Figure 22-2 illustrates how the level of education attained directly affects income.

Education increases your earning capacity.

FIGURE 22-2
Education and Income

HOW EDUCATION RAISES INCOME	
Heads of family*:	*Median family income**:*
5 or more years of college	$38,785
Finished college	$32,720
1 to 3 years of college	$26,873
Finished high school	$23,003
1 to 3 years of high school	$16,810
Finished grade school	$14,568

*25 years or older
**Based on 1981 figures

Reprinted from *U.S. News & World Report*
Copyright, 1982, U.S. News & World Report, Inc.

Security Level. A person acts and reacts in accordance with the degree of safety, security, and peace he or she enjoys. These factors include personal safety as well as personal freedoms and fears for life, liberty, and property. Being secure from physical harm—whether from civil conflicts or robbery and property damage—influences our perceptions and, therefore, our needs and wants. Job security is another important factor. If you feel secure and satisfied in your employment, your choices will be different from those you make when you feel threatened or dissatisfied.

Leisure Time. Individual needs and wants are often satisfied in our choices of pleasure and recreational activities. All of us have time after our work and chores are done. Those who are retired or not employed have more leisure time to allocate. Wise choices in this area can make life rewarding and satisfying. Wasting and making poor use of leisure time results in frustation, loneliness, and depression.

Leisure time needs careful planning.

Collective Values

Collective values are those things important to society as a whole; all citizens share in their costs and in their benefits. The society in which you live influences your values, goals, and choices because it demands from citizens and provides for citizens legal protection, employment, progress, quality environment, and public and government services.

Legal Protection. One of the first needs of the individual that is met by society is preservation of legal and personal rights, and protection from others who would deny you those rights. Law enforcement is the result of society's value of protection for citizens and property. Although it may not be often used directly by citizens, law enforcement is always made available. Laws are passed to protect freedoms and rights guaranteed by the Constitution or by local, state, and federal governments.

Legal and personal rights are important to society.

Employment. Society as a whole expects that its able members will be productive members. Employment is an acceptable measure of that productivity. Most people who are able will work in their lifetimes because it is expected and demanded in order to survive in the society. Most of us are aware of this subtle, yet very real, pressure to perform in the work arena. Therefore, we strive to do the best we can—to get a job that pays us well for the effort we put forth. In this way, we can be personally satisfied with our productivity and can, at the same time, satisfy society's demand for citizens who contribute.

Progress. The relative state of the country in which you live—its technological advances and feelings about their importance—will affect your personal goals. Our society is technologically advanced and places a high value on positive innovations. **Innovations** are new ideas, methods, or devices that bring about changes. Positive innovations, such as more efficient equipment or machinery, timesaving devices, or new solutions to old problems, bring about progress. Because we, as a society, place a high value on progress, we strive to achieve and discover new and more efficient methods and products. Discovery of new ideas, methods, or devices pays off, both financially and emotionally, because we are encouraged by our society to be innovative. A by-product of this encouragement is that citizens seek higher education and academic achievement to enhance their positions in society.

High value is placed on progress and innovation.

Quality Environment. Natural resources are of great value and concern to society as a whole because they are very limited, and some cannot be replaced. Because of our priority of preserving a quality environment

Quality of environment is a collective value.

for ourselves and future generations, we concentrate on activities such as land-use planning, preserving natural beauty and wildlife, and establishing air pollution standards. We also place a great importance on the environmental effects of a given product or service. Environmental quality is of great importance to society as a whole, and individuals respond to this concern by acting and purchasing accordingly.

Public and Government Services. Our country is organized to be "of the people, by the people, and for the people." We have a highly advanced and intricate system of government made up of the people, performing services for the people, with money contributed (through taxes) by the people. Our system of taxation takes money from those who earn it and redistributes this money to those who need it. High value is placed on providing services for all citizens—from police protection to public parks. Services, such as roads and highways, are provided for all citizens, regardless of how much the citizens are able to contribute to society. Most citizens have come to expect public goods and services automatically—as a right rather than a privilege. What is often forgotten or ignored is that these goods and services are provided because of taxation of productive workers, and that no one can be excluded from receiving their benefits.

Citizens receive all public services.

You may be able to identify other collective or societal values that influence your personal choices—each person has a different perception and reacts accordingly.

FACTORS OF PRODUCTION

A nation's productivity depends on the factors of production.

Factors of production are necessary for producing goods and services to meet consumer wants and needs. The quantity and quality of these factors determines a country's productive capacity. Effective use of factors of production determines a country's ability to meet the needs and wants of its own citizens and of others in the world. There are four factors of production that a firm uses to produce goods and services: land, labor, capital, and entrepreneurship.

Land

Land is our most limited productive resource.

Land is the factor of production that represents resources that are fixed or nonrenewable. Land includes water, climate, minerals, quantity of soil, and quality of soil. None of these resources can be easily changed or altered by humans. Natural resources either exist or do not exist in a given geographic area. *Rent* is the price paid for land.

Humans can use up natural resources, but only limited circumstances allow complete replacement of what has been used. Reforestation is one example of replacing a resource (our forests) that has been used. Once a resource such as oil is used up, there is no way to remake it. Consequently, increased usage of alternative sources of energy to decrease the dependence on oil is necessary. Once land and other natural resources have been used up, they cannot be replaced. Land is scarce and very valuable because it exists in limited quantities and qualities and cannot be replaced.

Labor

Labor is the human factor of production. The labor force is the human resources available within a country to work and produce the necessary goods and services. The labor force in the United States numbers slightly less than half of the total population, estimated to be 226 million (1980 census). All persons ages 16 to 70 who are regularly employed for 35 hours or more a week (not including temporary or part-time employment) are considered to be in the labor force. Persons under age 16 are not considered a part of the labor force because they are required to attend school until age 16.

The labor force directly affects a country's productivity. When the labor force changes in quantity or quality, its productivity changes proportionately. For example, women are now entering into the labor force in large numbers. Almost half of the total number of American households are two-income families; most women work outside the home at some time during their lives. There are more than 3 million women business owners and sole proprietors now in the U.S. Figure 22-3 illustrates how the labor force has changed in 40 years. As you can see, the largest increase in new workers to the labor force is caused by women entering into paid employment. Labor statistics from 1981 show that 52.3 percent of all women, age 16 and over, are in the work force.

The quality of the work force is affected by such things as level of education attained. An increased standard of living is directly related to a higher educational level (see Figure 22-2). The nation as a whole is affected when we do or do not educate our citizens. Education, from the standpoint of labor productivity, is for the benefit of all, not just those currently receiving an education.

Another factor affecting the quality of the work force is the general health of the nation. Whether or not national health insurance is the solution, all persons need good medical care and services. The reason is clear: when people do not feel well, they do not work well.

The quantity and quality of the labor force determines its productivity.

Public education benefits everyone.

FIGURE 22-3
The Labor Force

JOBS AND INCOME

In 1941 there were 55.9 million workers in the civilian labor force. By 1981 there were 106.7 million in the labor force, an increase of 91 percent.

	1941	1981	Change
Per capita income, after taxes	$691	$8,872	+1,184%
In 1981 dollars	$4,073	$8,872	+118%
Men in labor force	43,070,000	60,734,000	+41%
As percentage of all men	83.8%	76.8%	—
Women in labor force	14,650,000	46,002,000	+214%
As percentage of all women	28.5%	52.3%	—
Unemployment rate	9.9%	8.0%	—
Union members	14,489,000	22,366,000	+54%
As percentage of total work force	18.2%	20.9%	—
Manufacturing workers	13,192,000	20,225,000	+53%
As percentage of all nonfarm workers	36.1%	22.0%	—

Reprinted from *U.S. News & World Report*
Copyright, 1981, U.S. News & World Report, Inc.

Motivation can make a great deal of difference in productivity, too. Factors that motivate workers include rate of pay, working conditions, performance incentives, and fair labor agreements. In a "work ethic" society such as ours, productive employment is considered a positive goal.

Payment for the labor force is in the form of wages. **Wages** are total compensation for employment and include gross pay, insurance, sick pay, fringe benefits, and all other types of direct or indirect compensation. Wage level acts as an indication to the employee of his or her worth and value to the employer in terms of quality and quantity of work performed. Wage increase is the greatest incentive for higher productivity.

Employment is viewed as a positive contribution to society.

Capital

Capital is the factor of production that represents the durable, but depreciable, input in the production process. Machines, tools, and buildings are capital. Capital is used to make the investment in equipment, raw materials, and human resources needed to produce necessary goods and services. The price paid for using capital is **interest**.

Capital is an economic term.

Money is a *measure* of the productivity of capital. Money is NOT capital. In order to produce goods and services, all factors of production—land, labor, capital (natural and human resources, tools and machines, etc.), and entrepreneurship—are necessary. Capital is not wanted for its own use; it is used to invest in factors necessary for production.

The United States has great capacity for generating capital and productive capital equipment (machinery, factories, tools) and the knowledge to use them both effectively. Capital is also used in our personal lives. Home devices that save time and money, such as washing machines and dishwashers, office computers, and communication systems are examples of capital investments.

Entrepreneurship

Entrepreneurs take the risk of ownership.

Entrepreneurship is the factor of production that represents management, innovation, and risk-taking. The entrepreneurs are the owners or persons who are taking the risk of loss for owning land, investing in capital equipment, or hiring labor. The return for entrepreneurship is **profit.** If a profit is made, the entrepreneur knows he or she has an effective combination of land, labor, and capital to produce a product or service. The profit is the excess income received from the sale of a product or service over the cost of the land, labor, and capital used to make the product or provide the service. In other words, sale price less cost of production equals profit. Profit is the compensation to the owner for the risk that has been taken. Businesses sometimes refer to profit as "net profit" or "net income" because it represents what is left over after all income is collected and all expenses have been paid.

PRODUCTIVITY ANALYSIS

Production is the result when the factors of production (land, labor, capital, and entrepreneurship) are effectively combined into one successful venture. Entrepreneurs must use internal controls and external controls in order to make wise decisions that result in a profit.

Internal Controls

Decision making is responsibility for success or failure.

The entrepreneur collects data and is responsible for the decisions that ultimately lead to the success or failure of a company or business. The entrepreneur must decide the following:

1. What and how much should be produced (product/quantity decision)
2. How production should take place (production decision)
3. How what is produced should be distributed among the population (distribution decision)

If the entrepreneur's decisions are accurate and well planned, the result is success and profit.

External Controls

To make the preceding decisions, the entrepreneur must also consider the following:

1. Laws that may prohibit and dictate production or nonproduction, quantities, qualities, or other decision factors
2. Customs that dictate that some things are necessary while others are luxuries

Owners do not have total power to make decisions.

3. Government restrictions, controls, guidelines, or standards to be met
4. Amount, quality, and cost of available resources
5. Company goals and plans as well as profitability requirements (Generally, that which will generate the greatest profit will be produced.)
6. Economic concerns and stability of the nation, including interest rates and loan costs, times of peace or conflict, and issues of importance to citizens

Failure to consider one of these important items may cost a company in the salability of a product. Therefore, all of these considerations must be weighed carefully by the entrepreneur before a decision is made.

Time

Time is the element of production that refers to the crucial timing of production so that a product or service is available for consumption when it is desired by the consumer. Time has three significant characteristics that affect production decisions:

1. Once time has been invested, it cannot be recaptured. Time is money; once it has been used (spent), it is gone.
2. Time cannot be stored.
3. Time is limited in quantity and, therefore, is very valuable in terms of production.

Time is an important factor to consider.

Time is an important part of production. Once a decision has been made and time is invested, then the decision has incurred a cost that cannot be recovered. That is, it is too late to make a change. Perhaps the most important decisions an entrepreneur makes relate to time because it is the one element of production that is unchanging in relation to other conditions.

Space

Space is limited and expensive.

Space is the physical attribute of production that is concerned with dimensional, geographic, and measurable commitments of productive resources. Space is also very limited in quantity and must be considered in the following arenas:

1. Amount of living or producing space that is available to the citizen or to the entrepreneur
2. Population of the area in which production is being considered (Is it large enough to pay the costs of production? Will enough be purchased to make production worthwhile?)
3. Distances to be traveled in the process of production or distribution

The entrepreneur must decide issues that involve wise use of the available space in relation to cost, projected profit, storage, and many other areas of concern. Space, like time, is expensive in terms of production.

VOCABULARY

Directions: Can you find the definition for each of the following terms used in Chapter 22?

economics	basic needs
formal education	median
innovations	collective values
land	factors of production
labor	rent
capital	wages
interest	entrepreneurship
profit	time
space	

1. The study of human efforts to solve the problem of making scarce resources meet the unlimited needs and wants of society.

2. The physical attribute of production that relates to dimensional, geographic, or measurable commitments of productive resources.

3. The element of production referring to the crucial planning of production to assure that a product is available for sale when it is demanded.

4. Ingredients necessary for maintaining physical life.

5. The excess amount earned by the entrepreneur over the cost of production.

6. The price paid for using capital.

7. A statistical middle amount.

8. Knowledge gained through attending formal institutions of learning, such as colleges and universities.

9. Things that are important to society as a whole; all citizens share in their benefit and in their cost.

10. New ideas, methods, or devices that bring about changes.

11. Ingredients necessary to produce goods and services.

12. A factor of production that is provided by nature, such as water, climate, and soil.

13. A factor of production that is the human work force necessary to work and produce within a country.

14. The factor of production necessary to produce other goods and services.

15. The price paid for land.

16. The return or payoff to those who make up the labor force.

17. The factor of production that represents management, innovation, and risk-taking.

ITEMS FOR DISCUSSION

1. What are the basic needs for survival?

2. List five life-improving wants and needs.

3. Of the life-improving needs and wants, how many are met in your life?

4. If your family income is $40,000 or more, into what income range do you fall?

5. How does level of income relate to amount of education attained?

6. Why are natural resources expensive and valuable?

7. List the factors of production.

8. Who makes the decisions about what and how much is to be produced, and for whom?

9. What types of external controls affect production decisions?

10. What three important facts about time must be considered in production?

11. What are the three space considerations in production?

APPLICATIONS

1. Why is it important for everyone to have a good basic understanding of economics?

2. List the life-fulfilling and improving needs and wants that you have now and expect to have in the future. Prioritize them, placing a numeral *1* by very important wants and a *5* by your least important wants. How do you expect that each of these needs and wants will be met in your life (by self, parents, government, others)?

3. Explain what your achieved level of education has to do with the amount and the types of wants and needs you will have and will be able to meet.

4. As a citizen, what types of societal values do you consider important? List them and prioritize them, giving very important values a *1* and least important values a *5*. How are these societal values provided?

5. What types of things are being done in your local area and state to preserve natural resources, land use, and air quality?

6. What types of public goods and services do you expect to receive as a citizen? Are most of these taken for granted? How are these goods and services provided for all?

7. Most countries that are in deep poverty lack one major productive resource—capital. How can American entrepreneurs assist these countries? (Send them money? Send them food? Help them to be productive?)

CASE PROBLEMS AND ACTIVITIES

1. An innovation is a new idea, method, or product. As an inventor who has a great idea for a new product or service, what things do you have to consider before implementing a plan to produce your innovation and sell it to consumers?

2. When a farmer sells fresh corn in a vegetable stand at the side of the road, he or she sells what was planted, raised, and harvested. To do this, farm labor is hired during the summer growing months. In addition, farm equipment and tools, sprinklers, and fertilizers are purchased at the store. Yearly, the farmer plants crops, and when there is a good crop and expenses are low, the farmer makes a good profit. But when expenses of production are too high, labor costs too much, or bad weather causes a poor crop, the farmer is likely to lose money.

    Identify the factors of production the farmer used in the case above.

3. Describe a recent money-making project at your school or in your community. List the factors of production that went into that project, and list the payoff for each resource used. Who makes the decisions regarding whether or not to do the money-making projects? What is the basis (how do they reach this decision) of going ahead with, or deciding not to have, a certain project?

4. An underdeveloped country is unable to meet its citizens' needs for food, clothing, and shelter. Yet in this country is a vast untapped potential for economic prosperity because of its underground copper and uranium fields. How could we, the United States, help this underdeveloped country to feed its citizens? Choose one of the following options and explain why you think it would be the best way to help the underdeveloped country:

    (a) Send them food.

    (b) Give them money.

    (c) Help them build capital equipment and teach them how to use it.

CHAPTER 23

WE NEED EACH OTHER

> **CHAPTER OBJECTIVES**
> *After studying this chapter and completing the activities, you will be able to:*
>
> 1. Discuss economic concepts of scarcity and choice in terms of individuals and societies.
> 2. Explain trade-offs and opportunity costs and how they are described by a production possibilities curve.
> 3. List the characteristics of a market economy and describe how each plays a vital part in making the market economy productive.

SCARCITY AND CONSUMER BEHAVIOR

In Chapter 22, we defined the economic concept of scarcity. We will explore this topic further and learn how scarcity affects consumer decisions and actions.

Production of goods and services is limited by the factors of production. Consequently, everything we desire cannot be produced in quantities large enough for all people to have what they want at a low cost. Scarcity affects consumer behavior: because of scarcity, choices must be made. Our decisions will affect the American people and persons in other countries around the world. For example, if farmers in the United States decide to cut production of wheat and corn, the world's supply of food will be reduced. Other countries that depend on purchasing our surplus grains will have to buy elsewhere or do without.

Our choices affect others around the world.

There are ways in which consumers can act to resolve or minimize the problem of scarcity. Decreasing wants and needs, developing alternative resources, improving the quality of existing resources, making better use of existing resources, and redistributing goods and services are five methods used to lesson the effects of scarcity.

Decreasing Wants and Needs

Individually and collectively, we can make an effort to reduce consumption of some goods or services. For example, we can make an effort to drive less, combine trips, car pool, buy more energy-efficient cars, and find all possible alternatives to using the automobile. As a result of such conservation measures, we can save our fuel resources for future dates. Decreasing wants and needs affects our standard and style of living and often involves sacrificing and choosing alternatives that are not so pleasing or desirable. In order to take the city bus rather than drive to work, it may be necessary to get up an hour earlier in the morning. We may have to walk a few extra blocks.

As individuals we can reduce our consumption.

Decreasing wants and needs is not always possible, and in some cases it is only a temporary solution. For example, by conserving our supply of fuel oil, we can make it last longer. But the oil supply will run out eventually.

Developing Alternative Resources

In some cases, it is not possible to increase our supply of certain resources: we are limited in the quantity and quality of land, water, climate, etc. We can, however, attempt to develop alternative resources. For instance, using solar power or coal rather than electricity and oil for heating is one method of supplementing old sources of energy with new ones. We can increase our supply of human resources by encouraging older and younger workers, through pay and work incentives, to join the labor force.

Alternate sources conserve existing supplies of scarce resources.

Improving the Quality of Existing Resources

We can increase product output by improving the quality of our existing labor resources. For example, the quality of a nation's labor force is an important part of that nation's productive capacity. Quality can be increased by better educating our citizens, increasing safety and working conditions, and providing medical care for all citizens. *Motivators* are incentives that inspire workers to produce more and better quality goods and services. The best motivator is good pay; close behind are good working conditions, fringe benefits, health care plans, vacation and sick pay, and other benefits. Eliminating demotivators can also increase quality and quantity of goods and services produced. *Demotivators* are conditions and policies that create dissatisfaction and produce low employee morale and productivity. Demotivators include such things as poor management policies, lack of communication, low pay, few work incentives, uncertain and ambiguous policies and procedures, inconsistent hiring and firing policies, and lack of company organization.

The best motivation is higher pay.

Production tools are expensive because technology and research are often involved in their development. As new methods of production are created, more and better products can be produced. The process of creating new capital is lengthy and requires planning, innovation, and encouragement from government and society.

Making Better Use of Existing Resources

The wise use of scarce resources is known as *conservation*. Careful choices made after examining all possible uses will ensure that our scarce resources are conserved and used wisely. For example, because land is limited in quantity and quality for producing certain foods, the soil most conducive to producing fruits should be used for that purpose. Using machinery and tools can increase the amount of fruit that can we grown and harvested. By using fertilizers and sprays, we can save even more

Soil should be used for its most productive purpose.

fruit. Wise marketing procedures can save some of it from rotting on the way to the market or arriving in poor condition. Thus, we can make the best use of the resources we have.

Redistributing Goods and Services

The basic economic problem for all societies is deciding what goods and services shall be produced, what shall not be produced, and what can be postponed or produced in limited quantities. Decisions then follow of when to produce, how best to allocate resources, and how to use resources for other purposes if needed. The final decision concerns who will receive or will not receive the goods and services produced.

To make better use of the existing resources to meet total needs, we could simply send goods and services where they are most needed. We could decide that artichokes and avocados are not necessary and produce only carrots and peas. We could decide that taxis and vans are no longer to be used for family or private purposes and divert them for public transportation only. While this eliminates freedom of choice for some citizens, it gives others the goods and services they might not otherwise be able to acquire.

Redistribution results in loss of freedom of choice.

But the process of redistribution has many disadvantages in an economic society based on freedom of choice; it is unlikely to be accepted by most people. Redistribution of goods and services means more governmental control. Decisions as to who receives what and how much are made by the government. Citizens do not have freedom of choice. Because consumers do not have the power to determine what is produced, the supply and demand curves for the selected products change. When the price is lowered, producers are no longer willing to manufacture certain goods and services. Government intervention increases on both sides—production and consumption.

Let us take an example. Suppose the government determines that there are too many automobiles in our country because air pollution is out of control, and the government must take action to control who has a car, when it is driven, and how it is used. In this case, the government might set a rule that every family is entitled to only one vehicle. Government might also decide that every family will be provided one vehicle and that those who cannot afford to buy one will be given one. Consequently, any families having more than one car will have to sell the other one(s). Further, the government might also stipulate that no fewer than three persons can travel in a vehicle at one time to save fuel and to cut down exhaust fumes.

Most citizens do not favor this type of governmental control in our society. Producers of automobiles would be outraged because the prices would be controlled by government, which would also determine who would get the cars. Government could even regulate car sizes, engine sizes, and quality and number of cars produced.

CHOICE

We all make choices in our daily lives. Most of these choices are dependent on our ability to earn and the wants and needs we have as individuals and as families. Individuals make choices based on needs to optimize and economize. External factors affect choices of individuals and of society.

Optimizing

Optimizing is spreading resources to go as far as possible.

The procedure of *optimizing* is getting the most from all available resources—spreading the resources to cover as many needs as possible. Optimizing does not attempt to limit or do away with needs, but tries to cover all needs as well as possible. A family that optimizes divides its income into categories of a budget and determines how the total income shall be best allocated to meet as many needs and wants as possible. If, at the end of the year, some money is left over in one area, it can be used to increase or offset another need or desired purchase. But all areas are initially provided for so that maximum use is made of money that is available to the family.

Economizing

Economizing is saving and eliminating uses.

The procedure of *economizing* is saving and eliminating uses to make a product or resource last as long as possible. Rather than keeping a budget, the family that economizes starts each month with a record and spends as little as possible, cutting corners whenever possible. Living on a day-to-day basis, the family spends money only when essential. Less expensive alternatives are continually being sought to eliminate any possible waste and stretch and save the money so it will go as far as possible. Money not spent is set aside for future needs. Economizing is cutting back and saving whenever possible.

External Factors

Just as individuals make choices in their lives, groups of people and societies must make decisions for the benefit of all. Individual decisions must take into consideration any societal choices that may limit or affect the desirability of the decision. Some of these limitations and considerations are laws, customs, and expectations.

Laws. *Laws* are rules of conduct accepted by people and enforced to protect people. Environmental protection laws have been passed in our country to protect the air, water, and quality of environment for all citizens, present and future. Factories must meet standards established for clean air. Automobiles are made with devices to limit the pollutant content of exhaust. As individual citizens, we must consider what is acceptable to society when making our choices.

Laws are passed to protect the environment.

Customs. Many customs are so much a part of our lives that we may not realize they are not written laws. For example, it is customary in our country to sit down in a restaurant, order a meal and eat it, then pay for it. In many other countries, you must pay for the meal before you can eat it. Customs affect many of our purchasing decisions and choices. Holidays are the customary times for families to gather for celebrations, large dinners, and reunions.

Expectations. We are affected by our own self-expectations, those that significant others in our lives have for us, and those that are valued by society. Our society places a high value on education and expects that those capable will graduate from high school and pursue further educational opportunities. Parents and friends likewise expect that each of us will use our abilities to their fullest. As a result, we set self-expectations that are the basis of goal setting and values for our lives. Many expectations are unstated and subtle; others are very obvious and apparent in our daily lives.

Self-expectations are affected by society.

TRADE-OFFS AND OPPORTUNITY COST

Whenever a decision or choice is made, something is gained and something is lost (not chosen). An *opportunity cost* is something that you must give up to get something else that you also want. Uusually, it is not a direct monetary cost. For example, you may be part of a group that will decide what to do with 100 acres of land. The land could be used for parks and recreation, or it could be used for timber harvesting. By choosing one option, you are giving up part or all of the other option, foregoing one opportunity for another.

A *trade-off* is what you are making when you choose one option over another. When scarce resources are used for a particular purpose, the opportunity cost may be less than another choice. What you do receive, the trade-off, must be weighed carefully and be more valued than the choice given up.

When a trade-off is chosen, an opportunity cost is incurred.

Economists use a graph commonly called a production possibilities curve to illustrate the choices and combinations possible when decisions are made about scarce resources. A *production possibilities curve* plots combinations of two goods that can be produced with a given level of resources and technology. Figure 23-1 is a production possibilities curve that shows the possible combinations of lumber production and recreational park area on a 100-acre tract of land.

Possibilities for production are found in the production possibilities curve.

FIGURE 23-1
Production
Possibilities
Curve

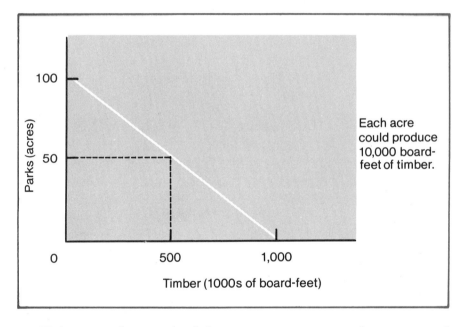

Within a production possibilities curve, we can see the concepts of scarcity, choice, opportunity cost, and trade-off. In Figure 23-1, when all 100 acres are used for parks, there is no land left to use for timber production. When all 100 acres are used for timber production, a total of one million board-feet of timber can be produced. The decision, then, is to choose what number of acres will be used for timber and what number of acres will be used for parks. We can see from the graph that as the amount of parkland increases, the amount of timber production decreases. The opportunity cost is the value of the parkland or timberland forfeited, while the trade-off is the timberland or parkland gained.

To produce all of one product eliminates production of others.

In our example, 50 acres could be used for parks, and 50 acres could be used for timber production. Fifty acres would produce 500,000 board-feet of timber. Timber is another resource in limited supply. Yet natural wilderness areas and parks are also scarce and valuable. A choice must be made because there is not enough land to allow all the timber production we could want and need and provide for all the parks and wilderness areas we want and need as well. Individuals and societies must make choices that trade off one potential benefit in return for another.

Choices can allow compromise situations where more people are satisfied.

PRICE AND THE MARKETPLACE

According to economists, the United States uses a ***market economy*** system, which is characterized by private property ownership, self-interest behavior, consumer sovereignty, and competition. Our market economy is often called capitalism, free enterprise, and democracy. All these terms are used interchangeably for a market economy but are not equally descriptive of the actual type of exchange that takes place in the marketplace.

Private Property Ownership

Private property is a means of production.

Individuals have the right to buy, sell, and own property, including land and natural resources, houses, tools, machinery, and equipment. We own and exchange private property, which is a means of production. Without ownership of private property, a market economy could not exist.

The concept of private property ownership is often called capitalism. In a free enterprise economic system, private individuals and groups—not governments—control the factors of production. While there is government participation, as seen in Chapter 24, the government does not play the major role in controlling what is produced and consumed. For the most part, consumers decide what will be produced by their dollar votes. The market system based on supply and demand will determine price, provided the necessary ingredients are present—competition, informed consumers, self-interest behavior.

In communist societies, the government controls the amount of economic activity of the nation, including individual rights and spending. Government owns or totally controls all the means of production in the society. In countries typical of this system, such as the U.S.S.R., the ruling party, called the Communist party, makes decisions for the country. Party officers decide whether to make guns or shoes, cars or boots. With a central government making all the decisions, there is very little freedom of choice left for citizens, who must purchase whatever the government makes available to them. There is little decision making, other than by government.

Socialism is between capitalism and communism: it supports governmental control of the factors of production, yet does not take all decisions away from citizens. In socialist societies, such as Sweden, many services are provided to all citizens. Through government all people have security. Yet there is also private enterprise that cooperates with government to provide other goods and services. Consumers have choices in some purchases, but no choices in others. Generally, taxes are very high to provide extensive government services, such as health care, for everyone.

It should be noted that there is no such thing as a pure system capitalism contains some elements of socialist and communist societies. Likewise, socialism contains some elements of a private enterprise system, and communism still contains a few elements of choice.

Private citizens can own tools of production (capital).

In our market economy, each person is entitled to ownership and control of his or her productive capacity—including property owned, tools of production, investment capital, and entrepreneurship abilities. The rewards (profits) are earned by those who make the best decisions and wisest choices in the allocation of scarce and valuable resources into production possibilities.

Self-Interest Behavior

Each person owning his or her share of the resources will act with his or her own best interests in mind. This is an important element of the market economy. Each person will desire to make the most of the resources available to him or her for the purpose of making the largest possible profit. The profit motive is quite evident throughout our country's history. The automobile would not have been produced and sold if the producers were not interested in making a profit; the clothing you wear and food you eat are the result of the profit anticipated by the entrepreneurs who made the decision to produce these goods.

Producers and consumers exhibit self-interest behavior in a market economy.

Not only businesses exhibit the self-interest motive. Workers and consumers must also function with their own best interests in mind to make the market economy most efficient. While producers are expecting to sell their products for the highest profit, consumers are also looking for the best possible product for the least amount of money. Workers are seeking the highest-paying jobs with the best working conditions and benefits.

Everybody within the market economy must pursue his or her own best interests: this is what makes the system operate most effectively. If workers did not care how much they got paid, if pay level was controlled by government, if producers did not care what kind of product they produced because there was no profit incentive, then resources would cease to be used wisely with the best production decisions.

Some people contend that self-interest behavior is selfish and wasteful. But there is no better motive for maximum efficiency and productivity than self-interest. Self-interest is the best possible incentive to conserve and make wise decisions—when you do your best and make the best decisions, then the profit is higher.

The best decisions bring the highest profits.

Consumer Sovereignty

Consumer *sovereignty* is the power or ability of consumers to affect what is being produced and consumed. The consumer will ultimately decide what will be produced and how resources will be allocated. If, for example, consumers demand a certain product and reject another (do not buy it), the profit motive will dictate that the product that will continue to be produced is the one the consumer prefers to buy.

Consumers have power in a market economy because they freely choose what they will buy. Although their decisions are based on external controls, such as laws, customs, and expectations, these factors are taken into consideration before products are made. As we shall see later, producers discover first and make decisions as to what is likely to be a good selling product long before it is actually produced.

As a consumer, you vote with your dollars on whether a product should or should not be made. Every time you purchase a product, you are casting a vote for that product at that purchase price. Each dollar you spend represents your choices, your opportunity costs (what you could have had with the same money), and your trade-offs (what you got). You want the most for each dollar you spend. When you refuse to pay a price for a product, the price will be lowered. If the product cannot be produced for the price demanded with a reasonable profit added to the cost, the product will not be made. Before a new product is introduced to the marketplace, the producer must decide what price to ask for it. Usually a market analysis or research project is done to find out what the demand might be for the product at different prices. The information collected is used to prepare a demand curve.

Each dollar you spend represents a dollar vote for the good or service purchased.

Figure 23-2 is a demand curve illustrating that demand is based on price: as price decreases, demand increases, and vice versa. At a price of

FIGURE 23-2
Demand Curve

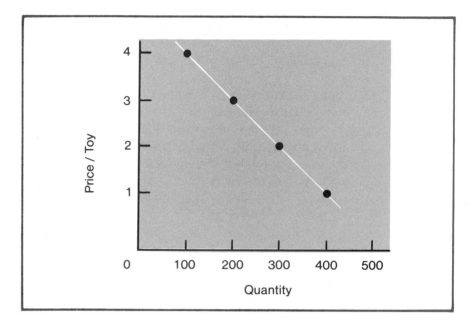

$1 each, 400 people will buy the toy in our example. But at a price of $4 each, only 100 people will buy the toy.

Competition

The fourth vital factor essential to the proper functioning of a market economy is competition. Competition is vital because it ensures that producers will produce at the cheapest price possible what is demanded by the consumer. If one producer will not supply the product demanded at an attractive price, other producers (competitors) will, and the competitors' products will be purchased. Whenever a new product or industry comes into being and big profits are generated, new producers freely enter the market and begin producing the product as well. This competition forces prices down because all producers are trying to get the consumer's support for their products.

Competition ensures a fair trade price for a product.

Competition also plays an important part in the allocation of scarce resources. Producers will seek to make the most efficient use of resources available in order to keep prices down. This way they can sell the most and make the most profit from the limited quantity of resources available.

Government interference in a market economy is limited.

In a market economy, government involvement and interference in the production and consumption of goods and services must be very limited. Our country is not a pure market economy, where there is no government involvement. The term *mixed economy* is often used interchangeably with the term **market economy** because we do have an active government that produces, consumes, and also controls production and consumption within the society to some extent. In a market economy, some controls must exist to prevent outrageous or selfish activities from damaging a majority of the citizens of the country.

When the activities of private ownership, self-interest behavior, consumer sovereignty, and competition mix with a modest amount of government participation, a circular flow of economic activity results in consistent and steady productivity. Figure 23-3 shows a circular flow diagram to illustrate how all the elements of the market economy interact to make productivity efficient.

FIGURE 23-3
Circular Flow
Diagram

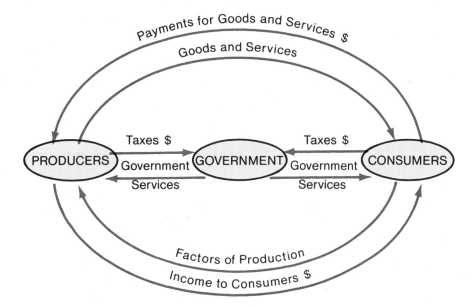

Consumers are purchasers of goods and services and suppliers of factors of production. Producers are purchasers of factors of production and suppliers of goods and services. The monetary flow that accompanies the flow of goods and services to consumers is called payments for goods and services. The monetary flow from producers to consumers is called income. Government taxes consumers and producers and provides services for consumers and producers.

In a market economy, competition transforms self-interest behavior into socially desirable ends. Competition limits the self-interest of entrepreneurs to ensure that they do not have the power to promote their own interests at the expense of public interests. Consumers direct the market system; self-interest behavior motivates the people to act; and competition regulates their behavior.

Competition has
socially desirable ends.

Competition benefits everyone in a market economy because (*a*) it encourages producers to increase production in those areas where consumer demand is strong; (*b*) it keeps prices low as producers compete for consumers' dollar votes; and (*c*) it forces producers to improve the quality of their products, thereby achieving the most efficient allocation of scarce economic resources.

VOCABULARY

Directions: Can you find the definition for each of the following terms used in Chapter 23?

motivators   sovereignty
conservation   demotivators
production possibilities curve   market economy
trade-off   opportunity cost
laws   optimizing
economizing

1. The wise use of scarce resources.

2. Something that you must give up to get something else that you also want.

3. Incentives that inspire workers to produce more and better quality goods and services.

4. The power and ability of consumers to affect what will be produced and consumed in a market economy.

5. Conditions that create dissatisfaction among workers, lowering their morale and productivity.

6. Rules of conduct established and enforced for the benefit of all citizens.

7. Getting the most from all available resources; spreading the resources to all possible areas of use.

8. Saving and eliminating uses to make a product or resource last as long as possible.

9. To choose one option over another.

10. A system characterized by private ownership, self-interest behavior, consumer power, and competition.

11. A graph to illustrate choices and combinations when decisions are being made about use of scarce resources.

ITEMS FOR DISCUSSION

1. What are five ways of solving or minimizing the problem of scarcity?

2. What are some motivators to increase labor force productivity and quality of work?

3. What are external factors that affect consumer buying choices?

4. What is the difference between a law and a custom?

5. What is the purpose of a production possibilities curve?

6. What are the four major characteristics of a market economy?

7. How do consumers have the ultimate power of deciding what will or will not be produced?

8. Why does the demand curve slope in a downward direction?

9. How much government involvement is there in a market economy? a socialist economy? a communist economy?

APPLICATIONS

1. Why is scarcity a basic economic problem?

2. Who makes the choices regarding scarce resources in a market economy? What external factors determine many of those choices?

3. Explain how we can increase the quality of the labor force.

4. Why does it take so long for new capital (machinery, factories) to come into existence when consumers demand a new product?

5. Conservation can save resources for longer periods of time. But some natural resources will eventually be gone and new sources will be needed to replace these resources. Give an example of a resource that will need to be replaced.

6. How is economizing different from optimizing?

7. How do environmental protection laws benefit you?

8. What are your self-expectations for the next five years of your life? What are your parents' expectations for you? Do you feel your decisions for those five years are affected by others around you, including subtle societal expectations?

9. Explain the meaning of the production possibilities curve—why does it curve downward from one axis to the other?

10. Explain how the self-interest behavior of wanting a profit makes for higher quality goods and services at the lowest possible prices.

11. Why is it important for consumers to cast their dollar votes wisely?

12. What is the natural result in a market economy when someone finds a unique way to produce a product that is in high demand by consumers for a high profit?

13. Explain how the circular flow diagram operates.

CASE PROBLEMS AND ACTIVITIES

1. As student body treasurer, you have been given the responsibility of allocating student body funds this school year. There are sixteen groups and clubs that are requesting funds. You have only $1,000. The junior class has asked for more money than other groups because of special needs, such as financing the prom. Explain how the $1,000 could best meet needs—by economizing or by optimizing.

2. You and a friend have just invented a new fuel additive that will increase gasoline or diesel efficiency and will allow an automobile to go from zero to eighty miles an hour in eight seconds. With your product, the average car can get fifty miles a gallon. What types of laws, customs, and expectations can you expect to run into when pursuing the production of this new invention?

3. Abdul is a very bright student, and had good grades in high school. He has wanted to be a teacher for a long time; his parents have encouraged him to go to college. Abdul owns a car and has a part-time job at the cannery. His employer has offered him a promotion to shift manager and says Abdul could be plant manager in five to ten years. After carefully considering the choices, Abdul has decided to quit his job and go to college. What was his opportunity cost? What were his trade-offs?

4. In times of high unemployment (recession), more people go to school for retraining and to further their education. In this situation, why would their opportunity costs be low?

5. You have worked all summer to save up $500 for clothes for school. School starts in four weeks. Your brother comes to you and has an emergency. He needs parts for his motorcycle that cost $300. He does not know when he can pay you back. Will you loan the money? Identify your opportunity costs and your trade-offs.

6. Mrs. Schwartz owns a bakery. Mr. Dimitri owns a bakery three blocks away. Mrs. Schwartz just discovered a unique way to make bagels that are very tasty and twice as big as Mr. Dimitri's bagels. She sells them for 50 cents each, including cream cheese. Soon her business is booming. Then Mr. Dimitri discovers a similar method and starts selling his giant bagels for 45 cents. Mrs. Schwartz's business drops. Mrs. Schwartz lowers her price to 39 cents and business booms again. Explain the concept of competition as illustrated in this case. How did self-interest behavior bring prices down?

CHAPTER 24

HOW THE SYSTEM WORKS

CHAPTER OBJECTIVES

After studying this chapter and completing the activities, you will be able to:

1. Compare the different economic systems and characteristics of each.
2. Describe specialization, division of labor, marginalism, and interdependence.
3. Explain the role of government in a market economy.

ECONOMIC SYSTEMS

An ***economic system*** is the way a group of people or a society chooses to organize its economic life and make economic decisions of what will be produced, when, how much, and for whom. There are three major economic systems: the traditional economy, the command economy, and the market economy. While no society falls absolutely within one of these categories, we classify most countries into one of them based on how their systems operate in general.

There is no pure economic system.

Traditional Economy

In the traditional economy, sometimes called the subsistence economy, fundamental questions are answered by appeals to tradition. People repeat what has been done in the past and accept it as what is supposed to happen. What will be produced, how, how much, and for whom have been taught for centuries; there are no questions about what actions would be best. What is produced is what the young have been taught by their parents to hunt, to gather, or to plant. How to produce has been passed on from generation to generation. The amount of production is dependent on good fortune. Distribution is also traditionally determined. The society that uses a traditional economy is a static one that changes slowly, but maintains a steady and constant pace. Japan is a good example of this type of system. The purest example, with little influences from our type of system or any other system, is found in primitive African villages where people exist today as their ancestors did many generations ago.

Children do as their parents did in a traditional economy.

Command Economy

In the planned or command economy, all questions are answered through planning or through central command and control. The decisions on what, how, how much, and for whom to produce are spelled out and documented. Detailed plans and orders are sent to producers, and these instructions carry the weight of law. Citizens are not free to purchase and sell at their own discretion. Planners determine wage rates and the amount of production of consumer goods. Socialist and communist countries often use this type of system.

Command systems exist to a degree in most countries. In times of war, citizens accept the directives of their government because of the emergency. Normal production is altered to meet the needs of national security. The gas and food rationing the United States experienced during World War II are examples of a command system operating during a national emergency.

Market Economy

A market economy operates according to the forces of supply and demand. Consumers are in control of a market economy. Self-interest motivates the people to act, and competition regulates the behavior of the market. Economic questions of what, how, how much, and for whom to produce are decided mostly by individuals in the marketplace.

Economic questions are decided in the marketplace in a market economy.

The market economy is unsympathetic; a good or service will be produced only as long as there is a profit to be made. A market economy is a price system: when a consumer buys a product, the purchase encourages further production of that product. In the market economy, the consumer determines what and how much will be produced. There is some government intervention, which means it is not a pure market economy. Therefore, a market economy is sometimes called a mixed economy. A *mixed*

A market economy is called a mixed economy because some government intervention is necessary.

economy is partly determined by market forces, but is aided by government policies to produce better overall results.

BASIC ECONOMIC PRINCIPLES

An increase in output of goods and services using the same resources can result from the use of specialization, interdependence, mechanization, and division of labor. In a complex economic system, we need to understand the underlying principles of productivity and total output. These principles include specialization, division of labor, marginalism, interdependence, and maximization behavior.

Specialization

Scarce resources are conserved and used to their fullest extent (economized and optimized) when specialization takes place. *Specialization* occurs when one person produces only one or a limited number of goods and services, but consumes many of them. For example, everyone in our country does not raise his or her own food. Instead most citizens work at a particular job, earn money, and buy their food from someone else. Most farmers do not grow all crops, but choose one or two main crops that are best suited to the climate and soil conditions of the geographic area.

Everyone cannot produce everything he or she consumes.

Everyone cannot do all things for themselves nor produce all that they need to eat, wear, and consume. It is more efficient for each person to learn to be productive in one specific area rather than to attempt to do all things less efficiently.

Certain areas of the country specialize in producing certain products. Warm southern states produce fruits and vegetables. Plains areas with rolling hills produce grain crops and herds of grazing animals. Within states, some areas are more conducive to certain crops. To produce what

To specialize is to have the greatest efficiency.

is best for that area is to increase efficiency. This is the principle of *comparative advantage*, which states that the greatest gain in total output will occur if each country (or state) specializes in producing those goods and services that can be produced with the greatest efficiency and imports goods that would have to be produced at great cost.

Farmers in the state of Hawaii produce half of the world's supply of sugar cane. They do so because they have the comparative advantage—the climate and soil in Hawaii are very suitable for sugar cane, and Hawaiians are able to produce this crop very easily. If, however, Hawaiian farmers attempted to divide their land to produce small amounts of several kinds of crops, they would find that the quality of their crops

would be much lower, and they would have very little to export. By trying to produce all they need to survive, Hawaiian farmers would lose their comparative advantage, and the land would not be used to its maximum potential.

Division of Labor

Closely related to specialization and comparative advantage is the concept of division of labor. *Division of labor* means that tasks are divided among workers to speed up production and make it more efficient. Task specialization takes place when one worker does not attempt to do all things, but learns one small part of the total production process. An automobile assembly line is a good example of this principle: one person along the line inserts a small part of the progressing product. This task may seem insignificant, but it is vital to the finished product. As the automobile being assembled moves down the assembly line, each specialized worker adds a part until the product is fully assembled. If one person tried to follow the product all the way through, she or he would have to know all the parts and processes. Division of labor can also take the form of specialization by trade or profession. Each person becomes very proficient in a particular kind of work, such as dentistry, cosmetology, or law.

Each person contributes a small but vital part.

Division of labor pro-
motes efficiency.

Division of labor promotes increased efficiency, avoids loss of time from switching activities, and has provided the primary source of economic growth in this country.

Marginalism

Marginal, in economic terms, means added or extra. It refers to the added value or benefit—the effect of buying or selling one more item.

Individually, consumers make marginal decisions daily. When shopping for groceries, you decide how many bananas, oranges, or cans of soup to purchase. You try to come up with the right combination so that you do not run out before the next shopping day. You also do not want to waste any groceries or allow any to spoil because you bought too many.

Marginalism is a technique used to analyze problems in which the results of small changes in quantity are examined. At 10 cents a pound, oranges are very inexpensive. You know that you are getting a good deal if you purchase 25 pounds of oranges for only $2.50. But you also have to consider whether you can consume 25 pounds of oranges before they spoil. If 20 pounds of oranges would go to waste, then any oranges you would purchase above the 5 pounds you are certain could be consumed

Marginalism is added
or extra benefits.

are said to be marginal. You must weigh the added benefit of getting 20 pounds of extra oranges to eat against the added cost—$2.00 worth of merchandise that might spoil.

Producers also have marginal decisions to make. They must decide whether to produce additional units of output and how many extra workers to hire. If a producer feels that the added benefit (increased profits) would pay for the extra costs (salary of additional workers), then he or she will choose to increase production. Producers must know where the break-even point is, and all points above that are marginal. Will the added revenue exceed extra costs incurred by hiring one more worker or producing one more unit?

The break-even point is called *equilibrium*—the point at which there is very little risk. The producer or consumer knows that up to that point

Producers are safe up
to the break-even point.

all products will be sold or consumed. There are times when the equilibrium point changes. When inflation reduces the consumer's buying power, then producers must decrease production or face a large inventory of unsold products that consumers are unable to buy. When this happens, a new equilibrium exists and production decisions by producers are weighed accordingly.

The study of marginalism is often called marginal analysis. It is often said to be a mathematical concept. An economist might describe the concept of marginal analysis in the following way: Don't look at the whole, examine the parts. For each additional product produced over the base (equilibrium) quantity, minimize production costs to get the most return for the amount spent. At each point beyond the equilibrium, you must compare the added benefits to the added costs to be sure you are still making a profit.

Remember that the marginal cost is the *additional* cost, not the *total* cost. Every time you take a new step—make or buy one more item—you must be better off than before you took that step.

The *sunken cost* is the amount already spent, or the amount it costs to have reached equilibrium. Once money has been spent or invested, there is nothing you can do about it. But you must decide if you want to spend (or invest) more. For example, a person spends $1,000 for a car. This $1,000 is the sunken cost. After a few weeks, he or she discovers that the car needs new brakes. For $75 the car will again run safely. Marginal analysis is used to make the decision of whether the added cost ($75) will return to the owner added miles of service. The $1,000 is already spent (sunken) and is not a consideration. If adding another $75 to the car will give sufficient return, then it is a good investment. If the car needs a lot of other work, too, spending more money on it might be wasted because it would not increase the value of the car, nor would it give enough added use to the car.

The sunken cost is not considered in marginalism.

Interdependence

Specialization stretches resources; as a nation and as individuals, we should produce that for which we have a comparative advantage. In a market economy, we can all benefit from each other's strengths.

In a *zero-sum game*, one person or group wins at the expense of the other. For every winner there is a loser. For example, in a basketball game, one team wins and the other team loses. But in a market economy, everyone benefits when someone else excels. This is the economic concept of *interdependence*—each unit depends on other units to do what each can do best.

We can all benefit from each other's gains.

The United States has a comparative advantage in the production of many types of food. Other countries depend on us for much of their grain and vegetable supplies because their comparative advantages lie in other productive areas. A country that consists of mostly desert regions could hardly make wisest use of its resources by trying to grow food. Instead, they drill oil and minerals from the land and sell them. With the money they receive, they purchase food and other items they are unable to produce.

Produce what you can do best; import the rest.

Suppose you are a medical doctor. During high school, you learned to type. Is it the best use of your productive capacity to type all your own correspondence? Probably not. You would not be as efficient as someone who is well trained as a secretary. Furthermore, your time could be much better spent in dealing with medical problems—a task for which you spent years in training.

Therefore, with specialization and comparative advantage that bring increased productivity, also come problems of interdependence. We depend on other countries to meet some of our needs. Likewise, as individuals, we also depend on others a great deal. On a personal level, the following two statements usually are true:

Increased productivity results from specialization and interdependence.

1. Everything one person does has an effect on someone else (economic decisions).
2. How well-off one person becomes depends, to some extent, on other persons.

The *product market* is the composite (total) of all the individual markets in which buyers and sellers interact to exchange goods and services. Anytime a buyer and seller get together to buy and sell, a market exists. All these markets put together are called the product market; it includes business transactions, household purchases, and government activities.

The *resource market* is the composite of all productive resources in which economic resources are purchased and used. It includes all labor hired, all natural resources consumer or used in production, all investment in capital equipment, and all innovations by entrepreneurs to produce new and existing goods and services.

To understand interdependence, let us look at the circular flow from a product market and resource market viewpoint. The circular flow of activity shown in Figure 24-1 illustrates how each part of the market is interdependent on other parts.

The circular flow of economic activity illustrates the interdependence of the ingredients of the market economy. Government taxes income of businesses and individuals. It also purchases goods and services from businesses and individuals (labor). Government produces and consumes products; it buys and sells resources through its controls. Consumers, represented by households, private individuals, and investors, participate actively by purchasing and selling goods and services in the product market; resources are consumed and sold through the resource market. In other words, individuals own the resources and are able to sell them to other individuals as well as to businesses and government for consumption. Businesses likewise purchase and sell resources and make and sell products using the resources. The primary goal of business is profit; the

FIGURE 24-1
Circular Flow of
Economic
Activity

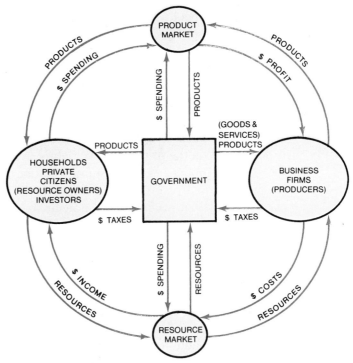

primary goal of investors is interest. Individuals earn wages, interest, and profit through these sources of income.

When something happens to stimulate or to depress the circular flow, the result is called a *ripple effect*. Imagine dropping a rock in the middle of a pond. The ripples go outward in ever larger circles until they reach the sides of the pond. Then the ripples hit the sides and bounce back toward the center, continuing to disrupt the pattern in the water. The pond water eventually settles into a new equilibrium, which is now different because of the presence in the pond of the rock that was not there before.

In an economy, a major event has the same effect. For example, suppose a new product that uses a scarce resource is invented. If the product is in demand, such as a new medical discovery, resources are allocated to that product. Businesses invest in capital or borrow money to develop the new product, new employees are hired, and new purchases are made. Individuals are able to sell goods and services; some are purchased from government and other businesses. Government may have regulations to be met, such as testing. The new product is introduced to the product market. Consumers and government purchase the product; profits are increased for the producers. Because of increased profits, wages, dividends, and interest on loans, more revenue is generated for government.

As the government receives more money, it is able to spend more money on goods and services, transfer payments, and legislative priorities. As the government spends money, those who receive it are given more purchasing power; and thus the cycle continues in a ripple effect until a new balance is achieved. Assuming the product continues to be successful, the marketplace then settles down to a new level that includes the successful new product.

Circular flow depends on voluntary exchange.

Interdependence, as shown in the circular flow of economic activity, is dependent on the principle of voluntary exchange. ***Voluntary exchange*** means each producer and consumer voluntarily gives up something that has been earned or produced in order to gain something that someone else has earned or produced. As individuals, groups, and regions, we specialize in producing goods and services. We produce more of them than we can consume ourselves, and we desire to exchange those left over for something else that we cannot readily specialize in producing.

Without voluntary exchange, a market could not exist. In most cases, the exchange consists of goods and services being purchased with money. The money that is earned is used to purchase goods and services from others.

Interdependence benefits both producers and consumers.

Businesses and producers are dependent on individuals and groups to buy their goods and services. Individuals and groups are dependent on businesses to hire them and pay them wages to produce goods and services. As a result of their interdependence, both businesses and individuals are able to benefit, and the best possible use is made of scarce and valuable resources.

Maximization Behavior

The motivational dimension of the market is based on two basic assumptions: (*a*) consumers attempt to maximize their well-being (utility), and (*b*) businesses seek to make the highest possible profit.

To make the highest profit, businesses seek to produce at the lowest possible cost. By lowering costs a bigger profit is made. To lower costs, businesses seek the following:

1. More efficient techniques of production
2. Less expensive combinations of factors to produce the product
3. A more efficient level or size of production

Total sales (gross profits) should be the maximum distance from costs of producing the product.

When a business can produce a product more efficiently than its competitors, the firm makes greater profits. Competition results when other businesses find ways to cut costs and thereby lower prices. *Normal profit* is the minimum return or payment necessary to maintain a business—pay its costs of operation and a reasonable return above that to continue in business through investment, additional purchases, etc. *Extra profits* are above normal profits; they are excess revenues that make it possible to expand, pay large dividends to stockholders, and achieve larger production.

ECONOMIC DECISIONS

Decisions as to what and how much to produce and to whom the product will be distributed are not easy decisions to make. These economic decisions are based on a number of factors, including economic goals and social costs.

Economic Goals

The people (consumers, producers, and government) of a society must set economic goals that are compatible with the economic system. The United States, being a free enterprise system, based on a market economy, has the following economic goals:

1. Economic freedom
2. Economic growth
3. Economic stability and security
4. Economic efficiency
5. Economic equity

Economic freedom is the right of individuals, with minimal interference by government, to make their own decisions—where to work, how to invest, how to spend—concerning their money and economic assets. Economic growth is the rising standard of living—a greater output of goods and services per capita. Without economic growth, there is little hope for future generations. Economic stability and security guarantee employment that is stable without high inflation, where all citizens can expect to support themselves in a reasonable level of existence and meet their economic and personal goals. Economic efficiency is the wise use of scarce resources to their maximum potential and at the lowest possible cost. Finally, economic equity is the element of fairness in the entire process. The free enterprise system is a fair system because everyone has an equal opportunity to enter, exit, invest or spend, and participate in self-interest behavior at will—all actions that can benefit others as well.

Social Costs

The producer's cost of producing each unit of goods or services may not reflect all the hidden costs. These hidden costs are usually not included in the price of the product, but are borne by the rest of society. Waste and by-products created in production that have to be disposed of, cleaned up, or somehow dealt with by society can be considered social costs of our economic decisions. Examples include air pollution created by a factory or smoke and dirt produced by industrial plants. Sometimes the production process can result in great social cost. Radioactive sludge, for example, is a by-product of the production process that represents a danger to health and is difficult and costly to dispose of. If it remains untreated and is allowed to accumulate, it can poison an area's water supply and destroy the quality of the environment. In the case of radioactive sludge, then, an economic decision to produce brings with it a great social cost that must be considered before other economic decisions are made.

ROLE OF GOVERNMENT

Our discussion would be incomplete without an explanation of the role of government in a market economy. In a *pure* market economy, consumers are in total control. In a *mixed* market economy, decisions of what, how, how much, and for whom are not left entirely to the market; there is some government intervention.

Government has several important roles in a market economy, all of which vitally affect the decisions that are made. Government controls production of some goods and services, such as our national defense, system of justice, and highway systems. In this light, we can say that government is a producer. Government hires many employees to carry out the functions and directives of the people. To do this, government purchases goods and services and is therefore a consumer.

Government provides goods and services.

The government produces public goods and services that have three unique characteristics that make them unlikely prospects for production by private business:

1. All persons receive the benefits, either directly or indirectly, from government services.
2. No one can be excluded from receiving the benefits, either directly or indirectly, from government services.
3. There is no way to adequately place a price tag on the value, and therefore the price, of government services. Nor is there any way to determine who will be charged for the cost of producing public goods and services. For example, weather warning systems, clean air

standards, public campgrounds, fire and police protection, and streets and highways are all maintained by government. Everyone receives benefits and everyone is entitled to use the services. Everyone also shares in paying for the services through taxation.

The government also regulates and controls certain aspects of the marketplace, ranging from labeling requirements of the FDA to minimum wage laws. All of these regulations and controls are made law by Congress in the best interest of a majority of the citizens and are necessary regulations and controls within the marketplace.

Government's most significant activity is that of taxation and income redistribution. The government taxes businesses and individuals based on income. It redistributes the funds collected to others through social security, welfare, and unemployment compensation payments. These government activities affect what and how much will be produced, how it will be produced, and how it will be distributed among the citizens of the country. Left alone, the marketplace most likely would not care for the nonproductive members of society; consequently, government takes over the role of caretaker. Government involvement is apparent in subsidies and legislative priorities.

The government takes care of what the marketplace would abandon.

Government provides what private business could not.

Subsidies

The government contributes money to, or subsidizes, programs or agencies that deal with selected problems. *Subsidies* are partial and temporary payments to help relieve financial burdens. They are based on need and are in the best interests of a society as a whole. Veteran's programs, business assistance plans, and natural disaster improvement loans are all examples of government subsidies or subsidized programs. Subsidies are also made directly to individuals and businesses from time to time when a clear and specific need is demonstrated.

Subsidies are based on need.

Legislative Priorities

The final distribution of revenue is by decision of the U.S. Congress, which meets annually to determine the distribution priorities. Congress creates programs according to the needs apparent in our country and others. It designs a federal budget and spending program to meet the country's needs, as designated by the president and committees in the Congress and Senate. Programs such as CETA (now called JTPA—Job Training Partnership Act), WIN (Work Incentive Program), and school lunch program assistance are examples of federally subsidized programs legislated by Congress.

The federal budget is designed to meet the nation's needs.

VOCABULARY

Directions: Can you find the definition for each of the following terms used in Chapter 24?

economic system
mixed economy
marginalism
sunken cost
interdependence
resource market
specialization

comparative advantage
division of labor
equilibrium
zero-sum game
product market
voluntary exchange
subsidies

1. Partial and temporary payments to help relieve financial burdens.

2. A situation in which one person wins at the expense of another.

3. To willingly give what you produce in exchange for something that someone else has produced.

4. A concept of each person depending on others to do what each can do best.

5. The result when one person produces one or a limited number of goods and services, but consumes many of them.

6. A principle stating that total output is greatest when a country produces only that which it can produce with greatest efficiency.

7. Dividing productive tasks among workers to speed up production and make it more efficient.

8. The way a group of people or a society chooses to organize its economic life and make economic decisions.

9. An economy partly determined by market forces and aided by a certain amount of government policies to produce better overall results.

10. A technique used to analyze problems, in which the results of small changes in quantity are examined.

11. The break-even point, at which there is very little risk.

12. The amount already spent to reach equilibrium.

13. The composite of all individual markets where buyers and sellers interact.

14. The composite of all productive resources in which resources are purchased and used to make goods and services.

ITEMS FOR DISCUSSION

1. What is a traditional economy?

2. What is a command economy?

3. Do we in the United States have a pure market economy?

4. What are the incentives that keep the market economy productive?

5. What is a marginal decision?

6. Why is specialization in a market economy not considered a zero-sum game?

7. How is the product market different from the resource market?

8. Why is voluntary exchange necessary in an economy based on specialization and interdependence?

APPLICATIONS

1. Explain how a command economy exists at times in most societies, even in a market economy.

2. Explain how specialization leads to comparative advantage and interdependence among nations and societies.

3. Can you think of a business that is run without any division of labor (one person does all tasks in operating the business)? Is it a profitable business? Could it be more profitable if there were division of labor and thus increased production?

4. Why is marginal analysis a look at the parts rather than the whole?

5. How is government a producer? a consumer?

CASE PROBLEMS AND ACTIVITIES

1. You have been assigned the task of distributing a limited number of ice cream cones to your class. There are not enough cones to give one to everyone in the class. You decide there are three options:

   (a) Begin distribution by giving to the oldest person first until all cones are gone, or distribute by some status until all cones are gone.

(b) Have the teacher determine who will receive the cones.

(c) Have the students bid for the ice cream cones; use the money that is received to buy more cones for the students who were left out.

Explain which of the alternatives is a command economy, which is a traditional economy, and which is a market economy. Can you think of any other methods of distribution, including combinations of these systems?

2. What products does your state or local area specialize in producing to sell elsewhere for profit? What types of products do you receive from other regions of the state or country because you are unable to produce them, but want to have them?

3. You have purchased an airline ticket and are waiting in the lobby of the airport for your flight to be called. With five minutes remaining before flight boarding time, a young man walks to the ticket counter and asks the ticket agent if there are any seats left. The agent says yes, there are five seats remaining. The young man offers the ticket agent half price for one of the remaining seats. Should the ticket agent accept it? Why or why not? Use marginal analysis as the basis for your decision, as well as airline policies.

4. Explain how it is possible that your economic decisions have an effect on others; how are you affected by decisions made by others? First, assume that you are a consumer working for a big corporation. Then, assume that you are a big corporation making and selling sewing machines. How does interdependence operate in the circular flow of economic activity to influence all citizens in a market economy?

CHAPTER 25

MICROECONOMICS

CHAPTER OBJECTIVES
After studying this chapter and completing the activities, you will be able to:

1. Describe the four market structures of pure competition, pure monopoly, monopolistic competition, and oligopoly.
2. Define and explain demand, supply, equilibrium price, price ceiling, price floor, and utility.
3. List the reasons for failure in our economic system.

THE PRICE SYSTEM

We now begin our study of *microeconomics*, which is a study of individual market interactions. Microeconomics examines choices of the individual unit—one consumer, one product, one firm, one industry. Central to the study of microeconomics is an understanding of demand and supply. The price mechanism is the basis of our market system; it is used to answer the questions of what, how, how much, and for whom to produce. Price affects kind and quantity of supply, determines resource allocation, and affects product rationing.

The price mechanism is the basis of the market system.

Kind and Quantity of Supply

In our free enterprise system, price determines the production of the kinds and quantities of goods and services that consumers want. Prices move up and down freely. An increase in the price of video games will result in the production of more video games. If the price of these video

When the price is high, more will be produced.

417

games is higher than production costs, more video games will be produced. If the demand for video games decreases and the price decreases, fewer video games will be produced.

Resource Allocation

In our economic system, land, labor, capital, and entrepreneurship are used to produce those goods and services that producers find most profitable. As the value of a given resource proves to be higher in one use over another, the resource will be used in the most profitable manner. For example, if two crops can be grown equally well on the limited acreage available, the crop that sells for the highest profit will be grown. That is, the land will be allocated for use in growing corn over wheat if corn will yield the highest profit, all other things being equal.

The most valued resource will be used in the most profitable manner.

Product Rationing

Price is used to determine who will and will not purchase products. Consumers who are willing and able to pay the price of a certain good or service that they want will do so. Those consumers who are unable or unwilling to pay the price of a certain good or service will not be users of that good or service.

Advantages of the Price System

The price system that is the basis for a free enterprise economy has the following advantages:

The consumer is the director of the price show.

1. The consumer is the primary director of the economy. The consumer is sovereign not as an individual, but as a society. Society is a group that collectively signals its wants and needs and guides and controls the productive efforts through the market mechanism.
2. The self-interest motive keeps all factors in balance. Consumers seek satisfaction in the purchase of goods and services. Producers seek to produce those with the highest return on investment (profit). Because both groups are working for their own best interests, they keep each other in balance and continually weigh decisions of need and want, desirability, and profitability. The profit motivation is the drive to maximize income while minimizing expenditures. The automatic, or built-in, regulator of the market system is competition. Competition pits seller against seller and buyer against buyer; this is true in the resource market as well as in the product market.
3. The market system is free to operate with little government interference, assistance, or controls. Through the free market system, those

A market system rewards those who do the best job of satisfying consumers.

who do the best job of satisfying consumers are rewarded with large profits. Those who produce inferior products suffer large losses. The government does not try to save businesses that fail. Each year there are millions of small businesses that fail—they fail because they have made unwise decisions or because they are not producing goods and services at prices demanded by consumers. Likewise, the government allows businesses to freely enter and leave the marketplace—to start business and go out of business at the appropriate times. Those who do the best planning make the biggest profits. Those who fail to meet the needs and demands of the marketplace go out of business, to be replaced by others who more fully meet needs and wants.

Disadvantages of the Price System

Because the price system is based on freedom of choice and self-interest behavior, it also has some disadvantages:

1. Producers do not necessarily want to produce what is most needed in our society. They may decide to allocate scarce resources to the production of something that brings them more profit but that is of less functional value to society. When profit is the motive, producers will pursue their own best interests first.

2. People, being subject to change and emotions, do not always make the best decisions for their own good. They may seek more pleasure

while resources need to be spent toward meeting basic needs of food, clothing, or shelter. People are not always rational; they may perceive their own needs differently from the way in which government or business might see them. People are not always predictable. A producer may foresee a demand for a particular product, but consumers may, for one reason or another, reject the product. A great deal of market strategy—getting the products from the manufacturer into the homes—is subjective and unpredictable. When one small part of the market system is out of balance, the entire mechanism can malfunction. For example, informed consumers are a necessary ingredient. Yet, it often takes consumers weeks or longer to find out about new products, try them, and make wise decisions. A product may be very successful initially, but fail after a good market saturation.

> *Informed consumers are necessary.*

3. Mistakes can be costly. The production of goods and services requires the consumption of resources and the production of by-products and waste products. These may be environmentally unsafe or unhealthy. As a whole, society pays for the mistakes of industry and the inefficiencies that result in contamination of air and water and reduced quality of life. Many years are often required to make appropriate changes in industrial equipment to make waste products satisfactory to the environment. Likewise, errors and miscalculations in products themselves may result in hazards for consumers.

MARKET STRUCTURES

Prices are determined by demand and supply under a condition of competition. In this chapter, we will discuss four market structures that create and affect competition: pure competition, pure monopoly, monopolistic competition, and oligopoly.

Pure Competition

When a marketplace is characterized by *pure competition*, there are a large number of buyers and sellers all interacting at the same time within the marketplace. The firms produce a homogeneous product, and there is free entry and exit of these firms to and from the industry. Homogeneous products are basically the same as other products produced by each firm in the industry; buyers have no preference for the product of one seller over another.

> *Pure competition allows the lowest prices.*

The large number of sellers of the product means that no single seller's production can affect price. Also, the large number of buyers means that no one buyer can affect the price in any noticeable way. No single purchaser has any significant market power. *Market power* is the ability of firms or buyers to affect price. Large numbers of buyers and sellers ensure that no one buyer or seller affects price.

Pure Monopoly

When a marketplace is characterized by *pure monopoly*, there is only one producer of a particular good or service, and there are no substitutes available for that product. Therefore, large numbers of consumers have no choice but to buy the product or do without it. Until recently, many geographic areas were serviced by only one telephone system. In almost every city or town, there is only one seller of electricity. If consumers in these areas wanted telephone or electrical service, they had no choice but to use the only supplier available for each.

Some industries lend themselves entirely to monopoly.

When a monopoly exists, governmental regulations are often present to prevent practices that are not in the best interest of consumers. When government regulates a monopoly, the controlling company must request permission to raise rates or fees. The controlling company does not have the authority to make production decisions as does a private company in an industry not characterized as a monopoly.

Monopolistic Competition

Monopolistic competition exists where there are many sellers of products that are not exactly the same, but very similar. The products are differentiated—there is a difference in the product of one firm when compared to others. The differences may be actual physical differences, or they may be superficial or imaginary. In addition, the differences may be in function, quality or brand, trademark, or package.

Hetereogeneous products compete based on style, quality, and uniqueness.

The automobile industry is a good example of monopolistic competition. Each of the major automobile producers is a giant corporation that produces a uniquely different product. The automobile manufacturers do not compete strongly with each other on price. But the auto manufacturers do try to differentiate between their products on style, mileage estimates, fuel efficiency, status, price discounts, rebates, or warranties. Monopolistic competition is closely monitored by the government and by consumer groups to ensure that price fixing and other unfair trade practices do not occur. Consumer legislation of the automobile industry has been enacted to assure that safety and minimum emission standards are met and that certain standard equipment is provided.

Oligopoly

An oligopoly has more than one producer.

The market situation characterized by very few firms is an ***oligopoly***. Because of their small number, firms recognize their mutual interdependence. As a result, a firm will forecast or expect a certain response from its rivals to any price or production decision that it makes. An oligopoly is similar to a monopoly, except that there is more than one producer in the marketplace. An oligopoly, like a monopoly, offers little choice of style or quality, yet there are many different brands from which to choose.

Oligopolies become more common as a society becomes more specialized and efficient.

An example of an oligopoly is the automobile tire industry. While there are only a few large producers of automobile tires, each producer offers a large number of choices of tires that are similar to those produced by all other tire producers. Oligopolies become frequent as a society becomes more specialized and makes more efficient use of resources.

While oligopoly means higher prices than pure competition, it also means lower prices than when a monopoly exists.

DEMAND AND SUPPLY

The price system of a market economy is based on the interaction of demand and supply. The shape of the total market demand for a good or service will incorporate individuals' demands, households' demands, and companies' demands as consumers and producers—everyone who is a part of the market individually and all producers and consumers collectively—come together in any marketplace to buy or sell goods or services. To arrive at the total supply of any product that will be available, all the individual quantities supplied at each price are added together. The higher the price, the more that will be produced.

Demand

Consumers buy more when prices are lower.

Demand on an individual level is what a person is willing and able to purchase at various prices during a given period of time. Factors that affect demand include income, individual tastes, cost of credit, and the general economic climate. The ***law of demand*** states that consumers will buy more at lower prices than at higher prices, if everything else is constant. That is, the quantity demanded of a good or service has an inverse relationship to its price.

A ***demand curve*** illustrates the relationship between price and quantity demanded. A demand curve slopes downward to the right because at the higher price, fewer units are sold. Figure 25-1 shows a demand curve for candy bars. At 10 cents each, a company could sell about 200,000 candy bars a week. But at 30 cents each, the company estimates that it can sell only about 50,000 candy bars a week. As the price increases, demand for the candy bars decreases.

FIGURE 25-1
Demand Curve
for Candy Bars

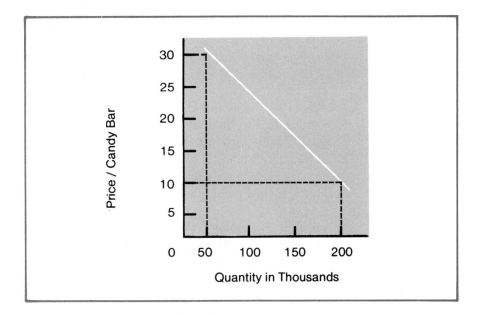

Price / Candy Bar

Quantity in Thousands

Utility

Marginal utility is the added satisfaction received.

Utility is the satisfaction that an individual receives from consuming a good or service. A consumer will demand any product if she or he feels that the product will give the desired return or satisfaction. *Marginal utility* is the added satisfaction (utility) that is received when an additional unit is consumed. The more units that are purchased, the less added or marginal satisfaction each gives. For example, if you purchase five candy bars and begin to eat them, each additional candy bar consumed will be less enjoyable than the previous candy bar. If you eat all five candy bars at the same sitting, you may find that the fifth candy bar is the least enjoyable and is perhaps even unpleasant to consume.

Supply

Supply is the quantity of a product or service that a producer is willing and able to offer for sale at a given price and time, or at a particular place. Everything that affects supply works through one of four factors:

price of a product, price of the factors of production, level of technology, and expectations.

Price of a Product. The lower the price, the smaller the quantity of the product supplied. At higher prices, producers are willing to produce larger quantities because profits are higher. If the price is high enough, but not too high for consumers to buy the product, a profit is generated. But a price that is too low results in loss and, unless the government subsidizes production of this item, it will probably not be produced.

At higher prices, producers are more willing to sell products.

Price of the Factors of Production. As costs of production rise, the total price of the final product also rises. As this price rises, demand decreases for the product. Therefore, producers want to keep the cost as low as possible while still producing a reasonable profit. As the cost of the factors of production increases, the incentive to make products decreases, because the final incentive (profit) decreases.

Level of Technology. Because new and creative ideas are considered necessary in our society, it is important to introduce new and stimulating products to the marketplace. As new ideas are found, suppliers want to be the first to introduce the new product. New technology, inventions, and improvements on old ways of doing things are in great demand. Because supply is slower to change, it is very sensitive to the needs of society, yet careful in choosing the ones to which it will respond. The higher the level of technology, the quicker the supply can be met to meet the demands of consumers. Improved technology thus brings better products at lower prices.

Technology brings better products at lower prices.

Expectations. We as a society are spoiled. We expect to have a multitude of products in a variety of colors, sizes, and shapes. We expect the marketplace to satisfy our wants and needs instantly. That is, when something new is found, we want to have it and benefit from it immediately. We invest millions of dollars in research each year; we expect results.

There are 752 different models of cars and trucks sold in the U.S. each year. If you want a subcompact, you can choose from 126 different types. You can shop for light bulbs at a store that sells 2,500 types of light bulbs. There are more than 200 brands of cigarettes from which to choose. All of these examples demonstrate how expectations affect supply in the marketplace.

The *law of supply* states that the higher the price, the greater the quantity that will be produced or supplied, if everything else is constant.

The quantity supplied of a good or service has a positive relationship to price.

A *supply curve* illustrates the quantity supplied at various prices. The supply curve will slope upward because as the price increases, the supply increases. Figure 25-2 shows a supply curve for candy bars. At 10 cents each, only 50,000 candy bars will be offered for sale. But at 30 cents each, 200,000 candy bars will be offered for sale.

FIGURE 25-2
Supply Curve for
Candy Bars

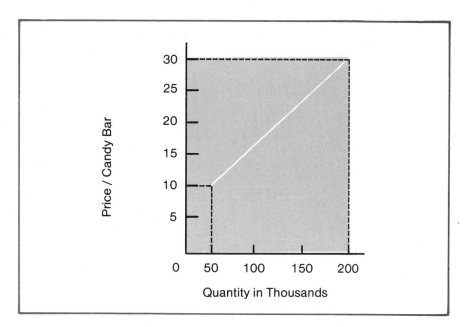

Equilibrium Price

Product prices are determined by the interaction of demand and supply in the marketplace. The price of a product set by the competitive interaction of demand and supply is the *equilibrium price*. It is the point at which the demand curve intersects the supply curve. Figure 25-3 shows the intersection of the demand and supply curves for candy bars. The equilibrium price of the candy bars is 20 cents each. At that price, the producer could safely produce and sell about 125,000 candy bars a week. If the price is higher, fewer candy bars will be sold. If the price is lower, more candy bars will be sold.

Equilibrium price is the balance where producers are sure they can sell what is produced.

The demand curve changes quickly. One day consumers may want to have a certain product. The next day a government study may reveal a potential health hazard posed by that product, and the product will be

FIGURE 25-3
Equilibrium Price
for Candy Bars

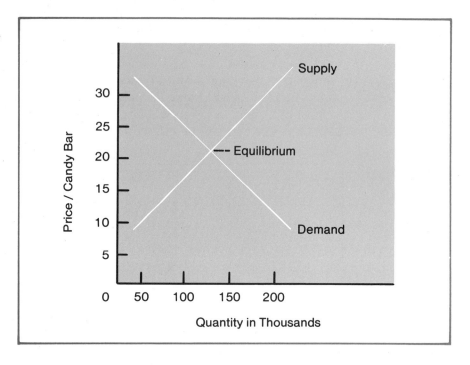

unsalable. The supply curve is slow to change. When consumers indicate a desire to buy goods and services, those products may not be instantly produced. Before producers can begin production of a good or service, they must do considerable work and research. A market study is often done to determine whether there is a genuine demand for a certain product. Substitutes are studied. The costs of production are calculated and a potential profit is determined. Often a product is made in a limited quantity and test marketed. This means that the product is sent to a specific geographic area for sale and use by consumers. If the product does well in the test market, then it is produced for sale to a larger population.

Because there is a great deal of work and expense involved in preparing to produce a product, the supply curve is slow to change. Costs of production can be extensive. Therefore, the producer must carefully calculate the price to determine if a reasonable profit can be made. If the price is too high, consumers will not buy the product. Demand and supply curves are used in market research to determine the quantity of a product that will sell at a given price. When the equilibrium price is determined, then the producer must decide if the profit margin is large enough to justify the expenses of production. Costs of production that go into making a good or service include land, labor, capital, advertising, overhead, and

Before beginning production of a new product, much work is required.

The supply curve is slow to change.

taxes. The price of the good or service will include the costs of production, transportation, distribution, advertising, and profit.

BALANCING DEMAND AND SUPPLY

Price serves to balance demand and supply in a market economy.

In a market economy, demand and supply are usually balanced by price. Price serves to allocate resources—as the value of a given resource is higher in one use than another, those resources will be pulled to the higher-priced use. Price serves to ration—those individuals who cannot pay the equilibrium price are rationed out of the market. A high level of competition among producers of a product will permit the supply and demand conditions in the market to set the price. The more competition and the less preference for brand names and artificial differentiation between products, the lower the equilibrium price. Monopolies, large businesses and unions, higher wages, scarce resources—all are reasons for higher prices. Each product market has its own special characteristics that determine the balance of demand and supply.

Elasticity of Demand

A microeconomist uses the elasticity measurement to describe demand and supply. *Elasticity* is the measure of responsiveness of quantity demanded or quantity supplied to changes in price and other factors. The first measure is elasticity of demand. The way in which a change in price affects the quantity demanded is *elasticity of demand.* If demand for a product is elastic, demand increases greatly when price is lowered. When the price is raised, demand decreases. For example, the demand for candy bars is usually very elastic. The more the price is lowered, the more candy bars are sold.

When demand is inelastic, price has little effect.

When there is no response in quantity demanded to changes in price, demand is *inelastic.* When demand for a product is inelastic, price has little effect on the quantity demanded. For example, the demand for surgery is considered to be inelastic. Regardless of the cost of a gallbladder operation, you will not rush out and have one. However, if you need gallbladder surgery, you will probably have it done, regardless of the cost.

The most important consideration separating elastic from inelastic demand is the availability of good substitutes. If an acceptable substitute is available for a good or service, then consumers will turn to the substitute when the price of the original product goes up. For example, when coffee prices jumped drastically in the mid-70s, consumers switched to tea. The more readily substitutes are available, the more elastic the demand for a product becomes.

Price Ceiling

A *price ceiling* is a maximum price set by government that is below the market equilibrium price. A price ceiling set below the equilibrium price prohibits the market from clearing out all supplies of the product. The quantity that consumers wish to purchase at the ceiling price is greater than the quantity suppliers are willing to supply at this price. The result is a shortage. A *shortage* occurs when the quantity that consumers wish to purchase at some price exceeds the quantity suppliers wish to supply. The shortage is created by the ceiling and can only occur on a lasting basis when a ceiling is in effect.

A price ceiling will create a shortage of a product.

Figure 25-4 illustrates the concept of a price ceiling. The price ceiling is set at $1.75. The equilibrium price, however, is $2.50. At a price of $2.50, producers are willing to produce only 1,000 units; but consumers want to purchase about 1,600 units. The shortage is 600 units.

FIGURE 25-4
Price Ceiling

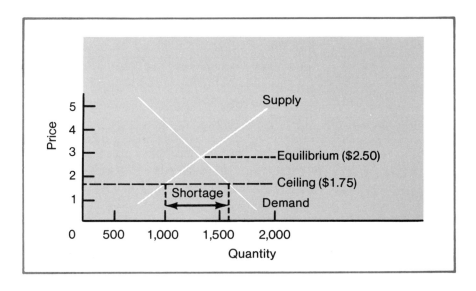

Price Floor

A *price floor* is a minimum price set by government that is above the equilibrium price. A price floor set above the equilibrium price prohibits the market from clearing. The quantity that suppliers offer for sale at the floor price is greater than the quantity consumers wish to purchase at this

A price floor will create a surplus of a product.

price. The result is a surplus. A *surplus* is when the quantity that suppliers wish to supply at some price exceeds the quantity that consumers wish to purchase. The surplus is created by the price floor and can only occur on a lasting basis when a price floor is in effect. Minimum wage is a price floor in the labor market.

Figure 25-5 illustrates the concept of a price floor using minimum wage. The equilibrium wage is $2.50 an hour. However, government has set the minimum wage at $3.75 an hour. At $3.75 an hour, almost 2,000 workers are willing to go to work. However, at $3.75 an hour, businesses are willing to employ only 850 or 900 workers. The result is a surplus of 1,100 or more workers. At the equilibrium wage, 1,400 workers would be employed.

FIGURE 25-5
Price Floor

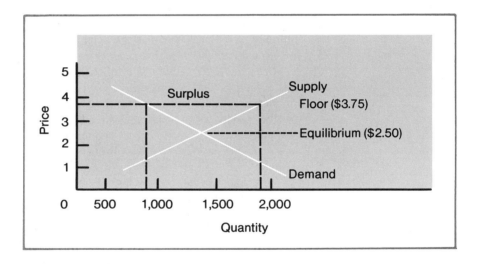

Government exerts controls, such as price ceilings and floors, to protect businesses, workers, and consumers as needed. Without some price floors, large producers would be able to undercut prices and put small businesses out of business. Minimum wage laws were written to protect workers from unfair wage levels. Rent control is an example of a price ceiling intended to protect consumers from exorbitant rent payments. Unfortunately, at a price less than the market clearing price, there will be a shortage of rental units. The number of rental units available will be less than the number of people looking for them. Because there are a number of people waiting to rent each apartment, the landlord can be selective in choosing tenants. Prospective tenants who are young or old, or who have children or pets, may be excluded because there are numerous other people to rent the apartments.

Minimum wage laws are price floors that create surplus (unemployment).

FAILURES IN OUR ECONOMIC SYSTEM

Our economic system is very complex, yet very efficient. It does not give preference to any product, good or service, producer or consumer. You may be wondering why it is, then, that so many small businesses, and a few large ones, fail each year. Failure occurs because the market is unsympathetic to those who do not produce what consumers want, at the appropriate price, the most efficiently. Few exceptions exist. The federal government rescued a large corporation, Chrysler, because it felt the Chrysler employees were a significant factor to be considered. Generally, when a business has failed to meet the demands of the consumer, it will go out of business. These are the basic reasons why some businesses fail:

Businesses are free to enter and leave the marketplace.

1. Lack of information. They did not forecast the market that existed for their product. In some cases, consumers were not adequately informed of the availability or characteristics of the product.
2. Resource immobility. The resources needed for the product are too expensive to move or cannot be utilized efficiently enough to produce a product that is competitive in price.
3. Competition. There are too many similar products being produced by other producers; the market is already saturated.
4. Unstable market. During times of economic recession, inflation, or other unstable periods such as high unemployment, consumer buying habits may be unsatisfactory. This could cause a product otherwise in demand to be replaced by a cheaper product.
5. Government intervention. Because of government controls, taxation, or regulations, a business might be prevented from producing or distributing an otherwise profitable product.

Most businesses that do not meet the needs of consumers go out of business.

6. Poor management and planning. Making a business profitable requires a lot of financial planning and expertise.

By understanding and applying basic economic concepts such as supply, demand, equilibrium, utility, and others, businesses can avoid many of the problems that can lead to failure in the marketplace.

VOCABULARY

Directions: Can you find the definition for each of the following terms used in Chapter 25?

microeconomics   pure competition
pure monopoly   monopolistic competition

oligopoly   market power
law of demand   demand curve
law of supply   supply curve
utility   elasticity
marginal utility   inelastic
equilibrium price   elasticity of demand
price ceiling   price floor
shortage   surplus

1. A market structure characterized by only a few sellers and a homogeneous product.

2. An economic law that states that consumers will buy more at lower prices than at higher prices, if everything else is constant.

3. The point at which the supply curve intersects the demand curve.

4. A theory describing the way in which a change in price affects the quantity demanded.

5. The maximum price that can be charged for a product, good, or service.

6. The ability of firms or buyers to affect price.

7. A market structure characterized by many sellers of products that are not exactly the same but very similar.

8. A graph that illustrates the relationship between price and quantity demanded.

9. A term to describe satisfaction per unit consumed.

10. A large number of buyers and sellers interacting at the same time in the marketplace. The firms produce a homogeneous product.

11. The minimum price set for goods and services.

12. A study of individual market interactions.

13. The added satisfaction received when an additional unit is consumed.

14. An economic law that states that the higher the price, the greater the quantity produced or supplied, if everything else is constant.

15. The measure of responsiveness of quantity demanded or quantity supplied to changes in price and other factors.

16. A market structure in which there is only one producer of a product, good, or service, and there are no substitutes available for that product.

17. The result when the quantity that consumers wish to purchase at some price exceeds the quantity suppliers wish to supply.

18. A description of demand when there is no response in quantity demanded to changes in price.

19. The result when the quantity that suppliers wish to supply at some price exceeds the quantity that consumers wish to purchase.

20. A graph illustrating the quantity supplied at various prices.

ITEMS FOR DISCUSSION

1. What is the basis of our market system?

2. Explain the four market structures that exist within our market price system.

3. List four reasons why businesses fail in a market economy.

4. Explain the law of demand. Use a chart, showing a demand curve.

5. Explain the law of supply. Use a chart, showing a supply curve.

6. Combine your demand chart with your supply chart and illustrate equilibrium price.

7. What are the three functions performed by price in a market system?

8. What are three advantages of the price system?

9. What are three disadvantages of the price system?

10. List two or three products for which demand is very elastic.

11. List two or three products for which demand is very inelastic.

12. What is the result when a price ceiling is set for a good or service?

13. What is the result when a price floor is set for a good or service?

APPLICATIONS

1. List several businesses in your area that fit into each of these market structures:

   (a) Pure competition

   (b) Pure monopoly

(c) Monopolistic competition

(d) Oligopoly

2. Is there a business in your local area that has failed in the last year? Why do you think the business did not succeed?

3. Determine which of the products listed below have elastic or inelastic demand. List substitutes that are available for each, if any.

(a) Tonsilectomy   (f) Cantaloupe

(b) Haircut   (g) Milk

(c) Taxi fare   (h) Gasoline

(d) Coffee   (i) Clothing

(e) Dental exam   (j) Tetanus shot

4. Explain marginal utility with an example.

CASE PROBLEMS AND ACTIVITIES

1. A local merchant sees that the market for 26-inch, 10-speed bicycles is this: at $150 the merchant is able to sell 10 bicycles a week; at $125 the merchant can sell 20 bicycles a week. The lower the price, the more bicycles the merchant will sell.

(a) From the information given below, construct a demand curve:

If price is:	Consumers would buy:
$150	10/week
125	20/week
100	30/week
90	40/week
80	50/week

(b) Now construct a supply curve. Draw the supply curve on the same chart as the demand curve. The bicycle merchant can produce and offer for sale the following:

If price is:	Producer willing to sell:
$150	50/week
125	40/week
100	30/week
90	20/week
80	10/week

What is the approximate equilibrium price? At this price, how many bicycles will be sold?

2. A market survey shows that high school students are interested in buying calculators for use in school and personal work. The results of the study are as follows:

At a price of:	Students would buy:
$ 5.00	950/month
7.50	750/month
10.00	500/month
15.00	250/month
20.00	0/month

After computing costs of production and a reasonable profit margin, producers of calculators are willing to produce the calculators as follows:

At a price of:	Producers willing to sell:
$25.00	1,000/month
20.00	800/month
15.00	600/month
10.00	450/month
5.00	100/month

(a) Draw a demand curve and a supply curve on the same graph. What is the approximate equilibrium price? At this price, how many calculators will be sold?

(b) Based on the same demand and supply curves, draw in a ceiling price of $7.50. How much of a shortage (in total units) will result?

(c) Based on the same demand and supply curves, draw a floor price of $15.00. How much of a surplus (in total units) will result?

CHAPTER 26
MACROECONOMICS

CHAPTER OBJECTIVES

After studying this chapter and completing the activities, you will be able to:

1. Define the macroeconomic concepts of aggregate supply and aggregate demand and explain how the economy grows through saving and investment.
2. Compare and contrast monetary and fiscal policy, explaining how each works to control inflation and unemployment and to stimulate the economy.
3. Discuss the different measures of economic growth—GNP, CPI, PPI, and the Index of Leading Economic Indicators.

THE ECONOMIC SYSTEM AS A WHOLE

Macroeconomics is the study of how the economy as a whole functions. Macroeconomics is concerned with policy issues such as output of the economy, employment, capacity to produce, capacity to spend, and economic growth and stability. When information on all these topics is put together and studied, economic decisions can be made that will result in a healthy economy. We have studied demand and supply on the individual level. Now we will study demand and supply as they relate to the aggregate, or collective, level.

Economic decisions are based on macroeconomics.

Aggregate Supply

The total amount of goods and services available to purchasers is the *aggregate supply*. Aggregate supply depends upon productive capacity, which is fixed at any given moment in time. Productive capacity depends on land, labor, capital, entrepreneurship, and technology, as well as how rapidly an industry is able to move forward into new and unknown paths. Thus, the aggregate supply curve is slow to change because decisions to increase or decrease productive capacity involve many risks and large capital investments. There are several ways to change productive capacity in a nation:

Aggregate supply is slow to change.

1. Change the size and quality of the labor force.
2. Change the quantity and quality of capital used in the production of goods and services.
3. Discover new resources, replenish diminishing resources, and create new types of products that replace demand for scarce and irreplaceable resources.
4. Make new technological advances that improve the quality of life (but not at the expense of using all scarce resources).

Productive capacity is fixed at a moment in time.

Productive capacity, fixed at a moment in time, can grow over time with the addition of one or more of the above factors. Improvement of the education or skill level of workers would substantially affect the nation's capacity to produce.

Aggregate Demand

The total demand of all consumers for all goods and services produced in an economy is **aggregate demand**. Consumption includes all purchases by individuals, households, businesses, and government. When aggregate demand falls short of what the economy is producing (aggregate supply), the result is recession, or a slowing down of the economy. When aggregate demand is greater than aggregate supply, at a full-employment level, the result is inflation. The goal of a market economy is to attempt to balance the forces of aggregate demand and aggregate supply. When aggregate demand and aggregate supply get out of balance, other economic events occur. In our study of macroeconomics, we will look at some of these occurrences, how to control them and how to prevent them.

Imbalance in macroeconomics leads to other economic events.

The condition of full employment exists when all persons who are able and willing to work are able to find employment. It should be noted that some unemployment always exists because (*a*) inadequate training or education makes some people unemployable; (*b*) depressed areas of the country often lack industries; (*c*) discrimination in hiring may occur; and (*d*) industries are replaced by newer technologies and ideas. During periods of normal, healthy economic growth, unemployment rates are generally less than 6 percent. During the Great Depression (1929-1941), however, the unemployment rate was over 25 percent. Similarly, during the recession period of 1981-1983, unemployment rose to almost 11 percent nationwide. Some areas—Michigan, for example—reported over 15 percent unemployment.

Aggregate demand can be affected by the following:

1. Government taxation, which takes away spending power of individuals and businesses
2. Government spending, which stimulates spending power of individuals and businesses
3. A change in the amount of money available caused by changes in credit and interest rates
4. National or societal expectations, priorities, and emphases during a given period of time

The interaction of aggregate demand and aggregate supply influences the level of prices, of output, and of employment. Thus, changes in aggregate demand or aggregate supply have dramatic effects. For example, inflation can enter the picture. There are three basic types of inflation: demand-pull inflation, cost-push inflation, and real cost inflation.

Demand-pull inflation is a rise in the general level of prices caused by too high a level of aggregate demand in relation to aggregate supply. Buyers are, in effect, bidding up prices, or demanding more than the supply is providing. In other words, when you go into a store, you buy whatever product you are seeking. You do not look for the best buy and compare prices, but purchase what you want without considering cost. Because consumers demand more goods and services than are being produced, those in existence are "bidded up." Merchants who have such products are able to raise the prices because they know supplies are limited and therefore consumers will pay the higher prices.

Cost-push inflation is a rise in the general level of prices that is caused by increased costs of making and selling goods. The costs rise, but the quality and quantity of goods does not increase. For example, wages increase for workers, but productivity remains unchanged. Therefore, the cost of the item being produced increases, while more or better units are not being produced to compensate for increased price.

Real cost inflation occurs when costs of the factors of production increase. For example, natural resources may become more valuable and therefore cost more. As supplies of natural resources continue to diminish, their value increases, and the real costs of producing goods and services cannot be controlled.

The result of inflation often is a spiral. As prices increase, workers need raises to pay for the increased cost of living. But increased wages create higher production costs, which result in higher prices. Unfortunately, when the inflation spiral begins, wages tend, for most people, not to keep pace with the increasing cost of living.

SAVINGS AND INVESTMENT

Savings and investment make growth possible.

At the base of growth and productivity are savings and investment. An increase in capital contributes both to increased production and increased productivity.

Savings

Saving occurs when individuals and businesses do not consume all of their current income. Saving affects the growth and productivity of the whole economy and can have both positive and negative aspects. Many consumers do not want to postpone current spending in order to have buying power at a later time. But as we have discussed previously, savings are necessary—we need to set aside money to provide for future expected and unexpected needs.

On a nationwide scale, savings is a leakage from the flow of productivity when it is not invested by banks. When money is saved, not spent, it is not available to businesses for reinvestment in capital equipment, inventories, or wages. When consumers choose to save and buy fewer goods and services, production slows down, and eventually higher prices result. Saving does not result in lower production and higher prices, however, if the money you save is reinvested by the bank or savings and loan where you deposit your money. In this case, when you save, you are indirectly investing in capital along with many other depositors who save money.

Savings must be reinvested to help increase productivity.

The prime interest rate is the rate charged by banks to their most credit worthy business customers. Most consumers will pay higher rates than businesses pay for loans. When the prime rate is high, spending slows down because money is too expensive to borrow. People begin to save more, since they can get higher rates for their savings through time certificates and other programs.

The housing industry is one of the first to suffer during times of high interest rates. Most people must buy their homes on credit and finance them over 25 or 30 years. Construction loans, which are temporary loans given to builders to make houses, have higher rates than ordinary loans. But when rates are very high, most builders cannot afford to get the loans because of the risk of being unable to sell the home when it is finished.

Construction loans are only temporary loans.

Federal Reserve Bank—Cleveland Branch

Investment

Investment occurs when money is used to increase the productive capacity of industry by developing new technology and building new capital equipment, buildings, factories, roads, or tools. Money invested by savers directly or through the banks in which they put their savings can be an important part of increasing productivity.

Like savings, investment can have both positive and negative effects. Investment provides for capital assets, adds to the nation's total productive assets, and serves to increase inventory and equipment potential. Yet investment is also less stable than savings and involves a great risk. Investment means that money that could have been spent for family purchases and goals is instead being used to increase productivity. For the economy as a whole, investment is a very positive factor; but for the individual investor it involves risk and illiquidity.

Investment often involves a great deal of risk.

Government policies and actions also have effects on investment and productivity. Government generally wants more productivity and growth; therefore, it increases its investment in education, transportation, and research. Other government actions and programs, such as taxation, welfare programs, and price ceilings, restrict and control growth. These policies adversely affect saving and investment and prevent the most efficient use of resources.

Economic Institutions

There are four formal economic institutions in our society: (*a*) households, the largest source of spending and saving; (*b*) corporations and businesses; (*c*) banks, credit unions, and savings and loan associations; and (*d*) labor unions and groups of people who gather for strength and power. Each of these institutions acts both as consumer and producer. Each citizen is involved in one or more of these economic institutions.

Economic institutions are both consumers and producers.

Figure 26-1 illustrates the flow of saving and investment and the productivity that results from the interaction of the economic institutions with government. When saving is invested, productivity increases. But when saving is taken out and not reinvested, productivity decreases, leading to unemployment.

FIGURE 26-1
Productivity

Savings decrease the output of a nation when not reinvested into capital equipment. In Figure 26-1, the small bucket at the side represents savings that are not reinvested. The nation as a whole does not benefit; productivity is actually slowed down because that money is taken out of circulation.

Our economy is fueled by capital equipment.

The logs in the figure (fuel for the fire) represent capital equipment—investment in the tools of production whereby more goods and services can be produced, transported, and sold in the marketplace. The fire represents the national economy—a continually active, growing, and measurable output of goods and services. Within the pot are consumers, producers, businesses, and government, all interacting and producing goods and services that are consumed, taxed, invested in, and benefited from by individuals, businesses, and government. Without the fire, the pot slows down its boiling. When the fire (economy) cools, the results can be unemployment, inflation, recession, and depression.

Economic principles describe a nation's efficiency.

In order for an economy to continue to grow and achieve higher productivity, and thus for its citizens to have higher standards of living, more and better goods and services must be produced. The first step in economic growth is saving. The second step is directing the savings accumulated to the production of capital goods that are needed to make the labor force more productive and to realize the efficiencies of mass production, specialization, division of labor, and comparative advantage. Consumers have, over the past two decades, consistently saved about 6 to 7 percent of their disposable income each year.

MONETARY AND FISCAL POLICY

There are two major methods of keeping the aggregate supply in balance with the aggregate demand: monetary policy and fiscal policy. Through these two controls, productivity is increased or decreased, unemployment is affected, and inflation rates are controlled.

Monetary policy

Monetary policy is a macroeconomic concept used to control inflation.

Monetary policy is activity by the Federal Reserve System (the Fed) to influence money supply growth, credit conditions, and the level of interest rates. The Fed was created by President Wilson in 1913 to provide an "elastic currency" and a more effective supervision of banking. A responsibility of the Fed is setting reserve requirements, which are the percentages of deposits that banks must hold in reserve and not use to make loans. The Fed also is responsible for maintaining good credit conditions, an orderly and systematic flow of money, and discount rates. The chairman of the Federal Reserve System is appointed by the president of the United States to serve a four-year term. The 7 members of the Fed's Board of Governors are appointed by the president with approval of Congress to serve 14-year terms. There are 12 Federal Reserve Banks and 25 branches, with approximately 6,000 member banks across the United States. Nearly 80 percent of all the nation's demand deposits are in those 6,000 banks, which represent about 40 percent of the total number of banks in the nation. The 12 Federal Reserve Banks are located in San Francisco, Minneapolis, Kansas City, Dallas, Chicago, St. Louis, Cleveland, Atlanta, Boston, New York, Philadelphia, and Richmond. The head offices of the Fed are in Washington, D.C.

There are 12 Federal Reserve Banks.

Through the banking system, the Fed operates to control money. Money is not a productive resource, but merely a measure of productivity and growth. Money is found in currency and demand deposits in the country's financial institutions. Currency is minted or coined by the U.S. Department of the Treasury, while demand deposits are created and controlled by the banking system.

Loaning of money creates new demand deposits and increases the money supply.

The money supply is increased when loans are made to individuals or businesses who then open accounts. Opening of new accounts creates new demand deposits. A certain percentage of demand deposits, usually around 80 percent, can be loaned out by banks. The effect is to increase the money supply.

If the Fed wants to tighten the money supply, it requires banks to hold a higher percentage of deposits—such as 25 to 30 percent of deposits—in reserve. But if the Fed wants to increase the supply of money, it lowers this reserve requirement to less than 20 percent. When banks have more money to loan, the interest rates are generally lower, and loans are easier to get.

The Federal Reserve System also provides a way for checks to flow from one part of the country to another. Through the check-clearing process, a check you write to a business in another state can be returned to your home bank.

The Fed uses four types of controls in exercising monetary policy.

The Fed can influence money supply growth, credit conditions, and the level of interest rates through use of one or more controls. The Fed can change bank reserve requirements, lower or raise interest rates, control open-market transactions, and establish direct controls.

Change Bank Reserve Requirements. The reserve requirement is usually approximately 20 percent of all deposits held by banks. The Fed raises and lowers the requirement to meet economic needs. By raising the rate, the Fed slows the economy down because there is less money to borrow, and consequently consumers cannot buy as much.

Lower or Raise Interest Rates. The discount rate is the rate of interest that the Fed charges its member banks to borrow money. As the discount rate increases, the rate charged to consumers and businesses also increases. To raise the discount rate is to tighten the money supply and discourage spending and the use of credit.

Control Open-Market Transactions. The Fed owns a large portion of the national debt. Bonds constitute government debts. When government bonds are purchased or sold, interest rates are affected. When the Fed buys more bonds, that gives the government more money to circulate and distribute. But when the Fed sells bonds, it takes money away from the government and out of the hands of the people.

To give more money to the government is to stimulate the economy and increase the money supply.

Establish Direct Controls. The Fed can change amounts of down payments needed for bank loans, as well as lengths of loans, repayment amounts, and rates of interest. It can limit the use of credit cards and allow fees to be added. Requirements to obtain bank credit cards were tightened by the Fed in the late 1970s. Higher monthly payments on credit card balances were required; interest rates increased substantially, from 12 to over 21 percent in many cases; and banks began charging annual fees for bank credit cards. These controls are used to slow down spending, lower inflation, and curb demand.

Fiscal Policy

Fiscal policy is the changing of government spending and taxing in order to move the economy toward a socially desirable level of income and output. When the government increases spending through direct purchases of goods and services or through transfer payments, aggregate demand is increased. This action stimulates the economy toward full employment, but also leads to inflation. When the government reduces spending, the economy is pushed toward lower inflation, but higher unemployment. When taxation is increased, purchasing power is taken away from the workers, and the economy slows down.

Government increases spending to increase aggregate demand and stimulate the economy.

The government operates under a federal budget, which is prepared by the president and is presented to Congress for approval. Anticipated revenues (income) and anticipated or desired expenses are listed in the budget. Often there is a budget deficit, which means there are not enough revenues to cover the desired expenditures.

The chief objective of fiscal policy is to control recession or inflation. The economy is said to be in a recession when production (output) has declined for two or more quarters (six months), when there is rising and widespread unemployment because of decreased production, and when profits of entrepreneurs and the purchasing power of consumers are diminished.

A depression is a severe recession. The decline in production during a depression is more dramatic than during a recession and lasts for a year or more, with unemployment above 10 percent nationally. The Great Depression resulted in many people losing everything they had, including their homes, because they were unable to get work and pay their bills. Real national income (income that reflects true purchasing power) dropped from $87 billion in 1927 to $40 billion in 1933.

A recession occurs when people stop buying—when demand is greatly reduced. Because purchases are down, production is cut back and employees are dismissed. We have had a number of recessions that have lasted a year or two. The reason none of them has become a disaster like the Great Depression is that government fiscal policy has been effective in controlling the severity of each recession.

In effecting fiscal policy, the government has three avenues. These include consumer spending, government spending, and business investment spending.

Consumers prefer to stimulate the economy through tax cuts, because individuals have more purchasing power. Most consumers spend the money gained through tax cuts rather than save. Because sales increase, the economy is stimulated.

Government spending programs are often called automatic stabilizers. *Automatic stabilizers* are immediate benefits that prevent consumers from losing purchasing power or being unable to survive. Automatic stabilizers include transfer payments, subsidies, social security benefits, and other payments automatically made to citizens when they need them. A progressive tax system is also said to be an automatic stabilizer because as you earn less, you are also taxed less. Government spending has an advantage over tax cuts as an effective fiscal policy because it does not involve a time lag. The time lag is the period of time between the tax cut and the increased purchasing power of individuals to buy goods and services. For example, a tax cut is approved in May, but does not go into effect until the following January. Individuals do not see a change in pay for a month or more. This is the time lag.

Fiscal policy is a governmental action to control inflation and other economic conditions.

Effective fiscal policy controls periods of recession and prevents depressions from occurring.

Automatic stabilizers protect citizens from economic disaster.

Timing can be crucial in using fiscal policies. In a recession, unemployment may reach 10 or 11 percent. This means that 10 or 11 percent of the total work force is unemployed and actively seeking employment. The president and Congress are constantly searching for ways to stabilize the economy. The president has a Council of Economic Advisors to watch the economy and advise him when action is needed.

We are constantly seeking ways to stabilize the economy.

Other types of fiscal policies include wage and price controls, hiring of public employees, grants to state and local governments, work projects, and revenue sharing. During the early 1970s, President Nixon imposed wage and price controls to fight inflation. Employers were not allowed to give raises, and retailers were not allowed to raise prices. The controls were somewhat effective. But after a few months, more and more exceptions were allowed so that many prices were climbing, yet wages remained frozen. Many workers lost purchasing power during that period of time.

Discretionary fiscal policy is performed by Congress.

Discretionary fiscal policy refers to an act by Congress in response to an economic situation, whereas automatic fiscal policy is the automatic stabilizer system that takes effect without special actions on the part of the president or Congress. One discretionary fiscal policy that the government can employ is investment tax credit. **Investment tax credit** (ITC) is a tax write-off or credit given to business for undertaking investment spending. By giving businesses a tax incentive to buy new plant equipment and invest in tools of production, the government stimulates production and employment. Those who gain new jobs also have new purchasing power, which further stimulates the economy.

Cost-push inflation needs special care in fiscal or monetary policies.

Fiscal policy is quite effective in dealing with demand-pull inflation, as is monetary policy. But careful application of either monetary or fiscal measures is needed for cost-push inflation. While cost-push inflation could be temporarily controlled by wage and price freezes, we learned from the Nixon administration's use of the freezes that the results can be harmful. Figure 26-2 is a comparison of fiscal and monetary policies.

ECONOMIC GROWTH

Economic growth needs to be steady, planned, and slow.

Economic growth is the increase over a period of time of the total output and production of an entire economy as a unit. Economic growth is desirable, but growing too fast means inflation. Growing too slowly results in unemployment. Growth must be controlled and planned to provide an equilibrium or balance of healthy growth, low inflation, and low unemployment. Real economic growth is determined after inflation has been

FIGURE 26-2
Fiscal and Mon-
etary Policies

FISCAL POLICY	MONETARY POLICY

Government controls to stimulate or shrink the economy.
 	
Major purpose is to control recession and inflation.
 	
Basis is the federal budget.
 	
Balances revenues and expenses; by manipulating these, it can control or counteract the economic forces.
 	
Discretionary fiscal policy:
    Taxation (increase or decrease)
    Government spending
    Investment credit
    Wage and price controls
 	
Automatic fiscal policy:
    Progressive taxes
    Transfer payments
    (unemployment compensa-
    tion, social security, and
    welfare payments).
	The Fed controls the supply and cost of money to stimulate or shrink the economy.
	
	Major purpose is to control spending and inflation.
	
	Works within the banking system to expand or shrink the purchasing power of individuals and businesses with interest rates and credit.
	
	Federal Reserve Board has power to:
	  1. Set reserve requirements
	  2. Set discount rate
	  3. Control open-market operations
	  4. Establish direct controls
	
	These policies are effective when interest rates are very high, but do not hit the economy with same impact in that some businesses and individuals rely more heavily on credit (e.g., housing industry and small businesses).

taken into consideration. Let us look at a few ways of measuring real economic growth.

Gross National Product

The **Gross National Product** (GNP) is the total value of all final goods and services produced in an economy over a given period of time. GNP measures the dollar value of the performance of an economic system. It is not a measure of quality of life or happiness; nor does it measure illegal activities that produce income. There are also omissions and duplications in a measurement of this scope. Everything that has a price tag and goes through the marketplace is counted in the GNP. Intermediate goods, such as the materials used in production, are not counted into the GNP. To count intermediate materials would be to count their value twice and would overstate the value of our total national output. Government contributions are included at their cost rather than market value: for example, police protection is valued at total cost.

GNP has deficiencies in its measurement.

A 3 percent growth in
GNP is considered
healthy.

If the GNP goes up 3 percent, the economy is experiencing a normal, steady growth. Population increases have been about 1.8 percent a year, including births and immigrations. Therefore, if we experience a 3 percent rise in GNP we know that productivity is increasing at a faster rate than population is increasing.

When government stimulates the economy by giving consumers more money to spend through a new jobs bill, increased transfer payments, or an immediate tax cut, consumers buy more. Added spending increases aggregate demand. Producers are able to hire more workers to meet the increase in demand. New wages create more purchasing power, and the effect continues to multiply and stimulate growth in the economy. This is called a multiplier effect. A *multiplier effect* is the concept that any change in policy affects total demand and total income by an amount larger than the amount of the change in policy. The multiplier effect is reflected in a high GNP.

Consumer Price Index

The *Consumer Price Index* (CPI) is an index showing changes in the average price of a basket of goods purchased by consumers. A market basket is a selection of goods and services that is studied for price increases. The selection is comprised of products that people buy for day-to-day living. The quantity and quality of these items is kept unchanged between major revisions so that only price changes are compared. Prices listed in the CPI are based on an index in relation to the base year of 1967. Index points indicate how much prices have risen above the 1967 level.

The CPI consists of
items people buy every
day.

Figure 26-3 is an excerpt from the April, 1983, CPI, which shows a summary of all items, including food, housing, clothing, transportation, medical care, entertainment, commodities, services, and other items. All items, as a whole, are indexed at 293.1 in January of 1983. This means prices have risen 193.1 points, since the base year, 1967, is indexed at 100.

The CPI covers two groups of the population: (*a*) All Urban Consumers and (*b*) Urban Wage Earners and Clerical Workers. In addition to wage earners and clerical workers, the All Urban Consumers group includes professional, managerial, technical, self-employed, and short-term workers, plus the unemployed, retirees, and others not in the labor force. Data are collected from more than 24,000 retail establishments and 24,000 tenants in 85 urban areas across the country.

The CPI measures reg-
ular shelf prices.

The CPI has weaknesses. It only measures regular shelf prices. It does not measure prices for military or for farmers. Things you might buy may not be listed in the index. Included in the CPI are such items as the single

19. Consumer Price Index for All Urban Consumers and revised CPI for Urban Wage Earners and Clerical Workers, U.S. city average—general summary and groups, subgroups, and selected items

[1967 = 100 unless otherwise specified]

General summary	All Urban Consumers							Urban Wage Earners and Clerical Workers						
	1982						1983	1982						1983
	Jan.	Aug.	Sept.	Oct.	Nov.	Dec.	Jan.	Jan.	Aug.	Sept.	Oct.	Nov.	Dec.	Jan.
All items	282.5	292.8	293.3	294.1	293.6	292.4	293.1	282.1	292.4	292.8	293.6	293.2	292.0	291.1
Food and beverages	273.6	279.9	280.1	279.6	279.1	279.1	280.7	273.9	280.2	280.4	279.9	279.4	279.6	281.1
Housing	306.1	320.1	319.7	320.7	319.0	316.3	317.9	305.6	320.5	320.0	321.2	319.6	316.8	317.0
Apparel and upkeep	187.3	191.8	194.9	195.5	195.4	193.6	191.0	186.5	190.7	184.1	194.6	194.4	192.8	190.0
Transportation	289.9	296.2	295.3	295.5	295.8	294.8	293.0	291.6	298.0	296.9	297.0	297.3	296.3	294.3
Medical care	313.4	333.3	336.0	338.7	342.2	344.3	347.8	312.0	331.3	333.9	336.5	339.8	341.8	345.3
Entertainment	229.2	237.4	238.3	240.3	239.9	240.1	241.5	226.1	233.9	234.8	236.5	236.1	236.5	237.7
Other goods and services	248.4	258.3	266.6	271.2	273.8	276.6	279.9	245.0	255.7	262.8	267.8	270.9	274.0	277.8
Commodities	258.8	266.4	266.6	267.5	267.8	267.7	267.2	259.3	266.8	267.0	267.9	268.2	268.2	268.0
Commodities less food and beverages	248.0	255.9	256.1	257.6	258.2	258.0	256.5	248.7	256.5	256.8	258.3	258.9	258.8	257.8
Nondurables less food and beverages	265.6	268.8	269.9	271.0	271.4	270.0	267.4	267.8	270.7	271.8	272.9	273.3	271.9	269.3
Durables	233.4	244.6	244.1	246.0	246.6	247.3	247.3	232.4	244.0	243.6	245.4	246.2	247.0	247.3
Services	323.9	338.9	339.7	340.3	338.6	335.6	337.9	324.3	340.0	340.5	341.2	339.3	336.2	336.9
Rent, residential	217.8	226.0	226.9	228.9	230.2	230.8	232.2	217.4	225.5	226.4	228.4	229.7	230.2	231.7
Household services less rent of shelter (12/82 = 100)	....	....	....	....	....	100.0	100.9	....	....	....	....	....	100.0	100.7
Transportation services	286.6	297.8	298.7	300.5	299.9	299.4	300.1	285.9	296.5	296.0	298.4	297.5	296.7	297.1
Medical care services	339.4	361.0	364.0	366.9	371.0	373.4	377.4	337.5	358.3	361.1	363.9	367.7	370.1	374.0
Other services	251.7	259.7	266.3	268.4	269.2	270.0	271.5	250.0	258.4	264.0	266.1	266.8	267.5	269.1
Special indexes:														
All items less food	281.4	292.5	292.9	294.0	293.6	292.1	292.6	281.3	292.4	292.8	293.9	293.5	292.1	291.9
All items less mortgage interest costs	266.1	275.6	276.7	278.0	278.2	278.4	....	266.4	275.8	276.7	277.9	278.1	278.3	278.5
Commodities less food	245.9	253.8	253.9	255.4	256.0	255.8	254.4	246.6	255.4	254.7	256.1	256.7	256.6	255.7
Nondurables less food	260.2	263.6	264.6	265.7	266.1	264.7	262.4	262.4	265.4	266.5	267.5	267.9	266.6	264.2
Nondurables less food and apparel	301.0	304.2	304.2	305.5	306.2	305.2	303.1	302.6	305.5	305.6	306.9	307.5	306.5	304.4
Nondurables	270.8	275.5	276.2	276.5	276.4	275.8	275.2	271.9	276.5	277.2	277.4	277.4	276.8	276.2
Services less rent of shelter (12/82 = 100)	....	....	....	....	....	100.0	100.7	....	....	....	....	....	....	....
Services less medical care	320.0	334.1	334.8	335.1	332.9	329.3	331.4	320.5	335.6	335.8	336.3	334.0	330.4	330.7
Domestically produced farm foods	262.4	268.4	268.0	266.6	265.3	264.8	265.7	261.4	267.4	267.0	265.5	264.4	264.0	265.0
Selected beef cuts	269.6	280.8	279.3	272.0	271.9	270.0	271.2	271.1	281.9	280.7	273.2	273.2	271.2	272.5
Energy [1]	416.4	424.5	424.2	425.0	422.6	419.9	414.5	419.0	426.1	425.6	426.0	423.7	420.8	415.1
Energy commodities [1]	446.4	436.6	433.3	431.9	431.6	425.4	414.9	447.0	437.3	433.8	423.3	431.8	425.6	282.2
All items less energy	272.1	282.7	283.1	284.0	283.6	282.5	283.8	270.9	281.5	281.9	282.8	282.5	281.5	279.3
All items less food and energy	268.5	279.8	280.4	281.5	281.2	279.9	281.1	267.1	278.7	279.2	280.4	280.2	279.0	237.1
Commodities less food and energy	223.7	233.6	234.1	236.0	236.6	237.1	237.1	222.8	232.8	233.6	235.4	236.2	236.8	415.2
Services less energy	320.5	333.6	334.4	334.4	333.1	329.6	331.8	321.0	334.7	334.8	335.2	333.7	330.1	330.5
Purchasing power of the consumer dollar, 1967 = $1	$0.354	$0.342	0.341	$0.340	$0.341	$0.342	$0.341	$0.354	$0.342	$0.342	$0.341	$0.341	$0.342	$0.342

See footnotes at end of table.

Source: *Monthly Labor Review*, April, 1983, page 66.

FIGURE 26-3 Consumer Price Index

family home. If you already own your home or do not buy a home, the CPI numbers will reflect a higher-than-reality housing price increase for you. New technology may have put many items in your market basket not included in that index of items. If the CPI shows a 12 percent increase in the general index, your actual personal cost is probably closer to 9 percent because you will not buy all the goods and services listed.

The CPI is a widely used index. For example, social security payments are increased on the basis of CPI figures.

Producer Price Index

The *Producer Price Index* (PPI) is an index showing changes in the average price of goods that are of particular interest to producers. It measures average changes in prices by producers of commodities in all stages

The PPI measures price changes in commodities being produced for sale.

of processing. The samples used for calculations contain about 2,800 commodities and 10,000 quotations a month. These samples represent the movement of prices from all commodities produced in manufacturing, agriculture, forestry, fishing, mining, gas and electricity, and public utilities sectors.

Leading Economic Indicators

The *Index of Leading Economic Indicators* is the government's gauge of future economic activity. Based on all its reports and information gathered, the government makes a composite rating. When the rating shows a 1.2 percent increase for one month, that is over 12 percent annual growth. When this is translated into a GNP figure, it is likely to equal about 3 percent, which is a steady, healthy economic growth. The composite rating is affected by all possible areas of input—interest rates; foreign trade; the strength of the dollar at home and overseas; inflation and credit; and the actions of the Fed, the president, and Congress.

VOCABULARY

Directions: Can you find the definition for each of the following terms used in Chapter 26?

macroeconomics	aggregate supply
aggregate demand	demand-pull inflation
cost-push inflation	real cost inflation
monetary policy	Gross National Product
fiscal policy	Consumer Price Index
automatic stabilizers	Index of Leading Economic
investment tax credit	Indicators
Producer Price Index	multiplier effect

1. An activity to influence money supply growth, credit conditions, and the level of interest rates.

2. The result of buyers bidding up prices or demanding more than is being supplied.

3. A rise in the general level of prices that is caused by increased costs of making and selling goods.

4. The concept that any change in policy affects total demand and total income by an amount larger than the amount of the change in policy.

5. The changing of government spending and taxing in order to move the economy toward a socially desirable level of income and output.

6. Immediate benefits that prevent consumers from losing purchasing power.

7. An incentive given by government to encourage business to undertake investment spending.

8. The result of an increase in the costs of the factors of production.

9. The total demand of all consumers for all goods and services produced in an economy.

10. An index showing changes in the average price of a basket of goods purchased by consumers.

11. The total value of all final goods and services produced in an economy over a given period of time.

12. The government's composite gauge of future economic activity.

13. The total amount of goods and services available to purchasers.

14. The study of how the economy as a whole functions.

15. An index showing changes in the average price of goods that are of particular interest to producers.

ITEMS FOR DISCUSSION

1. How can productive capacity within a nation be changed?

2. What can affect aggregate demand?

3. List and define the three types of inflation.

4. What are the four formal economic institutions in the U.S.?

5. What government agency is in charge of monetary policy?

6. List the four types of controls that are exercised by the Federal Reserve System.

7. What happens during a recession?

8. List some automatic stabilizers that prevent citizens from losing their purchasing power.

9. List four ways of measuring economic growth that are used in this country.

10. List three weaknesses of the CPI.

APPLICATIONS

1. Why is productive capacity fixed at a given point in time?

2. What happens when aggregate demand is greater than aggregate supply?

3. Why will we never experience full employment?

4. How can saving hurt the productive capacity of a nation?

5. Explain how the money supply can be increased by banks.

6. Who is responsible for printing and coining all money?

7. How does changing bank reserve requirements affect the cost of credit?

8. Explain how the Fed can tighten the money supply through direct controls.

CASE PROBLEMS AND ACTIVITIES

1. The Economic Recovery Act of 1981 was proposed by President Reagan and provided for tax cuts totaling 25 percent over three years. What is this economic policy called? Using current periodicals as a source of information (between 1981 and 1983), summarize the purpose of the tax cuts as a part of Reaganomics and the overall policies that the president proposed to aid the economy that was then in a recession.

2. Collect information from different years on the average annual income of different occupational groups in the country that are of interest to you. This can be found in the *Monthly Labor Review*, a magazine published by the U.S. Department of Labor. Write a brief summary of the type of information that can be found in this publication.

3. The Fed has just changed its required reserves in banks from 22 percent to 19 percent. Explain the purpose of this type of action and

how it would multiply down to affect you if you wanted to borrow money.

4. When you receive additional money because of raises, tax cuts, or a decreased cost of living, you can either spend it or save it. If you choose to save the money, how are you responsible for capital investment?

5. What is the current GNP and anticipated growth as reported in current newspapers and periodicals? What types of monetary and fiscal policies are being used to counteract economic forces of recession, inflation, unemployment, or other areas needing attention? Write a paragraph summarizing what you find in two sources.

APPENDIX

(The following Appendix is presented for the convenience of the student and illustrates the application of the annual percentage rate formula, discussed in Chapter 13, and the Rule of 78.)

ANNUAL PERCENTAGE RATE FORMULA

The simplified methods of computing interest (finance charges) shown in Chapter 13 are adequate for most comparison purposes. The formula shown here is used in colleges and advanced courses in finance and economics to illustrate an effective method of computing installment interest. The annual percentage rate (APR) formula is used when there is a down payment, payments to be made on the principal that include interest, and agreements requiring more than one regular payment.

By completing this relatively complicated formula, the annual percentage rate can be determined fairly accurately. Other methods exist, but this formula always proves to be accurate within tenths of a percent. The annual percentage rate is expressed first as a decimal, carried to the fourth decimal place. Then it is changed to a percent by moving the decimal point two places to the right and rounding to the tenths—9.8 percent from .0981. The formula is as follows:

$$R = \frac{2mI}{P(n+1)}$$

Where

R = the annual percentage rate
2 = a constant (always used)

m = the method of payment (m = 12 if monthly payments are made, m = 4 if quarterly payments are made, and m = 1 if annual payments are made.)

I = the dollar amount of interest

P = the principal (total amount borrowed—not including the down payment)

n = the total number of payments

1 = a constant

An examination of the important parts of this formula is essential in order to make it work properly.

Method of Payment

The method of payment is always 12 when monthly payments are made. Most loans are based on monthly payments. If quarterly payments (four times a year) are made, m = 4. If annual payments (once a year) are made, m = 1 (even if there is only one annual payment).

Down Payment

A down payment is often called a deposit, or amount given as security to ensure that other payments will be made. When a car is purchased, a trade-in is often considered as the down payment because the old car is worth money. The down payment must be subtracted from the purchase price because interest will not be charged on the amount that is paid in the beginning. Most merchants require that the down payment be 10 percent or more of the purchase price. Then the purchaser will have an incentive to keep making the payments and not lose the down payment.

Number of Payments

The actual number of payments to be made under the agreement is entered and 1 is added before any multiplication is done. For instance, if you were to multiply the principal by 36 and then add 1, you would have a much different answer than if you multiplied the principal by 37.

Case Problems

Let us do a case problem to see how this formula works. Assume that a person buys a car for $6,000, making a $400 down payment. The buyer will make 36 equal monthly payments of $170.

ANNUAL PERCENTAGE RATE

$$R = \frac{2ml}{P(n + 1)}$$

$$R = \frac{2(12)l}{P(36 + 1)}$$

$$R = \frac{2(12)520}{5,600(37)}$$

$$R = \frac{24(520)}{207,200}$$

$$R = \frac{12,480}{207,200}$$

$$R = .0602$$

$$R = 6\%$$

I is found by multiplying the total number of monthly payments by the amount of each payment:

$$36 \times \$170 = \$6,120$$

Then subtract the principal from that amount:

$$\$6,120 - \$5,600 = \$520$$

P is found by subtracting the down payment from the purchase price:

$$\$6,000 - \$400 = \$5,600$$

Remember to do what is in the parentheses first (i.e., add 36 and 1 before multiplying).

Use of a calculator will greatly speed these computations.

To make this formula work best, you need to fill in each missing item and then follow through mathematically. Let us work through another example. In this case the purchase price is $1,200, with a down payment of $200 and 12 equal monthly payments of $90.

ANNUAL PERCENTAGE RATE

$$R = \frac{2ml}{P(n + 1)}$$

$$R = \frac{2(12)l}{P(12 + 1)}$$

$$R = \frac{24(80)}{1,000(13)}$$

$$R = \frac{1,920}{13,000}$$

$$R = .1477$$

$$R = 14.8\%$$

P is found by subtracting the down payment from the purchase price:

$$\$1,200 - \$200 = \$1,000$$

I is found by multiplying the total number of payments by the amount of each payment:

$$\$90 \times 12 = \$1,080$$

Then subtract the principal from that amount:

$$\$1,080 - \$1,000 = \$80$$

When using a calculator, carry out your answer to the fourth decimal place. Then round to a tenth of a percent.

PROBLEMS FOR USING THE APR FORMULA

Use a separate sheet of paper on which to work each problem and record the answers.

1. Use the formula, $R = \dfrac{2mI}{P(n + 1)}$, to compute the annual percentage rate (R) for each of the problems below. Show your work.

(a) R = ?
 m = 12 (monthly payments)
 I = $240.00
 P = $2,000.00
 n = 24 monthly payments

(b) R = ?
 m = 12 (monthly payments)
 I = $16.00
 P = $344.00
 n = 4 monthly payments

(c) R = ?
 m = 12 (monthly payments)
 I = $292.00
 P = $4,000.00
 n = 18 monthly payments

(d) R = ?
 m = 2 (semiannual payments)
 I = $13.42
 P = $101.00
 n = 2 payments

2. In most cases, installment credit involves a down payment, which reduces the principal amount of the loan. In order to determine the dollar interest cost, you need to multiply the amount of payment by the number of payments being made. This is the amount you will pay back. By subtracting the principal from this figure, you will know the cost of credit (interest). Use the formula, $R = \dfrac{2mI}{P(n + 1)}$, to compute the APR for each of the problems below.

(a) The car costs $6,000. The down payment (trade-in) is worth $1,000. Payments will be $180 a month for the next 36 months. Compute the annual percentage rate.

R = ?
m = 12
I = ?
P = ?
n = 36

Remember, principal is the purchase price less the down payment ($6,000 − $1,000).

To find the interest, multiply the amount of each payment by the number of payments. Then subtract the principal (36 × $180 − $5,000).

(b) A refrigerator costs $800. The down payment is 10 percent ($80). Payments are $80 a month for the next 10 months. Compute the annual percentage rate.

(c) An installment contract provides for a purchase price of $8,000, a down payment of $1,200, and monthly payments of $330 for 24 months. What is the annual percentage rate?

(d) Purchasing furniture totaling $1,800, you make a $300 cash down payment and agree to pay the rest over 18 months at $100 a month. What is the annual percentage rate?

3. You are buying a television set for $500, putting down $50 cash, and paying the balance at $40 a month for the next 12 months. What is the annual percentage rate?

4. You borrowed $400 for 8 months. You will make 8 equal monthly payments of $55. What is the annual percentage rate?

5. You are buying a house for $80,000, with a down payment of $8,000, and are paying on the balance for 30 years (360 payments) at $750 a month. What is the annual percentage rate?

6. You are purchasing an automobile for $10,200 with a trade-in valued at $2,100. You will pay the balance at $280 a month for 36 months. What is the annual percentage rate?

7. You are borrowing $58 to buy a quality calculator. You will pay your uncle $6 a month for the next 12 months. What is the annual percentage rate?

8. You have agreed to buy a used typewriter for $280, paying $30 down and the balance at $25 a month for 12 months. What is the annual percentage rate?

9. Compute the annual percentage rate.

(a) R = ?
     P = $2,000
     I = $300
     n = 24 monthly
         payments
     m = 12

(d) Purchase price = $8,000
     Down payment = $1,000
     24 monthly payments of
         $325 each

(b) R = ?
     P = $1,000
     I = $100
     n = 12 payments
     m = 12

(e) Purchase price = $1,000
     Down payment = 10 percent
     36 monthly payments of
         $30 each

(c) R = ?
     P = $500
     I = $75
     n = 18 payments
     m = 12

(f) Purchase price = $6,800
     Trade-in = $1,200
     30 monthly payments of
         $240 each

10. You are buying a stereo for $800, less a down payment of $80. You will pay off the balance in 24 equal monthly payments of $40 a month. What is the annual percentage rate?

RULE OF 78

The Rule of 78 is a method of computing the amount of interest the consumer will save by paying off a debt early. The interest refund schedule is based on the number 78, which is the total of the digits for each month of the first year $(12 + 11 + 10 + 9 + 8 + 7 + 6 + 5 + 4 + 3 + 2 + 1 = 78)$. The first month, representing the first monthly payment, has 12 as a factor. Therefore, if you pay off a 12-month loan after you make the first payment, you pay 12/78 of the total interest. The rest of the interest is unearned and, therefore, saved and refunded to you. If you pay the loan off after the third month, you add 12 (first month) + 11 (second month) + 10 (third month) for a total of 33. You will pay 22/78 of the total interest. This calculation is done by dividing 33 by 78 (.4231). The total amount of interest due (example: $30) is multiplied by .4231 to get the amount of interest paid after 3 months ($30 $\times$ .4231 = $12.69). The amount of interest paid ($12.69) is then subtracted from the total amount of interest due ($30) to determine how much interest is saved by paying off the loan early ($30 $-$ $12.69 = $17.31). The chart below shows the amounts of interest saved when one-year loans are paid off early.

RULE OF 78				
Length of Loan	Total Interest	Date of Early Payment	Interest Paid	Interest Saved
1 year	$300.00	After 4th month	(42/78) $161.54	(36/78) $138.46
1 year	$150.00	After 8th month	(68/78) $130.77	(10/78) $19.23
1 year	$100.00	After 1st month	(12/78) $15.38	(66/78) $84.62

When a loan is extended for more than one year, a new base is used. For example, 2 years is $24 + 23 + 22 + \ldots + 3 + 2 + 1 = 300$. Three years begin at 36 and total 666; 4 years begin at 48 and total 1,176. A 3-year loan paid off after 3 months is 105/666 interest paid. To determine the amount of interest paid on a loan of more than one year, you count backwards—the first month of the loan has the highest factor. If it is a 24-month loan, the first month has the factor of 24. When the loan is paid off early, you count backwards: 24, 23, 22, etc. If you pay off a 2-year loan after the first month, you pay 24/300 of the interest and save the remainder, or unearned interest.

Below are examples of the Rule of 78 when computed on loans of longer than 1 year.

RULE OF 78 (for loans of longer than one year)				
Length of Loan	Total Interest	Date of Early Payment	Interest Paid	Interest Saved
2 years (300)	$240.00	After 2d month	(47/300) $37.61	(253/300) $202.39
3 years (666)	$168.00	After 4th month	(138/666) $34.81	(528/666) $133.19
4 years (1,176)	$818.00	After 11th month	(473/1,176) $329.01	(703/1,176) $488.99

The amount of interest already paid on the 2-year loan is computed by adding together 24 + 23, which is 47. Then 47/300 is the percentage of interest already paid. Multiply 47/300 by $240 to get the dollar amount of interest paid, $37.61. The rest of the interest ($240 − $37.61) is unearned and refunded to you ($202.39).

Not all businesses use the Rule of 78 plan of refunding unearned interest, but each business will outline and explain in the loan agreement the system used. On most revolving accounts, the interest merely stops when the entire balance is paid off. No unearned interest is accumulated because it is computed on the new balance each month. However, a plan for refunding unearned interest is needed on installment accounts because the regular monthly payments include both principal and interest and are calculated to pay off the loan after a set number of months.

PROBLEMS FOR USING THE RULE OF 78

Use a separate sheet of paper to work the following problems using the Rule of 78. Show your computations and underline your answers.

1.	Length of Loan	Total Interest	Date of Early Payment	Interest Paid	Interest Saved
(a)	1 year	$410	After 3d month	_____	_____

	Length of Loan	Total Interest	Date of Early Payment	Interest Paid	Interest Saved
(b)	2 years	$131	After 6th month	———	———
(c)	2 years	$68	After 2d month	———	———
(d)	1 year	$24	After 9th month	———	———
(e)	3 years	$180	After 2d month	———	———
(f)	4 years	$2,000	After 8th month	———	———
(g)	3 years	$160	After 11th month	———	———
(h)	4 years	$811	After 16th month	———	———
(i)	2 years	$160	After 14th month	———	———

2.

	Length of Loan	Date of Early Payment	Finance Charge	Interest Paid	Interest Saved
(a)	1 year	After 2d month	$30	———	———
(b)	1 year	After 11th month	$42	———	———
(c)	2 years	After 3d month	$26	———	———
(d)	3 years	After 6th month	$211	———	———
(e)	3 years	After 18th month	$108	———	———
(f)	4 years	After 2d month	$120	———	———
(g)	4 years	After 6th month	$120	———	———
(h)	4 years	After 28th month	$800	———	———

	Length of Loan	Date of Early Payment	Finance Charge	Interest Paid	Interest Saved
(i)	4 years	After 11th month	$324	_____	_____
(j)	3 years	After 8th month	$216	_____	_____
(k)	3 years	After 22d month	$308	_____	_____
(l)	2 years	After 18th month	$200	_____	_____
(m)	2 years	After 20th month	$380	_____	_____
(n)	1 year	After 6th month	$42	_____	_____

(o) What is the base for a one-year loan? $(12 + 11 + \ldots + 2 + 1 =)$ _____

What is the base for a two-year loan? _____ a three-year loan? _____ four-year? _____

GLOSSARY

Abstract. A summary of all previous transactions involving a piece of property.

Acceptance. When a seller accepts an offer exactly as stated.

Actuarial table. A table of premium rates based on ages and life expectancies.

Actuary. One who calculates insurance and annuity premiums; a specialist on insurance statistics.

Add-on interest. Interest added to the principal; equal payments that include principal and interest are made each month.

Adjusted balance method. Method of computing finance charges in which the monthly payment is subtracted from the balance due before the finance charge is computed.

Adjusted gross income. Income minus allowable exclusions.

Administrative agencies. Groups established by Congress and authorized by the executive branch of government that have the power to enforce administrative laws.

Ad valorem tax. A tax based on the value of a possession (e.g., property tax).

Advertising. The communication of product information through mass media to the consumer for the purpose of increasing the demand for a good or service.

Agent. A trained professional acting for an insurance company in negotiating, servicing, or writing a policy.

Aggregate demand. The total demand of all consumers for all goods and services produced in an economy.

Aggregate supply. The total amount of goods and services available to purchasers.

Agricultural Marketing Service. Agency that inspects food to ensure wholesomeness and truthful labeling, develops official grade standards, and provides grading services.

Alimony. Money paid to support a former spouse.

Allowances. Persons who are dependent on your income for support.

American Bankers Association (ABA) number. A number that appears in fraction form in the upper right corner of a check. The top half of the fraction identifies the location and district of the bank from which the check is drawn.

Annual percentage rate. The rate of interest charged on installment contracts.

Appellate court. A court that has the authority to review the judgment of a lower court.

Aptitude. A natural physical or mental ability that permits you to do certain tasks well.

Arbitration. A process whereby a decision is made by a neutral third party.

Assets. Items of value that a person owns.

Attractive nuisance. A dangerous place, condition, or object that is particularly attractive to children.

Audit. The examination of your tax records by the Internal Revenue Service.

Automatic stabilizers. Immediate benefits that prevent consumers from losing purchasing power or being unable to survive.

Average daily balance method. A method of computing finance charges based on the average outstanding balance during a given period.

Bait and switch. An insincere offer by a merchant who attracts the buyer into the store by advertising an exciting bargain, then switches the customer's interest to a more expensive product.

Balance due. The total amount that remains due on a loan, including both principal and interest.

Bankrupt. Legally insolvent—not capable of paying bills.

Bearer. Anyone who presents a coupon bond check to the bank for payment on the date of the coupon.

Beneficiary. A person named on an insurance policy to receive the benefits of the policy.

Benefits. Sums of money to be paid for specific types of losses under the terms of an insurance policy.

Better Business Bureau (BBB). On state and local levels, a clearinghouse of information about local businesses.

Billing (closing) date. The last date of the month that any purchases or payments made are recorded in your account.

Blank endorsement. The signature of the payee written on the back of the check exactly as it appears on the front of the check.

Bond indenture. A written proof of a secured bond debt.

Borrower. The person who borrows money or uses another form of credit.

Brokers. Members of a stock exchange who do the buying and selling of stocks that are listed with the exchange.

Budgeting. A process wherein expected income is matched to expected outflow.

Business venture. The creation of a business to sell a specific idea, product, or service.

Canceled checks. Checks the bank has processed.

Capital. Property possessed that is worth more than debts owed; a factor of production representing equipment, machines, and other durable but depreciable inputs to the production process.

Carrying charge. *See* Service charge.

Cashier's check. A check written by a bank on its own funds.

Cash management accounts. Money market accounts—services for persons wishing to invest their money at higher rates of return, but with liquidity.

Cash value. The amount of money payable to the policyholder upon discontinuation of a life insurance policy.

Certificate of deposit. A time certificate—a sum of money deposited for a set length of time.

Certified check. A personal check that the bank guarantees to be good.

Chapter 7 bankruptcy. A straight bankruptcy proceeding that wipes out most, but not all, debts.

Chapter 13 bankruptcy. The wage earner's plan of bankruptcy, wherein debtors keep all their property and repay a portion of their debts over a period of time under a court-enforced plan.

Checkbook register. A record of deposits to and withdrawals from a checking account.

Checking account. A banking service wherein money is deposited into an account, and checks are written to withdraw money as needed.

Check safekeeping. The practice of some financial institutions of not returning canceled checks to the customer.

Cherry picker. A customer who buys only loss leaders and super sale items.

Child support. Money paid to a former spouse for support of dependent children.

Civil court. A court that has the authority to hear disputes involving the violation of the private rights of individuals.

Claim. A demand for payment for loss under the terms of an insurance policy.

Class action. A lawsuit filed in behalf of many people who may have been affected by the defendant's actions in the same way.

Collateral. Personal property pledged to a lender to secure a loan.

Collectibles. Valuable or rare items, from art pieces to comic books.

Collective bargaining. The process of negotiating the terms of employment for union members.

Collective values. Those things important to society as a whole.

Collision coverage. Coverage of the insured's own car in the event of an accident.

Commodities. Quantities of goods or interests in tangible assets.

Common stock. A security representing a share in the ownership of a company.

Company advertising. Advertising to promote the image of a store, company, or retail chain.

Comparative advantage. The principle that the greatest gain in total output will occur if each country or state specializes in producing those goods and services that can be produced with the greatest efficiency and imports goods that could be produced only at great cost.

Competent parties. Persons who are legally able to give sane and intelligent assent.

Competition. A situation wherein there exists more than one producer or supplier of a good or service.

Compound interest. Interest computed on the sum of the principal plus interest already earned.

Comprehensive insurance. Insurance that covers damage to your car from events other than collision or upset.

Conservation. The wise use of scarce resources.

Consideration. Something of value that each party to a contract must receive.

Consumer advocate. One who promotes and protects consumer interests.

Consumer Price Index (CPI). An index showing changes in the average price of a basket of goods purchased by consumers.

Consumer redress. The resolution of a problem with a product or service.

Consumer Reports. A monthly magazine published by Consumers Union.

Consumers. Citizens and businesses that purchase and use the goods and services produced for sale.

Consumers' Research Magazine. A magazine published by Consumers' Research, Inc., that gives test results and product ratings.

Contacts. Relatives, friends, people you have worked for, and others who may be able to provide inside information on job openings.

Contract. A legally enforceable agreement between two or more parties to do or not to do something.

Cooperative Extension Services. An agency that provides consumer education materials.

Cooperative work experience program. A program in which students receive high school credits for on-the-job experiences that directly relate to classroom studies in a chosen career area.

Corporate note. The written promise of a corporation to repay loans it has accepted from private citizens.

Cosigner. A person with an acceptable credit rating who promises in writing to repay a promissory note if the maker fails to do so.

Cost-push inflation. A rise in the general level of prices that is caused by increased costs of production.

Counterclaim. A statement asserting the defendant's belief that the plaintiff is at fault and demanding damages as a result of the plaintiff's actions.

Counteroffer. A new offer made in response to an original offer.

Coupon bonds. Bonds that have individual coupons attached for each interest payment.

Court. A tribunal established by the government to decide matters properly brought before it, to give redress to the injured or enforce punishment against wrongdoers, and to prevent wrongs.

Coverage. Protection provided by the terms of an insurance policy.

Credit. What you use when you buy something now and agree to pay for it later, or borrow money and promise to pay it back later.

Credit bureau. A company that operates for profit in the business of accumulating, storing, and distributing credit information.

Credit file. A summary of a person's credit history.

Credit history. The complete record of your credit performance.

Creditor. Any person to whom one owes money or goods.

Credit report. A written report issued by a credit bureau that contains relevant information about a person's credit worthiness.

Criminal court. A court for the trial of crimes regarded as violations of duties to society and disturbances of public peace and order.

Currency. Paper money.

Custom. A long-established practice that may be considered an unwritten law.

Debenture. An unsecured corporate note.

Debit cards. Cards that allow immediate deductions from a checking account to pay for purchases.

Debt collector. A person or company hired by a creditor to collect the balance due on an account.

Decreasing term. A type of insurance policy for which the coverage value decreases each year while the premium remains the same.

Decree. A final statement of the dissolution of a marriage.

Deductible. A specified amount subtracted from covered losses. The insurance company pays only the amount in excess of the amount subtracted.

Deductions. Amounts subtracted from gross pay; expenses the law allows the taxpayer to subtract from gross income.

Defendant. The person against whom the plaintiff is making a complaint.

Defensive driving. Watching for the bad driving decisions of others.

Deferred payment price. The total amount, including principal and interest, that will be paid under a credit agreement.

Deficit spending. Spending by the government of more money than it collects.

Demand. The willingness and ability of consumers to purchase goods and services at certain prices.

Demand curve. A graph that illustrates the relationship between price and quantity demanded.

Demand deposit. An account wherein you can demand portions of your deposited funds at will.

Demand-pull inflation. A rise in the general level of prices caused by too high a level of aggregate demand in relation to aggregate supply.

Demotivators. Conditions and policies that create dissatisfaction and produce low employee morale and low productivity.

Dental insurance. A group insurance plan that covers such expenses as repair of damage to teeth, examinations, fillings, and other specified procedures.

Deposit. A pledge or down payment.

Depositions. Written, sworn statements of witnesses taken before court appearances in order to preserve the memory of the issues.

Deposit slip. A form completed each time you deposit money to your checking account.

Disability income insurance. Insurance that helps to replace the income of a wage earner who cannot work for a prolonged period of time because of an illness or injury.

Discharged. A debt that is no longer owed after declaration of bankruptcy.

Discount bond. A bond you buy for less than its cash-in value.

Discount brokerage. A service through which individuals can buy and sell stocks for a reduced fee.

Discount rate. The rate of interest that banks are charged to borrow money from the Federal Reserve System.

Discretionary income. Income left over after the bills are paid.

Disposable income. The money you have to spend as you wish after taxes, social security, and other required and optional deductions have been withheld from your gross pay.

Dissolution of marriage. Divorce.

Diversification. The practice of purchasing a variety of investments to protect against large losses and increase the rate of return.

Division of labor. The practice of dividing tasks among workers to speed up production and increase efficiency.

Docket. The schedule of cases, dates, and times for issues to be heard in a particular court.

Down payment. A percentage of the purchase price paid to secure the purchase.

Drafts. Checks.

Drawer. The depositor to a checking account.

Due date. The date on or before which a credit payment is due.

Earnest money offer. A formal, written offer to buy a home.

Economics. The study of society's attempts to fill unlimited needs and wants with scarce resources.

Economic system. The way a society organizes its economic life and makes decisions on what will be produced, when, how much, and for whom.

Economizing. Saving and eliminating uses to stretch the life of a product or resource.

Economy. The system or structure of economic life in a country.

Elasticity. The measure of responsiveness of quantity demanded or quantity supplied to changes in price and other factors.

Elasticity of demand. The way in which a change in price affects the quantity demanded.

Electronic funds transfer. A banking transaction made using an automated teller machine.

Endorse. To sign a check across the left end of the back so that the check may be cashed.

Endowment insurance. An expensive type of life insurance policy that functions primarily as a savings contract.

Entrepreneurship. The factor of production that represents management, innovation, and risk-taking.

Equilibrium. The point at which there is very little risk—up to that point all products will be sold or consumed.

Equilibrium price. The price of a product set by the competitive interaction of demand and supply.

Equitable relief. A legal action that allows a previous order to be rescinded, requires a situation to be restored to its previous state, or provides for the performance of a specific act.

Equity. The difference between the appraised value of a property and the debt owed on the property.

Escrow. The process whereby a neutral third party holds the deed and works through the details of a transaction for the purchase of a property.

Eviction. A landlord's legal demand that a tenant move from the premises.

Excellent credit rating. A credit rating earned by paying all bills before their due dates.

Exclusion. A part of income that is not, by special exception, taxable; a circumstance or loss that is not covered under the terms of an insurance policy.

Exempted item. An item of value or a possession that a bankrupt is allowed to retain a certain equity in because it is considered necessary for survival.

Exemption. An allowance a taxpayer claims for each person dependent on the taxpayer's income.

Exempt status. A claim that allows you to have no federal income tax withheld from your paycheck.

Expenses. Money you will need for day-to-day purchases.

Express contract. A contract in which the terms have been agreed upon between the parties.

Extended coverage. An insurance endorsement added to a basic policy so that the insured is covered against loss caused by windstorm, hail, riot, civil commotion, and other specified perils.

Face amount. The death benefit of a life insurance policy.

Factors of production. Land, labor, capital, and entrepreneurship—the components necessary for producing goods and services to meet consumer wants and needs.

Fair credit rating. A rating earned by a customer who usually pays all bills within the grace period, but occasionally takes longer.

Fake sale. A situation wherein a merchant advertises a big sale, but items are at regular prices, or the price tags are disguised to show a price reduction when there actually is none.

Federal Communications Commission (FCC). A government agency that regulates radio and television broadcasting and interstate telephone and telegraph companies.

Federal Deposit Insurance Corporation (FDIC). A company that insures bank deposits.

Federal Savings and Loan Insurance Corporation (FSLIC). A company that insures deposits in savings and loans.

Federal Trade Commission (FTC). A government agency concerned with protecting consumers from unfair methods of competition, false or deceptive advertising, deceptive product labeling, inaccurate or obsolete information on credit reports, and disclosure of the true cost of credit.

Finance charge (handling charge). The interest or money charged the borrower for the use of credit.

Financial planning. An orderly program for spending, saving, and investing the money you earn.

Financial resources. Sources of income.

Finger dexterity. The ability to use your fingers to move small objects quickly and accurately.

Fire insurance. Insurance that will cover losses from fire damage to your home and possessions.

Fiscal policy. The changing of government spending and taxing to control output, recession, inflation, and unemployment.

Fixed expenses. Expenses that remain constant.

Floating a check. The practice of writing a check on insufficient funds and hoping to make a deposit to cover the check before it is cashed.

Food and Drug Administration (FDA). A government agency charged with enforcing laws and regulations to prevent distribution of mislabeled foods, drugs, cosmetics, and medical devices.

Food and Nutrition Service. An agency that provides food assistance programs and information on diets, nutrition, and menu preparation.

Formal education. Knowledge gained through attending formal institutions of learning.

Formal wedding. A wedding for which all guests and participants wear formal attire.

Form W-4, Employee's Withholding Allowance Certificate. A form completed for income tax withholding purposes.

Form W-2, Wage and Tax Statement. A form that lists income earned during the year and all amounts withheld by the employer in your behalf.

Free and clear. A term describing a possession that has no debt of any kind owed against it.

Free checking. Checking with no service fees involved.

Fringe benefits. Optional or extra benefits provided for union employees.

Full coverage. Liability, collision, comprehensive, and personal injury protection insurances all combined into one policy.

Full disclosure. To reveal to a purchaser in complete detail every possible charge or cost involved in the granting of credit.

Full-service bank. A bank that offers every possible kind of financial service.

Furnished. A residence supplied with basic furnishings and essential appliances.

Futures contract. A contract to buy or sell a commodity on a specified date at a specified price.

Gems. Natural precious stones, such as diamonds and rubies.

Generic. A general term for a product having the same qualities or contents as a well-known brand-name product.

Goal. An end toward which efforts are directed.

Good credit rating. A rating earned by paying bills on their due dates or within a five-day grace period.

Grace period. The period following the due date of an unpaid premium during which an insurance policy is still in effect.

Gross income. All taxable income received, including wages, tips, salaries, interest, dividends, unemployment compensation, alimony, and so forth.

Gross National Product (GNP). The total value of all final goods and services produced in an economy over a given period of time.

Gross pay. The total salary, before any deductions are made.

Group health insurance. Insurance that provides coverage for employees or other large groups of people.

Handling charge. *See* Finance charge.

Health insurance. A plan for sharing the risk of financial loss due to accident or illness.

Help wanted ads. Brief descriptions of job openings that appear in the classified section of the newspaper.

High book value. The low book value of a used car, plus the value of the car's added features.

Holographic will. A will written in a person's own handwriting.

Homeowners insurance. A policy that combines fire, loss and theft, and liability coverages.

Hospital and surgical insurance. Insurance that pays for all or part of hospital bills, surgeons' fees, and other in-hospital services.

Identity. Who and what you are.

Illiquid. Not easily converted into cash.

Implied agreement. An agreement that is understood, though not necessarily discussed.

Incentive. A way to encourage employees to do more and better quality work.

Index of Leading Economic Indicators. The government's gauge of future economic activity.

Individual health insurance. An expensive policy covering only a single person or a household.

Industry advertising. Advertising to promote a general product group, without regard to where these products are purchased.

Inelastic. Demand that does not respond to changes in price.

Inflation. The increased cost of living.

Informal wedding. A wedding for which no special clothing is required for the wedding party or the guests.

Initiative. A quality that allows you to do things on your own, without being told to.

Innovations. New ideas, methods, or devices that bring about changes.

Insolvent. A term describing a poor credit position, in which one's liabilities are greater than one's assets.

Installment contract. A written agreement to make regular payments on a specific purchase.

Insurable interest. A condition of insurance contracts, wherein the insured must be in a position to sustain a financial loss if the event insured against occurs.

Insurance. A cooperative system of sharing the risk of financial loss.

Insured. The person, partnership, or corporation protected against loss by an insurance policy.

Interdependence. A condition wherein each person or unit depends on others to do what each can do best.

Interest. Money paid by the financial institution to the saver for the use of his or her money; the amount paid for the use of credit; the price paid for using capital.

Interest checking accounts. Accounts on which interest is paid if the depositor maintains a certain minimum balance.

Intermediate goals. Goals you wish to accomplish in the next few months or years.

Internal Revenue Service (IRS). An agency designed to collect taxes and turn them over to the government for the payment of debts, commitments, and benefits.

Intestate. What you are said to be if, when you die, you do not have a will, but own property that will not automatically pass to another person.

Investment. The outlay of money in the hope of realizing a profit.

Investment club. A group of people that pools its money, votes on spending decisions, and shares the profits.

Investment tax credit. A tax credit given to businesses for undertaking investment spending.

Involuntary bankruptcy. A financial situation that occurs when creditors file a petition with the court, asking the court to declare a debtor unable to meet his or her bills.

Itinerary. A detailed schedule of events, times, and places.

Job interview. A situation in which a potential employer asks questions about the answers an applicant has provided on the application for employment.

Joint account. An account opened by two or more persons.

Joint endorsement. The signature, on the back of a check, of both persons named as payees on the front of the check.

Jurisdiction. The legal right and authority of the court to hear and decide a case.

Jury. A body of citizens sworn by a court to hear the facts submitted to them during a trial and to render a verdict.

Labor. The human factor of production.

Labor unions. Groups of people who work in the same or similar occupations, organized for the benefit of all employees in these occupations.

Land. The factor of production that represents resources that are fixed or nonrenewable.

Landlord. The owner of the property that is rented or leased to another person.

Law of demand. Consumers will buy more at lower prices than at higher prices, if everything else is constant.

Law of supply. The higher the price, the greater the quantity that will be produced or supplied, if everything else is constant.

Laws. Rules of conduct accepted by people and enforced to protect people.

Layaway. A credit plan whereby merchandise is laid away in your name, and you make regular payments and claim the merchandise when it has been paid for in full.

Lease. A written agreement to rent certain property at a certain price for a specified time period.

Lease option. A lease agreement wherein each rent payment applies toward the purchase of the item or property leased.

Lethal. Deadly or dangerous.

Letter of application. A letter that introduces you to a potential employer and gives you a chance to sell your qualifications.

Letter of reference. A statement, in letter form, written by someone who can be relied upon to give a sincere report on your character, abilities, and experience.

Level term. A type of insurance that is renewable at set intervals, no proof of insurability being required.

Liabilities. Amounts of money that are owed to others.

Liability coverage. A policy that protects the insured against claims for personal injury or damage when the insured is driving his or her car or someone else's car.

Life insurance. Protection against the financial disaster that might otherwise result when a family's primary wage earner dies.

Life-style. The way people choose to live their lives, based on the values they have chosen or rejected.

Limited-payment life. A type of whole life insurance on which premiums are higher because the payment period is limited to a specific number of years.

Liquidation. A sale held to turn inventory into cash quickly.

Liquidity. The quality of being easily converted into cash.

Lo-balling. Advertising a repair service special at an unusually low price to lure customers, then attempting to persuade the customer that additional services are needed.

Lobbying. Supporting legislation and political action that is beneficial to a certain profession.

Locked into (a job). The state of feeling trapped in a job because you cannot afford to take the cut in pay that may accompany starting over.

Long-term goals. Activities or plans that will materialize in five to ten years or longer.

Loss. An unexpected reduction or disappearance of an economic value.

Loss leader. An item of merchandise marked down to an unusually low price, sometimes below actual cost.

Macroeconomics. The study of how the economy as a whole functions.

Major Appliance Consumer Action Panel (MACAP). A group comprised of representatives of the home appliance industry that provides assistance in resolving consumer problems in the purchase and use of home appliances.

Major medical insurance. Insurance that covers both hospitalization and medical services and may be purchased as a separate policy.

Maker. The person who creates and signs a negotiable instrument, agreeing to pay it on a certain date; the person authorized to write checks on an account.

Manual dexterity. The ability to move your hands skillfully.

Marginal. Added or extra.

Marginalism. A technique used to analyze problems in which the results of small changes in quantity are examined.

Marginal utility. The added satisfaction that is received when an additional unit is consumed.

Marketable. A term describing work of quality such that the employer can use or sell it.

Market economy. An economic system characterized by private property ownership, self-interest behavior, consumer sovereignty, and competition.

Market power. The ability of firms or buyers to affect price.

Market value. The highest price a property will bring in a competitive and open market.

Markup. The amount added by the dealer to the suggested retail price of a car.

Maturity date. The date on which you must renew a time certificate, cash it in, or purchase a new one.

Median. The statistical middle of a list of figures.

Medicaid. A government health insurance program for indigent persons, regardless of age, who do not qualify for Medicare.

Medical expense insurance. Insurance that pays for doctors' fees for office visits and for routine services other than those connected with hospital care.

Medicare. A medical and hospital insurance program under social security for persons over age 65.

Microeconomics. A study of individual market interactions.

Minimum wage. The legally established lower limit on wages employers may pay.

Minors. Persons under the age of legal majority.

Mixed economy. An economic system in which both producers and consumers play active roles; a market economy in which there is some government intervention.

Monetary policy. Activity by the Fed to influence money supply growth, credit conditions, and the level of interest rates.

Money market fund. An investment plan for small investors that concentrates on buying short-term government, bank, and corporate notes.

Money orders. Certificates purchased for use when cash or a check cannot be used.

Monopolistic competition. The market situation characterized by many sellers of products that are not exactly the same, but are very similar.

Month-to-month tenancy agreement. A written or oral agreement to rent certain property at a set price on a month-to-month basis.

Motivators. Incentives that inspire workers to produce more and better quality goods and services.

Multiple listing service. An organization of real estate offices through which all listings from each office are combined into one book. All salespeople within that geographic area have access to all real estate listings and can sell any one of them to a buyer.

Multiplier effect. The concept that any change in policy affects total demand and total income by an amount larger than the amount of the change in policy.

Mutual assent. Agreement to all terms of the contract by all parties to the contract.

Mutual fund. An investment wherein someone else is paid to choose and buy various securities for the investor.

NADA Blue Book. The National Automobile Dealers Association book that lists a low book value for a basic used car for six years.

National Bureau of Standards (NBS). An agency within the Department of Commerce that sets measurement, product, and safety standards.

National Credit Union Administration (NCUA). An agency that insures deposits in credit unions.

Negotiable. Legally collectible.

Negotiable instrument. A document that contains promises to pay monies and is legally collectible.

Net pay. The amount left after all deductions have been taken out of your gross pay.

Net weight. The weight of a product without the container or package.

Net worth. The difference between assets and liabilities.

No-fault insurance. Insurance that provides for the repair or replacement of your car, regardless of who is at fault at the scene of an accident.

Nominal rate. The rate of interest calculated on the principal amount only (does not include compounding).

NOW accounts. Accounts designed to provide the convenience of a checking account with short-term savings gains.

NSF check (not-sufficient-funds check). A check written without sufficient money in an account to cover it.

Odd-number pricing. The practice of putting odd numbers on price tags to make an item appear inexpensive.

Office of Consumer Affairs. An agency that represents consumer interests in federal agency proceedings, develops consumer information materials, and assists other agencies in responding to consumer complaints.

Oligopoly. The market situation characterized by very few firms.

Open-ended credit. Credit wherein the lender places a limit on how much a qualifying customer can borrow during a given period.

Opportunity cost. What you must give up to get something else that you also want.

Optimizing. Getting the most from all available resources.

Optional benefits. Benefits that are not required as part of the total wage package.

Overbooked. A term used to describe the situation in which tickets have been sold to more people than can be accommodated.

Overdraft. A check that is written that cannot be covered by the funds in an account.

Overextension. A situation wherein purchases exceed what can be handled comfortably with present income.

Over-the-counter exchange. The buying and selling of securities through brokers, but not through a stock exchange.

Overtime. Hours worked in addition to the regular hours.

Oxidize. To permanently lose the shine of a car's finish due to exposure to weather and sun.

Paid holidays. Holidays full-time employees who are receiving a salary are entitled to have off, with pay.

Pawnshop. A legal business in which loans are made against the value of specific personal possessions.

Payee. The person to whom a negotiable instrument is made payable.

Pediatrician. A doctor who specializes in the care and treatment of diseases of small children.

Peril. An exposure to the risk of loss.

Personal factors. Those influences in a person's or a family's life that determine spending patterns, preferences, and choices.

Personal information. Data given on a résumé, such as name, address, and telephone number.

Personal injury protection (PIP). Automobile insurance that pays for medical, hospital, and funeral costs of the insured and his or her family and passengers, regardless of fault.

Personality. Personal qualities and traits that make one unique.

Personal property floater. Additional property insurance coverage purchased to protect certain specified items of property without regard to location at the time of loss or damage.

Personal resources. Time, money, energy, skills and abilities, and available credit.

Pigeon drop. Any method used by experienced con artists to convince vulnerable people to invest in swindles.

Placement services. Organizations that help students find employment, usually without charge.

Plaintiff. The person filing a legal complaint.

Point system. A method used in rating consumers' credit worthiness wherein a credit applicant is given points for employment, amount of income, length of residence, type of residence, and other factors.

Poor credit rating. A rating earned by a customer who does not make regular payments, or who misses payments and must be reminded frequently of debts outstanding.

Postal Inspection Service. An organization within the United States Post Office that deals with consumer problems pertaining to illegal use of the mails.

Postdate. To write in a future date on a check.

Precious metals. Tangible, beautiful, desirable substances of great value, such as gold, silver, and platinum.

Preferred stocks. Stocks on which dividends are paid first in the event of company liquidation.

Premium. The sum of money the policyholder agrees to pay to an insurance company periodically for an insurance policy.

Prenatal expense. A cost that is incurred before a baby is born.

Previous balance method. A method of computing finance charges in which the charge is added to the previous balance, then the payment made during the last billing period is subtracted to determine the new balance in the account.

Price ceiling. A maximum product price set by government that is below the market equilibrium price.

Price fixing. The practice of some producers who are supposed to be competitors of conspiring to set the same prices on the same goods or services.

Price floor. A minimum product price set by the government that is above the equilibrium price.

Prime rate. The rate of interest lenders offer their best commercial (business) customers.

Principal. The amount of money deposited by the saver; the total amount that is financed or borrowed and on which interest is computed.

Producer Price Index (PPI). An index showing changes in the average price of goods that are of particular interest to producers.

Producers. Citizens and businesses that make products and services available for others to purchase.

Product advertising. Advertising to convince consumers to buy a specific good or service.

Production possibilities curve. A graph showing combinations of two goods that can be produced with a given level of resources and technology.

Product market. The composite of all individual markets in which buyers and sellers interact to exchange goods and services.

Professional organizations. Groups that collect dues from members of a profession and provide support services.

Profit. The entrepreneur's reward for taking risk.

Progressive taxes. Taxes that increase in proportion to income.

Promissory note. A written promise to pay a certain sum of money to another person or to the holder of the note on a specified date.

Proof of loss. The written verification of the amount of a loss that must be provided by the insured to the insurance company before a claim can be settled.

Property liability insurance. Insurance that protects the property owner against legal claims by persons injured while on the insured's property.

Property settlement agreement. A court-approved document specifying the division of property and assets agreed to by the parties in a divorce proceeding.

Proportional share. A percentage of a bankrupt's assets paid to a creditor, based on the total debt owed the creditor.

Proportional taxes. Taxes for which the tax rate remains constant, regardless of the amount of income.

Prorate. To divide, as to divide a charge, proportionately over a period of time.

Purchasing power. The power to buy goods and services, based on the amount of money owned.

Pure competition. The market situation in which there are a large number of buyers and sellers interacting at the same time.

Pure monopoly. The market situation that occurs when there is only one producer of a particular good or service, and there are no substitutes available for that product.

Pyramid sales. Selling schemes, illegal in many states, in which sellers are promised a lot of money quickly and with little effort for selling a product.

Rate. The interest charge, expressed as a percentage of the principal.

Reaffirmation. When debtors agree to pay some or all of their debts after bankruptcy is completed.

Real cost inflation. Inflation caused by an increase in the cost of the factors of production.

Real estate. Land and anything permanently attached to it.

Recall. A procedure whereby the manufacturer of a product stops production and refunds the purchase price of items already sold.

Reconciliation. The process of matching your checkbook register with your bank statement.

Recorded. Term describing some document or event that has been made a public record.

Recourse. The remedy for situations in which an employee believes that he or she has not received benefits as required by law.

References. Persons who have known you for at least one year and who can provide information about your character and achievements. References should be over age 18 and not related to you.

Referral sale. A selling method wherein a merchant promises a money rebate, prize, or discount if the buyer can provide names of friends and acquaintances who are prospective customers.

Registered bonds. Bonds for which the corporation keeps a record of the owners.

Regressive taxes. Taxes that decrease in proportion to income increases.

Rent. The price paid for land.

Reservation. An advance commitment that assures you of service.

Resource market. The composite of all productive resources in which economic resources are purchased and used.

Restrictive endorsement. An endorsement that restricts or limits the use of a check.

Résumé. A concise summary of personal information.

Retail stores. Stores that purchase goods from wholesalers and sell directly to customers.

Revenue. Money collected by the government from citizens and companies in the form of taxes.

Risk. The chance of loss.

Safe-deposit boxes. Boxes in banks rented for safe-keeping of valuables.

Salutation. A greeting to the receiver of a letter.

Save. To set aside money for future needs.

Secured loan. A loan that is guaranteed by a pledge of property or other assets to assure the creditor of repayment.

Semiformal wedding. A wedding to which guests wear less formal attire, such as special occasion suits and dresses.

Semiprecious stones. Smaller stones of less commercial value than diamonds, such as garnets, spinels, and opals.

Seniority. The policy that the last ones hired should be the first ones laid off.

Service charge (carrying charge). The amount charged borrowers by merchants or banks for servicing an account or loan.

Service credit. Credit for a service rendered (telephone, doctor).

Share accounts. Savings accounts at a credit union.

Share draft accounts. Credit union checking accounts that have no minimum balance requirements, no service fees, and interest payments based on your lowest monthly balance.

Shortage. A market situation that occurs when the quantity of a product that consumers wish to purchase at some price exceeds the quantity that suppliers wish to supply.

Short-term goal. A goal that is to be achieved in the next few days or weeks.

Simple interest. Interest computed on the principal only. The formula for computing simple interest is $I = P \times R \times T$.

Simple will. A short one- or two-page document that lists spouse and children and provides how each shall inherit.

Small loan companies. Finance companies that charge high rates of interest for the use of their money.

Social Security Act. The first national social insurance program, enacted to provide federal aid for the elderly and for disabled workers.

Social security number. A permanent work identification number.

Solvent. A favorable credit position in which assets are greater than liabilities.

Sovereignty. The power or ability of consumers to affect what is being produced and consumed.

Space. The physical attribute of production that is concerned with dimensional, geographic, and measurable commitments of productive resources.

Special checking account. An account offered to customers who will write only a small number of checks each month.

Special endorsement (endorsement in full). An endorsement that instructs the bank to pay the amount of a check to a third party.

Specialization. The production of only one or a limited number of goods and services by a person or group that consumes many goods and services.

Standard account. A checking account that usually has a set monthly service fee, but no per-check fee.

Standard policy. A contract form that has been adopted by many insurance companies, approved by state insurance departments, or prescribed by law.

Statement. An itemized bill showing charges, credits, and payments posted to an account during a billing period.

Statement of account. A monthly listing of checks received and processed by the bank, plus all other withdrawals and deposits made and service fees charged.

Statute of Limitations. A law that restricts the length of time in which court action may be taken on various complaints.

Stock exchange. A place where stocks and bonds of larger companies are bought and sold.

Stock market. A general term that describes the securities market—the place where supply and demand for investment alternatives meet.

Stop payment order. A request that the bank not cash or process a specific check.

Straight life. A type of whole life policy on which premiums are paid throughout life and the face value is paid at death.

Strike. A process whereby the members of a union refuse to work until an agreement is reached.

Subscribers. Creditors who pay an annual fee to a credit bureau for use of its credit reports.

Subsidies. Partial and temporary payments to help relieve financial burdens.

Sunken cost. The amount already spent, or the amount it costs to have reached equilibrium.

Supply. The quantity of goods and services producers are willing and able to manufacture.

Supply curve. A graph that illustrates the quantity supplied at various prices.

Surplus. A situation that occurs when the quantity suppliers wish to supply at some price exceeds the quantity consumers wish to purchase.

Survivorship account. A joint account, so called because any person authorized to sign on the account has the right to the entire amount deposited.

Take-home pay. The net amount of your paycheck.

Target audience. A specific consumer group to which the advertisements for a product are directed.

Taxable income. Gross income minus deductions, exemptions, etc.

Tax-deferred annuity. A contract wherein you agree to set aside a certain amount of money each month and defer paying taxes on the earnings until a later date.

Tax evasion. Willful failure to pay taxes.

Tax liability. The amount of taxes due from you, based on your taxable income.

Tax shelter. A legal method of avoiding paying taxes on present earnings.

Tenant. One who rents or leases a residence from a landlord.

Term life insurance. A type of life insurance that protects you for a set period of time.

Testator. The person who makes a will.

Time. The period the borrower will take to repay a loan; the crucial timing of production so that a product or service is available for consumption when it is desired by the consumer.

Toxic. Poisonous.

Trade-in. An older vehicle of some type used to reduce the price of the new car by the amount of money the dealer will give you on your old vehicle.

Trade-off. A situation in which you must choose one option over another.

Trade section. The part of a credit report that shows the consumer's present credit status.

Transfer payments. Moneys collected from employers and workers and distributed to those who do not work.

Travel agency. An authorized agent for all airlines to issue tickets and make reservations in the customer's behalf.

Trial court. A court that has the authority to hear a dispute when it is first brought into court.

True annual percentage rate. The effective rate received when money is compounded and interest is received on interest already earned.

True daily interest. Interest computed on each day of deposit.

Trust will. A very complicated will that lists specific provisions for holding property, assets, and money for minor children and others.

20/10 Rule. Never borrow more each year than 20 percent of your yearly take-home pay, and never agree to monthly payments that are more than 10 percent of your monthly take-home pay.

Unearned premium. The portion of the original premium that has not been earned by the insurance company and is returned to the policyholder when a policy is canceled.

Unemployment insurance. Insurance that provides benefits to workers who lose their jobs through no fault of their own.

Unfurnished. A rental residence that may or may not include basic kitchen appliances such as stove and refrigerator.

Uninsured motorist coverage. Insurance that protects you as a pedestrian when hit by a car that is uninsured.

Unions. Units or groups of people joined together for a common purpose.

Unit pricing. The determination of the cost per unit of items sold in quantity.

Unlisted securities. Stocks not listed with an exchange.

Unlisted telephone number. A telephone number that is not listed in the telephone directory and cannot be obtained through directory assistance.

Unused credit. The amount of credit above what you owe that you could charge, to a maximum amount.

Usury laws. Laws setting maximum interest rates that lenders may charge.

Utility. A service such as light, power, or water provided by a public utility company; the satisfaction received from consuming a good or service.

Valid contracts. Contracts that contain mutual assent, consideration, competent parties, a lawful objective, an agreed upon period of time, and a legal format.

Values. The things in life that are important to you.

Variable expenses. Expenses that change according to needs and short-term goals.

Void. To cancel a check.

Voidable contracts. Contracts that contain an element that makes them potentially void.

Void contracts. Contracts that are missing one or more of the essential elements and are, therefore, null and void.

Voluntary bankruptcy. A financial situation that occurs when a debtor files a petition with a federal court asking to be declared unable to meet his or her debts.

Voluntary compliance. The expectation that all employed citizens will prepare and file income tax returns.

Voluntary exchange. A situation in which producers and consumers willingly give up something that they have earned or produced in order to gain something that someone else has earned or produced.

Wage and Hour Act (Fair Labor Standards Act of 1938). A statute providing that persons working in interstate commerce or a related industry could not be paid less than a minimum wage of 25 cents an hour. This act was the basis of current minimum wage policies.

Wages. The total compensation for employment, including gross pay, insurance, sick pay, fringe benefits, and all other types of direct or indirect compensation.

Warranty. An assurance of product quality or of responsibility of the seller.

Wedding party. The persons who are active participants in a wedding ceremony.

Well-baby visits. Regular visits of a baby to a doctor during the first year or two of infancy for the purpose of receiving immunizations and checkups.

Whole life insurance. Insurance that pays the face amount to the beneficiaries on the death of the insured.

Workers' compensation. Benefits paid to workers and their families in the event of injury, illness, or death that occurs as a result of the job or working conditions.

Work history. A record of all jobs held and the length of time spent with each employer.

Work permit. A form allowing a minor to work.

Yellow Pages. An alphabetic, subject listing of businesses advertising their services in the telephone directory.

Zero bracket amount. The minimum dollar amount of deductions you need before it is worth it to you to itemize your deductions.

Zero-sum game. A situation in which one person or group wins at the expense of another.

INDEX